A Functional Competition Policy For India

 Pradeep S Mehta (57) is the founder Secretary General of the Jaipur-based Consumer Unity & Trust Society (CUTS), a leading research and advocacy group established in India in 1984. CUTS now operates out of six offices in India, and one each in Zambia, Kenya and UK. Mehta has studied commerce at the Calcutta University and law at the Rajasthan University, Jaipur.

Mehta serves on several policy-making bodies of the Government of India, related to trade, environment and consumer affairs. He is the Chairman of the Advisory Board of the South Asia Watch on Trade, Economics and Environment (SAWTEE), Kathmandu, and Co-Chairman of the International Network of Civil Society Organisations on Competition. In the past, he has served on the governing boards of the International Centre for Trade and Sustainable Development (ICTSD), Geneva, Life Insurance Corporation of India, Mumbai, Consumer Coordination Council, New Delhi and on the Global Policy and Campaigns Committee on Economic Issues of Consumers International, London.

He also serves on the advisory bodies of the Manchester University's Centre on Regulation and Competition, and on Loyola University's Institute of Antitrust and Consumer Protection. He is a Visiting Fellow to the Centre on Trade and Investment, Government of Rajasthan. Furthermore, he serves on the WTO Director General's Informal NGO Advisory Body.

Mehta writes extensively in the press in India and abroad, and has published several papers and books, which include: Essays on the International Trading System; Multilateralisation of Sovereignty; Environmental Conditions in International Trade; Analysis of the Interaction between Trade and Competition Policy; State of the Indian Consumer; Numbers at What Cost ? ; and a serial publication: Globalisation and India — Myths & Realities. The last is addressed to the common person in India, which helps to clarify many basic issues about economic reforms and trade liberalisation.

A Functional Competition Policy For India

Edited by

Pradeep S Mehta

Published by Academic Foundation, New Delhi
in association with Consumer Unity and Trust Society
(CUTS International), Jaipur

CUTS Centre for Competition,
Investment & Economic Regulation
(C-CIER), Jaipur

Academic Foundation

NEW DELHI

First published in 2006 by

Academic Foundation
4772-73 / 23 Bharat Ram Road, (23 Ansari Road), Darya Ganj, New Delhi - 110 002 (India).
Phones : 23245001 / 02 / 03 / 04. Fax : +91-11-23245005. E-mail : academic@vsnl.com
www : academicfoundation.com

Published in association with :

Consumer Unity and Trust Society
(CUTS International), Jaipur
www.cuts-international.org

A Functional Competition Policy for India
edited by Pradeep S Mehta.

ISBN 81-7188-493-8

Designed and typeset by Italics India, New Delhi.
Printed and bound in India.

Contents

1. Introduction

2005, "Can-Do" Year for India
What is Competition?
Why a Competition Law?
Competition Policy and Other Policies
Promoting Competitiveness through Competition
Competition Policy and Development
Promoting Effective Markets through Competition
The Report

PART I

Competition Law in India

2. Evolution of Competition Policy and Law in India

Introduction
Historical Developments Leading to the Enactment of the MRTP Act
Enactment of the MRTP Act, 1969
Economic Reforms and Impact on the MRTP Act
Experience with the Working of the MRTP Act
Metamorphosis from MRTP Act, 1969 to Competition Act, 2002
Role of Third Parties
Consumer Protection Act, 1986

PART IV

Competition Policy in Agriculture

PART V

Competition Policy in Manufacturing Sector

PART VI

Competition Policy in Infrastructure Sector

PART VII

Competition Policy in Services

PART VIII

Competition Policy in New Economy Areas

List of Tables, Figures and Boxes

Figures

Boxes

Foreword

The adoption of a new competition law in India, in 2002, was a major development in the history of economic policy-making in the country. It did not cheer up many in the business as well as economists. The spectre of a continued inspector *raj* started worrying people. Would it not stifle the growth of entrepreneurship and business when the economy has just started showing good results? Will we not get a new *avatar* of the Monopolies & Restrictive Trade Practices Commission (MRTPC), which did not exactly play an encouraging role in its heydays? These were some of the questions that were dogging the public discourse.

Theoretically speaking, trade liberalisation is one of the most effective measures to curb abuse of market power and the rent seeking behaviour of business. However, even this has its limits. Imported goods cannot reach the consumers directly and the well entrenched market players may have a grip over the distribution channels, which may nullify the gains of liberalised trade. Then, there are goods and services which are not tradable. There are goods which are tradable but only within a limited market. Cement being a classic example of this. Due to its bulky nature it is not economical to transport it to distant markets. As a result even geographical segments of a national market can be successfully monopolised or cartelised.

Thus, it is not surprising to see that while countries have gone for more and more trade liberalisation over the last one decade, more and more countries have also embraced competition laws, with many adopting new laws after scrapping their old ones. In the beginning of 1990, there were about 30 odd countries with a competition law. However, at present, the number is about 100 and many more are in the queue. Obviously there is a greater acceptance of the fact that trade liberalisation may not always be a perfect remedy for an abuse of market power.

In any discussion on the usefulness of a competition authority in India, the performance of the MRTPC cannot be ignored. Expectedly so, as the MRTP Act is being replaced by the Competition Act. Industries still remember MRTP Act for its negative role in the pre-reforms era when most big companies would be designated as monopoly companies. The MRTPA would be used to stifle growth of companies.

Given this context, there could not be a more appropriate time for this volume to be published. As a matter of fact I am not aware of any other study that has given such a comprehensive treatment to the issue of competition policy in India. It is a path breaking project. Contrary to popular perception the study does not treat competition policy as just adoption and implementation of a competition law but looks at it as a broader policy framework where competition is encouraged as a market process. Thus it rightly points out that along with the implementation of the Act, government policies need to be appropriately tuned at both central and state levels. The government at the centre has made competition a serious policy issue, therefore one hopes that the policymakers will take this volume as seriously as it deserves to be taken.

Through sectoral analyses, the study brings out the various dimensions of competition issues which need to be taken seriously not only by the competition authority and the governments, but also by different sectoral regulators, and all other stakeholders. An important aspect of the study is that it has looked at regulation not as an instrument of price control but as a process to bring forth competitive outcomes in a non-competitive situation.

As rightly articulated in the study, the competition policy would require that various institutions function properly, and these include the competition authority, the various branches of the government at centre and the states, along with sectoral regulators. This would require better accountability of all such bodies which can only become possible if all the stakeholders are aware of the relevant issues. The stakeholders include, in addition to governments and regulators, people in academia, media, trade unions and civil society organisations, particularly the consumer groups. It is thus imperative to build the capacity of all stakeholders.

The report would be useful to all those who are interested in economic policies in general and competition policy in particular. The present volume, through raising awareness and building capacity on competition policy issues particularly of the civil society, will ensure better accountability of governments and the regulators and thereby taking care of government failures to a large extent. I am assured by the fact that the demand for competition policy and law is coming not from armchair economists and policy-makers but from the consumer movement. I am highly optimistic about this, as this report, rich in analyses of the relevant issues, has come out not from an 'academic' institution but a consumer organisation.

I must also confess my deep admiration for CUTS and its head: Pradeep S. Mehta, the editor of this volume, for their crusade in pushing the system to work in favour of the common people. CUTS is a rare research and advocacy organisation, which works at the grassroot to the international levels simultaneously, on several policy issues. We need more such people and groups to push the reforms agenda, so that our nation constantly rises to higher levels of endeavour and achievement.

— **Vijay L. Kelkar**
*Chairman, IDFC Asset
Management Company Ltd.*

Preface

I do not propose to argue the case for an effective competition policy, and what such a policy could do to address consumer interests. Pradeep S. Mehta has done that very eloquently in the introductory chapter. A conducive climate for the new competition law to be understood and accepted is necessary to further economic reforms in India. I am, therefore, not surprised that CUTS, with its commitment to promote competition and through the process enhance consumer welfare, has brought out this report.

The contributors to this report are researchers, eminent academics and policymakers. I had the privilege of chairing an illustrious Steering Committee which guided the project. I had initially feared that a meeting of such talented and, perhaps, 'argumentative Indians', if one might borrow a phrase from the title of Professor Amartya Sen's book, would be one endless debate. My fears were misplaced. They were all so committed to the cause and so enthusiastic about the project that each meeting of the Steering Committee was crisp and productive, and a pleasure to attend. Two stimulating days were spent in the congenial surroundings of the village resort: *Chokhi Dhani* at Jaipur where all the papers were presented and critiqued. It was very much like a family gathering to discuss issues that were of common interest. The credit for all this goes almost entirely to Pradeep Mehta and his team of young, bright and energetic professionals at CUTS. Pradeep's enthusiasm and dedication were contagious.

I hope that the new competition authority will soon be in place and will find this report useful both for advocacy and in shaping its approaches to promote competition in sectors that are of importance to every Indian.

More importantly, I earnestly hope that the report would be used by governments, both at the centre and in the states, to address systemic problems and to mainstream competition policy in their economic and fiscal policies.

— **S. Sundar**

Distinguished Fellow,
The Energy & Resources Institute,
New Delhi

Acknowledgements

This report was prepared under the supervision of Pradeep S. Mehta, and the overall guidance of the Steering Committee, comprising of S. Sundar (Chairman), Shankar Acharya, T.C.A. Anant, Suman Bery, B.B. Bhattacharya, S. Chakravarthy, V.K. Dhall (special invitee), Shubhashis Gangopadhyay, Subir Gokarn, Shrawan Nigam, Manoj Pant, T.C.A. Srinivas Raghavan, S.L. Rao and Pronab Sen.

The foreword has been written by Vijay Kelkar.

The various chapters were written by Manish Agarwal, T.C.A. Anant, Aditya Bhattacharjea, S. Chakravarthy, Ramesh Chand, A. Damodaran, Prabhat Dayal, A.S. Firoz, Shubhashis Gangopadhyay, Sunil Jain, Bharath Jairaj, K.J. Joseph, Amirullah Khan, Devendra Kodwani, Pradeep S. Mehta, Praveen Mohanty, Nitya Nanda, K.V. Ramaswamy, Jaivir Singh, S. Sundar, and Mahesh Uppal.

Comments on chapters were received from Vivek Agarwal, Sanjeev S. Ahluwalia, Diwakar Babu, Laveesh Bhandari, S.S. Bhandare, T.H. Chowdary, Biswanath Goldar, Barbara Harriss-White, Surendra Kanstiya, Rajat Kathuria, K.L. Krishna, Bhanwar Lal, V.K. Mathur, Jiban K. Mukhopadhyay, R. Nagaraj, Raghav Narsalay, Anand Pathak, Amit Sengupta, N.S. Siddharthan, Pradeep Srivastava, N. Suresh, Suresh Tendulkar, P.N. Vijay and V.S. Vyas.

The report benefited from participants in a Brainstorming Session in New Delhi in March 2004, a Seminar on Functional Competition Policy for India held in Hyderabad in October 2004 and a Project Review Meeting in Jaipur in October 2004.

Inputs and comments were received during the various stages of preparation from: Pierre Arhel, Nazeeb Arif, T.K. Arun, T. Balachandran, Shantanu Banerjee, A.S. Bhall, T.P. Bhat, T.A. Bhavani, S. Bhattacharya, Philippe Brusick, Malti Chandkika, Bipul Chatterjee, M. K. Chaudhuri, R. Desikan, Dalia Dey, K.S. Galundiya, Reena George, Pushpa Girimaji, M. Gopalakrishna, Madan Giri Goswami, N.K. Jain, Usha Jumani, Amitabh Kumar, C.V. Kumar, Manoj Kumar, Ujjwal Kumar, Rajeev Mathur, Arvind Mayaram, V.D. Maalwade, R.K. Mishra, N.L. Mitra, Y.G. Muralidharan, A.K Padmanabhan, Ranjan Panda, Vinayak Pandey, Narendra Pani, S. Peer Mohamed, Sanjib Pohit, K.Y.U Durga Prasad, Marc Proksch, K. Raghu, P. Ravi Sekhara Raju, P.C. Ramakrishnan, A.V. Narasimha Rao, T.K. Rao, Dhanna Singh Rawat, C. Rami Reddy, D. Narasimha Reddy, Amrit Lal Saha, Bhaskar Samvat, S.K. Sarkar, Nabinananda Sen, N. Surya Senthil, U. Shankar, V.B. Shastry, Abhinav Shukla, A.R. Sihag, Harsh Vardhan Singh, Manjit Singh, Lakshmidevi Somnath, Mahendra Soni, K. Srinivasan, K. Swaminathan, G. Narayana Swamy, K.L. Thapar and Arif Waqif.

The financial support of the Department for International Development, UK is gratefully acknowledged. Gratitude is also expressed for all the above-named persons for their contribution to the project, and a special thanks to Manish Agarwal, the project manager, S. Sundar for steering the project, and to Vijay Kelkar for writing a most complimentary and encouraging foreword.

Assistance in the project management was provided by Shweta Agarwal, Vikash Batham, Nupur Mehta, Anudeepa Nair, Ayesha Patel, Sheela Rai, Ajit Singh and Vijay Singh.

Contributors to this Volume

Pradeep S. Mehta
Secretary General, CUTS International,
Jaipur.

S. Chakravarthy
Former Member, MRTP Commission,
Adviser/Consultant on Competition Policy and Law,
and Fellow, CUTS Centre for Competition,
Investment & Economic Regulation (C-CIER).

Manish Agarwal
Policy Analyst, CUTS Centre for Competition,
Investment & Economic Regulation (C-CIER).

Aditya Bhattacharjea
Reader, Department of Economics,
Delhi School of Economics,
University of Delhi, Delhi.

Nitya Nanda
Policy Analyst, CUTS Centre for Competition,
Investment & Economic Regulation (C-CIER).

T.C.A. Anant
Professor, Department of Economics,
Delhi School of Economics,
University of Delhi, Delhi.

Jaivir Singh
Assistant Professor, Centre for the Study of Law and Governance,
Jawaharlal Nehru University, New Delhi.

Prabhat Dayal
Fellow, CUTS Centre for Competition,
Investment & Economic Regulation (C-CIER).

Bharath Jairaj
Legal Coordinator, Citizen, consumer and civic Action Group, Chennai.

Ramesh Chand
Principal Scientist, National Centre for
Agriculture Economics and Policy Research, New Delhi.

K.V. Ramaswamy
Associate Professor, Indira Gandhi Institute of
Development Research (IGIDR), Mumbai.

A.S. Firoz
Chief Economist, Economic Research Unit,
Ministry of Steel, Government of India.

Amirullah Khan
Fellow, India Development Foundation, Gurgaon.

Mahesh Uppal
Director, Telecommunications & Computer Information Systems,
New Delhi.

Devendra Kodwani
Director, Tolani Institute of Management, Kutch, Gujarat.

Sunil Jain
Contributing Editor, Business Standard, New Delhi.

Shubhashis Gangopadhyay
Director, India Development Foundation, Gurgaon.

Praveen Mohanty
Prognosis Capital Advisor,
India Development Foundation, Gurgaon.

K.J. Joseph
Visiting Senior Fellow, Research and Information System
for the Non-Aligned and Other Developing Countries (RIS),
New Delhi.

A. Damodaran
Professor, Indian Institute of Management (IIM), Bangalore.

1 Introduction

Pradeep S. Mehta

In October 2004, I attended a grand dinner party at Jaipur where people from all walks of life were present. People were fawning over civil servants, as is the wont. Some of these fellows were quite pleasant, while many strutted around with their noses in the air. Who were the important people who were not there? – the officials of the Department of Telecommunications (DoT).

Why? A few years ago, telephone officials too strutted around such parties with their noses in the air, because people needed favours from them. For ordinary people like me, we needed a telephone, and one that worked. In any event, after getting a telephone, one would also have to grease the line-man etc., to ensure that it continued to work. Getting through long distance calls was another painful experience. I wonder how many people remember, sometime in the 1980s, when the former Chief Minister of Madhya Pradesh, Mr. P.C. Sethi, walked into a telephone exchange in New Delhi, brandishing a revolver because his trunk calls were not being realised.

What a sea change has taken place! I wonder how many people know the names of the telecom officials in their city any longer, because they don't need to. How many well-connected people make their way into the Telephone Advisory Committees? Hardly anyone, because it doesn't help any longer. Today, one can get different types of telephone services and make calls to anywhere at the drop of a hat. One no longer needs 'approach' to get a telephone connection. A similar story emerges if we look at the air transport sector. Earlier, employees of Indian Airlines too were wooed in order to get seats on over-booked flights. No longer. Now that there is competition, with many private airlines in the country, getting flight seats and at variable fares is no longer a mammoth task.

How does competition help us? Firstly, by ensuring that there are a large number of suppliers, as illustrated above, so that there is rivalry. Secondly, where there are natural monopolies, we require better regulation and price capping, so that we are not exploited. There is huge competition in the telecom sector, which is improving with new technologies available every day. Yet, the sector needs regulation. Rivals can collude, and thus negate the benefits of competition. Or, the tariff plans are made in such a way, that consumers cannot decipher. Thus, there is a Telecom Regulatory Authority of India (TRAI) at New Delhi, which governs the telecom sector including their performance standards.

TRAI is engaged in another area of regulation, which is also quite close to consumers, i.e. Cable TV. In this sector, there are a large number of suppliers i.e. the last mile operator, and a large number of consumers. Yet there is no perfect competition. Here we are stuck with natural monopolies, because they divide the territories among themselves. They too charge exploitative prices. We cannot even change our cable TV operator, or we risk getting no service at all. CUTS has done a nationwide survey on consumer satisfaction, results of which show just how dissatisfied they are. Then there are a huge number of other sectors, such as electricity, where too natural monopolies reign. There are regulatory institutions to govern these sectors, but their capacity is either limited or non-existent. This is made worse, as most regulators are manned with retired bureaucrats or judges, whose whole working life has been under a command and control regime. Their understanding of law and economics in the area of independent regulation is awful. Clearly, we have miles to go.

What is fortunate is that the new government at the centre is very serious about improving competition in the market place, and also to reform the regulatory structure that is in place. Currently, the Planning Commission is engaged in looking at the regulatory framework in infrastructure sectors and seeing how we can bring in best international practices to improve it. Thus, there is intent and the challenge to convert it into reality.

1.1 2005, "Can-Do" Year for India

"I do hope that in the New Year we can all work together to build a more equitable, competitive and humane India.... This is a doable agenda provided we can set aside our "make-do" attitude and adopt a "can-do" spirit. I want 2005 to be a "Can-Do" Year for every Indian." Dr. Manmohan Singh, Prime Minister of India, The Economic Times, December 25, 2004.

This Report "Towards a Functional Competition Policy for India" is dedicated to every Indian, the rich, the not-so-rich and the poor, so that we can build a more equitable, competitive and humane India. The process has to start now.

The Prime Minister's exhortation has its roots in the first days of the new government, which has made competition a serious policy issue. Extracted below are the relevant excerpts from the President's Address to the Parliament on 7th June 2004:

"Revival of industrial growth is of paramount importance. Incentives for boosting private investment will be introduced. Foreign Direct Investment will continue to be encouraged. Indian industry will be given every support to become productive and competitive. Competition, both domestic and external, will be deepened across industry with professionally run regulatory institutions in place to ensure that competition is free and fair.

"The Government will establish a National Manufacturing Competitiveness Council to provide a continuing forum for policy interactions to energise and sustain the growth of the manufacturing industry.

"The Government is committed to a strong and effective public sector, whose social objectives are met by its commercial functioning. But for this, there is need for selectivity and a strategic focus. My government will devolve full managerial and commercial autonomy to successful, profit-making companies operating in a competitive environment.

"My government believes that privatisation should increase competition, not decrease it".

The Common Minimum Programme adds: "It will not support the emergence of any monopoly that only restricts competition. All regulatory institutions will be strengthened to ensure that competition is free and fair. These institutions will be run professionally".

It is in this background, that CUTS' research project endeavours to find out what ails the economy, in the context of competition, and what can be done to improve the situation.

1.2 What is Competition?

Competition is a process of economic rivalry between market players to attract customers. These market players can be multinational companies, domestic companies, wholesalers, retailers (even our neighbourhood shopkeeper) or a cable operator. Such a competitive situation may also be affected by market contestability, where in competition comes not only from existing players, but also from new players that could enter and contest in the market.

In their pursuit to be better than other enterprises, market players adopt the following ways:

- *Fair*: This relates to the adoption of fair means such as producing quality goods, becoming cost efficient, adopting the best available technology, more research and development and the like. In this sense, firms do their best in terms of innovation, choice, quality and service.

- *Unfair*: This relates to the adoption of restrictive business practices such as predatory pricing, exclusive dealing, tied selling, resale-price maintenance, cartelisation, refusal to deal and the like.

In either situation, competition in the sense of economic rivalry leads to a concentrated market, as the number of firms operating in them is reduced while the size of those still active increases considerably, resulting in a greater market power. Thus, 'competition kills competition'. This is true, if one follows the inherent logic within competition; the natural tendency then would drive competition to result in monopoly.

Given this, the appropriate definition of competition is "a situation which ensures that markets always remain open to potential new entrants and that enterprises operate under the pressure of competition".

1.3 Why a Competition Law?

Theoretically speaking, trade liberalisation is one of the most effective measures to ensure competition in the market place and curb abuse of market power. However, even this has its limits. Imported goods cannot reach the consumers directly and the well entrenched market players may have a grip over the distribution channels, which may nullify the gains of liberalised trade. Then, there are goods and services which are not tradable. There are goods which are tradable but only within a limited market. Cement being a classic example of this. Due to its bulky nature it is not economical to transport it to distant markets. As a result, even geographical segments of a national market can be successfully monopolised or cartelised.

Thus, it is not surprising to see that while countries have gone for more and more trade liberalisation over the last one decade, more and more countries have also embraced competition laws, with many adopting new laws after scrapping their old ones. In the beginning of 1990, there were about 30 odd countries with a competition law. However, at present, the number is about 100 and many more are in the queue. Obviously, there is a greater acceptance of the fact that trade liberalisation may not always be a perfect remedy for an abuse of market power.

The need for a competition law, thus arises from the following factors:

- To take care of the anti-competitive practices designed to restrict the free play of competition in the market;

- To take care of the unfair means adopted by firms against the consumers in order to extract the maximum possible consumers' surplus; and

- To maintain and promote the competitive spirit in the market.

1.4 Competition Policy and Other Policies

Competition policy is an integral part of economic policy. The main objective of competition policy is to preserve and promote competition as a means to ensure efficient allocation of resources in an economy, resulting in the best possible choice of quality, the lowest prices and adequate supplies to consumers. Although a competition law may be quite narrow in its scope, Competition Policy is much more broad and comprehensive in its scope, and tries to bring harmony in all government policies that may encourage or adversely affect competition and consumer welfare. To put it differently, ensuring competition is just a means to achieve the above-stated objectives.

There are complex inter-relationships between competition and other public policies. This factor has a direct bearing on the extent to which competition policy objectives can be pursued without being constrained by or conflicting with other public policy objectives. Accordingly, even in the absence of a competition law or a stated competition policy, many of the related concerns can be addressed, at least partially, if there are other policies, which are favourable to competition.

Different government policies that may encourage or adversely affect competition and hence consumer welfare, particularly, in the context of the present globalising environment would include:

- Trade Policy

- Industrial Policy

- Regional Development Policy

- Privatisation/Disinvestment Policy

- Regulatory Reform Policy

- Fiscal Policy

- Intellectual Property Policy

- Consumer Policy

- Labour Policy, and

- Environment Policy

In addition, sector-specific policies in various areas, such as health, electricity, telecommunications, financial services etc., also affect competition in the economy.

Australia is a classic case! It has framed a National Competition Policy (NCP), which is a set of policy reforms adopted by provincial governments through out Australia. The objective is to encourage better use of the country's resources, and hence provide a higher standard of living, through increasing competition. NCP consists of a number of separate reforms, which, in aggregate, seek to deliver a widespread competitive revitalisation of the national economy. The policy is aimed at providing a consistent approach to the dismantling of barriers to competition across State borders as well as legislations to ensure that the same competitive rules apply to all sectors of the economy, regardless of ownership.

1.5 Promoting Competitiveness through Competition

Competition policy has a significant role to play in promoting competitiveness and growth. The term 'competitiveness' appears to have aroused considerable controversy in recent years. On the one hand, the word has become a kind of umbrella term for a wide ranging set of policies. On the other hand, the term evokes an analogy, which suggests that nation states compete in the same way that firms compete. It may be true that the nations do not compete but firms do. Nonetheless, it is equally true that while nations may not compete, they may help the firms compete more effectively by following a set of macro policies, which can create an enabling environment. For example, the issue of clearances to set up a business and how long it takes.

A study conducted by the World Bank[1] reveals that in India, entrepreneurs on average go through 11 steps to launch business, which takes 89 days on average, as against a regional average of 9 steps and 46 days. In a sample of 145 countries, India was placed at the 130th position in terms of the number of days it takes to get the procedural clearances. What a shame!

The term competitiveness gained wide currency after the introduction of the Competitiveness White Papers in the UK and the European Community in 1994. The backdrop of these white papers was slow productivity growth and decline in relative economic positions of the UK and Europe compared with Japan and the US. The economic malaise of the UK and European economies was thought to be poor competitiveness.

The decline in the UK's (and Europe's) relative economic performance prompted much debate about the appropriate response. In many ways, this debate was not new. The UK White Papers on competitiveness start from a recognition of the UK's relative decline and identify ten policy areas that influence competitiveness. One of these ten areas is the policy related to fair and open markets. Similarly, EU White Papers highlighted four areas for priority action:

• The promotion of investment in intangible assets;

• The development of co-operation between firms;

• Ensuring fair competition; and

• The modernisation of public authorities.

Thus, we see that both the white papers on competitiveness emphasise the need for ensuring fair competition in the market as an essential ingredient for enhancement and maintenance of competitiveness in the economy. These prescriptions apply to India as well.

Empirical evidence, though focusing mainly on the experience of developed countries, has confirmed that barriers to competition within an economy, whether due to governmental or private restraints, lead to losses in income and welfare. On the other hand, a well-designed and implemented competition policy promotes economic growth by ensuring better allocation of resources, as highlighted by the following examples:

A study carried out for the Australian economy estimates the expected benefits from a package of competition promoting and deregulatory reforms (including improvements in the competition rules) to incur an annual gain in real GDP of about 5.5 per cent, or A$23 billion where consumers would gain by almost A$9 billion besides having an increase in real wages, employment and government revenue.[2]

A report prepared for the UK Government illustrates the benefits of introducing competition into markets in which, previously, it had been absent. The chosen markets were: Retail Opticians, International Telephone Calls, Net Book Agreement, Passenger Flights in Europe, New Cars, and Replica Football Kits. It was found that competition policy led to large price reductions, innovations and product development.[3]

A book released by the McKinsey Global Institute (MGI)[4], based on research on the economies of 13 nations, argues that the key to reducing economic inequalities between rich and poor countries is productivity and its links to competition and consumption. MGI studied national economies from the ground up, and points out that global economic agencies underestimate the significance of a level playing field. Competition is more important than education or greater access to capital markets in lifting a country's gross domestic product. To reduce barriers to competition, policymakers must stand up to business special interests and focus more on the welfare of consumers.

In the context of developing countries, including India, there is a shortage of systematic analyses, regarding the benefits of adopting a competition policy and law. However, a relevant study of the Peruvian competition agency, Indecopi, found that in the first seven years of its operation, the economic benefits due to its operations amounted to $120m against operating costs of $20m, or six-fold.[5] A study by the Korean Fair Trade Commission in 2003 found that the benefit (consumer welfare increase and income transfer effect) outweighed the costs (KFTC's budget) of competition law enforcement in 2000 and 2001 by 34 times.[6]

Under the 7Up1 project[7], we found that the Government in India did not appear very serious about the competition regime, as the budgetary allocation to the MRTP Commission was just about 0.0009 per cent of the total government budget, when the ideal budget in other developing and developed countries was in the range of 0.0013 per cent of the total budget. Even a small poor country like Zambia had provided 0.005 per cent of its total budget to the Competition Commission.

1.6 Competition Policy and Development

An issue, often raised, while discussing Competition Policy in the context of a developing country, is the role of Competition Policy in the process of economic development of a country. The biggest challenge in the developing world today is to get rid of abject poverty that deprives a large section of their population a dignified life. An important approach to poverty reduction is to empower the poor, provide them with productive employment and increase their access to land, capital and other productive resources. But this approach may not be successful unless these people are linked to the markets and markets are made to work for the benefit of the poor people.

As stated in the World Development Report 2000-01,

"Markets work for the poor because poor people rely on formal and informal markets to sell their labour and products, to finance investment, and to insure against risks. Well-functioning markets are important in generating growth and expanding opportunities for poor people".

"Well-functioning" implies markets that work efficiently and without distortions. However, competition is often distorted by players, and it is essential that governments enact competition laws to regulate the distortions. What is very often ignored is the fact that the prevalence of anti-competitive practices in markets hurt the poor more. A rich person would not mind paying a dollar more for buying something but for people, living with less than a dollar a day, getting value for money for every cent they spend is more vital. This is the 'consumption' side.

If we turn to 'ability to pay' angle or the 'income' side, a sector that immediately comes to mind is agriculture. Of the 1.2 bn people of the globe who live in extreme poverty, approximately 75 per cent live and work in rural areas and about two-thirds of them draw their livelihood directly from agriculture[8]. The market for agricultural products is very often considered to be an example of a perfectly competitive market. However, there is a huge gap between the prices consumers pay and the prices farmers actually receive. This is because of the chain of intermediaries between consumers and farmers that do not always work in a competitive manner. These intermediaries abuse their monopolistic dominance in the market for final products, while in the markets for primary products, they abuse their monopsonistic dominance. In a country like India, where two-thirds of the population draw their livelihood directly from agriculture, the linkage between market imperfections in agriculture goods and poverty is manifest.

It needs to be realised that competition law is not a luxury of the developed world, but one of the necessary tools for developing countries, in their fight against poverty. Developing countries should not be dogmatic about withdrawing from the markets as distortions and failures in markets are quite ubiquitous and the state needs to play a role in promoting a fair and orderly market.

Competition Policy maximises consumer welfare, by ensuring goods and services at best possible quality, offered at lowest prices and available in adequate quantities. Alongside, competition policy also leads to business welfare, by ensuring, for instance, intermediate goods and services consumed by businesses are available through a competitive process.

1.7 Promoting Effective Markets through Competition

Competition, though seen as a means of attaining efficiency and fairness, may not necessarily promote these objectives. A perfectly competitive market with many small firms may achieve equality of opportunity (fairness) but may not achieve efficiency, as too many firms will mean that they will not be able to enjoy economies of scale. Obviously, competition policy must deal with trade-offs in its objectives and instruments. This concern has led to a shift from a structural approach to behavioural approach in enforcing competition in market. After all, in a fiercely competitive market, even a duopoly can produce an outcome that a perfectly competitive market generates. Thus, it may not be necessary to have a highly competitive market structure provided that appropriate rules of the game can be designed and enforced so that the behaviour of the market players remains competitive.

This approach may, however, become ineffective when there are natural monopolies and competition cannot be ensured as such. Situations could also arise where there might be a number of players in the market but the market itself is so segmented that the individual players become monopolists in the relevant market. The only way to get "competitive outcomes" in such markets is to put in place effective regulation. Thus, regulation in different sectors becomes an integral component of competition policy.

Obviously, competition policy is quite a complex issue. Unfortunately, there has not been much research on competition issues in India. In the past, efforts have been made by the Indian Institute of Management, Ahmedabad and CUTS, Jaipur. While the IIMA study did not go beyond policy level, a study by CUTS done under the 7-Up1 Project revealed a crying need to do further research in some sectors, which display typically anti-competitive behaviour: cement; trucking; services such as cable TV etc.

As the country is poised to implement a new competition law, a lack of understanding of the nature and extent of prevalence of different types of anti-competitive practices in India will pose a major challenge. CUTS has taken up this project to get a better understanding of the competition scenario in India. This will help:

- the government to draft and integrate a national competition policy;

- the competition authority to set priorities; and

- other stakeholders to understand the situation and make appropriate interventions.

The project has involved top experts of the country who have good understanding on competition issues, as well as different subjects. Each of their names appear in the relevant chapter. The project was guided by a Steering Committee, comprising eminent experts and economists.[9]

The report itself is being published as two separate volumes. The first one is an overview version, which carries all papers in a précis form, so that a busy reader can go through easily and get a flavour of what the issues are. The other one is a more detailed report, carrying all chapters in greater depth, and is meant for the policy community, particularly the research community. It is also addressed to the more serious policy implementers, including the various branches of the Government, the Planning Commission, the Competition Commission of India and the National Manufacturing Competitiveness Council, the consumer and business community etc., to see what further needs to be done. Both the reports are not detailed research reports, but will serve as curtain raisers and as a road map for future more in-depth work.

As an aside, the project has also established an e-discussion group:

FunComp@yahoogroups.com. This is being used regularly to post news and views relating to competition and regulatory issues, which can generate debate and thus better learning among a large economic policy community in India. The e-discussion group has over 200 members, and it continues to grow.

This project has been supported by the Department for International Development (DFID), UK as part of a CUTS project: 7Up2, which is engaged in a comparative study of competition regimes in five other countries of Asia: Nepal, Bangladesh, Vietnam, Laos and Cambodia. Part of this project dealing with the three Mekong countries has been supported by SECO, Government of Switzerland.

1.8 The Report

To begin with, this chapter on Introduction gives an overview of issues covered in the volume. The entire volume is divided into eight parts covering systemic as well as sectoral issues.

Part I brings out India's experience with competition law and some of the specific challenges that the newly formed Competition Commission of India would face in implementing its mandate.

Evolution of Competition Policy and Law in India (Chapter 2) highlights the economic policy scenario in India before and after the 1991 reforms, the extant competition law: Monopolies and Restrictive Trade Practices Act, 1969 and the evolution of the new competition law: Competition Act, 2002.

What is interesting is that the Monopolies and Restrictive Trade Practices Act, 1969 (MRTP Act) had its genesis in the Monopolies Inquiries Commission, 1965, which had uncovered strong concentration of economic power in various sectors of the economy. Consequently, the MRTP Act was enacted to prevent concentration of economic power, control monopolies, and prohibit monopolistic and restrictive trade practices. Unfair trade practices, a consumer protection provision covering deception, misleading claims and advertising etc., was brought in through an amendment in 1984. However, the MRTP Act was unable to deliver as expected, partly due to the weaknesses in its own structures and composition of the MRTP Commission (MRTPC), but also because it was created at a time when all the process attributes of competition such as entry, price, scale, location, etc. were regulated. The MRTPC had no influence over these attributes of competition, as these were part of a separate set of policies. What a paradox! The MRTP Act was enacted to check the various competition concerns that resulted from the then control regime, but had no say in changing the very elements of that regime.

It was in 1991 that widespread economic reforms were undertaken and consequently the march from a "command-and-control" regime to a regime based more on free market principles commenced its stride. The economic reforms undertaken since the early-1990s significantly changed the economic environment in the country. Major amendments were made to the MRTP Act in 1991 but even these were considered inadequate to deal with the emerging economic order. In view of this, India adopted a new competition law, the Competition Act, 2002 (the Act) to replace the MRTP Act.

Key provisions of the Act are presented in *Competition Act, 2002: The Approach* (Chapter 3). Certain distin-guishing features of the Act are noted. For instance, the Act emphasises the behavioural approach to examine competition in the market as against the structural approach followed by the MRTP Act. Importantly, the Competition Commission of India (CCI) has been given a competition advocacy role, which will help in creating a culture of competition. Other core areas on which the Act focuses are anti-competitive agreements, abuse of dominance and combinations regulations. One huge gap in the law is its inability to regulate abuse of intellectual property rights, even when it has been recommended in the TRIPs agreement.

A key reason for the ineffectiveness of the MRTP Commission was that it was poorly resourced. Hence, for the CCI to play its role effectively, it is imperative to resource it properly, including providing regular training exposure for capacity building of its personnel. The second drawback with the MRTPC was its inadequacy in dealing effectively with anti-competitive practices, which was due to lack of definitions, cumbersome procedures and scarce resources. The new law has tried to take care of these handicaps, but the resource issue will depend upon the political will of the government. However, it would bode well for the CCI to research some of the critical cases handled by the MRTPC, so that it can approach similar cases with greater confidence and cogency. Some of these cases could be the cement and tyre cartels, which were never cracked down by the MRTPC.

As part of the 1991 amendments, the MRTP Act was diluted by removing provisions on mergers & acquisitions (M&As), so as to allow unfettered growth. The 4th Chapter (*Mergers and Acquisitions in India: Implications for Competition*) looks at the nature of M&As, post-1991 amendments and shows that merger behaviour of erstwhile MRTP companies was such as it would have come under the scanner of the now diluted MRTP Act. In fact, certain mergers relating to foreign firms involved market shares of a magnitude that would attract the attention of competition authorities in most countries, but in India all M&A activities were beyond challenge, as there is no M&A regulation from competition perspective since the 1991 amendments. The Competition Act has provisions for combinations regulations, but these will be effective from the third year of its introduction. Be that as it may, the chapter argues that these provisions may not be very effective in regulating mergers. Firstly, the definition of combinations is very narrow in its scope. It doesn't

include joint ventures, alliances etc. Secondly, the threshold is so high, that many M&As will escape from its scrutiny. For effective M&A regulation, the CCI will also have to monitor those M&As which are out of the ambit of the Competition Act but may raise competition concerns.

As India integrates more and more into the global economy, it would become more prone to the anti-competitive practices operating on a global scale or originating elsewhere in the globe. *Cross-Border Competition Issues* (Chapter 5) addresses such issues and highlights the relevant provisions in the Competition Act, in particular that the Act has extra-territorial jurisdiction and embodies the 'effects doctrine'. To make these provisions effective the CCI would require substantial capacity building. It is suggested that efforts should be made to promote international cooperation at different levels: bilateral, regional and multilateral to tackle cross-border competition challenges.

Over the years, especially after economic reforms were initiated in the early-1990's various sectoral regulators, such as in power and telecommunications, have been established to attract private investment and create a predictable environment through the establishment of independent agencies. These regulators are also required to ensure healthy competition in the regulated sector. This can lead to overlaps with the competition law. However, we did not have any major problems until now, as our new competition authority has more or less been ineffective. So has been the case with some of our regulators as well. However, it is expected that the new competition authority and the regulators will be more active in the years to come. This may result in conflicts. Chapter 6: *Interface Between Regulation and Competition Law* has tried to identify potential areas of conflict. It has also made an effort in offering some solutions based on a study of different jurisdictions where problems arose and appropriate solutions found out.

The chapter on M&As brings out one such issue of overlapping jurisdiction, which relates to M&A regulation. Besides, the CCI, there are other agencies which regulate M&As such as the Telecom Regulatory Authority of India, Electricity Regulatory Commissions (federal as well as state level), Reserve Bank of India, Securities and Exchange Board of India, company benches of the high courts, etc. However, the objective of regulating M&As varies across these agencies. Proper coordination mechanisms would be required between the CCI and all other agencies for an effective regulation of M&As in the country.

There are complex inter-relationships between competition and other public policies. Government policies such as trade policy, industrial policy, regulatory reforms, etc. may encourage or impede competition and hence consumer welfare. Thus, although a competition law may be quite narrow in its scope, competition policy is much broader and comprehensive, and seeks to bring harmony in all the Government policies. Part II of the volume traces this interface between competition and various policies of the government, both at the federal level as well as state level.

Central Government Policies: Interface with Competition Policy Objectives (Chapter 7) shows that as policy outcomes are sought to be generated, it is a persistent practice in India to do so without taking into cognisance that policies need to be framed and implemented in harmony with the market process, and not in a manner so as to stall the process. This is true of both the pre-1991 control regime and even the liberalised regime followed since the early-1990's. Several examples of policies in the current economic milieu are provided, which are not in harmony with the market processes.

Besides Central Government policies, there are policies/practices or regulatory failures of state governments, which lead to anti-competitive outcomes. Unfortunately, these issues are most often ignored, partly because of lack of awareness and partly due to vested interests. Chapter 8 on *State Government Policies and Competition*, does a survey of five such issues *viz.*, procurement policy, excise policy, truck operations, bid-rigging in construction contracts and retail services. Anti-competitive practices are rampant at the state level and we need state-level competition agencies, backed by appropriate laws, to tackle them. In fact, by promoting competition, the state governments can protect consumer interest as well as increase their revenues.

The two chapters in part II suggest that all laws and government policies should be assessed on the touchstone of competition. Governments at the federal and the state level should frame and implement policies by acknowledging the market process. One good way to do it is through a systemic 'competition audit' of all policies, new and old.

Among other goals, Competition Policy aims to promote consumer welfare mainly in terms of lower prices, better quality of goods and services, more choice and easy availability. Part III of the volume highlights this aspect of competition policy.

Competition Policy and Consumer Welfare (Chapter 9) highlights that competition policy and law is just one of the tools in the larger context of other overarching public policies and approaches that need to be addressed for promoting consumer welfare. In the Indian context, besides the MRTP Act, an important central legislation to provide for the protection of interests of consumers is the "Consumer Protection Act, 1986" (COPRA). Both the outgoing MRTPA and the COPRA have similar provisions, particularly in the area of unfair trade practices (UTPs). However, the Competition Act, 2002 does not have provisions relating to UTPs, which henceforth will fall within the ambit of only the COPRA.

The chapter presents the experience with the working of the MRTP Act and COPRA in terms of protecting consumer interest. It is suggested that progressive legislations need to be encouraged to check market abuses and enhance consumer welfare. To help consumers either directly or through policy interventions, it is imperative to create and sustain a strong civil society movement.

For the new competition authority to become popular, without which it may face many hurdles thrown in by vested interests, it is necessary that it creates a public buy-in. It cannot do so by addressing only esoteric problems, such as cartels in the transmission tower industry etc. Not that it is unimportant to demolish cartels, which seem to pervade all our intermediate goods sectors. However, for getting a pro-people image, one way forward for the CCI is to take up systemic consumer abuses, which are ubiquitous at the local level. It could also do so in collaboration with the redressal agencies under COPRA, as retail level competition issues are covered under COPRA. Chapter 10: *Competition Abuses at Consumer Level: Study of Select Sectors*, has laid out a preliminary study of two consumer-level sectors: health services and school education to see how the prevailing anti-competitive practices at grassroots level are affecting the ordinary consumers.

So far, the report has addressed systemic and cross-cutting issues. In the subsequent parts, we take up sector-specific studies.

Part IV of the volume brings out competition concerns in the primary sector and discusses the issue of marketing of agriculture produce. In agriculture markets (Chapter 11, *Agriculture Markets in India: Implications for Competition*), there is a huge gap between the prices consumers pay and the prices farmers actually receive. This is because of the chain of intermediaries between consumers and farmers, who most often collude. In a country where two-thirds of the population draws their livelihood directly from agriculture, the linkage between market imperfections in agriculture goods and poverty is manifest.

Alternative avenues for sale and purchase through cooperative marketing agencies are found to dilute market power of private trade to some extent. In order to provide more competition at the retail level and to benefit consumers and producers, innovative marketing mechanisms like *apni mandi* and producer's sales counters in consumer centres should be promoted.

In the next part (Part V), we look at competition issues in the manufacturing sector, in general, as well as cement, steel and pharmaceuticals sectors in particular.

Chapter 12, *State of Competition in the Indian Manufacturing Industry* makes a preliminary assessment of the extent of competition in markets in the 1990's based on available evidence. It looks at changes in market concentration, impact of import competition and FDI, and price and profitability trends. What comes to the fore is that both domestic as well as foreign owned firms have taken dominant positions in many industries. Market concentration has risen in several industries as a consequence. The chapter highlights the need for developing a reliable and consistent data base. Linkage between industry, trade and FDI data needs to be established and maintained on a continuing basis. This would facilitate further in-depth studies.

The next three chapters look at specific sectors in the manufacturing sector. Cement (Chapter 13, *Competition Issues in the Indian Cement Industry*) is a basic good that is used mainly in infrastructure and hence its availability at competitive prices is very important for developing countries. However, because of its bulky nature, the cement industry is very often insulated from outside competition. World over it has gained notoriety for collusive practices. India is no exception. Indeed, cases were lodged with the competition authority a couple of times. But nothing came out. This is despite the fact that cartelisation in the Indian cement industry is an open secret. The weak provisions in the MRTP Act, along with weak investigation capacity due to resource constraints among other extraneous factors are the primary reasons for cartel formation going unchecked for years. The new law is a significant improvement in this regard with clearer provisions and leniency programme. Careful analysis of offers by different companies in Central and state government

bids can give important clues if there have been patterns of systematic rotation of winning bids, stable shares of companies in overall procurement etc. This information would also be helpful in detecting collusive behaviour in the market as well.

Crying hoarse over the shenanigans of the steel industry, the Union Steel Minister: Ram Vilas Paswan has been threatening to set up a steel regulator. It is not a workable proposal, because nowhere in the world is there an independent regulator for any commodity. The only exception is pharmaceuticals, which is usually governed by a regulator, but that too under the relevant ministry. Independent regulation is used for the service sector mainly. The Chapter 14: *Competition Scenario in the Indian Steel Industry* examines the history of evidence of collusive practices in the steel industry. Needless to say, no action could be taken in this sector too. The structure of the study is more or less on the same pattern as the cement sector.

The pharma retail trade has been exploiting the hapless Indian consumer by colluding and gouging the industry by squeezing out ridiculous commissions. Chapter 15, *Competition Policy for the Pharmaceuticals Sector in India* shows that in this sector, it is not only the industry, but the trade is a bigger culprit. It is difficult to promote and maintain competition because of the peculiarity of the pharmaceuticals market in the sense that consumers do not decide their purchases. There is a need for an effective regulatory framework to promote good prescribing behaviour among the doctors and to curb collusive/rent-seeking behaviour of the pharmacists. Mergers and Intellectual Property Right (IPR) related abuse of dominance are likely to raise competition concerns in coming years. There is a need to study the behaviour of the bulk drug market and if desirable there can be further decontrol in this regard.

Infrastructure is a critical determining factor to achieve and sustain a high growth rate. However, poor and inadequate infrastructure continues to remain a major obstacle. To boost investment in the infrastructure sector and ensure good quality and accessible services, the Central Government has resolved to create a regulatory framework that is transparent; independent of Government and, provides an impartial balance between public sector and private sector suppliers and is based on international best practices. Besides, the Planning Commission has been asked to prepare a policy paper indicating what the regulatory structure should be for each infrastructure area. Part VI of the report takes up three infrastructure areas: telecommunications, energy and transportation.

The telecom sector is widely recognised as a success story of regulation and competition in India. The number of telephone lines per person, has grown almost ten fold in the last decade. This is partly due to the advent of private players in the market. However, competition and investment though present, is yet to be seen in fixed line services, which are used by the majority of households even as mobile phones now outstrip fixed lines in number. There are several barriers to entry in these latter services where benefits of incumbency are largest. It is here that BSNL, the state-owned enterprise rules the roost. The existing regulatory regime has been largely unsuccessful in controlling BSNL's market power and regulating it effectively. The fact that BSNL is wholly government owned also provides important clues to the reason for the failure to regulate BSNL effectively. This reason is the conflict of interest that government and regulators face in taking decisions that will impact BSNL's position in the market place (Chapter 16, *Competition Issues in Telecommunication Sector*)

In India, government still dominates most of the primary as well as secondary energy sectors at large, though a beginning has been made to allow the private sector in the area. Chapter 17, *Competition and Regulation in Energy Sector in India*, brings out that issues of regulation and competition policy are complex in the energy sector. Any piecemeal approach to policy formulation or implementation would delay the development of competitive markets. A cohesive view of competition in the entire energy sector is missing so far. Recently, there were reports that the government is working towards developing a comprehensive energy policy. In such a case, it would be interesting to observe how much importance is given to make the sector competitive. It is advisable that keeping the bigger picture in mind, the choice between economic regulation *Vs.* competition be examined very carefully.

While the transport sector has grown at a healthy rate of 10 per cent a year during the last decade, this is the sector that has the greatest possibility to hold back India's GDP growth target of eight per cent. Despite several efforts made by the government, the sector remains inefficient. The reason for this sorry state of affairs eventually boils down to policies that inhibit competition and their poor regulation in the various transport sectors, as disclosed by Chapter 18, *Competition Issues in Transportation Sectors.*

In the case of the ports sector, for instance, despite allowing the private sector to invest in major ports,

there are few instances of this happening, as it is up to the port authority (the Government) to decide to allow competition. It is worse in the case of the railways. They are the primary medium for transporting containers across the country's vast hinterland and enjoy a total monopoly over this, through the Container Corporation of India (Concor). In the aviation sector, similarly, the Government is just about to allow private airlines to fly abroad, but the barriers to entry are still high, whilst the policy is loaded against the public sector carriers. Goods transport by road is often at the mercy of a cartel of transport operators, who through collusion dictate rent-seeking freight rates. The chapter argues that whatever needs to be done in the transport sector to make it more competitive has to be done by way of policy reforms. Since transport is inter-modal, creation of a single super regulator could also be explored.

Part VII covers competition issues in services.

Competition and Regulation in Financial Services (Chapter 19) focuses on issues relating to regulatory bodies and regulation. Regulatory bodies exist in the financial services sector because of the fact that markets may fail. Given that entities in the financial sector are taking up several activities related to different markets in the financial sector, for example banks are becoming universal banks; there is need to move away from sectoral regulation to functional regulation i.e. more coordination is required amongst the various sectoral regulators in the financial market. The chapter argues that a change is required in the regulatory mindset and suggests the appointment of a super regulator for the whole financial sector. There is also a need to build the capacity of the regulatory authorities to deal with the changing environment of the global financial system.

The key objective of regulators is to address the original source of market failure which may or may not be, promoting competition, as lack of competition may not be the source of market failure in the first place. However, competition plays an important role in regulated sectors. Chapter 20 (*Competition and Professional Services*) presents a case study of professional services in this regard.

The chapter focuses on three professions: accounting, law and medicine. Due to the idiosyncratic nature of the services provided, the sector is characterised by asymmetries of information. Certain characteristics of regulatory design in professional services from the point of view of competition are highlighted. For example, entry conditions are required to ensure that the practitioner is well qualified. The risk involved is that, if the profession is captured then we may end up in a situation where the entry condition is also used to maintain market return. Restriction on advertisements protects incumbency advantages, as somebody who is well established in a profession gets a huge advantage through word of mouth. It is suggested that the CCI should engage in deeper study through public hearings etc., and a dialogue with professional regulatory authorities for better market practices. Alternatively, co-regulation can be encouraged to discipline self-regulated professions. State level competition and regulatory agencies can be established *inter alia* to enforce standards of professional conduct *vis-à-vis* competition concerns. Managing the professions through New Delhi-based bodies is a sub-optimal experience.

Both the Information Technology and Biotechnology sectors are emerging sectors in the economy. It is widely believed that these two sectors have been doing extremely well. The last part (part VIII) of the volume analyses the two sectors.

Chapter 21, *Competition Issues in Information Technology Sector*, reveals that during the last decade India has emerged as a major player in the field of information technology. The analysis shows that in the case of hardware, the removal of tariff barriers and the presence of a large unbranded market act as sources of increased competition. However, the situation appears to be different in the case of software. The high market concentration in some of the software segments, especially in the operating system, seems to not only have the effect of making software high-priced but also dampens the development of applications software on account of the lack of access to source codes. The chapter underscores the need for creating a more competitive environment in the software sector *inter alia* by promoting open source software. In this context, it argues for an active state role, to provide appropriate incentives for the promotion of open source software and create demand by promoting its use in all the e-governance projects. From the hardware side, innovations like 'simputer' need to be encouraged so that hardware becomes more affordable and leads to greater demand.

Chapter 22, *Implications of Competition Policy on Biotechnology Industry in India* highlights that India's fast growing biotech sector has the potential of serious implications on the competition environment in the country. However, an array of pro-active legislations serves to ensure that competition is not impaired. India's IPR regimes, whilst affording protection to inventions that fulfil the criteria of novelty, non-obviousness and commercial application, do still carry with it the elements for regulating anti-competitive behaviour on the part of the firms concerned. The flexibilities inherent in India's IPR regimes, coupled with bio-safety, biodiversity and stringent food safety laws, could go a long way in promoting the biotech sector in a manner that is sustainable and economically advantageous.

Besides, there are certain sectors, such as media, retail sector, and postal services, which have not been included in the report. Anyhow, the typical competition issues in various sectors have already come up and there is little chance of value addition by studying more sectors.

In the media sector, for instance, the growth in readership created by price wars is disruptive and leads to some artificiality in the numbers. This creates a distortion in newspaper economics and they have to, willy-nilly, depend too heavily on advertising. In Delhi, when Times of India and Hindustan Times went into a price war, the newspaper hawkers were able to make money by not selling the copies at all. Price cuts reached a point where the news papers sold at Re. 1, while the number of pages was very high. Hawkers got 40 per cent commission and so the net price they paid to newspapers was pitiful. They actually gained by not selling the paper to the readers. This led to an artificial economics, which is not good for the industry. Over-reliance on advertising also affects media's role in promoting competition culture in the country. With increased dependence on ad budgets, it is difficult to imagine, media providing any space to news against a market player, whose advertising budget is attractive.

Organised retailing is a sector to watch out for in India, with the emergence of giant stores, such as Shoppers Stop and Big Bazaar. Big retail chains are getting more powerful, and as they flex their muscles, manufacturers are realising the importance of dealing with them in a different manner, as compared to the regular mom-and-pop stores or neighbourhood *kirana* outlets. So will the large retailer call the shots in the future? There have been several cases of enquiry in other countries that have found retailers using their market (buyer) power to the detriment of suppliers and competitors. China is facing a similar challenge, as monopolistic behaviour is said to exist in the retail sector. Considering this, the Competition Commission needs to keep a close tab on this emerging sector.

Another important sector, which affects a major section of the society, is postal services. The state-run Department of Posts is a dominant player in the sector; in fact, it has the exclusive franchise for delivery of 'letters'. However, promoting a government monopoly does not suit the times. In fact, healthy competition from the private sector will only lead to more efficiency and innovativeness by the Government postal service. One has already seen this happening in the form of a plethora of new, non-mail services offered by the Post Office, such as insurance, bill payment, and savings schemes as well as birth of Speed Post, to take on the overnight delivery services of private couriers. It also needs to be realised that the Post Office provides universal service, by servicing remote areas and carrying low priced post cards. Hence, any competitive field that is drawn up for postal services in the country, needs to clearly spell out the means by which the Post Office would be compensated for this loss-making service. If the private sector has to play a role in this compensation then the rules should be clear-cut and penalties stiff. The experience in the telecom sector, where private licensees failed to meet their rural connectivity obligations and have been let off by mild fines, needs to be avoided.

In brief, the volume brings out that there is a need to frame a National Competition Policy for the country, so that Government and other economic regulatory agencies are aware of and take into account the competition dimension in their own policy formulations and implementation. A draft National Competition Policy Statement is annexed to this report.

The role of the government needs to be rationalised to promote effective markets. And a 'competition audit' of all new and old policies will help the government to promote competition.

Furthermore, there is an imperative need to create State-level competition and regulatory agencies to resolve local problems. Even with regional offices, federal bodies cannot be effective as has been seen in the case of the MRTPA.

The Competition Commission should be made accountable through independent review by consumer organisations, external agencies and peer review by competition authorities from other countries. To ensure effective function of the competition authority, it is imperative to resource it properly. This includes recruitment of skilled staff.

Additionally, the consumer movement in the country needs to be adequately resourced and strengthened to enable the competition and regulatory agencies to perform their tasks and their advocacy roles.

Notes

1. *Doing Business in 2004: Understanding Regulation*, The World Bank.

2. http://www.unctad.org/en/docs//c2em_d10.en.pdf

3. *The Benefits from Competition: Some Illustrative UK Cases*, Centre for Competition Policy, University of East Anglia, May 2004.

4. William W. Lewis (2004). *The Power of Productivity*, McKinsey Global Institute, The University of Chicago Press.

5. See Caceres, A. (2000). *Indecopi's First Seven Years* in Beatriz Boza, ed., *The Role of the State in Competition and IP Policy in Latin America: Towards an Academic Audit of Indecopi*, Lima.

6. CUTS (2005). *Citizens' Report on the State of Competition Laws in the World*, CUTS/INCSOC, Jaipur.

7. CUTS (2003). *Pulling Up Our Socks - A Study of Competition Regimes of Seven Developing Countries of Africa and Asia: The 7-Up Project*, CUTS, Jaipur.

8. International Fund for Agricultural Development (IFAD), *Rural Poverty Report 2001: The Challenge of Ending Rural Poverty*, New York, OUP, 2001.

9. See list at Page 293.

Part I

Competition Law in India

2 Evolution of Competition Policy and Law in India

S. Chakravarthy

2.1 Introduction

This Chapter addresses the evolution of competition policy and law in India, tracing during its narrative course the economic scenario in India before and after the 1991 reforms, the extant competition law (Monopolies and Restrictive Trade Practices Act, 1969, briefly referred to as the MRTP Act) in the country and the evolution of the new competition law (Competition Act, 2002, briefly referred to as the Act) passed by the Parliament in December 2002. The new law is given a detailed treatment in Chapter 10 and its features, therefore, have been accorded only a cursory mention in the current Chapter.

Since attaining Independence in 1947, India, for the better part of half a century thereafter, adopted and followed policies comprising what are known as "Command-and-Control" laws, rules, regulations and executive orders. The competition law of India, namely, the MRTP Act was one such. It was in 1991 that widespread economic reforms were undertaken and consequently the march from "Command-and-Control" economy to one based more on free market principles commenced its stride. As is true of many countries, economic liberalisation has taken root in India and the need for an effective competition regime has also been recognised.

2.2 Historical Developments Leading to the Enactment of the MRTP Act

2.2.1 Constitutional Provisions

The Constitution of India, in its essay in building up a just society, has mandated the State to direct its policy towards securing that end. Articles 38 and 39 of the Constitution of India, which are part of the Directive Principles of State Policy, mandate, *inter alia,*

that the State shall strive to promote the welfare of the people by securing and protecting as effectively, as it may, a social order in which justice – social, economic and political – shall inform all the institutions of the national life, and the State shall, in particular, direct its policy towards securing:

- that the ownership and control of material resources of the community are so distributed as best to subserve the common good; and

- that the operation of the economic system does not result in the concentration of wealth and means of production to the common detriment.

The MRTP Act was in consequence of the aforesaid mandate in the Directive Principles in the Constitution of India, namely, prevention of concentration of economic power. We next highlight the circumstances that led to the need and enactment of the MRTP Act.

2.2.2 Development Strategy After Independence and its Impact

India adopted the strategy of planned economic development since the early 1950s. The Indian Industrial Policy, since Independence in 1947, commenced with the Industrial Policy Resolution of 1948, which defined the broad contours of the Industrial Policy and delineated the role of the State in industrial development, both as an entrepreneur and as an authority.

The next important watershed in Industrial Policy was the 1956 Resolution, which emphasised growth, social justice and self-reliance. It further defined the parameters of the government's regulatory mechanism. The most significant thrust of the 1956 Resolution was making industrialisation subject to government intervention and regulation. In particular, the private sector was allowed limited licensed capacity in the core sector and the public sector was given the mantle to achieve the "commanding heights" of the economy by being made responsible for the major share of production.

Government intervention and control pervaded almost all areas of economic activity in the country. For instance, there was no contestable market. This meant there was neither an easy entry nor an easy exit for enterprises. Government determined the plant sizes, their location, prices in a number of important sectors, and allocation of scarce financial resources. Their further interventions were characterised by high tariff walls, restrictions on foreign investments and quantitative restrictions. It may, thus, be seen that free competition in the market was under severe fetters, mainly because of governmental policies and strategies.

The licensing policy of the government favoured big business houses for they were in a better position to raise large amount of capital and had the managerial skill to run the industry. The business houses also had the advantage in securing financial assistance from the bankers and financial institutions. With no proper system of allocating licences in place, licensing authorities were naturally inclined to prefer men who had proved their competence by success in big industrial ventures in the past to men who had still to establish their ability. This also led to pre-empting of licences by a few business houses. Another reason why big businessmen succeeded in getting new licences was their ability to secure foreign collaboration.

Thus, the system of controls in the shape of industrial licensing restricted the freedom of entry into industry and also led to concentration of economic power in a few individuals or groups of business houses. This emergence of monopoly industries and the indulgence by industrial groups in restrictive trade practices were detrimental to the general public.

2.2.3 Trigger Cause

There were essentially three enquiries/studies, which acted as the lodestar for the enactment of the MRTP Act.

The first study was by a Committee chaired by Mr. Hazari, which studied the industrial licensing procedure under the Industries (Development and Regulation) Act, 1951. The Report of this Committee concluded that the working of the licensing system had resulted in disproportionate growth of some of the big business houses in India (Hazari, 1965).

The second study was by a Committee set up in October 1960 under the chairmanship of Professor Mahalonobis to study the distribution and levels of income in the country. The Committee, in its Report presented in February 1964, noted that the top 10 per cent of the population of India cornered as much as 40 per cent of the income (Mahalanobis, 1964). The Committee further noted that big business houses were emerging because of the "planned economy" model practised by the government in the country and suggested the need to collect comprehensive information relating to the various aspects of concentration of economic power.

The third study was known as the Monopolies Inquiry Commission (MIC), which was appointed by the Government in April, 1964 under the Chairmanship of Das Gupta. It was enjoined to enquire into the extent and effects of concentration of economic power in private hands and the prevalence of monopolistic and restrictive trade practices in important sectors of economic activity (other than agriculture). In particular, MIC was given the terms of reference:

- to ascertain the factors responsible for concentration of economic power and for monopolistic and restrictive trade practices,
- to ascertain their social and economic consequences, and
- to suggest suitable legislative and other measures to protect essential public interest.

MIC presented its Report in October 1965, noting therein that there was concentration of economic power in the form of product-wise and industry-wise concentration. The Commission also noted that a few industrial houses were controlling a large number of companies and there existed in the country large-scale restrictive and monopolistic trade practices (Monopolies Inquiry Commission, 1965).

As a corollary to its findings, the MIC drafted a Bill to provide for the operation of the economic system so as not to result in the concentration of economic power to the common detriment. The Bill provided for the control of monopolies and prohibition of monopolistic and restrictive trade practices, when prejudicial to public interest.

2.3 Enactment of the MRTP Act, 1969

The Bill, drafted by the MIC and amended by a Committee of the Parliament, became the Monopolies and Restrictive Trade Practices (MRTP) Act, 1969 and was enforced from 1st June 1970. The Act drew its inspiration from the mandate enshrined in the Directive Principles of State Policy in the Constitution, which aim at securing social justice with economic growth.

The Preamble to the Act says that the Statute is enacted to provide that the operation of the economic system does not result in the concentration of economic power to the common detriment, for the control of monopolies, for the prohibition of monopolistic and restrictive trade practices and for matters connected therewith or incidental thereto.

The MRTP Act drew heavily upon the laws embodied in the Sherman Act and the Clayton Act of the United States of America, the Monopolies and Restrictive Trade Practices (Inquiry and Control) Act, 1948, the Resale Prices Act, 1964 and the Restrictive Trade Practices Act, 1964 of the United Kingdom and also those enacted in Japan, Canada and Germany. The US Federal Trade Commission Act, 1914, as amended in 1938, and the Combines Investigation Act, 1910 of Canada also influenced the drafting of the MRTP Act.

The premises on which the MRTP Act rests are unrestrained interaction of competitive forces, maximum material progress through rational allocation of economic resources, availability of goods and services of quality at reasonable prices, and finally, a just and fair deal to the consumers. An interesting feature of the Statute is that it envelops, within its ambit, fields of production and distribution of both goods and services.

Thus, one of the products of the planned and controlled economy was the Monopolies and Restrictive Trade Practices Act, 1969 (MRTP Act). Its cousin, to regulate, control and grant foreign exchange, was born in 1973, christened the Foreign Exchange Regulation Act. In the planned and controlled regime, the market suffered from little or no competition resulting in detriment to economic efficiency and productivity. Self-reliance was synonymous with import substitution and consequently, indigenous availability criteria ensured automatic protection to domestic producers, regardless of cost, efficiency and comparative advantage.

2.3.1 Thrust Areas

The thrust of the MRTP Act is directed towards:

- the prevention of concentration of economic power to the common detriment;

- the control of monopolies;

- the prohibition of monopolistic trade practices; and

- the prohibition of unfair trade practices.

A criticism is often voiced that the Statute prohibits growth. This is fallacious and erroneous. The Statute regulates growth but does not prohibit it. Even in its regulatory capacity, it controls the growth only if it is detrimental to the common good.

In terms of competition law and consumer protection, the objective of the MRTP Act is to curb monopolistic, restrictive and unfair trade practices, which disturb competition in the trade and industry and which adversely affect the consumer interest (monopolistic, restrictive and unfair trade practices are described later in this chapter). A parallel legislation known as the Consumer Protection Act, 1986 (described towards the end of this chapter) has also come into being, which prevails in the realm of unfair trade practices.

The regulatory provisions in the MRTP Act apply to almost every area of business – production, distribution, pricing, investment, purchasing, packaging, advertising, sales promotion, mergers, amalgamations and take-over of undertakings (provisions relating to mergers, amalgamations and take-overs were deleted in the MRTP Act by the 1991 amendments to it). They seek to afford protection and support to consuming public by reducing, if not eliminating, monopolistic, restrictive and unfair trade practices from the market.

One of the main goals of the MRTP Act is to encourage fair play and fair deal in the market, besides promoting healthy competition. Under the MRTP Act, a regulatory authority called the MRTP Commission (briefly, Commission) has been set up to deal with offences falling under the Statute.

2.3.2 Objectives

The principal objectives sought to be achieved through the MRTP Act are:

i)   prevention of concentration of economic power to the common detriment;

ii) control of monopolies;

iii) prohibition of monopolistic trade practices;

iv) prohibition of restrictive trade practices;

v)   prohibition of unfair trade practices.

2.3.3 Doctrine Guiding the Act

Behavioural and reformist doctrines inform the MRTP Act. In terms of the behavioural doctrine, the conduct of the entities, undertakings and bodies, which indulge in trade practices in such a manner as to be detrimental to public interest, is examined with reference to whether the said practices constitute any monopolistic, restrictive or unfair trade practice.

In terms of the reformist doctrine, the provisions of the MRTP Act provide that if the MRTP Commission, on enquiry, comes to a conclusion that an errant undertaking has indulged either in restrictive or unfair trade practice, it can direct that undertaking to discontinue or not to repeat the undesirable trade practice. The MRTP Act also provides for the acceptance of an assurance from an errant undertaking that it has taken steps to ensure that the prejudicial effect of trade practice no more exists.

The veneer of the MRTP Act is essentially based on an advisory or reformist approach on the ground that mere deterrence by punishment approach is not the only way to make an errant undertaking to behave.

2.3.4 Amendments to the MRTP Act (1984)

Less than a decade had elapsed after the MRTP Act came in force, when the government appointed a high-powered expert committee on Companies and MRTP Acts, under the Chairmanship of Justice Rajindar Sachar to review and suggest changes required to be made to the MRTP Act in the light of experience gained in the administration and operation thereof.

The Committee observed that it (MRTPA) contained no provisions for the protection of consumers against false or misleading advertisements or other similar unfair trade practices and that they needed to be protected from practices which are resorted to by the trade and industry to mislead or dupe them (Sachar, 1978). To quote the Sachar Committee: "Advertisements and sales promotion have become well established modes of modern business techniques. That advertisements and representations to the consumers should not become deceptive has always been one of the points of conflict between business and consumers".

In many countries, in particular developing countries like India, a large number of consumers are illiterate and ill-informed and possess limited purchasing power, in an environment where there is shortage of goods. Very often, one witnesses the spectacle of a large number of non-essential, sub-standard, adulterated, unsafe and less useful products being pushed through by unscrupulous traders by means of unfair trade practices and deceptive methods. Subtle deception, half truths and misleading omissions inundate the advertisement media and instead of the consumer being provided with correct, meaningful and useful information on the products, they often get exposed to fictitious information, which tends to their making wrong buying decisions. Transparent information is missing and needs to be a goal to be chased.

The Sachar Committee, therefore, recommended that a separate Chapter should be added to the MRTP Act defining various unfair trade practices, so that the consumer, the manufacturer, the supplier, the trader and other persons in the market can conveniently identify the practices, which are prohibited. The 1984 amendments to the Act brought unfair trade practices within its ambit.

The 1984 Amendment also created a new authority, in the form of the Director-General of Investigation and Registration (DGIR), which was supposed to function in close liaison with the Commission. On matters relating to restrictive trade practices, unfair trade practices, and monopolistic trade practices, the DGIR has the power to make preliminary inquiries to assess the need for the Commission to initiate an inquiry. The Commission can also ask the DGIR to investigate such matters and submit reports to the Commission. Trade agreements that incorporate restrictive clauses must be registered with the office of the DGIR.

In addition, the 1984 amendments to the MRTP Act tightened certain provisions therein, like definitions of "dominant undertaking", "inter-connected undertakings", "group", "monopolistic trade practice" etc.

2.3.5 Ambit and Coverage of MRTP Act

The Indian Statute, as most competition laws in the world, encompasses within its ambit essentially three types of prohibited trade practices, namely, restrictive, unfair and monopolistic. Very briefly, the core of such practices is enumerated below.

2.3.5.1 Restrictive Trade Practice (RTP)

A Restrictive Trade Practice is generally one, which has the effect of preventing, distorting or restricting competition. In particular, a practice, which tends to obstruct the flow of capital or resources into the stream of production, is a RTP. Likewise, manipulation of prices and conditions of delivery or flow of supply in the market, which may have the effect of imposing on the consumer unjustified costs or restrictions are regarded as Restrictive Trade Practices.

Certain common types of Restrictive Trade Practices enumerated in the MRTP Act are:

i)   Refusal to deal

ii)   Tie-up sales

iii) Full line forcing

iv)   Exclusive dealings

v)   Concerted practice

vi)   Price discrimination

vii) Re-sale price maintenance

viii) Area restriction

ix)   Discriminatory pricing.

All Restrictive Trade Practices under the MRTP Act are deemed legally to be prejudicial to public interest. Therefore, the entity, body or undertaking charged with the perpetration of the Restrictive Trace Practice, can, after the establishment of the charge, only plead for gateways provided in the MRTP Act itself, to avoid being indicted.

If the gateways are satisfactory to the Commission, and if it is further satisfied that the restriction is not unreasonable, having regard to the balance between those circumstances and any detriment to the public interest or consumers likely to result from the operation of the restriction, the Commission may arrive at the conclusion that the RTP is not prejudicial to public interest and discharge the enquiry against the charged party.

The law in the UK frowns on anti-competitive arrangements, which are multilateral in character. The law in the USA, on the other hand, is wider and all that is required is that competition is impaired somewhere in the line of commerce. The Indian law, MRTP Act, is modelled on the UK pattern, but conceptually similar to the US pattern.

Furthermore, if a trade practice is expressly authorised by any law for the time being in force, the Commission is barred from passing any order against the charged party.

2.3.5.2 Unfair Trade Practice (UTP)

The 1984 amendments to the Act brought Unfair Trade Practices within its ambit. Essentially, Unfair Trade Practices fall under the following categories in the Indian law:

1. Misleading advertisements and false representations.

2. Bargain sales, bait and switch selling.

3. Offering of gifts or prizes with the intention of not providing them and conducting promotional contests.

4. Product safety standards.

5. Hoarding or destruction of goods.

Making false or misleading representation of facts, disparaging the goods, services or trade of another person is also a prohibited trade practice under the Indian law.

2.3.5.3 Monopolistic Trade Practice (MTP)

The definition of monopolistic trade practice was amended by the 1984 amendment to the Act. MTP is a trade practice, which has, or is likely to have, the effect of:

i)   maintaining the prices of goods or charges for services at an unreasonable level by limiting, reducing or otherwise controlling the production, supply or distribution of goods or the supply of any services or in any other manner;

ii) unreasonably preventing or lessening competition in the production, supply or distribution of any goods or in the supply of any services;

iii) limiting technical development or capital investment to the common detriment or allowing the quality of any goods produced, supplied or distributed, or any services rendered, in India, to deteriorate;

iv) increasing unreasonably:-

    a) the cost of production of any goods; or

    b) charges for the provision, or maintenance, of any services;

v)   increasing unreasonably:-

    a) the prices at which goods are, or may be, sold or re-sold, or the charges at which the services are, or may be, provided; or

    b) the profits which are, or may be, derived by the production, supply or distribution (including the sale or purchase of any goods or in the provision or maintenance of any goods or by the provision of any services);

vi) preventing or lessening competition in the production, supply or distribution of any goods or in the provision or maintenance of any services by the adoption of unfair methods or unfair or deceptive practices.

2.3.6 Dominance

In the MRTP Act, the basis of determining dominance is whether an undertaking has a share of one-fourth or more in the production, supply, distribution or control of goods or services.

2.3.7 MRTP Commission

Under the MRTP Act, a Commission has been established, the Chairman of which is required to be a person who is or has been or is qualified to be a judge of the Supreme Court or High Court (of a State). The Members of the Commission are required to be persons of ability, integrity and standing who have adequate knowledge or experience of, or have shown capacity in dealing with problems relating to economics, law, commerce, accountancy, industry, public affairs or administration. The Commission is assisted by the Director General of Investigation and Registration for carrying out investigations, for maintaining register of agreements and for undertaking carriage of proceedings during the enquiry before the MRTP Commission.

The powers of the Commission include the powers vested in a civil court and include further power:

i)   to direct an errant undertaking to discontinue a trade practice and not to repeat the same;

ii) to pass a 'cease and desist' order;

iii) to grant temporary injunction, restraining an errant undertaking from continuing an alleged trade practice;

iv) to award compensation for loss suffered or injury sustained on account of RTP, UTP or MTP;

v)   to direct parties to agreements containing restrictive clauses to modify the same;

vi) to direct parties to issue corrective advertisements;

vii) to recommend to the Central Government, division of undertakings or severance of inter-connection between undertakings, if their working is prejudicial to public interest or has led or is leading to MTP or RTP.

2.3.7.1 Investigation and Enquiries

The MRTP Commission can be approached with a complaint on Restrictive or Unfair Trade Practices by:

a) an individual consumer;

b) a registered association of consumers; or

c) a trade association.

The Commission can be moved by an application from the DGIR or by a reference by the Central or State Governments. The law provides for *suo motu* action on the part of the Commission, if it receives information from any source or on its own knowledge.

The procedure followed by the Commission is that on receipt of a complaint, the matter is, in many cases, referred to the DGIR for investigation and report. More often than not, the complainee is called upon to give his/her comments on the complaints received. Experience shows that in a large number of cases, the mere letter of investigation or letter of enquiry issued by the DGIR or the Commission results in the complainee providing the needed relief to the complainant. This has been noticed in cases relating to refunds in respect of bookings of scooters, repair or replacement of refrigerators, TV sets, replacement of defective parts during the warranty period and the like. Similarly, there have been cases of successful interventions relating to bookings of flats and plots and disputes relating to property.

The law provides for a temporary injunction against the continuance of alleged monopolistic, restrictive or unfair trade practices, pending enquiry by the Commission.

A salutary provision in the MRTP Act is the power of the Commission to award compensation for loss or damage suffered by a consumer, trader, class of traders or government as a result of any monopolistic/restrictive/unfair trade practice indulged in by any undertaking or person.

It is logical and equitable to provide that any person who is affected by any prohibited practice should have a remedy to recover damages and compensation from the guilty party.

2.4 Economic Reforms and Impact on the MRTP Act

2.4.1 Key Elements of Economic Reforms

It was in 1991 that India took the initiative in favour of economic reforms consisting essentially of liberalisation and de-regulation. In a manner of speaking, India embarked on what is described as the LPG regime, an acronym for liberalisation, privatisation and globalisation.

In the post-1991 LPG policy paradigm, a number of changes were introduced in policies relating to industrial licensing, foreign investment, technology imports, government monopolies and ownership, price and purchase preferences for the public sector, reservations for the small scale sector, financial sector, etc. The main objective has been, and is, to make the market driven by competitive forces, so that there could be incentives for raising productivity, improving efficiency and reducing costs.

The concept of size and monopoly, not viewed with prejudice any more, resulted in amendments to the MRTP Act. Furthermore, the licensing requirement became confined to a very short list of industries. The other features of the post-1991 paradigm include de-controlling, de-regulating, de-licensing, de-canalising and de-bureaucratising of industry and trade. Constraints of space prevent a description of the reforms in the various sectors of the economy. However, for certain important sectors, the reforms are given below in a capsule form herein.

1. Industrial Policy: Licensing has been abolished except in respect of six industries. Sugar industry was de-licensed in January 1999, though it remains subject to a number of other controls.

2. Public Sector: The monopoly of public sector industries, except those where security and strategic concerns still dominate (arms and ammunition, atomic energy, rail transport etc.), has been abolished. Major industries, like iron and steel, air transport, and telecommunication equipment, are now open for private sector investment.

Price preference for public sector has been discontinued, but purchase preference continues.

3. Small Scale Industries: The policy of reservation and preferential treatment for small-scale industries continues, but a large number of items have been removed from the reserved category.

4. Price Control: Price and quantity controls for a number of commodities have been relaxed.

5. Import Licensing: Originally, before the reforms, the export and import policy contained a negative list of imports, subject to licensing. Almost all consumer goods were subject to import licensing. In the export and import policies after the 1991 reforms, the list of restricted consumer goods has been pruned, the number of canalised items has been reduced and the import of some restrictive items has been liberalised. Tariffs have been reduced in a phased manner. The average applied tariff rate was 125 per cent in 1990-91 and now it is less than 35 per cent. India has done away with the quantitative restriction regime, as a result of WTO commitments.

6. Foreign Investment: Foreign direct investment, foreign technology agreements and compulsory licensing have been liberalised. The cap on foreign holdings has been increased in a number of sectors.

7. Financial Sector: The financial sector has been gradually de-regulated. Entry of domestic and private foreign banks has been permitted. Domestic financial institutions have been allowed to enter conventional banking activities. The office of the Controller of Capital Issues was abolished in 1992 and a National Stock Exchange was set up.

8. Exit Policies: Exit was and is difficult for Indian industry because of the labour and bankruptcy laws. Legislation has been enacted for a new insolvency law. The Industrial Disputes Act, 1947, which protects the interests of labour, is being examined to provide for easier exit for industry.

9. State Monopolies and Privatisation: Limited privatisation has taken place. In civil aviation, competition has been allowed. Power sector is being unbundled and independent regulatory authorities have been set up. Competition has been permitted in the area of telecommunications.

2.4.2 Amendments to the MRTP Act and their Impact

Major amendments were effected to the MRTP Act in 1991. Two of the five objectives mentioned earlier, namely, prevention of concentration of economic power to the common detriment; and control of monopolies, have been de-emphasised, after the 1991 amendments to the MRTP Act. In the context of the latter, to the extent monopolies tend to bring about monopolistic trade practices, the MRTP Act continues to exercise surveillance, which existed prior to the 1991 amendments. This is because a monopolistic trade practice is understood to be synonymous with anti-competitive practice.

Prior to the 1991 amendments, the MRTP Act essentially was implemented in terms of regulating the growth of big size companies, called the monopoly companies. In other words, there were pre-entry restrictions therein requiring undertakings and companies with assets of more than Rs. 100 crore (about US$25 million) to seek approval of government for setting up new undertakings, expansion of existing undertakings, etc.

Provisions relating to concentration of economic power and pre-entry restrictions with regard to prior approval of the Central Government for establishing a new undertaking, expanding an existing undertaking, amalgamations, mergers and takeovers of undertakings, were all deleted from the Statute through the amendments.

With the restructuring of the MRTP Act through the 1991 amendments, the thrust thereof is on curbing monopolistic, restrictive and unfair trade practices with a view to preserving competition in the economy and safeguarding the interest of consumers by providing them protection against false or misleading advertisements and/or deceptive trade practices. Size as a factor, to discourage concentration of economic power, has been, in a manner of speaking, given up.

2.4.3 Applicability of the MRTP Act

During the year 1991, a notification was issued by the government that the MRTP Act shall apply to public sector undertakings, whether owned by the government or by government companies, statutory corporations, undertakings under the management of various controllers appointed under any law, cooperative societies and financial institutions. Thus, there is no distinction, post-91, between the public sector undertakings and private sector companies in the matter of monopolistic, restrictive and unfair trade practices.

Indian Airlines, nationalised banks, Indian Railways, Post and Telegraphs and tele-communications undertakings, housing and urban development authorities, are all accountable if they indulge in MTP, RTP or UTP. There are of course a few entities, like defence undertakings, which are outside the ambit of the MRTP Act. It may also be mentioned here that after the amendment to the definition of "service", it includes the business of builders and real estate operators. This has brought a large number of buildings activity operators under the ambit of the MRTP Act.

2.4.4 Mergers and Amalgamation

Concentration of economic power may result from merger, amalgamation or take-over. The MRTP Act does not prohibit merger, amalgamation or take-over, but seeks to ensure that the arrangement sub-serves public interest.

Before the 1991 amendments, the MRTP Act frowned upon expansion of giant undertakings so as not to permit them to acquire power to put a stranglehold both on the market as well as on consumers, and further industrial expansion of the country.

After the 1991 amendments, the MRTP Act has been restructured and pre-entry restrictions with regard to prior approval of the government for amalgamation, merger or take-over have been removed. However, the MRTP Act still has power under provisions relating to restrictive trade practices and monopolistic trade practices to take action against mergers that are anti-competitive. This was posited by the Supreme Court in the Hindustan Lever Limited-Tomco merger case (Supreme Court, 1994). The Court observed that the MRTP Act, after the 1991 amendments, did not empower the Central Government to pre-emptively stop a merger, because it is likely to affect competition. Thus, the 1991 amendments to the MRTP Act removed the *ex ante* power of the said Statute to block merger deals. This vacuum has been plugged by the Competition Act, 2002, which gives *ex ante* power to the Competition Commission of India to block certain combinations, if found to adversely affect competition.

Furthermore, in relation to concentration of economic power, even after the 1991 amendments to the MRTP Act, the law retains provisions relating to the power of the Government to direct division of an undertaking and severance of inter-connection between undertakings, if the working of an undertaking is prejudicial to public interest or is likely to lead to the adoption of any monopolistic or restrictive trade practice. While the power to conduct an enquiry in this regard is vested with the Commission, only the Government can pass the order for division of understanding or severance of inter-connection, and thus the role of the Commission is advisory.

2.5 Experience with the Working of the MRTP Act

2.5.1 Disposal of Cases

The achievement of the Commission with regard to the disposal of cases relating to MTPs is indicated in Table 2.1.

TABLE 2.1

Statistics of Cases on Monopolistic Practices

	1997	1998	1999
Brought Forward	7	8	8
New Cases	1	0	0
Disposed off	0	0	0
No. of enquiries pending at the end of year	8	8	8

Source: CUTS, 2002.

During the three years 1997 to 1999, not a single new investigation relating to an MTP was launched by the Commission. The procedure to be followed by the Commission for an MTP enquiry is based on adversary proceedings, which are by their very nature time consuming.

TABLE 2.2

Statistics of Cases on Restrictive and Unfair Trade Practices with MRTPC

	1997	1998	1999
Brought Forward	6016	5666	6250
New Cases	1447	1024	749
Disposed off	1791	440	4695
No. of enquiries pending at the end of year	5666	6250	2404

Source: CUTS, 2002.

The Commission has been successful in dealing with cases relating to restrictive and unfair trade practices (Table 2.2). It disposed off nearly 4700 cases in 1999 and only 2404 cases were pending at the end of 1999. It can be seen from Table 2.2 that the number of new cases declined sharply during 1997 to 1999. The end of 2004 saw the pendency reduced to a little less than 500.

There have been cases in which a restrictive or unfair trade practice is adopted against an individual consumer unintentionally or due to ignorance of the provisions of the MRTP Act. In such cases and also in some other cases, the complaints of consumers or other aggrieved persons are sent to the respondents for comments. It has been noticed that in a large number of such cases, the respondent satisfies or redresses the grievance on the intervention of the Commission, and since the complainant gets the needed relief, no further action is taken. In this way, relief has been received by an innumerable consumers.

2.5.2 Inadequate Budget and Independence of the MRTP Commission

The Department of Company Affairs provides the budget of the MRTP Commission. Data collected for the four years 1996 to 1999 may be seen in Table 2.3.

The data in Table 2.3 shows that the Government subvention towards the budget of the MRTP Commission is a very small fraction of both the GDP and the budget of the Central Government. While there is no benchmark for the fraction, the relatively smaller proportion for India *vis-à-vis* some countries is well brought out in CUTS (2003), which provides comparative figures for eight countries, besides India. The percentage of the expenditure of the Competition Authority to the total government budget in all those countries is more than that of India. The inadequacy of the budget allocation by the Government is compounded by the need for the Commission to seek

the former's permission to incur expenditure beyond certain limits. The sanction for most posts at the senior level of the Commission has to be given by the Government. The autonomy of the Commission stands impaired to a great extent because of the above constraints.

TABLE 2.3

Annual Budget of the MRTP Commission

(Rs. in billions)

Year	Actual Expenditure	Budget	Budget of Central Government	(3) as Proportion of (4)	GDP	(3) as Proportion of (6)
(1)	(2)	(3)	(4)	(5)	(6)	(7)
1996	10.48	11.08	2010.07	0.005	13682.08	0.0008
1997	14.363	14.399	2320.68	0.006	15224.41	0.0009
1998	16.724	17.728	2793.60	0.006	17582.76	0.0010
1999	—	17.605	2980.84	0.0059	19569.97	0.0009

Source: CUTS, 2002.

2.5.3 Qualitative Output of the MRTP Commission and its Independence

The quantitative output of the MRTPC was given in para 5.1. A scan of the various decisions of the MRTPC over more than three decades shows that, by and large, they have been qualitatively good and well argued. They have been essentially in favour of the consumers, who were victims of restrictive and unfair trade practices. A criticism against the MRTPC has been that the cases brought before it consume a lot of time, thus delaying justice. It is true (from the author's experience as Member, MRTPC) that many cases took more than two years before they were disposed off. Essentially, the reason for the delay had been that the MRTPC, because of the Statute and the Statutory rules and regulations, was following the procedure outlined in the Code of Civil Procedure, 1908. Sequentially, after receipt of a complaint, there would be a reply from the respondent, a rejoinder from the complainant, framing of issues, evidence through interrogatories and discovery of documents, oral evidence of witnesses (with cross examination and re-examination), arguments by the advocates representing the parties and the final judgment. In other words, a full-fledged trial, like in the case of civil matters in civil courts, rather than a summary trial, governed the conduct of the cases.

The perception among the consumers, litigants and advocates has been that the MRTP Commission is independent in discharging its investigative and adjudicatory functions. It needs mention that Government has the discretion in the appointment of the Chairman and Members of the Commission, which one could argue may undermine its independence. But, there has been no complaint of the Commission being influenced by the Government because of the latter having discretionary powers for choosing persons for appointment to the Commission. The bar on Chairman and the Members of the Commission for seeking appointment in any undertaking, which falls within the ambit of the MRTP Act for a period of 5 years after demitting office, is designed to impart integrity to the functioning of the Commission.

Nonetheless, the MRTP Commission is independent in discharging its investigative and adjudicatory functions. The Commission acts like a civil court with powers to summon witnesses, recording their depositions, receiving affidavits and issuing commissions for the examination of witnesses and documents.

2.5.4 MRTP Act has Outlived its Utility

The MRTP Act was enacted, as noted earlier, at a time when India had the "command-and-control" paradigm for the administration of the economic activities of the country. Most of the process attributes of competition, such as entry, price, scale, location etc. were regulated. Thus, the MRTP Act had very little influence over these process attributes of competition, as they were part of a separate set of decisions and policies of the Government. As the new paradigm of economic reforms, namely, liberalisation, privatisation and globalisation (LPG) took root in the mid-80s and intensively from the early-90s, the MRTP Act was hardly adequate as a tool and a law to regulate the market and ensure the promotion of competition therein.

Paras 2.2.2 and 2.4.1 had traced briefly the impact of governmental policies on economic activities in the country. The MRTP Act, though a competition law, could not be effective in the absence of other governmental policies inhering the element of competition. For instance, the protections offered to public sector undertakings in the form of price and purchase preferences distorted competition in the market, where private sector was also operating. Indeed, this resulted in the public sector undertakings not attempting to be efficient and price competitive. Many of them did not even take care to technologically upgrade themselves when the Government provided them preference protection. A pre-requisite for competition

law is the creation of competition culture in the market, through putting in place by the Government a chain of policies relating to industrial, financial, fiscal, public sector, labour etc., with a competition perspective. In the absence of such policies, competition law, by itself, cannot exist in a vacuum and act as an effective tool to foster competition in the market.

The need for a new law, particularly after 1991, in line with the new LPG paradigm led to the enactment of Competition Act, 2002, described in Chapter 10.

2.6 Metamorphosis from MRTP Act, 1969 to Competition Act, 2002

During the administration of the MRTP Act over the last three decades and more, there have been a large number of rulings of the Supreme Court of India (binding on everyone in India) and also Bench decisions of the MRTP Commission. These decisions have interpreted the various provisions of the MRTP Act from time to time and have constituted precedents for the future. Thus, where the wording of the existing law has been considered inadequate by judicial pronouncements, redrafting the law to inhere the spirit of the law and the intention of the lawmakers became inevitable.

A perusal of the MRTP Act will show that there is neither definition nor even a mention of certain offending trade practices, which are restrictive in character. Some illustrations of these are:

- Abuse of Dominance
- Cartels, Collusion and Price Fixing
- Bid Rigging
- Predatory Pricing

In this context, a question arose if the existing MRTP Act could itself be suitably amended, instead of drafting and bringing a new law into force. An argument in support of the former, namely, amending the MRTP Act, is generally advanced that one particular generic provision [Section 2(o)] of the MRTP Act may cover all anti-competition practices, as it defines an RTP as a trade practice which prevents, distorts or restricts competition. But, the issue has to be viewed in another perspective. While complaints relating to anti-competition practices can be tried under the generic definition of a Restrictive Trade Practice, the absence of specification of identifiable anti-competition practices always gives room to different interpretations by different courts of law, with the result that the spirit of the law may sometimes escape being captured and enforced. While a generic definition may be necessary and may form the substantive foundation of the law, it is necessary to identify specific anti-competition practices and define them so that there is no scope for a valve or opening on technical grounds for the offending parties to escape indictment.

Some of the anti-competition practices like cartels, predatory pricing, bid rigging, etc. are not specifically mentioned in the MRTP Act, but the Commission, over the years, has attempted to fit such offences under one or more of its sections by way of interpretation of the language used therein.

Another dimension is the dynamic context of international as well as the domestic trade and market. When the MRTP Act was drafted in 1969, the economic and trade milieu prevalent at that time constituted the premise for its various provisions. There has been subsequently a sea change in the environment, with considerable movement towards liberalisation, privatisation and globalisation (LPG). The law has to yield to the changed and changing scenario on the economic and trade front. This is one important reason why a new competition law was framed. Many countries like the UK, Canada, Australia and the European Community have, in line with this thinking, enacted new competition laws and repealed their earlier laws governing fair-trading, etc. It may be added here that amendments to MRTP Act would have entailed cumbersome innumerable changes in its provisions. Instead, enacting a new law was considered a better option. Hence, the new law, the Competition Act, 2002.

2.6.1 *Expert Group on Interaction Between Trade and Competition Policy*

The 1996 Singapore Ministerial Conference of the WTO decided to set up, *inter alia*, a Working Group to study issues relating to the interaction between Trade and Competition Policy, including anti-competitive practices. The Ministry of Commerce, Government of India, in its turn set up an Expert Group on interaction between Trade and Competition Policy, as an offshoot of the Singapore Ministerial Declaration of 1996. The Expert Group presented its report to the Ministry of Commerce in January 1999. (The Working Group set up consequently on the Singapore Ministerial Declaration has also presented its report to the General Council of the WTO). The Expert Group (1999) addressed competition issues *qua*:

- Mergers, Amalgamations, Acquisitions and Take-overs
- Intellectual Property Rights
- Foreign Investment
- Anti-Dumping Measures, Subsidies and Countervailing Measures and Safeguard Measures
- State Monopolies, Exclusive Rights and Regulatory Policies
- Sanitary and Phytosanitary Measures
- Technical Barriers to Trade
- Professional Services
- Government Procurement
- WTO Provisions.

The common thread that runs through the Expert Group's report and recommendations is that there should be a regulatory agency to control and eliminate anti-competition practices that may surface during the operation of international trade and during the implementation of the WTO Agreements.

For instance, the owner of a copyright, patent or other forms of Intellectual Property Right may issue a licence for someone else to produce or copy the protected invention, design, work, trademark, etc., and in the process, the terms of the licensing contract may restrict competition or impede technology transfer. There should be in place a law to take action to prevent anti-competitive licensing that abuses Intellectual Property Rights.

The Expert Group observed that competition law or policy is an essential complement to investment liberalisation. A sound competition policy and law can contribute to securing an attractive environment for foreign investment, particularly foreign direct investment by providing a stable and transparent legal framework and signalling a commitment to market institutions and mechanisms. The competition law should be capable of providing safeguards against possible abuses of market power by foreign investors.

The Expert Group, therefore, recommended that there is a need for an appropriate competition law to protect fair competition and to control, if not eliminate, anti-competition practices in the trade and market. Many anti-competition practices may surface during the operation and implementation of WTO Agreements. It is in this context, that a sound and effective competition law and a Competition Law Authority became the need of the hour, ushering in the new law, namely, the Competition Act, 2002.

2.6.2. High Level Committee on Competition Policy and Law

In October 1999, the Government of India appointed a High Level Committee on Competition Policy and Law to advise a modern competition law for the country in line with international developments, and to suggest a legislative framework, which may entail a new law or appropriate amendments to the MRTP Act.

S.V.S. Raghavan, a senior official of the Central Government, chaired the Committee. Among others on the Committee were the Chairman of Hindustan Lever Limited, a large company manufacturing fast moving consumer goods; a Consumer Activist; an Economic Journalist; a Chartered Accountant; and an Advocate, besides the Joint Secretary in the Department of Company Affairs dealing with competition law. The Committee took evidence from the representatives of different Chambers of Industries and Commerce, Professional Institutes, Consumer Organisations (NGOs), Experts, Academics and Government Officials.

At the time of the High Level Committee's deliberations, there were available about 80 competition laws of different countries. No competition law of any one country was adopted as a model, but features of different competition laws considered relevant for India and its prevalent milieu, were reckoned in giving a shape to the report. The arguments and logic governing prescriptions for the new Indian competition law are described in Chapter 10 dealing with the Competition Act, 2002.

In terms of the evidence received by the Committee, there was almost unanimity among those who gave their depositions to the Committee that the MRTP Act had outlived its utility and that a new competition law was required for the country, in tune with the post-1991 LPG paradigm. Anterior to the constitution of the Committee, this was well reflected in the announcement of the Finance Minister in his budget speech in February 1999. He observed that,

"The MRTP Act has become obsolete in certain areas in the light of international economic developments relating to competition laws. We need to shift our focus from curbing monopolies to promoting competition. The Government has decided to appoint a committee to examine the range of issues, and propose a modern competition law suitable for our conditions" (Parliament, 1999).

The Committee presented its Competition Policy Report to the Government in May 2000. Most (but not all) of the recommendations were unanimous, but two Members attached their supplementary notes to the Committee's Report, advising calibrated introduction of the competition law and cautioning against rigid bureaucratic structure for the Competition Commission of India. There were two notes of dissent, one of which was ideologically against any competition law at all and the other against mandatory notification of combinations. What finally emerged, as would be seen in Chapter 10, is the adoption of a provision in the Act for voluntary notification of combinations, calibrated introduction of the provisions of the Act and a competition law (Act) in line with post-1991 liberal regime.

On the basis of the recommendations of the Committee, a draft competition law was prepared and presented in November 2000 to the Government, which thereupon held wide consultations with stakeholders, like Chambers of Commerce and Industry, Consumer Organisations etc. While the Chambers of Commerce and Industry favoured a lenient competition law (e.g. high threshold limits for combinations' regulation), the Consumer Organisations suggested a tight competition law with severe penalty provisions.

A bill on the new competition law was introduced in the Parliament, outlining the objects and reasons for its enactment. The Statement of Objects and Reasons on Competition Bill ran thus:

"In the pursuit of globalisation, India has responded by opening up its economy, removing controls and resorting to liberalisation. The natural corollary of this is that the Indian market should be geared to face competition from within the country and outside. The Monopolies and Restrictive Trade Practices Act, 1969, has become obsolete in certain respects in the light of international economic developments relating more particularly to competition laws, and there is a need to shift our focus from cubing monopolies to promoting competition...

The Competition Bill...seeks to ensure fair competition in India by prohibiting trade practices, which cause appreciable adverse effects on competition in markets within India, and, for this purpose, provide for the establishment of a quasi-judicial body to be called the Competition Commission of India (hereinafter referred to as CCI), which shall also undertake competition advocacy for creating awareness and imparting training on competition issues" (Mittal, 2003).

The Parliament remitted the Competition Bill to its Standing Committee for detailed scrutiny. The Standing Committee met with representatives of Financial Institutions, Chambers of Commerce and Industry, Consumer Organisations, Professional Institutes, Experts, Academics and the relevant Ministries of the Government and presented its report to the Parliament (Standing Committee, 2002). After considering the recommendations of the Standing Committee and effecting some refinements, the Parliament passed in December 2002 the new law, namely, the Competition Act, 2002.

2.6.3 *Trigger for Metamorphosis from MRTP Act, 1969 to Competition Act, 2002*

To sum up, the factors that gave rise to the trigger for the metamorphosis from MRTP Act, 1969 to Competition Act, 2002 and that influenced the shape of the new law are:

1. The recommendations of the Expert Group (1999).

2. The recommendations of the High Level Committee (2000).

3. The unanimity among those who deposed before the High Level Committee for repealing the MRTP Act and substituting it with a new competition law.

4. Appreciation of the fact that the MRTP Act was more concerned with curbing monopolies rather than with promoting competition.

5. Appreciation of the fact that the MRTP Act was enacted during the pre-1991 LPG regime and that a new law was needed for the post-1991 LPG regime.

6. The recommendations of the Standing Committee of the Parliament, and

7. Recognition that Indian undertakings are small in size and need to merge and grow to become competitive globally (thus leading to the prescription of fairly high threshold limits for combinations regulation).

[Please see Mittal (2003), High Level Committee (2000), Expert Group (1999) and Standing Committee (2002)].

2.6.4 *Rubric of the New Law, Competition Act, 2002*

The structure and features of the new Indian competition law, namely, Competition Act, 2002 have been described in Chapter 10 and have been therefore left out in this Chapter. Improvements over the outgoing MRTP Act in the new law, namely, the Competition Act, 2002, are synoptically touched in Chapter 10 (para 12.0)

2.7 Role of Third Parties

Both, the outgoing law – MRTP Act, 1969 – and the new law – Competition Act, 2002 – provide for third parties to bring action before the Competition Authority. Both the Statutes permit any person, consumer, consumer association or trade association to file a complaint before the MRTP Commission or the Competition Commission of India, as the case may be. Under the new law, a "person" includes an individual, a Hindu undivided family, a company, a firm, an association of persons or a body of individuals, any corporation established by the government or a government company, a cooperative society and a local authority. Thus, a challenge to any anti-competitive agreement or to abuse of dominance is available to third parties. It is to be hoped that consumer associations and consumer activists will act as watchdogs on competition in the market and invoke the provisions of the Act, where necessary, in the larger interest of consumers.

2.8 Consumer Protection Act, 1986

Besides the MRTP Act, an important central legislation to provide for the protection of interests of consumers is the "Consumer Protection Act, 1986". Its sole concern is the welfare of the consuming public. It is supplementary to and not in derogation of the MRTP Act/Competition Act. It can be said to be an offspring of the consumer movement in India.

The Consumer Protection Act, 1986 (COPRA), providing for the protection of interests of consumers has provisions for the establishment of consumer councils and other authorities for the settlement of consumer disputes and matters connected therewith.

The consumer councils essentially seek to promote and protect the rights of consumers, such as:

a) the right to be protected against marketing of goods hazardous to life and property;

b) the right to be informed about the quality, quantity, potency, purity, standard and price of goods to protect the consumers against Unfair Trade Practices;

c) the right to be assured access to a variety of goods at competitive prices;

d) the right to be heard and to be assured that consumers' interests will receive due consideration at appropriate fora;

e) the right to seek redressal against Unfair Trade Practices or unscrupulous exploitation of consumers;

f) the right to seek redressal against Restrictive Trade Practices, like tie-in sales, delays, etc; and

g) the right to consumer education.

Quasi-judicial machinery has been set up at the district, state and central levels, empowered to give relief to the consumers and to award compensation for the loss or injury suffered by them. For non-compliance of an order passed by a quasi-judicial body, COPRA provides for penalties. Thus, the COPRA has two approaches, the first to provide consumer education and the other to provide for a simplified, inexpensive and speedy remedy for redressal of grievances of consumers.

Among the relief available, to which the quasi-judicial bodies are empowered to direct the guilty party are:

a) to remove a defect in the goods in question;

b) to replace the goods with new goods of similar description, free from any defect;

c) to return to the complainant the price or charges paid by her/him; and

d) to pay such amount as may be awarded as compensation for the loss or injury suffered by the consumer due to the negligence of the guilty party.

Both, the outgoing MRTP Act and the COPRA, have similar provisions particularly in the area of unfair trade practices. Where the area of jurisdiction overlaps, the complainant has the option to choose either of the fora for seeking redressal of her/his grievances. As noted earlier, the Competition Act, 2002 does not have provisions relating to UTPs, which henceforth will fall within the ambit of only the COPRA.

2.9 Sectoral Regulatory Authorities

Over the years, especially after economic reforms were initiated in early-90s, a number of sectoral regulatory authorities have been formed. For telecom, there is the Telecommunications Regulatory Authority of India (TRAI) and an appellate tribunal. For electricity, there is Central Electricity Regulatory Commission (CERC) at the federal level and State Electricity Regulatory Commission (SERC) in most states. Securities and Exchange Board of India (SEBI) looks after the operation of the capital market while the banking and the financial sectors are regulated by the Reserve Bank of India, the central bank. Insurance Regulatory & Development Authority (IRDA) has been created to regulate the newly opened insurance sector. There are other statutory bodies for regulating some other sectors and some more are in the offing (e.g. biotechnology).

Regulatory authorities have been set up in several sectors to produce competitive outcomes, i.e. foster greater efficiency in resource allocation and consumer welfare through maintaining and promoting competition. The question of overlapping jurisdictions, between the competition authority and sectoral regulators, is going to be a challenge and would require a proper mechanism to resolve the same. Chapter six of the report deals with this issue in greater detail.

2.10 Way Ahead

The new Competition Act, 2002 is now a part of Indian jurisprudence. Made effective by a Government notification on March 31, 2003, certain sections of the new Act are now in force. Staff has been authorised and is operating. One member of the Commission has been appointed. While the Central Government appointed a Chairperson of the Commission, the Supreme Court of India objected and his appointment was withdrawn. The matter of the qualifications of the Chairperson is now *sub judice* before the Supreme Court of India.

While the Act specifies that there shall be a Chairperson and not less than two nor more than ten other Members to be appointed by the Central Government, one cannot predict exactly when the full Commission will be appointed, or when the Central Government will bring the other provisions of the new law into force, in view of the pendency of the case in the Supreme Court. In the meantime, the old MRTP Act is in operation and the MRTP Commission continues to function. How well the new regime will operate, and whether it will be an improvement over the MRTP regime it has been designed to replace, remains to be seen.

References

Ahluwalia, I.J. (1991). *Productivity and Growth in Indian Manufacturing*, Oxford University, Press, Delhi.

APEC (1999). *Competition Law for Developing Economies* – Asia-Pacific Economic Cooperation Trade and Investment Committee, Singapore.

Bhagwati, J.N. and Desai, P. (1970). *Planning for Industrialisation and Trade Policies Since 1951*, Oxford University Press, Delhi.

Bhagwati, J.N. and Srinivasan, T.N. (1975). "Foreign Trade Regimes and Economic Development: India," - *A Special Conference Series on Foreign Trade Regimes and Economic Development*, NBER, New York.

Chakravarthy (2002). "Competition Regimes Around the World" *Monograph*, Consumer Unity & Trust Society, CUTS CITEE, Jaipur.

—————. (2004). "India's New Competition Act 2002 – a Work Still in Progress" in *Business Law International*, Vol. 5 No. 2, International Bar Association, London.

CUTS (2002). *Reorienting Competition Policy and Law in India*, CUTS CITEE, Jaipur.

—————. (2003). "Pulling Up Our Socks – A Study of Competition Regimes of Seven Developing Countries of Africa and Asia under the 7Up Project" – *Report of CUTS CCIER*, Jaipur.

Expert Group (1999). *Report of the Expert Group on Interaction between Trade and Competition Policy*, Ministry of Commerce, Government of India.

Hazari (1965). *Hazari Committee Report on Industrial Licensing Procedure*, Ministry of Industry, Government of India, New Delhi.

High Level Committee (2000). *Report of The High Level Committee on Competition Policy and Law* – Department of Company Affairs, Government of India, New Delhi, 2000.

Industrial Policy (1991). *Industrial Policy Statement*, Ministry of Industrial Development, Government of India.

Khemani R.S. and Mark A. Dutz (1996). "The Instruments of Competition Policy and their Relevance for Economic Policy" *PSD Occasional Paper* No. 26, World Bank, Washington DC.

Khemani, R.S. (1997). "Role of Competition Law – Policy in the Development Process" – Paper presented at the Conference on *Competition Policy in a Global Economy* – New Delhi, 17-19 March, 1997.

Mahalanobis (1964). *Mahalanobis Committee Report on Distribution and Levels of Income*, Government of India, New Delhi.

Messerlin P.A. (1996). "Competition Policy and Anti-Dumping Reform: An Exercise in Transition" – *The World Trading System: Challenges Ahead*, (ed) J Scott, Institute for International Economics.

Mittal, D.P. (2003). *Competition Law* - Taxmann Allied Services (P) Ltd, New Delhi.

Monopolies Inquiry Commission (1965). *Monopolies Inquiry Commission Report*, Government of India, New Delhi.

MRTP Commission (1979). "In re: Raymond Woollens Ltd. – 49," *Company Cases*, p.686.

Parliament (1999). *Proceedings of the Parliament – Indian Parliament*, New Delhi.

Ramaiya, A. (1992). *Guide to the Companies Act* – Wadhwa and Company, Agra.

Sachar Committee (1978). *Report of the High-powered Expert Committee on Companies and MRTP Acts*, Ministry of Law, Justice and Company Affairs, Government of India, New Delhi, August.

Standing Committee (2002). *Report of the Standing Committee of the Parliament*, Parliament Secretariat, New Delhi.

Supreme Court (1994). Hindustan Lever Ltd. Vs. Tata Oil Mills Co., Ltd., SLP 11006/94 dated 24 October 1994.

World Bank (1999). *A Framework for the Design and Implementation of Competition Law and Policy*, World Bank, Washington DC, p.1.

Competition Act, 2002: The Approach

S. Chakravarthy

3.1 Introduction

The evolution of competition law in India was traced in Chapter 2, highlighting the metamorphosis of the outgoing MRTP Act, 1969 into a new law, namely, Competition Act, 2002. Description of the MRTP Act having been given in that Chapter, the present one will address the rubric and contours of·the Competition Act, 2002. The trigger cause for this metamorphosis was the new policy paradigm ushered in 1991 resulting in liberalisation of policies, rules, regulations and executive decisions that inform the Governmental role in the economic activities of the country.

3.1.1 Prefatory Note

Governments generally rely on several policy tools to ensure that markets remain contestable (easy entry, easy exit) and that competition in the markets is maintained as far as possible, so that economic growth and welfare are driven, by and large, by efficient and optimal allocation or use of resources. The more important policy tools comprise Trade Policy, Foreign Direct Investment Policy and Regulatory Policy with respect to domestic economic activity and Competition Policy. Axiomatically, the first three policies serve purposes indicated by their nomenclature including incidentally of maintaining competition. The last mentioned policy, namely, the competition policy relates specifically to the introduction and fostering of competition principles in the executive policies of the Government (including the first three policies mentioned above) and also relates to competition law implemented by the Competition Authority with respect to arrangements among enterprises and the conduct of individual enterprises.

Historically also, the objectives of competition policy in many countries have been to protect economic freedom and competitive process and protecting fairness in the process. A quotation from a joint World Bank and OECD study reflects this:

> "While many objectives have been ascribed to competition policy during the past hundred years, certain major themes stand out. The most common of these objectives cited is the maintenance of the competitive process or of free competition, or the protection or promotion of effective competition. These are seen as synonymous with striking down or preventing unreasonable restraints on competition. Associated objectives are freedom to trade, freedom of choice, and access to markets. In some countries, such as Germany, freedom of individual action is viewed as the economic equivalent of a more democratic constitutional system. In France, emphasis is placed on competition policy as a means of securing economic freedom, that is, freedom of competition" (World Bank – OECD, 1997).

The new competition law of India, namely, the Competition Act, 2002 (Act, for brief) in its preamble highlights its major objectives so as "to prevent practices having adverse effect on competition, to promote and sustain competition in markets, to protect the interests of consumers and to ensure freedom of trade carried on by other participants in markets in India" (the Act is available on the Internet at *http://dca.nic.in/competition_act2002.pdf*).

The preamble also mandates that the economic development of the country needs to be kept in view in implementing the Act's objectives. Singh argues that competition policy in developing economies should support their overall development path (Singh, 2002).

A survey of the literature shows that there is no agreed list of the elements of competition law but the following figure prominently in the laws of most countries (UNCTAD, 2002):

1. Measures relating to agreements between firms in the same market to restrain competition. These measures can include provisions banning

cartels as well as provisions allowing cartels under certain circumstances.

2. Measures relating to attempts by a large incumbent firm to independently exercise market power (sometimes referred to as abuse of dominant position).

3. Measures relating to firms that, acting collectively but in the absence of an explicit agreement between them, attempt to exercise market power. These measures are sometimes referred to as measures against collective dominance.

4. Measures relating to attempts by a firm or firms to drive one or more of their rivals out of a market. Laws prohibiting predatory pricing are an example of such measures.

5. Measures relating to collaboration between firms for the purposes of research, development, testing, marketing, and distribution of products.

6. Measures for control of mergers, amalgamations and acquisitions.

The above list of six measures, which occur in most competition laws, is not exhaustive nor does it suggest that each measure is given the same weight or described in the same terminology in each country with a functioning competition law.

The six measures above can be broadly grouped into three core areas, namely, anti-competitive agreements, abuse of dominance and merger surveillance.

3.2 Rubric of the New Law

There are three core areas, as noted above, of enforcement that provide the focus for most competition laws in the world today.[1]

- Anti-competitive agreements among enterprises
- Abuse of dominance
- Mergers or, more generally, combinations among enterprises

There are, however, differences in emphasis and interpretations across countries and over time within countries. The above-mentioned three areas are not mutually exclusive and there is considerable overlap between them.

The rubric of the new law, **Competition Act, 2002** (Act, for brief) has essentially four compartments:

- Anti-Competitive Agreements

- Abuse of Dominance
- Combinations Regulation
- Competition Advocacy

These four compartments are described in the narrative that follows:

3.3 Anti-Competitive Agreements

Firms enter into agreements, which may have the potential of restricting competition. Agreements could be formal written documents or oral understandings, whether or not enforceable by legal proceedings. A scan of the competition laws in the world will show that they make a distinction between "horizontal" and "vertical" agreements between firms. The former, namely the horizontal agreements are those among competitors and the latter, namely the vertical agreements are those relating to an actual or potential relationship of purchasing or selling to each other. A particularly pernicious type of horizontal agreements is the cartel. Vertical agreements are pernicious, if they are between firms in a position of dominance. Most competition laws view vertical agreements generally more leniently than horizontal agreements, as *prima facie*, horizontal agreements are more likely to reduce competition than agreements between firms in a purchaser-seller relationship.

3.3.1 Horizontal Agreements

Agreements between two or more enterprises that are at the same stage of the production chain and in the same market constitute the horizontal variety. An obvious example that comes to mind is an agreement between enterprises dealing in the same product or products. But the market for the product(s) is critical to the question, if the agreement trenches the law. The Act has taken care to define the **relevant market**.[2] To attract the provision of law, the products must be substitutes. If parties to the agreement are both producers or retailers (or wholesalers), they will be deemed to be at the same stage of the production chain.

The Act seeks to prevent economic agents from distorting the competitive process either through agreements with other companies or through unilateral actions designed to exclude actual or potential competitors. It frowns upon agreements among competing enterprises (horizontal agreements) on prices or other important aspects of their competitive interaction. Likewise, competition-harming agreements between firms at different levels of the manufacturing or distribution processes (vertical agreements, for example between a manufacturer and wholesaler) would be hit by the provisions of the Act, *albeit* they are less harmful than horizontal agreements.

In general, the "rule of reason" test is required for establishing that an agreement is illegal. However, for certain kinds of agreements, the presumption is generally that they cannot serve any useful or pro–competitive purpose. Because of this presumption, the lawmakers do not subject such agreements to the "rule of reason" test. The Act presumes that the following four types of agreements between enterprises, involved in the same or similar manufacturing or trading of goods or provision of services have an appreciable adverse effect on competition:

- **Agreements regarding prices:** These include all agreements that directly or indirectly fix the purchase or sale price.

- **Agreements regarding quantities:** These include agreements aimed at limiting or controlling production, supply, markets, technical development, investment or provision of services.

- **Agreements regarding bids** (collusive bidding or bid-rigging): These include tenders submitted as a result of any joint activity or agreement.

- **Agreements regarding market sharing:** These include agreements for sharing of markets or sources of production or provision of services by way of allocation of geographical area of market or type of goods or services or number of customers in the market or any other similar way.

Such horizontal agreements, which include membership of cartels, are presumed to lead to unreasonable restrictions of competition and are therefore presumed to have an appreciable adverse effect on competition. This would mean that there would be very limited scope for discretion and interpretation on the part of the prosecuting and adjudicating authorities and very little scope for the errant enterprises to rebut the presumption (the errant enterprises had the right to agitate gateways and penalties proposed to be imposed under the outgoing MRTP Act and the Restrictive Trade Practices Act of the U.K).

3.3.2 Vertical Agreements

By and large, as noted earlier, vertical agreements, in most competition regimes are not subjected to the rigours of the law. However, where a vertical agreement has the character of distorting or preventing competition, it is generally not spared from the ambit of the law.

For instance, the following types of agreements, *inter alia*, are subject to the "rule of reason" test under the Act:

- Tie-in arrangement;
- Exclusive supply agreement;
- Exclusive distribution agreement;
- Refusal to deal; and
- Resale price maintenance.

The Act lists the following factors to be taken into account for adjudicatory purposes to determine whether an agreement or a practice has an appreciable adverse effect on competition, namely,

a) creation of barriers to new entrants in the market,

b) driving existing competitors out of the market,

c) foreclosure of competition by hindering entry into the market,

d) accrual of benefits to consumers,

e) improvements in production or distribution of goods or provision of services, and

f) promotion of technical, scientific and economic development by means of production or distribution of goods or provision of services.

3.3.3 Exceptions

The provisions relating to anti-competition agreements will not restrict the right of any person to restrain any infringement of intellectual property rights or to impose such **reasonable conditions** as may be necessary for the purposes of protecting any of his rights which have been or may be conferred upon him under the various intellectual property right statutes.

The rationale for this exception is that the bundle of rights that are subsumed in intellectual property rights should not be disturbed in the interests of creativity and intellectual/innovative power of the human mind. No doubt, this bundle of rights essays an anti-competition character, even bordering on monopoly power. But without protecting such rights, there will be no incentive for innovation, new technology and enhancement in the quality of products and services.

What is called for is a balance between unjustified monopolies and protection of the property holders' investment.

The relationship between competition law control and Intellectual Property Rights is inherently contradictory as there is a potential conflict between the two, in that **the existence and the exercise** of Intellectual property Rights may often produce anti-competitive effects through the monopoly power granted to the holder of the rights.

3.3.4 Indian Case Laws under the MRTP Act

In India, Intellectual Property falls in the Union list of the Seventh Schedule under Article 246 of the Constitution, which has itemised the same as "patents, inventions and designs, copyright, trade marks and merchandise marks" (Item 49). From the nature of items brought together, the framers of the Indian Constitution have apparently intended to afford protection, incentive and encouragement to artists, men of letters, inventors and the like. Limited monopoly is provided by the Patents Act, 1970, the Copyright Act, 1951 and the Trade and Merchandise Marks Act, 1958 and other IPR Statutes balancing the interest of the owners of the right and public interest.

The conflict between IPRs and the competition law came up before the Monopolies and Restrictive Trade Practices Commission (MRTPC) in India in Vallal Peruman and another *Vs.* Godfrey Phillips (India) Limited (MRTP Commission, 1994). The Commission observed as follows:

> "Applying the above principles to the controversy at hand, it seems ...., that a certificate of registration held by an individual or an undertaking invests in him/it, an undoubted right to use trade mark/name etc. so long as the certificate of registration is in operation and more importantly, so long as the trade mark is used strictly in conformity with the terms and conditions subject to which it was granted. If however, while presenting the goods and merchandise for sale in the market or for promotion thereof, the holder of the certificate misuses the same by manipulation, distortion, contrivances and embellishments etc. so as to mislead or confuse the consumers, he would be exposing himself to an action .... of indulging in unfair trade practices. It will, thus, be seen that the provisions of the Monopolies and Restrictive Trade Practices Act would be attracted only when there is an abuse in exercise of the right protected ...." This principle was reiterated in Manju Bhardwaj's Case by the same Commission (MRTP Commission, 1996).

3.3.5 Competition Act Permits Only Reasonable Conditions

Having said this, it may be noted, that the new Indian competition law, namely, Competition Act, 2002 does not permit any **unreasonable condition** forming a part of protection or exploitation of intellectual property rights. Only reasonable conditions will pass muster in terms of the specific wording in the Act and in particular, the use of the expression "reasonable conditions" in section 3(5) thereof. In other words, licensing arrangements likely to affect adversely the prices, quantities, quality or varieties of goods and services will fall within the contours of competition law as long as they are not in reasonable juxtaposition with the bundle of rights that go with intellectual property rights.

3.3.6 Another Exception - Export Cartels

Yet another exception in the Act, to the applicability of the provisions relating to anti-competition agreements is the right of any person to export goods from India, to the extent to which, an agreement relates exclusively to the production, supply, distribution or control of goods or provision of services for such export. In a manner of speaking, export cartels are outside the purview of competition law. In most jurisdictions, export cartels are exempted from the application of competition law. A justification for this exemption is that most countries do not desire any shackles on their export effort in the interest of balance of trade and/or balance of payments. Holistically, however, exemption of export cartels is against the concept of free competition.

3.3.7 Leniency Provisions

While discussing cartels, it would be appropriate to briefly refer to the leniency provisions in the Act. These provisions allow for the imposition of a reduced penalty on a participant in a cartel, who makes a full disclosure of having violated the Act. But such reduction is possible only to the first participant who comes forward and is not available, if any proceedings or investigations have been instituted/directed. The logic behind these provisions is that cartels are a hard nut to crack. More often than not, cartels will not have formal or written agreements. Essentially, they operate on oral understandings. Consequently, proving a cartel or cartelisation is beset with practical difficulties and in particular, absence of evidence. But, if a participant in a cartel is prepared to blow the whistle, the CCI should be able to secure evidence through him/it and in return offer amnesty or reduction in penalty to the whistle blower. Aditya Bhattacharjea (2003) commenting on this provision, suggests that leniency should be available to more than one participant and at various stages of the proceedings in exchange for evidence that could be used to prosecute co-conspirators. He has cited the US and EU schemes in support. The suggestion is well taken and could be considered in due course for amending the Act, after gaining experience in implementing the Act, as it is today.

3.4 Abuse of Dominance

"Dominant Position" has been appropriately defined in the Act in terms of the "position of strength, enjoyed by an enterprise, in the relevant market, in India, which enables it to (i) operate independently of competitive forces prevailing in the relevant market; or (ii) affect its competitors or consumers or the relevant market, in its favour". This definition may perhaps appear to be somewhat ambiguous and to be capable of different interpretations by different judicial authorities. But then, this ambiguity has a justification having regard to the fact that even a firm with a low market share of just 20 per cent with the remaining 80 per cent diffusedly held by a large number of competitors may be in a position to abuse its dominance, while a firm with say 60 per. cent market share with the remaining 40 per cent held by a competitor may not be in a position to abuse its dominance because of the key rivalry in the market. Specifying a threshold or an arithmetical figure for defining dominance may either allow real offenders to escape (like in the first example above) or result in unnecessary litigation (like in the second example above). Hence, in a dynamic changing economic environment, a static arithmetical figure to define "dominance" may, perhaps, be an aberration. With the aforesaid broad definition, the Regulatory Authority under the Act, namely, the Competition Commission of India (CCI) will have the freedom to fix errant undertakings and encourage competitive market practices, even if there is a large player around. Abuse of dominance is key for the Act, in so far as dominant enterprises are concerned. It is important to note that the Act has been designed in such a way that its provisions on this count only take effect, if dominance is clearly established.

3.4.1 Relevant Market

Before assessing whether an undertaking is dominant, it is important, as in the case of horizontal agreements, to determine what the relevant market is. There are two dimensions to this – the product market and the geographical market. On the demand side, the relevant product market includes all such substitutes that the consumer would switch to, if the price of the product relevant to the investigation were to increase. From the supply side, this would include all producers who could, with their existing facilities, switch to the production of such substitute goods. The geographical boundaries of the relevant market can be similarly defined. Geographic dimension involves identification of the geographical area within which competition takes place. Relevant geographic markets could be local, national, international or occasionally even global, depending upon the facts in each case. Some factors relevant to geographic dimension are consumption and shipment patterns, transportation costs, perishability and existence of barriers to the shipment of products between adjoining geographic areas. For example, in view of the high transportation costs in cement, the relevant geographical market may be the region close to the manufacturing facility.

3.4.2 Abuse

In general, actions that are considered anti-competitive and illegal in the context of agreements are also illegal, if undertaken by a dominant firm. These would include charging or paying unfair prices, restriction of quantities, markets and technical development. Discriminatory behaviour and any other exercise of market power leading to the prevention, restriction or distortion of competition would obviously be included. It needs to be clarified that there is a fine distinction between defending one's market position or market share, which is perfectly legal and legitimate and may involve certain level of aggressive competitive behaviour and exclusionary and anti-competitive behaviour. However, as noted above, a greater threat to competition is from the action(s) of dominant firms that are inimical to future competition.

3.4.3 When Does Abuse of Dominance Attract the Law?

To attract the provision of the Act, it needs to be established whether the restraints create a barrier to new entry or force existing competitors out of the market. The key issue is the extent to which these arrangements foreclose the market to manufacturers (inter-brand rivalry) or retailers (intra-brand rivalry) and the extent to which these raise rivals' costs and/or dampen existing competition. The costs of such arrangements need to be weighed against the benefits. For example, some of these restraints help to overcome the free-rider problem and allow for the exploitation of scale economies in retailing.

Before proceeding to the next compartment, lists of factors from the Act constituting "dominance" and constituting "abuse of dominance" have been reproduced herein below.

Dominance is determined by taking into account one or more of the following factors:

- market share of the enterprise;

- size and resources of the enterprise;

- size and importance of the competitors;

- economic power of the enterprise including commercial advantages over competitors;

- vertical integration of the enterprise, or sale or service network of such enterprise;

- dependence of consumers on the enterprise;

- monopoly or dominant position whether acquired as a result of any Statute or by virtue of being a Government company or a public sector undertaking or otherwise;

- entry barriers including barriers such as regulatory barriers, financial risk, high capital cost of entry, marketing entry barriers, technical entry barriers, economies of scale, high cost of substitutable goods or service for consumers;

- countervailing buying power;

- market structure and size of market;

- social obligations and social costs;

- relative advantage, by way of the contribution to the economic development, by the enterprise enjoying a dominant position having or likely to have an appreciable adverse effect on competition;

- any other factor which the Commission may consider relevant for the inquiry.

Abuse of dominance having an appreciable adverse effect on competition occurs if an enterprise,

a) directly or indirectly, imposes unfair or discriminatory-

 (i) condition in purchase or sale of goods or service; or

 (ii) price in purchase or sale (including predatory price) of goods or service,

b) limits or restricts-

 (i) production of goods or provision of services or market therefor; or

 (ii) technical or scientific development relating to goods or services to the prejudice of consumers; or

c) indulges in practice or practices resulting in denial of market access; or

d) makes conclusion of contracts subject to acceptance by other parties of supplementary obligations which, by their nature or according to commercial usage, have no connection with the subject of such contracts; or

e) uses its dominant position in one relevant market to enter into, or protect, other relevant market.

It was noted earlier that the preamble of the Act refers to the development criterion by using the expression 'keeping in view of the (sic) economic development of the country' therein. This finds correspondence in one of the factors for determining dominance by the CCI. That factor is the contribution of the offending enterprise to the economic development of the country. A similar factor occurs among the factors for determining if a combination has appreciable adverse effect on competition (a treatment on combinations regulations is given in a later section). Aditya Bhattacharjea (2003) observes that "development" is a matter of subjective perception and that the provision may be used "to exonerate blatantly anti-competitive practices by large corporations that purport to be promoting development". He expresses his reservation that the Act leaves this matter entirely to the CCI's subjective understanding of 'development'. But he is quick to add that 'developmental clauses are redundant, since they in no way help to determine the impact of competition'.

When Act was at the drafting stage, the Government was of the view that efficiency serving or economic development serving practices by dominant enterprises as well as combining enterprises should not be discouraged and that this should be factored in by the CCI in its adjudicatory effort. This is the reason why the economic development criterion has been listed among the factors to be reckoned by the CCI in its adjudicatory exercise.

Predatory pricing is one of the pernicious forms of abuse of dominance and is, therefore, given a treatment in the following section.

3.4.4 Predatory Pricing

Predatory pricing occurs, where a dominant enterprise charges low prices over a long enough period of time so as to drive a competitor from the market or deter others from entering the market and then raises prices to recoup its losses. The greater the diversification of the activities of the enterprise in terms of products and markets and the greater its financial resources, the greater is its ability to engage in predatory behaviour.

"Predatory price" is defined in the Act to mean "the sale of goods or provision of services, at a price which is below the cost, as may be determined by regulations, of production of the goods or provision of services, with a view to reduce competition or eliminate the competitors" (the expression "regulations" means the regulations made by the Competition Commission of India).

But there is a danger of confusing pro-competitive pricing with predatory behaviour. In reality, predation is only established after the fact i.e. once the rival has left the market and the predator has acquired a monopoly position in the market. However, any law to prevent is meaningful, only if it takes effect before the fact i.e. before the competitor has left the market. The case law in Box 3.1 describes the ratio given by the MRTP Commission in a predatory pricing case, which perhaps could be followed in predatory pricing cases that may be filed in future under the new competition law, namely, the Act.

Aditya Bhattacharjea (2003) referring to the relevant section in the Act and its 'Explanations', has observed that "(m)odern economics does not regard price discrimination as necessarily bad; discrimination allows producers to cross–subsidise low income consumers who might not be served otherwise, and can be welfare–increasing. If, despite this, discrimination is to be made an offence, then perhaps it is sensible to allow pricing to meet competition as a defence. But the wording of the Explanation explicitly includes predatory pricing, which is defined in a subsequent 'Explanation' to the same section, as pricing below cost 'with a view to reduce competition or eliminate the competitors'". He apprehends that the wordings in the 'Explanations' (meeting competition and eliminating competition) may legitimise predatory pricing by firms with 'deep pockets', the financial resources to incur losses in order to drive out more efficient producers. This apprehension, with due respect to him, has no force, as predatory pricing as specifically explained in the Act, must have the *mens rea* of reducing competition or eliminating competitors.

Distinguishing predatory behaviour from legitimate competition is difficult. The distinction between low prices, which result from predatory behaviour and low prices, which result from legitimate competitive behaviour is often very thin and not easily ascertainable.

Indeed, it is sometimes argued that predatory behaviour is a necessary concomitant of competition. To

BOX 3.1

Predatory Pricing – Case Law Relating to Modern Food Industries

The MRTP Act does not explicitly use the expression "predatory pricing", but lists the practice as an agreement, which constitutes a Restrictive Trade Practice. According to the relevant provision in the said Act, an agreement to sell goods at such prices as would have effect of eliminating competition or competitor is a Restricted Trade Practice prejudicial to public interest. This kind of a provision may limit its applicability to coordinated predation by a group of enterprises and leave out predation by a single enterprise.

In a 1996 case (MRTP Commission, 1996) involving a complaint of predatory pricing against Modern Food Industries, which produces bread and bakery items, the MRTP Commission extended the aforesaid provision in the Act, to a single seller on the ground that "in fixing the prices, there is an understanding that the seller will sell the product at a particular price", bringing the practice within the purview of the relevant provision of the MRTP Act. The Commission observed that the essence of predatory pricing is pricing below cost with a view to eliminating a rival. Further, the Commission made it clear that the "mere offer of a price lower than the cost of production cannot automatically lead to an indictment of predatory pricing" and that evidence of "malafide intent to drive competitors out of business or to eliminate competition" is required. The logic underlying the caution of the Commission is that price-cutting may be for genuine reasons, for example in the case of inventory surplus. Price-cutting has, therefore, to be coupled with the *mens rea* of eliminating a competitor or competition to become an offence under competition law.

The two principles enunciated in this case—evidence of pricing below costs and intent to eliminate competition—are in conformity with the International practice in predatory pricing cases. The Commission used the principle resembling the well known Areeda-Turner test in comparing price to marginal cost whether it could be considered predatory.

quote Professor Jagdish Bhagwati from his book "A Stream of Windows":

"The notion that ..... companies..... compete in a benign fashion is faintly romantic and fully foolish. What the Cambridge economist Joan Robinson used to call the "animal spirits" of capitalist entrepreneurs surely are manifest..... The successful always appear more predatory. ...... With success, one gets one's share of envy and resentment" (Bhagwati, Jagdish, 1999).

It may, therefore, be seen that the Act does not frown upon dominance as such but frowns upon abuse of dominance.

3.5 Combinations Regulation

Combinations, in terms of the meaning given to them in the Act, include mergers, amalgamations, acquisitions and acquisitions of control. The compartment dealing with combinations was one of the most debated ones among the four compartments in the Act, when it was in its draft form (which was placed on the website inviting comments and suggestions). It is, therefore, necessary to give this compartment a detailed treatment.

3.5.1 The Act on Combinations Regulation

The Act makes it voluntary for the parties to notify their proposed agreement or combinations to the Mergers Bench (a part of the Competition Commission of India), if the aggregate assets of the combining parties have a value in excess of Rs. 1000 crore (US $ 220 million) or turnover in excess of Rs. 3000 crore (US $ 660 million). In the event either of the combining parties is outside India or both are outside, the threshold limits are US $ 500 million for assets and US $ 1500 million for turnover.

If one of the merging parties belongs to a group, which controls it, the threshold limits are Rs. 4000 crore (US $ 880 million) in terms of assets and Rs. 12000 crore (US $ 2640 million) in terms of turnover. If the group has assets or turnover outside India also, the threshold limits are US $ 2 billion for assets and US $ 6 billion for turnover. For this purpose a group means two or more enterprises, which directly or indirectly have:

* the ability to exercise 26 per cent or more of the voting rights in the other enterprise; or

* the ability to appoint more than half the members of the Board of Directors in the other enterprise; or

* the ability to control the affairs of the other enterprise.

Control (which expression occurs in the third bullet defining a 'group' above), has also been defined in the Act. Control includes controlling the affairs or management by

(i) one or more enterprises, either jointly or singly, over another enterprise or group;

(ii) one or more groups, either jointly or singly, over another group or enterprise.

The threshold limits of assets and of turnover would be revised every two years on the basis of the Wholesale Price Index or fluctuations in exchange rate of rupee or foreign currencies.

The Act has made the notification of combinations, voluntary and not mandatory and has laid down threshold limits for combinations to fall within its surveillance. The reasons that impelled the Government to opt for voluntary notifications and for threshold limits merit mention. The draft law that preceded the Act had mandatory notification provisions. Recommendations in favour of mandatory notification and threshold limits that fashioned the draft law and incorporated therein, were those of the High Level Committee (2000).

Before the Act was passed by the Parliament, the draft law was placed on the website and a number of suggestions were received particularly, on the provisions relating to combinations regulation. Many economists, experts and officials during their discussions[3] with the Government were of the view that at the present level of India's economic development, combinations control should not lead to the shying away of foreign direct investment and participation by major international companies in economic activities through the route of mergers and acquisitions. They suggested that combination approvals (above specified threshold limits) might not be made mandatory. Notification of combinations might, on the other hand, be made voluntary, *albeit* with the risk of the discovery of anti-competitive mergers at a later date with the concomitant cost of demergers etc. The trigger cause in the aforesaid suggestions was the felt need for companies in India to grow in size in order to become globally competitive. These suggestions carried favour with the Government, which effected amendments to the draft law leading to the final shape of the Act.

The Act, has, thus made the **pre-notification of combinations voluntary** for the parties concerned. However, if the parties to the combination choose not to notify the CCI as it is not mandatory to notify, they run the risk of a post-combination action by the CCI, if it is discovered subsequently, that the combination has an appreciable adverse effect on competition. There is a rider that the CCI shall not initiate an inquiry into a combination after the expiry of one year from the date on which the combination has taken effect.

On the prescription of threshold limits, the High Level Committee (2000) had this to say: "[i]t is extremely important that the law regarding mergers be very carefully framed and the provisions regarding prohibition of mergers be used very sparingly. This is particularly important at the current stage of India's corporate development. Relative to the size of major international companies, Indian firms are still small. With the opening of trade and Foreign Direct

Investment, Indian firms need to go through a period of consolidation in order to be competitive. Any law on merger regulation must take account of this reality."

Thus, the High Level Committee had advised that only big combinations should be placed under the regulations of competition law. Government in finalising the threshold limits in the Act reckoned the above advice and prescribed the limits in such a way that, by and large, only major combinations would fall within its ambit. In other words, small and medium combinations would be outside the pale of the Act.

The Act has listed several factors to be taken into account for the purpose of determining whether the combination would have the effect of or be likely to have an appreciable adverse effect on competition.

The Regulatory Authority, namely, the Mergers Bench of the Competition Commission of India is mandated to adjudicate on mergers by weighing potential efficiency losses against potential gains.

In order that the Competition Commission of India (Mergers Bench) should not delay its adjudication on whether a merger may pass through or may be stopped because of its anti-competitive nature, the Act admonishes the Regulatory Authority to hand in its adjudicatory decision within 90 working days, lest the merger will be deemed to have been approved.

3.6 Competition Advocacy

In line with the High Level Committee's recommendation, the Act extends the mandate of the Competition Commission of India beyond merely enforcing the law (High Level Committee, 2000). Competition advocacy creates a culture of competition. There are many possible valuable roles for competition advocacy, depending on a country's legal and economic circumstances. A report of the OECD noted as follows:

> "In virtually every member country where significant reform efforts have been undertaken, the competition agencies have been active participants in the reform process. This 'advocacy' ... can include persuasion offered behind the scenes, as well as publicity outside of formal proceedings. Some competition agencies have the power, at least in theory, to bring formal challenges against anti-competitive actions by other agencies or official or quasi-official bodies. More indirect, but still visible, is formal participation in another agency's public hearings and deliberations. What is appropriate depends on the particular institutional setting" (OECD, 1997).

The Competition Commission of India, in terms of the advocacy provisions in the Act, is enabled to participate in the formulation of the country's economic policies and to participate in the reviewing of laws related to competition at the instance of the Central Government. The Central Government can make a reference to the Competition Commission of India for its opinion on the possible effect of a policy under formulation or of an existing law related to competition.

In order to promote competition advocacy and create awareness about competition issues and also to accord training to all concerned (including the Chairperson and Members of the CCI and its officials), the Act enjoins the establishment of a fund christened as the **Competition Fund**. The Fund will be credited with the fees received for filing complaints and applications under the law, costs levied on the parties, grants and donations from the Government, and the interest accrued thereon. The four main compartments having been discussed above, a description of how the investigative and adjudicatory apparatus is designed, follows, which is an important part of the Act.

3.7 Investigation, Prosecution, Adjudication, Mergers Bench and Selection Procedure

3.7.1 Investigation and Prosecution

Adjudicative wing is distinct and separate from the investigative wing in the Act. At the apex level of the investigative wing, there is an official who has been designated as Director General (DG). The Director General will not have *suo motu* powers of investigation. He will only look into the complaints received from the CCI and submit his findings to it. The DG will be the prosecuting authority and has been vested under the Act with powers, which are conferred on the CCI, namely, summoning of witnesses, examining them on oath, requiring the discovery and production of documents, receiving evidence on affidavits, issuing commissions for the examination of witnesses etc.

The Act mandates that the investigation staff would need to be chosen from among those, who have experience in investigation and who are known for their integrity and outstanding ability. They should have knowledge of accountancy, management, business, public administration, international trade, law or economics. Hitherto, in terms of the dispensation under the MRTP Act, they were drawn routinely from those working in the Department of Company Affairs. The Act, thus, induces professionalism in the investigative wing, a step in the right direction.

3.7.2 Adjudication

Central to effective implementation and enforcement of competition policy and competition law is an appropriate competent and effective adjudicative body, in the instant case, the Competition Commission of India. CCI is the adjudicating body under the Act with autonomy and administrative powers.

CCI will be a multi-member body with its Chairperson and Members chosen for their expertise, knowledge and experience in Economics, Law, International Trade, Business, Commerce, Industry, Finance, Accountancy, Management, Public Affairs or Administration. The Act stipulates that the Chairperson and Members shall be selected from those, who have been, or are qualified to be Judges of the High Courts or from those who have special knowledge of any of the disciplines listed above. They should not only have special knowledge in one or more of the aforesaid areas, but also have experience of not less than 15 years therein. Besides, they need to be persons of ability, integrity and standing.

Each Bench will have a judicial member, as it will have the power of imposing sentences of imprisonment, in addition to levying fines.

For the cases of mergers, amalgamations etc., the Act has provided for a separate Mergers Bench, which is a part of the Competition Commission of India. This is to ensure that there is no avoidable delay in dealing with such scrutiny, as delays can prevent bodies corporate from being competitive globally.

3.7.3 Selection Procedure of Chairperson and Members of CCI

In order to ensure competent and effective implementation of competition policy and competition law, it is important and imperative to select suitable persons. It cannot be over-emphasised that Government ought to ensure that the CCI is free of political control. While, it is practically difficult to eliminate political favouritism, it can be minimised to a great extent by resorting to what may be described as a "Collegium Selection Process". With this in view, the High Level Committee (2000) suggested that the Collegium should collectively undertake and discharge the task and responsibility of choosing suitable persons for the posts of Chairperson and Members of the CCI. The Act, as passed by the Parliament, however, has left the selection procedure to the Government, which will therefore frame Rules in this regard.

The Government appointed two retired officials, one as the Chairperson and the other as a Member of the CCI. The appointments and some provisions of the new law, namely, the Act have been challenged in particular, the provisions relating to allowing non–judicial persons

to be Chairperson/Members. The case is presently pending in the Supreme Court which has observed some other reservations as well. The Government of India, on its part has proposed to make some changes in the Act. The Supreme Court has reserved its final judgement in the case till the time the proposed amendment is carried out.

3.7.4 Independence and Autonomy of CCI

There are certain provisions in the Act which undermine the independence and autonomy of CCI. These are listed and discussed below:

1. Prior approval of the Central Government is required before the Chairperson of the CCI can transfer a Member from one Bench situated in one city to another Bench situated in another city. This provision prejudices the autonomous functioning of the Chairperson.

2. The Central Government, after due appropriation made by Parliament, may make to the CCI "grants of such sums of money **as the Government may think fit**". If the CCI has to seek monies from the Government from time to time, there is a clear prejudice to its independence and autonomy.

3. There is a provision in the Act, that the CCI would "be bound by such directions on questions of policy, other than those relating to technical and administrative matters, as the Central Government may give in writing to it from time to time". The provision relating to issue of directions by the Government contravenes the spirit and letter of independence of the CCI, a requirement inevitable for its effectiveness.

4. Yet another provision, most serious in the context of independence of the CCI, is the one which gives power to the Government to supersede it on certain grounds, like circumstances in public interest, non-compliance of a direction given by the Government etc. If CCI has to effectively implement the Competition Act and bring about competitiveness in the market, the supersession provision is hardly likely to help.

The above listed provisions do prejudice the independence and autonomy of the CCI and need to be reviewed, even if not immediately, perhaps after gaining experience in implementing the Act over a period of say, 5 to 10 years.

3.8 Exemptions

The Act provides for the Government to bring into force its different provisions on different dates by a notification. Furthermore, it empowers the Central Government by notification to exempt from the application of the law or any part thereof for such period, as it deems fit,

(a) any class of enterprises if such exemption is necessary in the interest of security of the State or public interest;

(b) any practice or agreement arising out of and in accordance with any obligation assumed by India under any treaty, agreement or convention with any other country or countries;

(c) any enterprise which performs a sovereign function on behalf of the Central Government or a State Government.

3.9 Appeal and Review Provisions

Appeals against decisions and orders of the CCI lie to the Supreme Court within the limitation period of 60 days. Thus, the status given to the CCI is very high with only the Supreme Court having the power to overturn its orders. The CCI has power under the Act to review its own order on an application made by the party aggrieved by its order.

3.10 Extra-Territorial Reach

The Act has extra-territorial reach. Its arm extends beyond the geographical contours of India to deal with practices and actions outside India, which have an appreciable adverse affect on competition in the relevant market in India. The CCI has the power to enquire into an agreement, abuse of dominance position or combination, if it has or is likely to have appreciable adverse affect on competition in the relevant market in India, notwithstanding that,

(a) an agreement has been entered into outside India;

(b) any party to such agreement is outside India;

(c) any enterprise abusing the dominant position is outside India;

(d) a combination has taken place outside India;

(e) any party to combination is outside India; or

(f) any other matter or practice or action arising out of such agreement or dominant position or combination is outside India.

The above provisions are based on what is known as the 'effects doctrine'. This doctrine implies that even if an action or practice is outside the shores of India but has an impact or effect on competition in the relevant market in India, it can be brought within the ambit of the Act, provided the effect is appreciably adverse on competition. Box 3.2 below, describes a case law on extra-territorial jurisdiction of the outgoing MRTP Act, 1969. However, the Competition Act as passed by the Parliament includes a provision to overcome the problem covered in the ruling of the Supreme Court on extra-territorial jurisdiction and on imports.

BOX 3.2

Extra-Territorial Jurisdiction – Case Law Relating to Float Glass

In September, 1998 the All India Float Glass Manufacturers' Association (AIFGMA) filed a complaint to the MRTP Commission against three Indonesian companies manufacturing float glass alleging that the latter in association with Indian importers were resorting to restrictive and unfair trade practices and in particular, selling float glass at predatory prices in India. They further alleged that the sale of float glass by the Indonesian manufacturers at predatory prices would restrict, distort and prevent competition by pricing out Indian producers from the market. The MRTP Commission issued an injunction against the Indonesian companies from exporting float glass to India. This matter was carried in appeal to the Supreme Court. During the hearing of the case, the extra-territorial jurisdiction of the MRTP Commission came up for consideration by the Supreme Court. The Supreme Court (2002) while observing that "[A] competition law like the MRTP Act is a mechanism to counter cross border economic terrorism", ruled that the MRTP Commission had no extra-territorial jurisdiction in the float glass case. The Court added that allowing challenge to the actual import would tantamount to giving the MRTP Commission jurisdiction to adjudicate upon the legal validity of the provisions relating to import and that the Commission did not have jurisdiction. It observed that the Commission's jurisdiction would commence after the import was completed and any restrictive trade practice took place subsequently. To quote the Supreme Court: "The action of an exporter to India when performed outside India would not be amenable to jurisdiction of the MRTP Commission. The MRTP Commission cannot pass an order determining the export price of an exporter to India or prohibiting him to export to India at a low or predatory price". This decision of the Supreme Court led to arming the Competition Commission of India under the Competition Act, 2002 with the power to take extra-territorial action by restraining imports, on the ground that the imports (after effectuating) would contravene the substantive provisions of the law. How the Competition Commission of India would be dealing with such cases in future will be eagerly awaited.

3.11 New Wine in a New Bottle

The Act is, therefore, a new wine in a new bottle. The extant MRTP Act 1969 has aged for more than three decades and has given birth to the new law (the Act) in line with the changed and changing economic scenario in India and rest of the world and in line with the current economic thinking comprising the post-1991 liberalisation/reforms paradigm.

The differences between the old law (extant law, namely the MRTP Act, 1969) and the new law (Competition Act, 2002) may perhaps be best captured in the form of a Table 3.1.

TABLE 3.1

Difference between MRPT Act, 1969 and Competition Act, 2002

S. No.	MRTP Act, 1969	Competition Act, 2002
1.	Based on pre-reforms command and control regime	Based on post-reforms liberalised regime
2.	Based on size/structure as factor	Based on conduct as a factor
3.	Competition offences implicit and not defined	Competition offences explicit and defined
4.	Complex in arrangement and language	Simple in arrangement and language, and comprehensible
5.	Frowns upon dominance	Frowns upon abuse of dominance
6.	Registration of agreements compulsory	No requirement of registration of agreements
7.	No combinations regulations (post-1991 amendment)	Combination regulations beyond a high threshold limit
8.	No competition advocacy role for the MRTPC	CCI has competition advocacy role
9.	No penalties for offences	Penalties for offences
10.	Reactive and rigid	Proactive and flexible
11.	Unfair trade practices covered	Unfair trade practices omitted (Consumer Protection Act, 1986 will deal with them)
12.	Rule of law approach	Rule of reason approach
13.	Blanket exclusion of intellectual property rights	Exclusion of intellectual property rights, but unreasonable restrictions covered

3.12 Improvements in the Competition Act, 2002 over the MRTP Act, 1969

In Chapter 2, mention was made of the failings in the MRTP Act and the consequent problems faced by the MRTPC. The new Act has to some extent redressed the situation.

Firstly, explicit definitions have been accorded to the offences of Abuse of Dominance, Cartels, Bid-rigging, and Predatory Pricing etc., in the Act. Such explicit definitions are not available in the outgoing MRTPA. Secondly, the Act specifies criteria for assessing whether a practice has an appreciable adverse effect on competition. The MRTPA is rather ambiguous and subjective in this regard by not providing any criteria for defining a restrictive trade practice or a monopolistic trade practice. The criterion in that Statute is

"reasonableness", which lends itself to differing rulings by the MRTPC, depending on the disposition of the Chairperson and/or the Members sitting on the Bench in a particular case. Thirdly, the Act mandates that the CCI "shall not be bound by the procedure laid down by the Code of Civil Procedure, 1908" but shall be guided by the principles of natural justice. The CCI is empowered to regulate its own procedure. The thinking in the Government, when the new law was passed, was to make regulations so as to provide a summary trial for the cases, unless the CCI felt it necessary to deviate. Fourthly, the CCI under the Act may call upon such experts from the fields of economics, commerce, accountancy, international trade or from any other discipline as it deems necessary to assist it in the conduct of any enquiry or proceeding before it. Introduction of competition advocacy functions for the CCI is designed to increase the awareness among consumers, Chambers of Commerce and Industry, Professional Institutes and even the CCI and its officers regarding Competition as an important factor of market driven economy and activities and to create a competition culture in the country.

3.13 Phased Introduction of the Act

The Government has decided on a calibrated introduction of the Act. In other words, the main four compartments of the Act will be introduced in a phased manner. In the first phase, during the first year of the coming into force of the Act, the CCI has been called upon to carry on only competition advocacy functions. The first year is and will be devoted to imparting training to all concerned with the implementation and administration of the Act. The thinking of Government is that the Members of the Parliament and Legislatures should also be educated on the features and implications of the Act. Competition advocacy functions would also include measures for creating awareness about competition issues among all concerned and in particular, the public and also include promoting in the country what can be described as 'competition culture' and creating and fostering a competition driven market in the country.

During the second year, the provisions relating to anti-competitive agreements and abuse of dominance would be brought into force. The MRTP Act would then stand repealed and MRTP Commission wound up. During the first year of the introduction of the Act, the MRTP Act would be operational, as the CCI would be addressing only competition advocacy functions. During the third year of the introduction of the Act, the provisions relating to combinations regulations would be brought into force.

This calibrated introduction of the Act is strategically a step in the right direction, as it will help the country to progress gradually on competition related matters but steadily and surely.

3.14 Concerns and Reservations on the Act

After the draft law, [before it was refined and made into a law (the Act)] was placed on the web-site, a number of suggestions, comments and concerns were received from different Chambers of Commerce and Industry, Professional Institutes, Consumer Groups, different Ministries of the Government, Academicians and Experts. A spate of conferences and seminars on the draft law and in general "competition" was held, which too threw up concerns and suggestions.[4] They are discussed below under separate captions for convenience.

3.14.1 Combinations Regulation

Most of the reservations and concerns relate to the provisions on combinations regulation. Earlier, in this narrative, the rationale for combinations regulation or mergers regulation has been spelt out. Essentially, the following dimensions will inform combinations regulation and address the concerns expressed:

1. Indian corporate sector requires consolidation with a view to bringing about reasonably sized companies and players to effectively compete in the domestic and international market.

2. The threshold limits asset-wise and turnover-wise are high enough so that most mergers will be outside the ambit of combinations regulation.

3. Beyond the threshold limits there is only a voluntary (and not mandatory) pre-merger notification obligation by the parties.

4. The coverage in the Act of the expression "combinations" does not include "joint ventures". Some of the Industry Chambers were apprehensive that if "joint ventures" were included, it would dampen industrialisation in the country, as the route of "joint ventures" was a pragmatic and popular one adopted by its constituents.

5. The "group" concept is included in the provisions relating to combinations regulation. There was a suggestion to exclude it on the ground that a possible and likely bureaucratic approach may lead to connecting unconnected undertakings. This may result in derailing many mergers on the sword of an undertaking being perceived as belonging to same group. Originally, in the MRTP Act, "group" was defined extensively running to a few pages. The new law, the Act, defines "group" in terms of just three dimensions, namely, share holding, management and control.

6. The 90 working days limit fixed for the adjudication exercise by the CCI, with caps on the time frame for calling for further information by the CCI and for receiving the same from the parties is worthy of note. Furthermore, the Act provides for a deemed approval in case the CCI does not give its verdict within the said 90 working days limit.

7. CCI in its adjudicatory effort is mandated to keep in view the benefits of a combination as to whether they outweigh its adverse impact on competition.

8. A detailed Mergers Manual is proposed to be prepared as guidance for the CCI, for the Industry and for service renderers.

3.14.2 Super Regulator

Concern has been voiced that CCI will become a Super Regulator in view of Section 21 of the Act, which empowers any statutory Authority regulating any utility or service to make a reference to the CCI, if an issue is raised that any decision of that Authority is or would be contrary to the provisions of the Act. As the Act stands, the statutory Authority has the discretion (not mandatory) to make a reference to the CCI, if an issue with a competition perspective is raised by any party. Thus, the Statutory Authority has the right to decide on the raised issue without making a reference to the CCI. If it deems fit, the Act gives it the power to make a reference to the CCI. What is more important is that the opinion of the CCI is not binding on the Statutory Authority and this should take care of the concern expressed above.

It needs to be emphasised that the Act is not another law supplementing the existing MRTP Act. On the other hand, it will supplant the MRTP Act. As explained in the Table 3.1, highlighting the differences between the MRTP Act and the Act, the new law is simpler, more flexible and more liberal than the outgoing law, namely, the MRTP Act, 1969.

However, in order to allay this fear, the CCI should be made accountable through independent review by consumer organisations, external agencies and peer review by competition authorities from other countries.

3.14.3 Unfair Trade Practices Not a Part of the Act

The MRTP Act deals with Restrictive Trade Practices, Unfair Trade Practices and Monopolistic Trade Practices. The RTPs and MTPs, with refinements and modifications in their content, language and meaning are included in the new law, namely the Act. The UTPs are totally left out of the Act. This is because the Consumer Protection Act, 1986 (COPRA) designed to protect the interests of consumers has provisions relating to UTPs. The MRTP Act and the COPRA suffered from a significant overlap on the provisions relating to UTPs. As a matter of fact, the definition of 'unfair trade practices' is literally the same in both the enactments, the MRTP Act and the COPRA.

The provisions relating to unfair trade practices need not figure in the Indian Competition Act as they are presently covered by the Consumer Protection Act, 1986. The pending UTP cases in the MRTP Commission may be transferred to the relevant Consumer Courts under the Consumer Protection Act, 1986. The Competition Act, 2002 has no provisions relating to UTPs, which will, henceforth, be in the domain of the COPRA except in cases where only business people are affected as they are not entitled to approach a consumer court.

With provisions on unfair trade practices removed, the CCI may face a major challenge to get the public buy-in, and to create a public image. Therefore, even with the handicap, the CCI should take up consumers' issues, which are of systemic nature, to create a public buy-in. These could include: tied sales in schools and colleges over uniforms and stationery or the tie-up of doctors with diagnostic clinics (see chapter ten on Competition Abuses at Consumer Level for these issues).

3.14.4 Consumer Concerns in the Act

Any consumer can move the CCI for action under the Act for offences relating to anti-competitive agreements and abuse of dominance. Consumer associations are similarly empowered to move the CCI. "Consumer" finds a comprehensive definition in the Act, which includes those who buy goods or hire or avail of services. The preamble of the Act specifically mandates that the legislation is intended to "protect the interests of consumers". While individual consumers who have suffered damage or loss consequent on an enterprise having provided him with a defective product or service have redress available

under the Consumer Protection Act, 1986 (mainly unfair trade practices), they have the right to move the CCI for action relating to anti-competitive practices or abuse of dominance. But such cases under the Act are likely to be wider in scope than those filed under the Consumer Protection Act, 1986, as they are likely to affect a large body of consumers, who suffer as a consequence of practices resulting in appreciable adverse effect on competition.

The gains sought through competition law can only be realised with effective enforcement. Weak enforcement of competition law is perhaps worse than the absence of competition law. Weak enforcement often reflects a number of factors such as inadequate funding of the enforcement authority. The Government should provide the required infrastructure and funds to make the CCI an effective regulator to prevent, if not eliminate anti-competition practices and also to play its role of competition advocacy.

Notes

1. Although it does not directly form a part of competition law, legislation regarding various regulatory authorities falls under the larger ambit of competition policy.

2. Relevant market is discussed in the narrative under "abuse of dominance", infra.

3. The author was present during the discussions.

4. The author had the privilege of attending a large number of such conferences and seminars, securing the benefit of discussions, suggestions and comments from the participants therein.

References

Bhattacharjea, Aditya (2003). "India's Competition Policy An Assessment" *Economic and Political Weekly*, Vol. XXXVIII, No.34, 23 August.

Bhagwati, Jagdish (1999). *A Stream of Windows – Unsettling Reflections on Trade, Immigration and Democracy*, Oxford University Press, New Delhi.

Chakravarthy, S. (2002). "Competition Regimes Around the World" *Monograph*, Consumer Unity & Trust Society, CUTS CITEE, Jaipur.

Court of Appeals (1980). Hoehling A.A. *Vs.* Universal City Studios Inc., 618 F. Ed 992.

──────. (1986). Windsurfing International Inc. *Vs.* AMF Inc. 782 F.2d 995.

European Court of Justice (1974). Centrafarm *Vs.* Sterling ECR 1147.

European Economic Commission (1986). *Ford Body Panels Settlement Bull-EC*, 1-1986, Point 2.1.49.

Evenett, S.J., M.C. Levenstein and V.Y. Suslow (2001). "International Cartel Enforcement: Lessons from the 1990s" – *The World Economy*, 24:1221-45.

Frazer, Tim (1988). *Monopoly, Competition and the Law: The Regulation of Business Activity in Britain, Europe and America* - St. Martin's Press, Inc., New York, 222.

High Level Committee (2000). *Report of The High Level Committee on Competition Policy and Law* – Dept. of Company Affairs, Govt. of India, New Delhi.

MRTP Commission (1994). Director General *Vs.* Deepak Fertilisers and Petro Chemicals Corporation Ltd – 1994 – 2 – CTJ – 253 – MRTPC, New Delhi.

──────. (1996). Decision of the Monopolies and Restrictive Trade Practices Commission in Modern Food Industries Ltd. case - 1996 3 Comp LJ 154, New Delhi.

—————. (1997). Alkali Manufacturers Association of India *Vs.* American Natural Soda Ash Corporation (ANSAC) and others – 1997 (5) CTJ, 288. MRTPC.

OECD (1997). *2 OECD Report on Regulatory Reform* 265.

—————. (2003). *Hard Core Cartels: Recent Progress and Challenges Ahead* – OECD, Paris.

—————. (2003a). "Coverage of Competition Law: Illustrative Examples of Exclusions"- *Document CNM/GF/COMP/TR*(2003)17, Paris.

Rosen (1986). "Licensing Restrictions in the US and the European Economic Community" - 55, *Antitrust Law Journal*.

Rule (1986). "The Administrative View: Antitrust Analysis After the Nine No-No's" - 55, *Antitrust Law Journal*, 365.

Singh A. (2002). "Competition and Competition Policy in Emerging Markets: International and Development Dimensions", *G-24 discussion paper Series*, Paper No. 18, United Nations, New York, 18 September.

Supreme Court (2002). "Haridas Exports *Vs.* All India Float Glass Manufacturers Association, 6 SCC 600.

UNCTAD (2002). "Closer Multilateral Cooperation on Competition Policy: The Development Dimension" – *Consolidated Report on issues discussed in seminars on Competition Policy*, UNCTAD, Geneva.

U.S.A. Court (1977). Continental T.V. *Vs.* GTE Sylvania Inc - 433 US 36; 53 L Ed 2d 568, Supreme Court.

World Bank – OECD (1997). *A Framework for the Design and Implementation of Competition Law and Policy*, World Bank and OECD, Paris.

4 Mergers and Acquisitions in India: Implications For Competition

Manish Agarwal

4.1 Introduction

'*Merger or amalgamation*' is defined as a combination of two companies wherein at least one loses its corporate existence. The surviving company, also called the merged company, acquires both the assets and liabilities of the company that loses its existence.

'*Acquisition or takeover*' on the other hand, means acquisition of a certain block of equity capital of a company, which enables the acquirer to exercise control over the affairs of the company thus acquired. In India, a holding of 26 per cent of equity of a company makes the holder a strategic partner and leads to the exercise of effective control.[1]

In terms of the nature of procedure involved, acquisition turns out to be relatively less cumbersome than a merger. Acquisitions have to be carried out in a time bound manner and this by itself acts as an incentive for the acquirer and entity getting acquired to re-organise their business in a very short time. In India, acquisitions are governed by the SEBI takeover code called the Securities and Exchange Board of India (Substantial Acquisition of Shares and Takeovers) Regulations, 1997 and the acquisition process normally gets over in about three months. On the other hand, in case of mergers, the parties involved in a merger have to take permission from their shareholders, and the High Court concerned. The legal proceedings that are part of a merger process take about a year and may sometimes cause delays and prove deleterious to the future performance of the merged entity.

4.1.1 Classification of M&As

In terms of markets involved, mergers and acquisitions (M&As) are broadly classified into the following three categories:

- *Horizontal* merger is one in which both firms are in the same product market. Merger of the two pharmaceutical companies, Glaxo and Smithkline Beecham is one such example.

- *Vertical* merger is between firms with potential or actual buyer-seller relationship. In this case, there is a merger of companies engaged in different stages of the production cycle. Vertical merger can either lead to a forward integration or a backward integration. An example of a backward-vertical merger is the merger of Uptron Colour Picture Tubes Ltd. (manufacturer of picture tubes used in colour television) with BPL Ltd. (a manufacturer of electronics including colour televisions).

- *Conglomerate* mergers are those mergers, which are neither horizontal nor vertical. In practice, the conglomerate merger category has been subdivided into three further classes as follows:

  - A *product extension merger* occurs when firms merge who sell non-competing products but use related marketing channels or production processes;

  - A *market extension merger* is the joining of two firms selling the same product but in separate geographic markets; and

  - There is the '*pure*' category of conglomerate mergers between firms with no relationship of any kind.

The paper analyses M&As in India from the perspective of competition policy and highlights the regulatory framework for overseeing M&As in India. Section two throws light on the nature of M&As in India. Section three highlights motives and characteristics of firms involved in M&As and section four talks about the impact of M&As on performance and product concentration. Section five highlights cases of M&As by multinational enterprises in India. Section six discusses the regulatory framework governing M&As in India. Section seven reviews the case of promoting national champions. Section eight makes certain recommendations and highlights issues for further research.

4.1.2 M&As from Competition Policy Perspective

Firms resort to M&As for a variety of reasons: to realise economies of scale, for expansion and growth, and to improve operating performance. While these motives are desirable, the concern arises when M&As lead to increased market power wielded by the merged entity.

This is most obvious in the case of *horizontal mergers*, as they provide the clearest example of possible anticompetitive effects. A merger between two firms in the same industry that increases the acquiring firm's market share may allow it to engage more effectively in tacit or explicit collusion with other firms in the industry and thereby to charge a higher price. Horizontal mergers can also increase barriers to entry if they are coupled with cost reductions. An existing or potential entrant may be deterred from competing with a larger firm in an industry if it knows that the firm's costs are lower and thus the incumbent would be better able to engage in a competitive price war than the potential competitor itself.

Vertical mergers can have similar potential effects as vertical integration, combined with substantial market power at one level, may permit an extension of that market power to the other level. For example, if a firm has a monopoly over the supply of a particular input and it integrates downstream into processing of the input into a finished product, an anti-competitive effect may arise if the firm charges a high price for the input supplies and a low price for the finished product. This differential price jeopardises the economic viability of all the other firms in the downstream finished product market. This practice is prevalent in the steel industry where integrated steel manufacturers follow differential pricing in hot-rolled coils to harm the interests of cold-rolled steel manufacturers, the downstream players.

In case of *conglomerate mergers,* the most obvious way it can harm competition is through agreements to remove potential competitors[2], applicable in the case where firms operate in related markets.

In effect, a merger leads to a 'bad' outcome only if it creates a dominant enterprise that subsequently abuses its dominance. To some extent, the issue overlaps with the issue of dominance and its abuse. Viewed in this way, there is probably no need to have provisions for merger control in competition law. The reason that such a provision exists in most laws is to pre-empt the potential abuse of dominance where it is probable, as subsequent unbundling can be both difficult and socially costly.

4.2 Nature of M&As in India

The policy regime since the early-1990's has greatly liberalised the possibility of industrial restructuring and consolidation through M&As by removing restrictions under the Industrial Licensing Policy, Foreign Exchange Regulation Act, and the Capital Issues Control Act. Besides, major amendments were made to the Monopolies and Restrictive Trade Practices Act (MRTPA) in 1991, which resulted in no pre-M&A scrutiny for MRTP companies.

Most of the studies on M&As in India pertain to the period of post-91 liberalised regime, reflecting the increased importance of M&As as a subject of academic interest during the reforms era. Though most of these studies highlight the period of 'nineties as one of heightened merger activity, their analysis is at best partial in nature as it does not compare the merger activity in the post-91 period with that of the pre-91 period.

In comparison, Agarwal (2002) has compiled a comprehensive database on mergers in India, which covers the period from 1973-74 to 2001-02. The study highlights that the delicensing policy of the government (during the late-eighties as well as that undertaken during the nineties) had a positive impact on merger activity. The analysis also highlights the positive impact of the 1991-amendments to MRTPA on merger behaviour of erstwhile MRTP companies. The study shows that MRTP companies could not respond to the deregulation measures of late-eighties as they were still restrained by the MRTP Act. However, the effects of deregulation measures of the nineties were more pronounced given the simultaneous amendment of the MRTPA. Even in this case, the effect of the nineties deregulation policy on merger behaviour of MRTP companies would have been insignificant in the absence of the 1991 amendments.

4.2.1 Merger Trends

For the purpose of this paper, merger data compiled by Agarwal (2002) was extended to 2002-03, and is presented in Figure 4.1. The database reports 2253 merger cases from 1973-74 to 2002-03. The entire period is divided into three phases based on the annual intensity of merger activity, such that the highest number of mergers in a year in one phase is lower than the lowest number of mergers in the immediately succeeding phase. A high level of merger activity is observed since 1995-96 with each subsequent year recording more than 100 deals. The following three distinct phases of merger activity in India have been identified:

I. Low and Stagnant Merger Activity (1973-74 to 1987-88)

II. Moderate Merger Activity (1988-89 to 1994-95)

III. High Merger Activity (1995-96 to 2002-03)

4.2.2 M&As by Type

Merger studies' reviewed for post-1991 regime highlight the importance of horizontal type of mergers. In Beena's (1998) sample of 45 merger cases, around 69 per cent were horizontal mergers. Roy (1999) observes that in most of the cases, company taken over is horizontally related to the acquirer company. Das (2000) found that 65 per cent of merger cases in her sample were of horizontal type. For a sample of 397 M&A cases during the 1990s, Basant (2000) found 60 per cent cases were of horizontal nature. Agarwal (2002) found majority (56 per cent) of mergers were between firms that belonged to the same product category, defined at two-digit level as per NIC.

In comparison to the horizontal type, share of vertical and conglomerate types is less and between the two, the picture is mixed. In Beena's sample, vertical

and conglomerate mergers were equally distributed. Das finds 16 per cent cases of vertical and nearly 19 per cent cases of conglomerate type. Basant's sample highlights 11 per cent cases of vertical M&As and also observes a significant share (28 per cent) of M&As of the conglomerate type.

In general, horizontal type of combination has been the main form of M&A in India. This pattern suggests that firms have been trying to consolidate in the same product market.

In a significant number of cases both acquirer and target belong to the same business group. For the post-1991 period, Beena (1998) observes dominance of mergers between firms belonging to the same business group with similar product lines. In this context, Roy (1999) observes, "an interesting feature about the majority of the mergers is that the companies that are being merged belong to the same business group". In a sample of 36 merger cases, Saple (2000) finds 24 cases between group companies. Basant (2000) observes that in about 74 per cent cases, merging companies belonged to the same business group.

Agarwal (2002) finds that 35 per cent of mergers reported during the 10-year period spanning 1991-92 to 2000-01, were between affiliated firms. The study also shows that incidence of group mergers increased as one moves from the first phase of *stagnant* merger activity to the third phase of *high* merger activity.

As argued by Basant (2000), over-diversification resulting from earlier business strategies, which was largely an outcome of the erstwhile licensing regime, is being corrected. The pre-1991 regulated regime often made companies within the group compete with each other for market share. The partial liberalisation measures of eighties and economic reforms of nineties created an environment for rectifying such anomalies as shown by the above trends.

The dominant pattern is therefore for consolidation at the business and/or group levels. It has also been argued that a high incidence of mergers among affiliated firms could partly be explained by the need of the management to increase its controlling block in order to guard against a takeover or a dilution of control.

4.2.3 M&As by Industry

M&As have been spread across various industry groups. Studies that have analysed M&As during the 1990s find that firms in beverages, spirits and vinegar, financial and other services, chemicals, drugs and pharmaceuticals, electrical machinery and electronics

FIGURE 4.1

Number of Mergers (1973-74 to 2002-03)

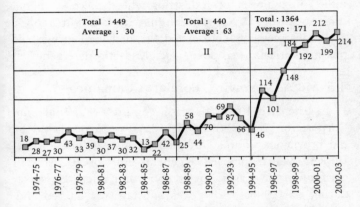

Source: Research & Statistics Division, Department of Company Affairs, Agarwal (2002).

sector have had relatively higher involvement in M&As activity (Basant, 2000; Das, 2000).

As per a recent analysis covering the period 1999-2004, M&As have been largely concentrated in machinery, chemicals, electronics, computer software, food and beverages, drugs and pharmaceuticals, and textiles (Dasgupta 2004).

With an exhaustive data on mergers, Agarwal (2002) identifies industries that were in the top-10 in terms of merger intensity during 1991-92 to 2000-01: Investments & Trust, Trading, Loan/credit activity, Electrical Machinery, Electronics, Textiles, Drugs & Pharmaceuticals, Construction, Beverages, and Iron & Steel. Together they account for about 57 per cent of mergers during the period.

4.3 Motives and Characteristics of Firms Involved in M&As

4.3.1 Motives

Beena (1998) argues that the merger wave in the early-1990s was more a means of internal restructuring aimed possibly at increasing size, deriving marketing and financial benefits, and exploiting scale economies. Moreover, there are signs of mergers aimed at synergies associated with vertical mergers; at linking more closely the production plans of related firms; and at increasing size. For the second half of the 1990s, Beena (2003) finds enhancing corporate control and market share as the key motivations. For a more recent period, Dasgupta (2004) finds that M&As have been used as a corporate strategy for consolidation and achievement of objectives such as scale economies, cost reduction and enhancement of market shares.

4.3.2 Characteristics of Firms

The various studies that have analysed M&As during the 1990s highlight that acquirer companies are generally characterised with higher profitability, larger size, higher growth rate, and higher liquidity than the target companies. Further, target companies, in general, have larger debt liability before merger than the corresponding acquirers.

4.4 Impact of M&As

4.4.1 On Performance

Das (2000) compares the pre-merger and post-merger operating profit margin for a sample of 14 acquiring companies and finds a decline in profitability in eight of these companies after merger. The study by Saple

(2000) shows that mergers did not lead to any improvement in performance as measured by profitability (return over net assets), adjusted for the industry average. Beena (1998) also finds no significant difference in the rate of return and profit margin between the periods before and after the merger. Overall, the results of these studies point to the possibility of merger driven by the managerial self-interest motive of growth maximisation rather than that of improving performance.

4.4.2 On Concentration

The study by Das (2000) examines the extent of concentration in the manufacturing sector in India in 15 product groups over the period of six years from 1993 to 1998. The study adopted the official notion of dominance as provided by the MRTPA whereby market share exceeding 25 per cent is considered to be an indicator of concentration of market power.

The study observed that in 11 out of 15 product groups level of market concentration was found to be high, out of which in 10 sectors concentration was 'consistently high' (micro-level concentration, greater than or equal to 25 per cent in at least five out of six years) over the relevant period. It is moderate (micro-level concentration, greater than or equal to 25 per cent in three out of six years) in one sector and low (micro-level concentration, greater than or equal to 25 per cent up to two out of six years and also micro-level concentration, consistently less than 25 per cent) only in the remaining three. The study, thus, finds high concentration ratios for most of the different product groups studied and also observes that as a consequence of dominance of horizontal mergers, concentration ratio in the product group level had gone up.

For a sample of 64 product lines, Beena (2003) finds an increase in concentration based on the Herfindahl index, in majority of industries where there is higher incidence of M&As. The industries are automobile ancillaries, cement, cotton and blended yarn, drugs and pharmaceuticals, tea, soap, and synthetic detergents.

4.5 M&As Involving Foreign Companies

In the pre-1991 'control regime' Multinational Corporation (MNC) related M&As were restricted by the provisions of the Foreign Exchange Regulation Act (FERA), which imposed a general limit of 40 per cent on foreign ownership in Indian companies. However, during the 1990s, FERA was substantially altered and, ultimately, replaced by the Foreign Exchange

Management Act (FEMA) in 1999. The New Industrial Policy of 1991 accords a much more liberal attitude to FDI inflows. Changes have been made to remove shareholding and business restrictions on MNCs and these relaxations are being continued year after year.

Given this liberalised policy framework since the early-1990s, MNCs have increasingly used the M&A route to enter and strengthen their presence in the country.

Kumar (2000) observes that the bulk of the deals relating to MNCs have materialised since 1996 and have mostly involved acquisitions rather than mergers. In terms of industry composition, an increasing proportion of MNC related M&As are found in the field of services, where multinational service enterprises are seeking to establish a place of business in the country by acquiring established domestic enterprises and their networks. In particular, an increasing interest of MNCs in financial services, advertising, travel agencies and other business services is notable. Further, consumer goods industries such as food and beverages, household appliances, pharmaceuticals and personal care products and automobiles have a high concentration of MNC related deals. This is because of the importance of a countrywide marketing, distribution and service network for these industries.

The deals relating to MNCs are predominantly horizontal in nature. Among other motives are: entering the Indian market and extending the scope of operations or consolidation of market share. There are also instances of mergers of foreign affiliates following the merger of their parents or as a part of group restructuring (Kumar, 2000).

According to Bhattacharjea (2003), certain mergers relating to foreign firms involved market shares of a magnitude that would attract the attention of competition authorities in most industrial countries, but in India all this merger and acquisition activity was beyond challenge. Thus, although the merger of Lipton and Brooke Bond into Hindustan Lever Limited's parent Unilever passed unchallenged in India, the Pakistan competition authority succeeded in getting Unilever to withdraw one of its brands and reduce its shareholding in Brooke Bond Pakistan to 40 per cent.

Dasgupta (2004) compares the M&A activity of Indian owned companies with that of foreign owned companies based on an analysis relating to 38 industry sectors and 19 service sectors for the period 1999-2004. The study finds that the number of acquisitions by Indian owned companies and number of mergers among Indian owned companies are higher than the number of acquisitions by foreign owned companies and the number of mergers among foreign owned companies, except for six industry sectors. In terms of value of acquisitions, in 52 per cent of the industry sectors, value of acquisitions by Indian owned companies is larger than those by foreign owned companies. For services, in 66 per cent of the sectors, value of acquisitions of Indian owned companies are higher than those of foreign owned companies. However, the study finds that the average size of acquisitions of foreign owned companies is higher than Indian owned companies.

4.6 M&A Regulation in India

4.6.1 Monopolies and Restrictive Trade Practices Act, 1969 (MRTPA)

MRTPA was passed to check concentration of economic power, control the growth of monopolies and prevent various trade practices detrimental to public interest. Mergers and acquisitions are separately dealt with in Chapter III of the MRTP Act. MRTP companies[3] were required to seek the Central Government's approval under sections 23 and 24 of MRTPA.

These provisions gave absolute power to the Central government in matters relating to M&As involving MRTP companies. Under the Act, an application had to be made to the Central Government, which, if it thought fit, referred the same to the MRTP Commission. But the government was not bound to do so. Further, the government was not bound to follow the recommendations of the MRTP Commission.

Armed with this power, the government often used the M&A provisions for reasons other than what related to competition policy. For example, the government filed a case to order a break-up of the Indian Express group of newspapers during the Emergency but the reason was political and not economic. This case was later withdrawn after the Congress party was defeated.

The provisions remained in vogue for over two decades until the economic liberalisation measures initiated during the early-nineties. The only exception was the 1985 amendments to MRTPA, which raised the minimum asset limit from Rs. 20 crore to Rs. 100 crore for referring a company to the MRTP Commission, thus limiting the applicability of the Act. With this amendment, companies with asset value of less than Rs. 100 crore no longer required pre-merger approval under the MRTPA.

Rao and Rao (1987) analyse a sample of 94 merger orders passed during 1970-86 by the Government of India under the auspices of the MRTPA. Their analysis shows that the existence of MRTPA determined the arguments advanced by the companies concerned for government's approval. The most frequently used argument for according approval was that both companies were interconnected and belonged to same group, and such merger would not result in any further concentration of economic power to the common detriment. The Central Government rejected **five** of these merger proposals. The government's argument were based on the criteria of concentration of economic power and the principles underlying the then industrial policy, such as the items manufactured by the acquirer company were not open to MRTP companies.

Major amendments were made to the MRTPA in 1991 when several sections (20 to 26 and 28 to 30) of Chapter III of the Act were deleted. These were in line with the structural adjustment measures initiated during the same time. Under the amendments, provisions relating to pre-entry restrictions with regard to prior approval of the Central government for any expansion, new investment or M&A activities were all deleted from the Statute. The causal thinking in support of the 1991 amendments is contained in the Statement of Objects and Reasons appended to the MRTP (Amendment) Bill, 1991, which states:

"With the growing complexity of industrial structure and the need for achieving economies of scale for ensuring higher productivity and competitive advantage in the international market, the thrust of the industrial policy has shifted to controlling and regulating the monopolistic, restrictive and unfair trade practices rather than making it necessary for certain undertakings to obtain prior approval of the Central Government for expansion, establishment of new undertakings, merger, amalgamation, takeover and appointment of directors. It has been the experience of the government that pre-entry restrictions under the MRTP Act on the investment decision of the corporate sector has outlived its utility and has become a hindrance to the speedy implementation of industrial projects. By eliminating the requirement of time-consuming procedures and prior approval of the government, it would be possible for all productive sections of the society to participate in efforts for maximisation of production."[4]

The scrapping of pre-entry restrictions was expected to encourage competition by reducing barriers to entry for new firms and to enable Indian firms to become large enough to compete effectively in global markets. With the 1991 amendments, focus of the Act shifted from prevention of concentration of economic power to the common detriment, to curbing monopolistic, restrictive and unfair trade practices. Size as a factor, to discourage concentration of economic power, was given up.

However, section 27 survived the amendments, which empowers the Central Government to order division of an undertaking or sever interconnections between undertakings if it is found to be prejudicial to public interest or is likely to lead to the adoption of any monopolistic or restrictive trade practice. The MRTPC can recommend de-merger and the process to carry it out to the Central Government, if approached by a consumer organisation, trade association, by a State government or by the Central Government itself, or even on its own. But this clause has not been used so far.

In the context of analysis, post-1991 amendment, Beena (1998) finds around 41 per cent (39 out of 94 merger cases studied during 1990-94) of the acquiring firms belonged to the asset-size class of Rs.100 crore and above, the cut-off asset figure in the now diluted MRTPA.

Agarwal (2002) finds for the five-year period pre-amendments that in 17 per cent mergers both the companies were affiliated to the same business group. However, for the five-year period post-amendments this percentage was significantly high at 63 per cent. Further, for the five-year period pre-91 amendments, in 38 per cent cases both companies belonged to the same product category. Interestingly this percentage was higher at 53 per cent for the five-year period post-91 amendments (Table 4.1). Most of these firms, which had been classified as MRTP firms pre-91 amendments, acquired another firm that belonged to the same management and produced a similar product. Further, based on econometric analysis, Agarwal (2002) finds that 1991-amendments to the MRTP Act had a positive and significant impact on merger behaviour by MRTP firms, as acquirer.

TABLE 4.1
Merger Behaviour of MRTP Companies (Pre- and Post-1991 Amendments)

	5-years pre-91 (1986-87 to 1990-91)	5-years post-91 (1992-93 to 1996-97)
Percentage of mergers where both companies belong to the same business group	17% (13 out of 77)	63% (60 out of 96)
Percentage of mergers where both companies belong to the same product category	38% (22 out of 58)	53% (48 out of 90)

Source: Agarwal (2002).

Hence, it can be argued from Table 4.1 that most of these MRTP firms could not have opted for this route of expansion if the government had not diluted the MRTPA. The removal of legislative barriers encouraged a few large Indian firms to redefine their product portfolios and reformulate their corporate and business strategies through the merger process.

4.6.1.1 Supreme Court Judgment in HLL-TOMCO Case Post-1991-Amendments

(Information provided in this section has been taken from Bhattacharjea (2003)

The first controversial merger post-1991 amendments that did not have to pass the acid test of the MRTPC was that between Hindustan Lever Limited (HLL) and Tata Oil Mills Company Ltd. (TOMCO), both significant players in the market for soaps and detergents. As 90 per cent of the shareholders had voted for the merger, the "reasonable" shareholder acknowledgement was satisfied. However, the merger was challenged on various grounds by the HLL employees' union.

The Supreme Court in its judgment did not favour the pre-merger scrutiny to be undertaken by the MRTP Commission. The Supreme Court ruled that after the 1991 amendment deleted the relevant section of the Act, no government approval was required because no other provision of the Act could be construed to require such approval. The merger could be questioned only if it was not carried out in accordance with the provisions of the Companies Act, or involved fraud or illegality. The plaintiffs also argued that the merger would result in a large share of the market being controlled by a multinational company, and that consumer interests might be adversely affected. On these grounds, they sought to invoke the public interest dimension.

However, the Court held that the merger could not be stopped on the grounds that it violated public interest or public policy. The judgment held that the MRTP and FERA amendments were specifically intended to allow foreign firms to do business in India more easily and what has been expressly authorised by the Statute cannot be struck down as being against public policy. The Court opined that consumer interests could be considered if after the merger it is found that the merged entity is working in a way, which brings it within the purview of the MRTP Act. Under such circumstances, the MRTP Commission can take any action as it deems fit. However, the concern is that section 27 of MRTPA, as noted above, has never been used.

Market share data compiled by the Centre for Monitoring Indian Economy (CMIE, 1999) shows that HLL's market share in soaps rose from 19.7 per cent in 1992-93 (the year before the merger with TOMCO) to 26 per cent in 1997-98; in synthetic detergents it rose from 33.1 per cent to 46.7 per cent. Market research data (Naidu 2000) put its share of toilet soaps and shampoos at over 60 per cent and detergent bars at 45 per cent.

4.6.2 Competition Act, 2002

The Competition Act, 2002 has provisions for regulations of "combinations", which include mergers, amalgamations, and acquisitions beyond a specified threshold limit. That is, those mergers and acquisitions, which fall below the threshold limits specified, are not considered in the expression "combinations" and are outside the ambit of the Act.

The threshold limit as specified in section 5 of the Act is Rs. 1,000 crore (US$208mn, on 2004 exchange rate) in terms of aggregate value of assets of the combining parties or Rs. 3,000 crore (US$625mn) in terms of turnover of the combining parties. In the event that either of the parties is outside India or both are outside, the threshold is US$500mn for assets and US$1500mn for turnover. If one of the merging parties belongs to a group, which controls it, the threshold is Rs. 4,000 crore (US$833mn) in terms of assets and Rs. 12,000 crore (US$2500mn) in terms of turnover. If the group has assets or turnover outside India also, the threshold limits are US$2bn for assets and US$6bn for turnover.

The threshold limits are subject to revision every two years on the basis of wholesale price index or fluctuations in exchange rate of the rupee or foreign currencies. These limits are prescribed in such a way that, by and large, only major mergers and acquisitions would fall within the ambit of the Act. As per current estimates, if assets/turnover of Indian companies were considered, the number of cases that would fall within the definition of "combinations" would not be more than 100.

The Act makes it voluntary for the companies concerned to notify their proposed combination to the Mergers Bench (a part of the Competition Commission of India), though the draft law that preceded the Act had mandatory notification provisions. The initial proposal for mandatory review of proposed mergers faced tremendous criticism from business lobbies, and was diluted by making pre-merger notification voluntary.

Even threshold limit was doubled due to business opposition. The trigger/cause for these changes was that companies in India needed to grow in size in order to become globally competitive.

Around 13 criteria have been built-in to determine the adverse effects of a combination on competition. Among the listed factors are:

- Level of competition through imports in the market;

- Extent of barriers to entry into the market;

- Extent of effective competition likely to sustain in a market;

- Extent to which substitutes are available;

- Market share in the relevant market;

- Nature of vertical integration in the market; and

- Nature and extent of innovation.

The merger bench of the CCI is mandated to adjudicate on combinations by weighing potential efficiency losses against potential gains. As per the provisions in the Act, approval is deemed to have been granted if no decision is reached in 90 days. However, the Act empowers the CCI to look into a combination **up to a year after it has taken effect** (emphasis added) and to undo or modify it, if the combination causes or is likely to cause an appreciable adverse effect on competition within the relevant market in India. But, unscrambling of merged firm's assets is likely to be a costly affair and will require technical expertise in the Commission. A similar provision exists in the MRTP Act, but no case has ever come up before it.

In comparison, in the USA, demergers have been carried out successfully in the past, such as the mini-Bells case, where AT&T, the giant telecom company, was broken up into seven companies in 1984, in response to a federal anti-trust suit.

With this backdrop, there are two concerns that arise relating to analysis of M&As under the Competition Act.

First, the definition of "combinations" as defined in the Act is very narrow in its scope. It does not include joint ventures, alliances, etc. The threshold is also so high, that many M&As, which may cause appreciable adverse effect on competition, will escape from its scrutiny. This is likely in cases where the overall market size is small or merger involves a product whose relevant market is local/regional in nature.

One such instance could be merger/acquisition between companies in the cement industry. The cement industry is of a regional nature, given that freight costs are a significant proportion of the final cost of cement. For example, the southern market in India, which is the largest market both in terms of consumption and installed capacity, is insulated from competition due to geographical location and transport costs. Recent consolidation in the cement industry has made it more concentrated. This has hiked the risk of firms resorting to collusive practices and uncompetitive behaviour, as market shares of a few companies have become significantly large when compared to other firms.

Given that formation of a cartel is *per se* illegal, companies in the cement industry that want to indulge in anti-competitive activities in a region will most likely resort to a merger or acquisition, as it would be relatively easy to carry out, given the high threshold limits specified in the Act. Hence, any merger/acquisition among top companies in the southern region might raise competition concerns but would be out of the ambit of the Competition Act because of high threshold limits.

Thus, for effective M&A regulation, the CCI will have to also monitor those M&As which are out of the ambit of the Competition Act but may raise competition concerns.

Second, the Act mentions that the CCI shall not initiate an inquiry into a combination after the expiry of one year from the date on which the combination has taken effect. Nonetheless, the effective date of merger is not specified in the Act, which is normally the date on which assets and liabilities of the target company gets vested in the acquirer company. It is observed that in most merger cases, effective date precedes the date on which the merger order is passed by the high court concerned. Given this, would the CCI initiate an inquiry when companies file their application with the high court concerned or whether it would be after the high court has passed an order?

In the former case, the CCI has to inform the high court concerned of the enquiry it has initiated and coordinate with the court in conducting the inquiry. In the latter case, the CCI may not even get time to conduct an inquiry if it takes the effective date of merger as defined above. This is because in several cases, a high court often takes a year to arrive at its decision. Even if the high court takes less than a year, the CCI would effectively have only a few months to conduct and complete the inquiry. This issue needs to be taken care of when Statutory Regulations are framed.

4.6.3 Companies Act, 1956

The general law relating to mergers/amalgamations is embodied in sections 391 to 396 of the Companies Act, 1956. Section 391 gives the High Court the power to sanction a compromise or arrangement with creditors and members (shareholders) subject to certain conditions. Section 392 gives the power to the High Court to enforce and supervise the carrying out of such compromises or arrangements with creditors and members. Section 393 provides for the availability of the information required by creditors and members of the company concerned when acceding to such an arrangement. Section 394 makes provisions for facilitating reconstruction and amalgamation of companies. Section 395 gives power and duty to acquire the shares of shareholders dissenting from the scheme or contract approved by the majority. Section 396 deals with the power of the central government to provide for an amalgamation of companies in the national interest.

The merging entities are supposed to apply to the High Court for merger and the court is expected to examine public interest implications of the proposed merger. In practice, however, public interest is understood **as protecting the interest of creditors and shareholders**. The high courts do not screen a merger from the competition angle.

The provisions relating to acquisition and transfer of shares is provided in Sections 108-A to 108-I of the Act. These provisions were originally a part of the MRTP Act and were incorporated in the Companies Act in the year 1991, following the 1991-amendment to the MRTP Act. These provisions apply only to dominant undertakings i.e. those with a market share of 25 per cent or more in the relevant market.

As per the provisions of the Act, an acquirer shall take prior approval of the Central Government for acquiring shares in a company, if the total shareholding post-acquisition exceeds 25 per cent of the paid-up equity capital of the target company. In case of transfer of shares, it is stipulated that a company, which holds at least ten per cent equity capital of any other company, shall provide intimation to the Central government if it wants to transfer such shares. Similar provisions exist for transfer of shares of foreign companies having an established place of business in India.

Where the Central Government is satisfied that as a result of the acquisition or transfer of shares of a company, a change in the controlling interest of the company is likely to take place and that such a change would be **prejudicial to the interest of the company or to the public interest**, the Government may not approve the acquisition or transfer of shares. The Central Government is given a time period of sixty days to refuse to grant such approvals, otherwise the approval is presumed to have been granted.

These provisions do not apply to government companies, statutory corporations, and financial institutions that are exempted from the purview of these sections.

From the above provisions, it is observed that market power or similar competition issues are not considered for granting approval to an acquisition or transfer of shares.

4.6.4 SEBI Takeover Code

The Securities and Exchange Board of India (SEBI) regulates substantial acquisitions of shares. As per SEBI (Substantial Acquisition of Shares and Takeovers) Regulations, 1997 (also known as the Takeover Code), any person acquiring 15 per cent or more of the voting capital of a company or securing control of the management of a company[5] has to make an offer to the remaining shareholders of the target company to acquire from them at least 20 per cent of the total shares. This is an open offer, which on several occasions offers attractive exit opportunities to other shareholders.

The Takeover Code provides for transparency relating to the acquisition of shares of listed companies and is designed to **protect shareholders' interest**. Competition issues are not considered.

4.6.5 Sectoral Acts/Regulations

M&A is governed under certain sectoral Acts/Regulations such as in Telecom, Electricity, Banking etc. The question of overlapping jurisdictions between the Competition Act and sectoral Acts/Regulations regarding M&A is going be a challenge and would require a proper mechanism to resolve the same. Relevant provisions from certain sectoral acts/regulations are given below.

4.6.5.1 Telecommunications

The Department of Telecommunications (DoT) has framed guidelines for intra-circle mergers and acquisitions, following the recommendations of the Telecom Regulatory Authority of India (TRAI) on the issue. All such M&As need DoT's approval. In order to ensure that **sufficient competition exists**, intra-circle merger/acquisition is allowed subject to the condition that, post-merger, there are at least three operators within the telecom circle for that service, and the market share of the merged entity in that service area does not exceed 67 per cent. While merger of companies holding different service licences is permitted, a standalone basic service licence cannot be merged with a standalone cellular service licence and *vice versa*.

4.6.5.2 Electricity

As per the Electricity Act, 2003, a licensee needs to take prior approval of the Appropriate Commission i.e. Central Electricity Regulatory Commission (CERC) at the federal level or State Electricity Regulatory Commission (SERC) at state level, to undertake any merger or acquisition. The Act further states that the Appropriate Commission may grant approval on the grounds of **public interest**.

4.6.5.3 Banking

A merger between public sector banks requires Parliamentary approval, as they are governed by the Bank Nationalisation Act and the Banking Regulation Act. Mergers or acquisitions among private sector banks are governed by the Companies Act and are subject to the approval of the Reserve Bank of India (RBI). Private sector banks also need the RBI's approval for merger or acquisition with a non-banking finance company. The latter, though, not a formal requirement under the current provisions of the Banking Regulation Act, is practiced by the Banking regulator on a case-by-case basis to ensure that the merger or acquisition is in **depositors' interest and public interest**. The RBI has in the past blocked several mergers on the grounds that it had concerns about the antecedents of the acquiring entity, for example, that of IndusInd Bank with Ashok Leyland Finance and that of restricting Chrys Capital from investing in Centurion Bank. In order to formalise this arrangement, the working group of the Indian Banks' Association has recommended to the Finance Ministry that the RBI should be the final authority to decide on all merger and acquisition issues, including swap ratios. This is to ensure strict financial discipline.

4.6.5.4 To sum up...

Except for the DoT guidelines, which take into account competition concerns, M&A provisions in other Acts/Regulations as studied above do not regulate M&A from the competition perspective. Accordingly, after the 1991 amendment and the 1994 judgment of the Supreme Court, and with the exception of the DoT

guidelines, there is at present no regulation of M&As in India from competition angle. The provisions relating to combinations regulations in the Competition Act would be brought into force during the third year of the operation of the Act. But even this will leave out certain M&As, which may pose competition concerns.

4.7 National Champions

The Finance Ministry is exploring the issue of merging country's public sector banks to create a few mammoth banks. There is also a move to set up a massive development financial institution (DFI) by merging all existing DFIs. The purpose is to create giant Indian financial entities that can take on competition in the global market. Similarly, the Petroleum Ministry is exploring options of merging companies in the oil sector to create oil behemoths that have financial capabilities to match firms in the international market. The Ministry has set up a committee to suggest ways to synergise the strengths of oil companies to create a strong and efficient public sector unit, fully competitive in both domestic and global markets.

Yet, there are both *pros* and *cons* to creating national champions.

BOX 4.1

'Pros' and 'Cons' to Creating National Champions

Pros...	... and Cons
• Economies of scale	• Abuse of dominance
• International competitiveness	• Anti-competitive behaviour
• R&D promotion	• Reduction of competition in relevant markets
• Spillover effects to stimulate other industries and economic development of home country	• Consumer interest concerns
• National security grounds	• Possible distortions to FDI, trade flows and frictions among trading partners
• Dynamic growth and development	• Possible misuse by special interest groups

World over, in the UK, and in the Netherlands, government intervention in the enforcement of competition policy in regulating mergers and acquisitions with regards to "national interests" is limited to national security grounds at most. But, in countries like Germany, Canada and Australia, the "national champion" argument has considerable significance.

For instance, in a merger case in 2002, Germany's Ministry of Economics overruled a Federal Cartel Office (FCO) decision, rejecting E.ON AG's proposed acquisition of Ruhrgas AG, Europe's largest gas importer. The country's Economics Ministry is empowered to approve a merger vetoed by the FCO, if the anti-competitive effects are outweighed by advantages to the entire economy or it is justified by a predominant public interest. Anyhow, the Ministry has rarely used this power, and this was only the ninth time. In the particular case, the Cartel office had vetoed the merger on competition grounds. Its argument was that the merger would have major implications due to vertical integration: Ruhrgas' gas import contracts and high-pressure pipelines were sought to be merged with E.ON's sizeable interests in regional and municipal gas distribution. This would have strengthened E.ON's already dominant position in gas and electricity distribution in Germany, and, in effect, reduced competition in these markets. The German Monopolies Commission as well as the German Minister of Consumer Affairs too gave negative evaluation of the mergers' implications for competition and for consumers. However, the Ministry of Economics approved the bid arguing that the merger will help create a global player that will benefit the Germany economy and secure Germany's gas supply, 90 per cent of which came from abroad.

In developing countries, the pro-national champion industrial policy has considerable force. The argument that less developed economies and small markets can, at best, sustain one or two firms in an industry capable of achieving economies of scale, undertaking research and development and securing world markets in competition with advanced trading partners and giant multinational corporations, as a stimulus for other sectors, has been used at times to give industrial policy precedence over competition policy. Besides, factors such as trade liberalisation, perceived to be threatening their national policy space and largely favouring multinationals, contribute to the desire to create globally competitive entities.

The experiences with pro-national champions industrial policy in certain countries illustrates the dynamic benefits that can be derived by helping domestic firms become more efficient and competitive. For example, the success of the Korean industrialisation programme relied on a big business-oriented growth strategy, together with regulations on entry and protection from foreign competition.

In Korea, the government helped create the giant corporation, the *Chaebol*, which went on to capture the world markets. During the second half of the 20th century, Korea has managed to transform itself into an industrially and technologically sophisticated economy. Though Korea has one of the highest levels of industrial concentration in the world, largely due to the lax enforcement of competition policy, the giant Korean *chaebols* were made to compete with each other for government support. The national champion policy in this case was strategically applied to bring maximum benefits for the country.

Still, the *chaebol*-led economic growth eventually took its toll on the Korean economy. The market structure became distorted due to existence of monopolistic practices leading to a strong public outcry in the 1980s. Recognising the need to remedy such distortion, the Korean government enacted the Monopoly Regulation and Fair Trade Act in 1980 and established the Korea Fair Trade Commission (FTC) in 1981. The matter of competition has been treated very seriously by Korea, as the head of the FTC is a member of the cabinet. This enables the competition authority to have its say in most economic policy matters.

The challenge is to strike the right balance, so that the pursuit of national development goals is not misused by special interest groups and wrong 'winners' picked, proving detrimental to competition and consumer welfare.

Given this, the relevant question is, will Bank of Baroda, for example, become a better bank if another PSU bank is merged into it? Bank of Baroda is already bigger than, for example, the HDFC bank. However, a comparison between the two shows that (Patnaik, 2004):

(i) HDFC bank does a business of Rs. 8.66 crore per employee as compared to only Rs. 2.53 crore for Bank of Baroda.

(ii) Secondly, while Bank of Baroda's assets are twice that of HDFC Bank's, its market value is just one-third.

According to Patnaik (2004), the Ministry of Finance should certainly worry about how Bank of Baroda can be brought to HDFC Bank's standards. But if size was of the essence, Bank of Baroda has that already. If size were of the essence in global competitiveness, then SBI and IDBI would have been exporters of financial services. The path to globally competitive finance does not lie in bigger PSU banks, but in asking questions about why Bank of Baroda and

IDBI are so far behind the well-run banks of India. If Dena Bank is merged into IDBI, we won't get a globally competitive bank. We'll just get a bigger IDBI.

Another aspect to consider is that when a PSU gets big, there are unique set of problems that come from it being so big that no government can accept bankruptcy. SBI has assets of Rs. 409,771 crore, and it is the Ministry of Finance that has to worry about SBI going bankrupt. The threat of bankruptcy is a central device through which a firm is kept honest. A policy of mergers will diminish this pressure on the PSUs and detract from efficiency (Patnaik, 2004).

In a merger case involving the four largest banks in Canada, the country's Finance Ministry rejected the merger proposals. In 1998, the Royal Bank of Canada and the Bank of Montreal announced their plans to merge. This was followed by a similar announcement involving the Canadian Imperial Bank of Commerce and the Toronto-Dominion Bank. However, the Finance Ministry rejected the two proposals and said that the mergers were not in the best interests of Canadians because they would lead to[6] a) an unacceptable concentration of economic power in the hands of fewer, very large banks, b) a significant reduction of competition, and c) reduced policy flexibility for the government to address potential future prudential concerns, as allowing two banks to operate will sharply increase the overall systemic risk in case one of them failed. It was also argued that between 20,000 to 40,000 jobs would be lost as a result of the proposed mergers.

On the last argument, interestingly, an employees' association of the Industrial Finance Corporation of India (IFCI) had in April 2004 asked the government to rethink the proposed mergers of IFCI-PNB, and IDFC-SBI and instead, explore the possibility of a mega merger of all the existing development financial institutions (DFI). It mooted this suggestion with a view to form a strong and vibrant DFI.

In the context of the oil sector, a discussion paper brought out by the Ministry of Petroleum and Natural Gas highlights that the PSU oil companies under-performed against their private sector rivals in core businesses. The higher profitability of PSUs came mostly from the dismantling of the administered pricing mechanism (resulting in cartelised pricing), lack of competition and higher international oil prices. Looking at the specifics, such as in the exploration and production business, where ONGC and Oil India are the major players, the performance over the last six years shows that the joint ventures and private sector companies, achieved a compound annual growth rate (CAGR) of 7.5 per cent in oil production while the PSUs only managed a negative CAGR of –0.5 per cent.

Be that as it may, in oil, big is truly beautiful and captivating. The world over, vertically integrated oil and gas businesses are the norm. The merger of Chevron and Texaco or that of Exxon and Mobil are two such examples. The oil and gas business is highly capital-intensive and requires serious risk-taking in exploration calling for deep pockets. And the standard practice is to foray downstream into retail sales of petroleum products to garner volumes. Anyhow, in the Indian public sector, the exploration and production major, ONGC, was restricted to the upstream, and the refining and retailing major, IOC, was confined to the downstream.

An important aspect to consider is that of competition in the two sectors. Both banking and oil suffer from a lack of competition. It is imperative for the government to create an open market and a level playing field to encourage competition for the companies to reach global standards of performance. The interests of the citizen will be ill served by more concentrated banking or more concentrated oil. It is important to ensure that the market process is acknowledged to realise the benefits from promoting national champions.

4.8 Recommendations and Issues for Further Research

- Competition Commission of India (CCI) should also monitor those M&As which are out of the ambit of the Competition Act but may raise competition concerns

- Proper coordination is required between the Competition Commission and other agencies that regulate M&As (i.e. sectoral regulators, RBI, SEBI, High Court etc.)

- To realise the benefits from promoting national champions, it is important to ensure that the market process is acknowledged

- Public interest is an important factor in approving a merger or acquisition proposal. Care should be taken to ensure that it is not misused by special interest groups at the cost of consumer welfare

- The country has witnessed a tremendous spurt in M&As ever since economic reforms were initiated. Conduct an impact analysis of M&As in terms of efficiency gains and market power.

Notes

1. Equity holding of 26 per cent or more is effective in the passing of special resolutions. According to the Companies Act, 1956 a special resolution requires a special majority to approve the resolution i.e. the votes in favour must at least be three times the votes cast against the resolution, if any. This implies that a holder of 26 per cent or more of equity shares of the company can block the special resolution. Some of the matters for which special resolution is required to be passed are – to alter the objects clause of memorandum (the objects clause defines the objects of the company and indicates the sphere of its activities); to alter Articles of Association (these are the bye-laws or rules and regulations that govern the management of its internal affairs and the conduct of its business. Hence, the articles regulate the internal management of a company).

2. An actual competitor is defined as one that "has existing productive and distributive facilities that could easily and economically be used to produce and sell the relevant product within a short period (generally, one year) in response to a small but significant and non-transitory increase in price". On the other hand, potential competitors are those that "must construct significant new productive or distributive facilities in order to produce and sell the relevant product". (Viscusi *et al.*)

3. A company was classified as MRTP company, when it by itself or together with its interconnected undertakings had asset value of at least Rs. 100 crore (raised from Rs. 20 crore during the 1985 amendments) or was dominant in the relevant market i.e. commanding a market share in excess of one-fourth.

4. *Report of the High Level Committee on Competition Policy and Law*, 2000, Chapter VII, Para 7.2.7.

5. A person can secure control of the management of a company by acquiring or agreeing to acquire, irrespective of the percentage of voting capital, securities of the directors or other members who control or manage the company.

6. *Source*: http://www.fin.gc.ca/news98/98-123e.html

References

Agarwal, Manish (2002). *Analyses of Mergers in India*, M.Phil. dissertation, University of Delhi.

Basant, Rakesh (2000). "Corporate Response to Economic Reforms," *Economic and Political Weekly*, March 4.

Beena, P.L. (1998). *Mergers and Amalgamations: An Analysis in the Changing Structure of Indian Oligopoly*, unpublished Ph.D thesis submitted to the Jawaharlal Nehru University, New Delhi.

————. (2003). "Understanding the Latest Phase of Merger Wave in India: A Comparative Perspective," paper presented at the *Conference on Globalisation in India*, sponsored by the School of Management of the Indian Institute of Technology, Bombay.

Bhattacharjea, Aditya (2003). "Trade, Investment, and Competition Policy: An Indian Perspective," in Aaditya Mattoo and Robert M. Stern ed., *India and the WTO*.

Das, Nandita (2000). *A Study of the Corporate Restructuring of Indian Industries in the Post-New Industrial Policy Regime – The Issue of Amalgamations/Mergers*, unpublished Ph.D thesis submitted to University of Calcutta, Calcutta.

Dasgupta, Paramita (2004). "Establishing an Effective Competition Policy System: the Challenges facing India in implementing its New Competition Law," presentation made at the WTO/UNESCO/ASCI Regional Seminar for *Asia and Pacific Economies on Competition Policy, Development and the Multilateral Trading System*, Hyderabad, India, 6-8 October.

High Level Committee (2000). Report of "The High Level Committee on Competition Policy and Law," Department of Company Affairs, Govt. of India, New Delhi.

Kumar, Nagesh (2000). "Mergers and Acquisitions by MNEs: Patterns and Implications," *Economic & Political Weekly*, August 5-11.

Ministry of Law and Justice (Legislative Department) (2003). "The Competition Act, 2002," *The Gazette of India*, No.12, January 14.

Monopolies Inquiry Commission (1965). *Monopolies Inquiry Commission Report*, Government of India, New Delhi.

Naidu, R. (2000). "Where Size Matters," *Business Standard Smart Investor*, April 17.

Patnaik, Ila (2004). "PSU Mergers: Are Bigger Things Better?" *Financial Express*, November 22.

Pham, Alice (2003). "National Champions – National Interests *Vs.* Competition: Where to Strike the Balance?" *CUTS Centre for Competition, Investment & Economic Regulation Briefing Paper* No. 8.

Rao, Narasimha V. and Dr. P.V. Krishna Rao (1987). "Regulation of Mergers under the MRTP Act 1969: A Critical Study," *Company News & Notes*, Vol. 25, No 6.

Roy, Malabika (1999). "Mergers and Takeovers: The Indian Scene during the 1990s," in Amiya Kumar Bagchi ed., *Economy & Organisation – Indian Institutions under the Neoliberal Regime*, Sage Publications.

Saple, Vardhana (2000). *Diversification, Merger and their Effect on Firm Performance: A Study of the Indian Corporate Sector*, unpublished Ph.D thesis submitted to the Indira Gandhi Institute of Development Research, Mumbai, May.

Viscusi, W. Kip, John M. Vernon, Joseph E. Harrington Jr., (2000). *Economics of Regulation and Antitrust*, Third Edition, Cambridge and London: MIT Press.

5 Cross-Border Competition Issues

Aditya Bhattacharjea • Nitya Nanda

5.1 Introduction

As countries integrate more and more into the global economy, they become more prone to the anti-competitive practices operating on a global scale or originating elsewhere in the globe. India is no exception to this. Transnational corporations (TNCs) have entered developing-country markets and/or increased their activities within these countries. The entering of TNCs can have many positive effects on developing countries' economies. At the same time, there is a serious concern among these nations that competition could suffer because of the entry of TNCs, as their ability to deal with cross-border competition problems is either inadequate or non-existent (Jenny 2000). When competition authorities from highly developed countries/blocks like the European Union face difficulties in handling cases with a cross-border dimension, it is clear that the authorities in developing countries face even greater and more serious problems.

One important issue concerns jurisdiction, since the origins of such practices are, by and large, outside the territorial jurisdiction of a country. Although there is a general presumption against the extra-territorial application of legislation, a number of states seek to apply their laws outside their territory in the context of competition policy. This is on the basis of the so-called 'effects' doctrine, according to which states have assumed jurisdiction over conduct having anti-competitive effects in their territory even if it takes place in another state.[1]

The recognition of challenges posed by cross-border competition problems, however, is not a recent phenomenon. The 1946 Havana Charter provided for the obligation of each member to take appropriate measures and cooperate to prevent business practices, by private or public commercial enterprises affecting international trade, which restrain competition, limit access to markets or foster monopolistic control, whenever such practices have harmful effects on the expansion of production or trade and interfere with the achievement of any of the other objectives set forth in the Charter. But the Charter could not be ratified by the US Congress, primarily because of the fear among the legislators that the proposed International Trade Organisation (ITO), would interfere too much with domestic governance. This concern was particularly pronounced in the regulation of restrictive business practices.

As the Charter was not adopted, efforts were made at the GATT, the UN and later UNCTAD to remedy the absence of rules on anti-competitive practices, but this did not get far. In December 1980, the UN General Assembly adopted by Resolution a "Set of Multilaterally Equitable Agreed Principles and Rules for the Control of Restrictive Business Practices" (popularly called the Set). But the developed countries distanced themselves from the agreement, probably due to the liberalisation in the US and EC approaches to competition matters. Developing countries, however, continued to support the idea of international rules on restrictive practices and, in fact, actively promoted, in the review conference convened in 1985, the upgrading of the Set to a binding instrument and of the Intergovernmental Group of Experts to a committee. These initiatives failed and the developed countries repeatedly turned back the efforts by the developing countries to make the code a binding international legal instrument.

In sum, developing countries have generally favoured the development of international disciplines on restrictive business practices, including under binding rules. The support for the UNCTAD Set and the insistence on the need of providing it with some teeth by making it into a binding instrument, are sufficiently illustrative in that regard. It is rather the group of developed countries, which has been on the defensive and which has so far blocked the establishment of a more solid basis for dealing with firms' anti-competitive practices (Evans, 1995).

Before we look further into the issue of tackling cross-border anti-competitive practices, let us briefly look into the various types of such practices that affect countries. The types of cross-border anti-competitive practices are quite similar to that of those perpetrated within national borders. The only difference lies in the cross-border (international) dimensions of the anti-competitive behaviour. A number of areas where enterprise behaviour is perceived to give rise to competition concerns with international dimensions are discussed here. There is no single way by which one can estimate the damage that these cross-border anti-competitive practices are causing. However, one can have a fair understanding of the nature and dimensions of the problems through the analysis of anecdotal evidence. These issues can broadly be classified into four groups:[2]

- Market power in global or export markets;
- Barriers to import competition;
- Foreign investment; and
- Intellectual property rights

5.2 Cross-Border Market Power

5.2.1 International Cartels

International cartels have attracted much attention in recent years. Competition (antitrust) agencies in the European Union and the United States have successfully prosecuted over forty such cartels that operated in their jurisdictions during the 1990s, and slapped multi-million dollar/Euro fines on several companies. Studies commissioned by the OECD (2003), the WTO Secretariat (Evenett, 2003), and the World Bank (revised version in Levenstein et al., 2003) summarise some of the evidence generated by these cases, and present estimates of the losses incurred by consumers in other jurisdictions, especially developing countries, as a result of the cartels' collusive price-fixing activities. Levenstein et al., put the volume of developing countries' imports of just 19 of these cartel-affected products in 1997 at $59.9 bn, representing 4.4 per cent of their total imports and 0.9 per cent of their GDP in that year. Another estimate shows that the vitamins cartel alone cost developing countries $3 bn

during the 1990s (Clarke and Evenett, 2002). Almost all these cartels are constituted by producers in developed countries, and Levenstein et al., also present evidence that they have attempted to penalise rivals in developing countries by launching anti-dumping actions against their exports and restricting their access to technology. However, apart from limited measures taken by Brazil, Korea and Mexico, no other developing country has made any attempt to take action against these cartels.

5.2.2 Export Cartels

The cartels discussed above came to light only because they operated in countries with strict anti-cartel laws and well-equipped competition authorities. But most countries exempt export cartels from their antitrust laws, as long as they do not have any anti-competitive effect on the domestic market. In some cases there is additional explicit exemption, in the form of separate legislation covering such cartels (e.g. the Webb-Pomerene and Export Trading Companies Acts in the United States), or provisions for exemption in the main competition legislation itself (e.g. Germany and Japan). In India. both the old MRTP Act and the new Competition Act exclude anti-competitive practices that have effects exclusively in export markets from their purview.

5.2.3 Mergers and Acquisitions with Cross-Border Dimensions

During the 1990s, there was a wave of mega-mergers, with firms merging with or acquiring controlling stakes in other firms, often in other countries. This was brought about by corporate restructuring in the much more globalised environment, technological changes, and a more relaxed approach to merger review in competition policy enforcement in Europe and the US, which was more receptive to arguments that such mergers created efficiencies and synergies. Such mergers, because of their size and the multinational operations of the merging firms, can restrict competition in all countries where the firms operate. Large companies merge in the developed world and consequently their subsidiaries and associates in developing countries too end up in new combinations. This can create positions of dominance for merging firms leading to subsequent abuse. Moreover, developing countries may also be affected by merger and acquisition (M&A) activities that take place outside their territory without any local presence. Because these companies operate in multiple markets, they can also adversely affect developing country markets.

Developing countries, to our knowledge, have dealt only with the first type of cases, i.e., subsidiaries merging as a result of a merger between parent companies internationally. But even stopping the subsidiaries from merging would not serve any purpose, as both will continue to be controlled by the same parent company. Even if its competition law embodies the effects doctrine, a developing country will find it very difficult to enforce any such action against offshore mergers between companies that are entirely based abroad but supplying goods and services through exports with no subsidiaries in the domestic territory. Similar actions are, however, quite common in the developed world, based on the effects doctrine. For example, the EU blocked the merger between GE and Honeywell, both US based corporations. Similarly, in the Philip Morris-Rothmans case, a merger between the US and British-South African companies was stalled by Germany.

5.2.4 Cross-Border Predatory Pricing

Predatory pricing, strictly speaking, is pricing below costs with the intention of driving out rival producers. Due to some striking similarities, cross-border predatory pricing is very often equated with dumping. However, the principle underlying anti-dumping is different from that underlying competition law in that the former seeks to protect domestic competitors while the latter seeks to protect competition. Low prices could simply reflect the greater efficiency of the foreign firm, and closure of the domestic firms may not be the result of any predatory intention on its part. Predatory pricing can be suspected only if it deliberately prices its exports below costs, and is assured of a monopoly if the domestic firm(s) are forced to exit. The latter requires that the alleged predator should have a large share of the importing country's market, which should also be characterised by barriers to entry so that the domestic firms or other foreign firms cannot enter. In contrast, dumping is simply pricing exports below "normal value" (explained below), not below costs, and can in fact be welfare enhancing unless it is predatory.

In this context, the parallel anti-dumping and competition-law cases relating to the sale of Japanese television sets in the US is interesting. Beginning in the 1960s, US producers sought relief from low-priced imports of Japanese television sets and other consumer electronics products initially under anti-dumping and subsequently under competition law. As a result, the US decided to impose anti-dumping duties on Japanese TVs in 1971. The competition law case was finally decided by the US Supreme Court in 1986, where, in a split decision, the majority expressed the view that the market for electronics products in the US was fundamentally incapable of being successfully monopolised through a predatory-pricing conspiracy.

The situation in most developing countries might be different due to the small size of markets and low levels of market contestability. Hence, there would be more convergence between anti-dumping and anti-predation actions. Until recently, the main users of anti-dumping laws were developed countries, though increasingly developing countries too are taking recourse to these laws. It has been suggested (Scherer, 1994) that applying the stricter standards required in predatory pricing cases would limit the misuse of anti-dumping for protectionist purposes. But with the proliferation of anti-dumping in both developed and developing countries, there seems to be little chance of a consensus on this. Both the EU and the US have opposed reform of the anti-dumping agreement to make them consistent with antitrust principles. We discuss in detail below the case of India, which has now emerged as the most active user of anti-dumping.

5.3 Barriers to Import Competition

Import cartels, vertical market restraints creating import barriers, private standard setting activities, abuse of monopsonistic dominance (dominance by a buyer) etc. may fall under this category.

Import cartels formed by domestic importers or buyers and similar arrangements (such as boycotts of, or collective refusals to deal with, foreign competitors) may be a threat to maintaining competition in a market. In principle, a national competition law may generally be able to tackle such market-access barriers to foreign supplies and suppliers. Import cartels whose function is solely to attempt to exercise monopsony power in order to get a better price from foreign suppliers may be viewed more favourably from a national efficiency and welfare perspective than cartels that also exercise market power domestically. But it may be difficult to make such a distinction or to separate the two types of activities.

Another related concern in this regard is inadequate domestic enforcement of competition law against private practices that restrict another country's exports. Such concerns prompted a revision of US guidelines regarding international enforcement to permit application of the US antitrust laws to foreign-based activities such as import cartels that restrict US producers' access to foreign markets. To date, however, the revised US guidelines have never been employed. Instead, it has been using the WTO dispute settlement mechanism. The best-known example is its complaint against Japan, in which it alleged that the Japanese competition authorities were not taking action against Fuji for effectively preventing Kodak's exports to the Japanese market by controlling the distribution channel. WTO Dispute Settlement Panel (DSP) did examine Japan's competition policy to see whether it was consistent with Japan's obligations under existing WTO agreements: that is, whether concessions made in respect of reduced trade barriers were being nullified by non-enforcement of competition laws against private anti-competitive practices directed against imports. Although the US lost that case, it has recently succeeded in convincing another Panel that the very general competition-related provisions in the agreement on telecommunications required Mexico to take action against a cartel of domestic telecom firms that was allegedly inhibiting foreign competition (Marsden, 2004).

5.4 Foreign Investment

Foreign direct investment (FDI) has now become an important way for companies to supply foreign markets. Foreign direct investment may increase competition in local markets, particularly in the investments of greenfield type. However, there is a possibility that over time such takeovers may make the markets increasingly concentrated to the extent of having one or a small number of dominant players. Moreover, even though a single instance of cross-border acquisition may seem to have no effect on competition from a narrow national-market perspective, it may lead to a lessening of effective competition in the market if the acquirer has been a major exporter to the country. Such acquisitions may be aimed at regional or global consolidation by TNCs.

5.5 Intellectual Property Rights

Intellectual property rights (IPRs) may generate or contribute towards a position of market power. The IP holders typically engage in licensing arrangements with firms in different countries. The territorial nature of property rights in such agreements means that frequently national law enables them to be used by rights holders to prevent parallel imports. In many cases, it has also been observed that cartels were built around patent cross licensing schemes and thereby foreclosed competition.

TRIPs has imposed an obligation on all countries to respect IPRs. It also empowers the countries to take necessary actions if IPRs are abused to give effect to anti-competitive practices. But the suggested remedy of compulsory licensing (licensing the product to another producer without the consent of the patent-holder) would not be available to a country that lacks domestic production capacity. On the eve of the 2003 Cancun Ministerial of the WTO, members agreed that in the case of public health emergencies, governments may issue compulsory licences to manufacturers in other developing countries. However, this applies to medicines only and small countries would have no remedy available for abuse of IPR in other products for which they lack manufacturing capability.

5.6 The Indian Experience

5.6.1 International Cartels

According to one estimate (Clarke & Evenett, 2002), the vitamins cartel alone cost India about $25mn in the 1990s due to overcharging. Country-specific estimates of losses are not available for other cartels. Some other important cartels that hit India very hard are those in heavy electrical equipment and flat rolled steel products. None of them were ever prosecuted but their existence and their agreements were exposed by the US House of Representatives. The operation of the international cartel on heavy electrical equipment, under the auspices of the International Electrical Association (involving most of the North American, European, some East European and Japanese firms) applied to all procurement outside of the EC and the US. India was one of the countries badly affected by the conspiracy (Jenny, 1997).

An international cartel on flat rolled steel products (which was in existence at least until end 1994, and may still exist) with participation of European, Korean and Japanese firms divided the world (other than the US) with the area West of Myanmar coming under the sphere of European suppliers and the area to the East under Korean and Japanese suppliers. This brought steel importers of Thailand, Indonesia, Malaysia or the Philippines under the influence of Japanese mills, while India, a large importer of hot rolled flat steel, could only import small amounts from Japan since it was under the sphere of European mills (Wolff, 1994). India has significant production capacity in some of the products but its producers were not part of the global cartel and they were sufficiently punished for that, especially at the time of global recession in the sector (Jenny, 1997).

5.6.2 Foreign Export Cartels and Predatory Pricing

The Indian MRTP Commission was unable to take any action against any of the international cartels that attracted the attention of other competition authorities for over-pricing. It did, however, respond to complaints by two Indian manufacturers' associations against groups of foreign companies who had been selling at **low** prices, but these orders were set aside by the Supreme Court. A brief account of these cases is instructive.

The American Natural Soda Ash Corporation (ANSAC) is a joint venture of six US soda ash producers registered under that country's Webb-Pomerene Act specifically for joint marketing of exports to other countries. In September 1996, ANSAC attempted to ship a consignment of soda ash to India. On a complaint by the Alkali Manufacturers Association of India (AMAI), whose members included the major Indian soda ash producers, the MRTP Commission ordered an *ex parte* interim injunction against ANSAC, restraining it from cartelised exports to India. In another case, involving a complaint by the All India Float Glass Manufacturers' Association against import of float glass from Indonesia in 1998, the MRTPC found evidence of predatory pricing and again restrained imports, expressing concern about the destruction of the Indian float glass industry even though the Indonesian firms accounted for only two per cent of the Indian market. Both ANSAC and Haridas Exports (the importer of the Indonesian float glass) appealed to the Supreme Court, which in a far-reaching verdict delivered in July 2002, overturned both the MRTPC orders. It did not go into the allegations of cartelisation or predatory pricing, but instead held that the wording of the MRTP Act did not give it any extra-territorial operation. The Commission could, therefore, not take action against foreign cartels or the pricing of exports to India, nor could it restrict imports. Action could be taken only if an anti-competitive agreement involving an Indian party could be proved, and that too only after the goods had been imported into India.[3] The consequences of this ruling have been undone in the new Competition Act, which is designed to replace the MRTP Act, and is further discussed below.

5.6.3 Private Barriers in Foreign Markets

Evidence concerning India in this area is not well documented. However, a couple of examples may be worth mentioning. It may be noted that the Swiss Watch Manufacturers Association prevented the Indian watch manufacturer, Titan, from exhibiting their products at the Basle Jewellery and Watch Fair in Switzerland, using the pretext of the prevailing quantitative restrictions in India, which did not allow them to export to India. Similarly, Indian traders were not allowed to participate in the Dutch Flower Auction.[4]

5.6.4 Anti-Dumping

As mentioned above, predatory pricing is often confused with dumping. But while the former is a relevant issue for competition policy, because it results in the elimination of competitors from the market, the latter is merely a form of price discrimination, which can even be beneficial to low-income consumers. Yet, the reduction of orthodox trade barriers has been accompanied by a proliferation of anti-dumping (AD) measures, in situations that could not possibly have been predatory pricing. The traditional users of AD have been the developed countries, particularly the US, EU, and Canada. Indian exports, particularly in the engineering and textiles sectors, have been repeatedly targeted by these countries, as well as by South Africa. But in recent years, developing countries have themselves become major users, with India now heading the list.

The Uruguay Round Agreement on Anti-dumping requires a member to establish that the imported goods are being dumped (exported at a price below "normal value"), injury to domestic producers, and a connection between dumping and injury. Evidence of how generously India is in interpreting these rules comes from the cases tabulated in the latest available (2002-03) Annual Report of the Directorate General of Anti-dumping and Allied Duties (DGAAD) of the Ministry of Commerce. During the period 1992-2003, 22 petitions did not result in initiation of investigations. Of the 153 cases that were initiated, 12 remained under investigation. Of the remaining 141, six had been closed for various reasons. It is striking that provisional or final AD duties were recommended or imposed in all the remaining 135 cases. Thus, Indian industries seeking AD relief from low-priced imports had an almost 83 per cent chance (135/(141+22)) of success, which is much higher than the success rate of petitioners in the developed countries which have been castigated for misusing anti-dumping.

It is easy to prove dumping based on comparing price with "normal value", because the rules allow petitioners to construct normal value based on an estimate of costs, including administrative expenses as well as normal profits. The rules also allow various measures of injury, and the anti-dumping authority can accept any of them. In several cases, the DGAAD has accepted an increase in the foreign firms' market share (which was only to be expected in a period of trade liberalisation) as evidence of injury, even though the Indian industry's sales and profits were increasing at the same time. AD duties or price undertakings were imposed so as to ensure a 'non-injurious' import price, which would guarantee a 'reasonable' rate of return to the domestic producers, based on their own cost data. This provided a cushion for inefficiency. What the DGAAD considers reasonable is entirely subjective and usually not made public, but in a rare case in which the appellate authority set aside its findings, it emerged that it had fixed the AD duty so as to yield a 22 per cent rate of return on capital to the Indian polyester industry! It also came to light that during the period of alleged dumping, the domestic industry was operating at full capacity and had, in fact, raised its prices (Jain 2004).

Could these anti-dumping measures have been legitimate responses to predatory pricing? Direct tests would require comparing the foreign firms' prices with their costs, which is out of the question. Instead, Singh (2003) uses a variety of statistical filters that have been employed in other countries to identify cases in which dumping might have been predatory. This is likely only if the foreign supplier has a large market share in India and the world and there are very few competitors in the world for the same product. Otherwise, the alleged predator cannot hope to recover the sacrifice incurred through dumping by later monopolising the market. Singh finds that only five of the 92 Indian cases studied by him could possibly have been consistent with predatory dumping. In almost all cases, therefore, AD remedies have been used to protect Indian industries, and not to preserve competition. Even though employees and shareholders of these industries have benefited, AD measures have inflicted higher import costs on user industries, as it is mainly intermediate goods industries in the chemicals sector that have succeeded in obtaining protection. The latter are almost always highly concentrated and capital-intensive, while production in many of the user industries is predominantly in small-scale, relatively labour-intensive units, which are being increasingly exposed to import competition. The Indian anti-dumping regime is, therefore, likely to have harmed rather than promoted competition and employment in the aggregate.

5.7 Cross-Border Issues in the Competition Act, 2002

The new Competition Act is yet to take effect at the time of writing, because the Indian government has announced that the first year of its operation would be used for competition advocacy and education, with its cartel provisions coming into effect only in the second year. A detailed assessment of its provisions is undertaken in Bhattacharjea (2003), and is beyond the scope of this chapter. However, some of its provisions relating to cross-border issues deserve comment. Section 3(5)(ii) states that "nothing in this section [on anti-competitive agreements] shall restrict ... the right of any person to export goods from India to the extent to which the agreement relates exclusively to the production, supply, distribution or control of goods or provision of services for such export". Section 32 states that, notwithstanding that any restrictive agreement, any party to such agreement, any enterprise abusing a dominant position, or any combination or party to combination, is outside India, the Competition Commission has the power to inquire into it if it has an anti-competitive effect within the relevant market in India. This clearly restates the effects doctrine, which should undo the Supreme Court's disabling of the MRTP Commission in that respect.

Another problem is sub-section 33(2) of the Act, which goes to the other extreme in undoing the effects of the Supreme Court's ruling. It allows the Competition Commission to grant a temporary injunction restraining any party from importing goods, if it can be established that such imports would contravene the Act's substantive provisions. This would once again enable misuse of the Act for protectionist purposes. If the foreign anti-competitive practice is a cartel, then this measure would only make a bad situation worse by further restricting competition. If it is predatory pricing, then an import restriction might be reasonable. But a WTO Dispute Settlement ruling of 2000 held, in respect of the United States, low-valued imports can only be tackled through anti-dumping remedies. Any other trade restriction would attract dispute settlement and retaliation by other WTO members.

Interestingly, the Competition Act also excludes efficiency-enhancing joint ventures from the prohibition of hard-core cartels in Section 3. It remains to be seen, therefore, whether the domestic soda ash industry will again try to obtain an injunction against imports from ANSAC under section 33(2) the new Act, whether ANSAC (which describes itself as a joint venture, and pressed its claims to efficiency even before the MRTP Commission) will employ this loophole, and whether the new Commission will accept it.

A more general concern is that the Competition Act lists detailed economic criteria to be taken into account while assessing whether a firm is dominant or a merger is anti-competitive. These criteria, which were not there in the old MRTP Act, require proficiency in fairly advanced economic and statistical techniques, and also access to industry data. The new Competition Commission, staffed at present by a handful of civil servants, will have to be equipped with the necessary resources, but the required expertise is scarce in India. Instead, multinational companies, which usually have professional staff and consultants with the requisite skills, and experience of fighting antitrust cases in countries where such criteria have been used for many years, will have a decisive advantage. Inexperienced Indian firms might bear the brunt of enforcement, while foreign firms get away with similar violations.

5.8 The Way Forward

In order to face the cross-border competition challenges, a well-functioning national competition regime may be necessary but not sufficient. Developing country competition authorities, in general, do not have the resources or the experience to tackle international competition challenges. Cartel cases are notoriously difficult to prove, even for the American and European authorities dealing with companies based in their territories. It will, therefore, be almost impossible for a developing country to carry out the tedious case work, and conduct necessary investigations leading to prosecution. The provision of extra-territorial jurisdiction in a national competition law will have a very limited capability, if at all, especially in developing countries. Moreover, some of the international competition problems are essentially global in nature and there cannot be any local solution. Nevertheless, countries have entered into bilateral or regional agreements to deal with such problems.

The US, the EU and Canada have signed a number of bilateral agreements with other countries to cooperate in the area of competition law. While the US has agreements with Australia, Brazil, Canada, Germany, Israel, Japan and Mexico, the EU has such an agreement with Canada. Similarly, Canada has signed bilateral agreements with Chile and Mexico. It has also entered into a tripartite cooperation agreement with Australia and New Zealand. Competition provisions can be found in many of the bilateral trade agreements. However, in such agreements, the focus is on the market access issue and hence the competition provisions are not comprehensive enough to deal with the range of competition issues.

A comprehensive regional approach to competition policy was first adopted by the EU and subsequently by CARICOM. While the primary objective of adopting a regional competition policy within the EU was to use it as a vehicle to further integrate the common market, the main objective of CARICOM regional competition policy is to apply competition rules in respect of cross-border anti-competitive business conduct; promote competition in the Community; and coordinate the implementation of the Community Competition Policy. Such an approach is at various stages of discussion/adoption in many other regional groupings, such as the Nordic countries and the Andean Common Market. Regional approach is quite popular as the definition of the market in which competition is to be applied becomes somewhat more meaningful. Moreover, for political economy reasons as well, a regional approach is easier to sell. However, regional competition regimes will only focus on those cases in which anti-competitive practices have a regional dimension. Needless to say that bilateral agreements will have very limited impact. Thus, they can be best dealt with in a multilateral framework, rather than on a bilateral or regional basis.

As mentioned before, the global community has been discussing the issue of a possible international framework on competition since the days of the Havana Charter in the late 1940s. The discussions got a significant boost after the issue was introduced in the WTO agenda during its Ministerial Conference in Singapore in 1996. However, as the proposal for a competition agreement at the WTO allegedly played one of the spoilsports at the 2003 Ministerial meeting at Cancun, the issue seems to have taken a backseat. In fact, the framework agreement that was reached at the WTO General Council meeting held in Geneva in July 2004 to break the deadlock explicitly dropped it from the work programme of the Doha Round. There is, by and large, an overall consensus that there is a case for a multilateral competition framework, but there is no agreement as to:

• What should be its scope and contours, and

• Where it should be institutionally situated.

Apart from UNCTAD and the WTO, the issue has been discussed at the OECD, which has a Standing Committee on Competition Policy and Law. The OECD has been regularly cooperating with a variety of non-OECD countries to provide capacity building support. With the advent of the OECD's Global Forum on Competition, it claims, its cooperation with non-OECD countries will extend beyond capacity building to include high-level policy dialogues to build mutual understanding, identify 'best practices', and provide informal advice and feedback on the entire range of competition-policy issues.

The competition authorities of different countries have come together to promote the International Competition Network (ICN). ICN is intended to encourage the dissemination of competition experience and best practices, promote the advocacy role of competition agencies and seek to facilitate international cooperation. ICN has already adopted a common set of guiding principles for merger notification and review. However, the guidelines are focussed on facilitating smooth mergers of companies with presence in multiple markets requiring them to get their deals cleared in multiple jurisdictions. The fact that such mergers may lead to substantial lessening of competition in many markets and the fact that they may not have the necessary capabilities to tackle such mergers unilaterally are yet to be addressed. Moreover, the ICN is yet to take initiatives in other areas of competition enforcement, though in its latest annual conference at Seoul it has created a working group on cartels.

The proposals at the WTO focused on getting members to enact domestic competition laws prohibiting hard-core cartels, with the core WTO principles of non-discrimination, transparency and procedural fairness. There was also discussion on a framework for international cooperation for cross-border issues, and for technical assistance for developing countries. India and other developing countries, while well aware of the dangers posed by cartels, are opposed to an agreement at the WTO. India has expressed its opposition to making the core principle of National Treatment (non-discrimination between domestic and foreign firms) mandatory in competition policy, arguing that developing countries must have the right to allow domestic firms to enter into mergers and cartels for industrial rationalisation and restructuring.

Early academic proponents of an agreement argued that the principal benefits accruing to developing countries from a multilateral agreement would be the control of international cartels that overcharge them for imports, and the replacement of arbitrary anti-dumping barriers to their exports with more stringent predatory pricing rules. The latter is most definitely not on the agenda of the WTO, being opposed by both the EU and the US. On the former, while evidence of international cartel activities is now plentiful, the case for a WTO agreement is questionable. Prosecution of foreign cartels requires cooperation from the authorities in their countries to obtain evidence. But such cooperation is lacking even between the member countries of the OECD, amongst whom a fair amount of communication and institutional convergence has occurred on antitrust matters. A recent official review has expressed disappointment about restrictions imposed by various members on sharing even non-confidential information obtained in the course of an inquiry (OECD, 2003). Active cooperation occurs only between a handful of developed countries, notably the US, the EU, Canada, Australia and New Zealand. Much of the funding that these countries and international organisations have devoted to so-called capacity building in developing countries has actually been to convince them of the virtues of a competition agreement, rather than to develop their technical skills.

Moreover, the EU and the US will not contemplate a WTO agreement that would require them to extend cooperation on anything other than a voluntary basis to the competition authorities of other countries. They also oppose the extension of the WTO's MFN principle (prohibiting discrimination between members) to the bilateral cooperation agreements they have entered into with each other and some selected partners. The US also insists that its export cartels will continue to be exempted from antitrust scrutiny, and that its laws do not allow for prosecuting firms that have adverse effects only on foreign parties. With no promise of effective international cooperation, developing countries are being asked to set aside financial and human resources to set up competition agencies and crack down on their own cartels, in pursuit of the mirage of the supposedly huge gains that will accrue to them once international cartels are magically brought to heel.[5]

Considering the present geo-political situation, it is highly unlikely that a consensus could emerge on a competition agreement at the WTO. However, the consumers (and many producers too) would continue to pay for the anti-competitive practices operating at the global level. Hence, there is a feeling that other forums or initiatives to promote international co-operation on competition should be strengthened or launched instead of pushing for a competition agreement at the WTO. Merely establishing standards for national competition rules, which was the proposal before the WTO, is not enough. A global framework that will promote development, competitiveness and poverty reduction in developing countries will require global rules on competition.

Some suggest that UNCTAD already has a long history of dealing with competition issues, in the course of periodically reviewing the UNCTAD Set and studying the activities of multinational companies. It is also perceived as more friendly to developing countries. Hence, it is regarded as the best place to anchor a multilateral competition framework. However, the US is not particularly fond of UNCTAD. Perhaps, the international community will need to find a forum where everyone is comfortable. The feasibility of the International Competition Network may also be explored in this regard. However, this will require significant reforms in the ICN, which remains dominated by some advanced countries.

Developing countries, including India, would find it difficult to commit to an agreement on competition at the WTO unless they were convinced of its benefits. This would be possible only if they have experience. Their experience in bilateral or regional agreements is also almost non-existent. Thus, the best way forward in this regard would be to evolve a competition framework at a non-controversial forum. A limited agreement on competition, involving market access issues, may be negotiated but only at a later date when there is an "explicit consensus". If members agree at any point of time, the proposed framework may also be transferred to the WTO. This can happen only if the WTO goes through drastic reforms to adopt a pro-development image. However, the bottom line is that it should be done only if there is positive willingness and understanding among all members and not through pressure tactics.

Notes

1. Although the 'effects' doctrine could theoretically be applied to all kind of activities, it has been most energetically maintained in the area of antitrust or competition regulation, particularly by the United States. In the famous *Alcoa*-case the US Supreme Court declared that 'any state may impose liabilities, even upon persons not within its allegiance, for the conduct outside its borders that has consequences within its borders which the state reprehends' (*United States Vs. Aluminium Co. of America*, 148 F.2nd 416 (1945)).

2. This categorisation is borrowed from "Special Study on Trade and Competition Policy" as included in Chapter Four of the *WTO Annual Report* for 1997.

3. *Haridas Exports Vs. All India Float Glass Manufacturers' Association*, (2002) 6 SCC 600. A discussion on the wider implications of this judgment, and Indian competition policy in relation to international trade, in greater detail can be found in Bhattacharjea (2003).

4. See "Communication from India" at the WTO Working Group on the Interaction between Trade and Competition Policy (WT/WGTCP/W/111).

5. For a more detailed critique of the case for a competition agreement at the WTO, see Bhattacharjea (2003), Section IV.

References

Bhattacharjea, Aditya (2003). "India's Competition Policy: An Assessment," *Economic and Political Weekly*, 23 August (accessible at www.epw.org.in).

Clarke, J.L. and S.J. Evenett (2002). *The Deterrent Effects of National Anti-Cartel Laws: Evidence from the International Vitamins Cartel*, AEI-Brookings Joint Centre for Regulatory Studies, Working Paper 02-13, Washington DC.

Evans, P. (1995). *Internationalisation of Competition Policy: A Way Forward for Consumers?* International Conference on Fair Trading, June 28-30, Hong Kong, organised by the Hong Kong Consumer Council and Consumers International.

Evenett, S.J. (2003). *Study on Issues Relating to a Possible Multilateral Framework on Competition Policy*, WTO document WT/WGTCP/W/228 (Geneva).

Jain, Sunil (2004). "Increase your returns to 22 per cent!" *Business Standard*, 5 July.

Jenny, Frédéric (1997). "The Interface between Competition Policy and Trade, Investment And Economic Development" (*mimeo*), paper presented at the *International Training Programme on Competition Policy*, Seoul, 4-8 August 1997.

———. (2000). "Globalisation, Competition and Trade Policy: Convergence, Divergence and Cooperation" (Paper presented at the WTO Regional Workshop on Competition Policy, *Economic Development and the Multilateral Trading System: Overview of the Issues and Options for the Future*), Phuket, Thailand, July 6-8.

Levenstein, M., V.Y. Suslow and L.J. Oswald (2003). "Contemporary International Cartels and Developing Countries: Economic Effects and Implications for Competition Policy," *NBER Working Paper 9511* (www.nber.org). Forthcoming in *Antitrust Law Journal*.

Marsden, Philip (2004). "WTO decides first competition case – with disappointing results," *Competition Law Insight*, May.

OECD (2003). *Hard Core Cartels: Recent Progress and Challenges Ahead*. Paris.

Scherer, F.M. (1994). *Competition Policies for an Integrated World Economy*. Brookings, Washington DC.

Singh, Samir K. (2003). *An Analysis of Antidumping Cases in India*, Unpublished M.Phil. dissertation, Department of Economics, University of Delhi.

Wolff, Alan Wm. (1994). "The Problems of Market Access in the Global Economy: Trade And Competition Policy," Remarks before the OECD Market Access Roundtable, Paris, June 30 (www.dbtrade.com/publications/181733a.htm).

6

Interface Between Regulation and Competition Law

T.C.A. Anant • **S. Sundar**

6.1 Introduction

The decade of the '90s has seen a paradigm shift in the approach to economic management in India. There has been a greater recognition of the value and significance in the use of markets and market-friendly processes in the economy. The benefits of competitive markets are standard material for courses in economic theory. Equally, it is well recognised that for a variety of reasons, competitive markets may not exist or yield desirable results. The factors typically identified are externalities; economies of scale and scope; imperfect and asymmetric information; and imperfect competition.

Because of these different reasons for market failure, it is argued that crucial economic sectors cannot be left to unregulated markets and a case is made for some form of intervention in the market process. The nature and character of the desired intervention would clearly depend on the source of the failure. But, for purposes of analysis, we can classify two broad types of interventions. The first seeks to restore efficiency in a particular market through the creation of a sectoral regulator. So, we have regulators[1] in power, telecom, and the different elements of the financial sector, and so on. This is a centralised process in which decisions are made about tariffs, quality standards, entry conditions, service obligations, and investments. Wherever full-scale competition is not feasible, regulation is essentially considered as a surrogate to achieve competitive outcomes.

The second seeks to create an entitlement for competition through a competition law, which seeks to promote competition and competitive practices in markets. It is a decentralised process that aims at attaining the situation where individual service providers, driven by profit motives, offer services to consumers and compete with each other. The form of intervention is clearly the most useful in correcting problems created by imperfect competition.

The difference between the two forms of intervention is in their nature. Regulation tells the firms as to what they have to do. Competition rules, on the contrary, operate in a negative form, as they tell the firms what they should not do. Such economy-wide rules cover predatory pricing, price-fixing, cartels and collusion, discriminatory treatment and several other aspects.

Regulation is clearly in the executive domain with the regulator examining issues of technology, costs and processes in the regulated industry. Promotion and maintenance of competition is closer to an adjudicatory process, where the authority, either on its own, or on receipt of complaints, acts on anticompetitive practices. It needs to be underlined that as against the extant MRTP Act, the Competition Act 2002 creates a proactive obligation on the Competition Commission of India to promote competition in the market place (See Chapter on Competition Act 2002: The Approach).

The separation between the executive and adjudicatory functions is not perfect, since competition authorities, in exercise of merger jurisdiction, for instance, function in an executive capacity and regulators are routinely empowered to adjudicate disputes amongst players on issues related to interconnect charges, access and so on. In addition to the functional separation, the sectoral regulator typically has a narrow focus, whereas the competition agency has an economy-wide remit. Here too, one must point out, that some regulators, like environmental regulators, also have economy-wide remits.

6.2 Instruments of Regulation

Typically, regulators have a variety of powers to implement their brief. On that account, regulators can determine conditions of entry, as we see in professional services, such as chartered accountants, lawyers and doctors. In each case, the respective professional body regulates the qualification process through standards and certification. (See Chapter on Competition and Professional Services).

The central/state regulatory commissions can issue licenses for entities to be able to transmit, distribute, or trade in electricity. Yet, in some cases, as in telecom, the power to regulate entry and/or modify license conditions is with the government. The regulators, in addition, influence conduct through standards and norms, as well as through explicit directions on prices, use of technology, and, at times, may even specify quantities that may be offered on the market. The exact choice of instruments is partly influenced by the characteristics of the industry and partly by the objectives to be served. Be that as it may, different instruments require different types of information and different institutional structures at times to implement them.[2] Different regulators have a different blend of powers allowed to them under the legislation. For instance, in telecom, licensing condition is a prerogative of the government, and as we have noted in electricity, that power is given to the regulator.

6.3 Regulatory Failure

Anyhow, sectoral regulators have been criticised on a number of grounds and these can be summarised as:

1. *Narrow Technical Focus*: The technical and skill requirements of regulation imply that regulators are drawn from the industry they seek to regulate. This implies that regulators often approach issues from their technical standpoint, rather than considering the effects on social welfare. A related concern is one of regulatory capture.

2. *Regulatory Capture*: The close proximity of the regulator to the industry being regulated, leads it to give a higher value to the industries' requirements, than to consumers or market welfare. In the bargain, regulators who are dependent on the industry to provide them with skills and personnel are more vulnerable to capture.

A consequence of both these types of concerns is that the regulator may not adequately take account of the requirements of efficiency and welfare. For instance, in the acquisition of ABN AMRO Bank by Citibank, the Central Bank of Kenya (CBK) dealt with the matter. Competition concerns were not taken on board as a vital factor in evaluating the case for the CBK, and neither was the competition authority, Monopolies & Prices Commission, consulted. Post-merger, the combined entity became the fourth largest bank in the country, and quite possibly, the transaction might have raised competition concerns in the market.

In addition to the limitations of a single regulator, the presence of multiple regulators in closely related fields leads to concerns arising out of regulatory overlaps.

3. *Technological change/convergence/overlap*: Telecom, cable TV and Internet services are increasingly seen as areas where the interests of different providers are in conflict. The potential conflict increases once we realise that optic fibre cables laid by the railways and electricity companies also offer potential sources of competition.

A similar situation is seen in financial services, with converging interests of banks, insurance companies and stock market players. In spite of this convergence in the financial sector, we see capital markets and insurance activities, which were once regulated by the Ministry of Finance, are now with Securities & Exchange Board of India (SEBI) and Insurance Regulatory and Development Authority (IRDA), respectively.

The RBI regulates most banks and development of financial institutions. The Department of Company Affairs (DCA) regulates deposit-taking activities of corporate entities, other than banks and non-banking financial companies. And banking cooperatives are under the dual authority of the RBI and the various state registrars of cooperative societies. In telecommunications, and broadcasting and cable services, the picture was earlier similar, but recently the Government has nominated TRAI to be a unified regulator.

The trouble is that different regulators have differing objectives. Consequently, while the Reserve Bank of India is more concerned with systemic stability, the concerns of SEBI are investor protection and information disclosure. These may, at times, be in conflict. The other trouble with overlapping jurisdiction is that different regulators have varied powers to enforce and punish.

One more problem is that the objectives of the regulator differ, depending on the maturity of the market. In this manner, the insurance regulator has a stated objective to develop the insurance market. Similarly, the TRAI is obliged to increase tele-density. The market development objective, at times, requires the regulator to allow the regulated firms to make larger profits on existing operations to enable them to meet the costs of market development. To this extent, the approaches of a regulator facing a mature market may well differ from one facing an undeveloped market.

Regulation is often perceived to be a free good, available at no cost, but it is not so. There are the costs of administering regulation, of compliance, and there are also structural costs. Excessive or inappropriate regulation can stifle efficiency. As a result, leading to the natural question as to what is the appropriate domain for regulatory intervention and to what extent can we leave matters to the free play of market forces?

6.4 Sectoral Regulators and the Competition Authority

The creation of a statutory competition authority raises additional concerns about the relationship between Statutory regulators and the competition authority. In India, the relationship is somewhat ambiguous. On the one hand, there is a very clear statement in the TRAI Act that it will be subject to the rulings of the MRTP Commission,[3] and its power to determine entry, mergers or other matters relating to competition are primarily recommendatory. The TRAI, as per the amended Act, is directed to determine standards and terms and conditions of inter-connectivity; technical compatibility and effective inter-connection; revenue sharing; quality of service and compliance with universal service obligations. These have major implications for competition in the sector.

On the other hand, the Electricity Act creates ambiguities, as the preamble clearly talks about the objective of promoting competition in the electricity market. The commission (central or state) is empowered to regulate production, supply or consumption to promote competition (Sec 23), and further, section 60 allows it to regulate generation and distribution to prevent abuse of dominance.[4] Thus, the law clearly

---

BOX 6.1

Regulation and Competition Interface in Pakistan

As historically the case with most countries, in Pakistan there has been a proliferation of sectoral regulators, with the emergence of the National Electric Power Regulatory Authority; the Pakistan Telecommunication Authority; the Oil and Gas Regulatory Authority; and the Atomic Energy Regulatory Authority. These regulators operate independent of each other and the Monopoly Control Authority (MCA), Pakistan's national competition authority. They may consult with the MCA, but they are not legally bound to accept its advice. Therefore, in countries such as Pakistan, where the interaction amongst regulatory authorities with overlapping responsibilities is ill defined, the opportunities for turf-disputes and legal wrangling are multiplied.

Similarly, under Pakistan's Banking Companies Ordinance, 1962, the State Bank of Pakistan (SBP) is fully authorised to regulate and supervise banks and financial institutions. However, the SBP's supervisory policy does not take cognisance of competition issues in the sector. As a result, regulatory issues related to the acquisition of ANZ Grindlays by Standard Chartered Bank were evaluated only by the SBP, and the competition authority was not involved. The deal had a smooth sailing, even though it has corporate banking market segment.

Source: Sampson, Cezley and Faye, *Briefing Paper: Competition and Sectoral Regulation Interface,* CUTS, 2003.

---

directs the regulator to act in a manner so as to promote competition and efficiency. What's more, they are also required to advise the government on measures to promote competition. In a similar manner, we see that in the financial sector, the RBI is authorised on all matters relating to bank licensing, mergers and other similar practices.

On the other hand, the nature of the competition authority's power *vis-a-vis* Statutory regulators, is ambiguous. Section 21 of the Competition Act implicitly recognises that sectoral regulators have a role to play in competition matters and says that Statutory regulators may refer competition matters to the competition authority[5], but to what extent the competition authority can influence the regulators in the absence of such requests is not clear. And even where the competition authority's advice is sought, it is not necessarily binding on the sectoral regulators. This ambiguity could create conflicts between the competition authority and the sectoral regulators and lead to forum shopping.

The critical areas where competition rules interact with industry specific rules are interconnection, monopoly-pricing, anti-competitive agreements and merger control.

BOX 6.2

Nature of Function of South Asian Regulators

Country	Regulated Sector	Nature of Mandate vis-à-vis Competition
India	Telecom	Recommendatory/ Advisory
	Electricity	Mandatory
Bangladesh	Energy	Mandatory
Sri Lanka	Telecom, electricity, water, gas, transport	Mandatory
Nepal	Telecom	Mandatory
Pakistan	Telecom, electricity, oil and gas,	Mandatory

Source: Apurva Sanghi and S.K. Sarkar, "Institutional approach to regulation and competition in South Asian Infrastructure Sectors," International Journal of Regulation and Governance, 2004.

In integrated monopoly enterprises, regulatory rules seek to define entry conditions. However, in network industries, where the monopoly segments have been separated from potentially competitive elements, the question of access to the monopoly's 'essential facility' demands regulation so that free and non-discriminatory entry could be ensured. For instance, in the US, competition rules and judicial precedents prohibit the misuse of market position on interconnection. Such an arrangement might be sufficient to deal with the problem. However, since the sector-specific regulatory bodies are often responsible to define 'entry conditions', their actions directly affect the nature of competition once the entry has been made. Consequently, conflicts between sectoral regulators and competition authorities could arise.

Also, while dealing with pricing issues, the sectoral regulator may find the competition rules on price fixing as vague and inadequate to address the sectoral concerns. In case the pricing rules imposed by the competition authority to restrict excessive or unjust prices do not coincide with the sectoral regulator's objectives, the situation may lead to a conflict between two regulators.

Similarly, whenever a vertically integrated monopoly is unbundled to open up for competition, the competition rules could be used to challenge the co-operative arrangements, which are acceptable for sectoral regulation. Quite often, sectoral regulators restrict mergers between utilities or reintegration. In such a situation, there are good chances for a possible conflict with respect to interpretation of sectoral regulatory rules and the competition rules.

BOX 6.3

Role of Competition Commission in Sectoral Regulation in Mexico

The sectoral regulators are empowered to establish tariffs and maximum prices for their respective sectors. Appeals against such determinations by firms, within the respective sectors, are made to the Federal Competition Commission (FCC) for relief.

The sectoral regulator is also permitted to solicit the opinion of the FCC on sectoral regulation, regarding the existence of effective competitive conditions in the market.

The sector regulator is empowered to establish a pricing regime, as long as the conditions dictate. Depending upon the finding, the Commission can require that price regulations be lifted, or modified, within 30 days. The provision has been applied to various sectors, and, in particular, the transport, port, telecommunication and energy sectors (natural gas and petroleum). The Commission's role, in addition to economy-wide competition jurisdiction, also covers appellate matters.

Source: Sampson, Cezley and Faye, Briefing Paper: Competition and Sectoral Regulation Interface, CUTS, 2003.

The practice in other countries has been to recognise these problems, and derive a variety of solutions to them.[6]

In the UK, the Director General of Fair Trading and each regulator are represented on the Concurrency Working Party, chaired by a representative of the Office of Fair Trading. The Working Party was formed in 1997 to ensure full co-ordination between regulators and the Director General of Fair Trading, to consider the practical working arrangements between them. This includes ensuring that more than one authority would not investigate a single case; ensuring consistency of approach in casework; co-ordinating the use of the concurrent powers; and preparing the guidelines issued under section 52 of the Act. In The Netherlands, protocols have been established to determine which agency would be responsible for a particular case.

In Australia, many of the utility sectors are regulated by the competition authority and not by an independent regulator. On the other hand, there are competition agencies and regulatory authorities in some provinces, which are all members of the Utility Regulators Forum, where provincial regulators and competition authorities meet regularly to ensure better coordination. The Competition Act of South Africa makes the Competition Commission responsible for negotiating agreements with other regulatory authorities to coordinate and harmonise exercise of jurisdiction over competition matters within the relevant industry or sector, and ensure consistent application of the principles of the Competition Act.

The Act also authorises the Commission to participate in the proceedings of any regulatory authority, and to advise, or receive advice from any such authority. In some other countries (Korea, for instance), statutory authorities are required to consult the KFTC if they are planning any rule that may have an anti-competitive effect. Alternatively, the Competition Authority (CA), as in Canada, may represent its views before the regulators at their request, or on its own initiative, with respect to competition issues.

BOX 6.4

Embedding Competition Scrutiny in UK

Important steps have recently been taken to make competition scrutiny of regulation in the UK more systematic.

First, the Enterprise Act has strengthened the powers of the Office of Fair Trading (OFT) and the Competition Commission (CC) to examine and make recommendations to government on regulatory restrictions and distortions of competition. The OFT proposes to amend its guidance on market investigation references in order to enhance further the potential role of the CC in this regard.

Second, since the year 2002, competition scrutiny has been built into the regulatory impact assessment of legislative proposals. Government departments primarily do this assessment. OFT provides guidance to government departments on when and how to carry out competition assessment, and assists on cases as necessary.

Third, a cross-government forum called Competition Forum has been established to discuss the relationships between market competition and government bodies. The Forum helps to identify markets where competition appears not to be working well.

Source: Presentation made by John Vickers, Chairman, Office of Fair Trading, at the Competition Policy Conference of the Regulatory Policy Institute, Oxford, September 15, 2004.

As we can see, a variety of arrangements are possible. The key issue is to select one pattern and stay with it. The problem is that in the absence of clear statutory or administrative rules/principles, it would be difficult to ensure compliance.

A logical question to ask would be that, should we exclude the competition authority from oversight in all statutorily regulated sectors? This would not be desirable for three reasons:

- First, the possibility of capture alluded to above,

- Second, the conflict between the alternative objectives and the technical background of most sectoral regulators may make them poorly equipped to make assessments on competitive impact, and

- Finally, the possibility of overlap across different sectoral regulators means that an economy-wide authority may in fact be in a better position to assess efficiency problems.

At the same time, it would not be prudent to exclude the sector regulators from addressing competition issues in their sectors, as they would have a much better understanding of the sector than an economy-wide competition authority. The answer, as follows, is to provide for and encourage cooperation between the sectoral regulators and the competition authority.

The problem arises because there is no uniform framework that is followed when we are designing regulatory authorities. Uniform guidelines are not adhered to[7] and it would be ideal if such provisions could be included in any law. It might be best to amend the Competition Act to provide for coordination between the competition authority and the sector regulators, and ultimately for the competition authority to have an oversight in the regulated sectors on competition issues. Even in the absence of legal provisions relating to coordination, it can be achieved in a number of ways:

- First, authorities can enter into formal cooperation protocols for deciding on agency that would have jurisdiction in a particular matter, for sharing information and seeking advice.

- Second, we could consider a single appellate authority so that jurisdictional conflicts are not escalated to the appellate level, and can be resolved by a single appellate tribunal. Since the technical expertise is in the domain of fact assessment, there would be no loss of functionality by merging the appellate powers. In the UK, the Competition Commission hears appeals against all sectoral regulators' orders, thus promoting harmony.

To sum up, we see that if the competition authority is to be successful, it must face up to the challenge of interfacing with sectoral regulators. Till this can be done statutorily, it should be pointed out that it could, and may be should, use its *suo moto* and advocacy powers and represent before sectoral regulators on matters relating to competition concerns. Since typically all regulatory proposals are put up for public discussion, it would be useful for the competition authority to provide its input into them. For instance, the CERC issued a consultation paper in 2004 on competition, and the competition authority should be providing official feedback using its power of advocacy.

The TRAI too regularly publishes discussion papers on various issues, many of which relate to competition concerns, on which the CCI can send its inputs.

Even as we encourage cooperation between the competition authority and sectoral regulators, we need to review the legislation through which sectoral regulators have been established, and also the competition law to provide for formal working arrangements between them to ensure coordination and avoid conflicts of jurisdiction and needless turf battles.

Given the federal structure of India, the provisions in the relevant central and state legislation and the institutional arrangements in vogue, an appropriate way forward could be as follows:

BOX 6.5

Proposed Regulatory Structure for India

One ministry in the Government of India should be identified as the nodal ministry for furthering sectoral regulation and overseeing the implementation of the competition law. Ideally, it should be the Department of Economic Affairs in the Ministry of Finance, as that Department has the overall responsibility for macroeconomic management and is also familiar with regulation in the financial sector. This Ministry – or Department – should be made responsible for developing an integrated approach to regulatory issues.

In the first instance, the Ministry should review all the sector specific legislations establishing sectoral regulators and the competition law to delete provisions that are ambiguous and could create conflicts, and introduce provisions that would require sectoral regulators and the competition authority to work harmoniously in addressing competition issues.

At the national level, specialised regulatory bodies should be established, as far as possible, for sectors such as energy, communication & broadcasting, transportation and not for each industry or sub-sector, such as coal, power, and oil, or civil aviation, railways and road transport. This would facilitate a co-ordinated approach to the different sectors and avoid multiplicity of regulators.

At the state level, two regulatory agencies, namely State Utility Services Regulatory Commission (SUSRC) and State Professional Services Regulatory Commission (SPSRC) can be constituted to cover the entire spectrum of utilities and services. The SUSRC should deal with infrastructure services such as energy, communication, transportation, water etc; while the other body, SPSRC, should regulate the sectors including education, medical, law, entertainment, among others. Inclusion of a particular sector under the regulatory purview will have to be decided locally and has to be priority-based. Besides, these state level bodies can create a common forum to institutionalise the process of information exchange and cross-fertilisation of ideas.

The multi-sectoral state regulator could draw the necessary specialised technical support from central sectoral regulatory authorities, as they will work as knowledge hubs. For

Contd...

...Contd...

instance, all SUSRCs will have access to the specialised opinions/database of the Central Electricity Regulatory Commission. This arrangement will also help in achieving a degree of uniformity in regulatory approach across the states.

A Central Appellate Tribunal (CAT) can be constituted as the sole appellate body for all central and state sectoral regulators and the CCI. However, the jurisdiction of the appellate tribunal should be restricted to issues of law and not facts.

Competition Councils could be constituted both at the national and the state levels to advise governments and the sector regulators on competition issues. These councils could comprise of representatives of government, the competition authority, the sector regulators, representatives of trade and industry, civil society organisations, academia, media and the legal fraternity.

The objective of these Councils would essentially be to promote competition advocacy, encourage sectoral regulators to become competition-conscious and facilitate integration of competition policy with the economic and fiscal policies of the concerned government.

Notes

1. In this paper the phrase 'regulator' will be used exclusively to refer to statutory or non-statutory sectoral regulators and the competition authority will be referred to as the CA.

2. See Anant & Singh (2001).

3. **TRAI:** Amendment of Section 11.

(1) Notwithstanding anything contained in the Indian Telegraph Act, 1885, the functions of the Authority shall be to:

(a) *make recommendations*, either *suo moto* or on a request from the licensor, on the following matters:

   (i) need and timing for introduction of a new service provider;

   (ii) terms and conditions of license to a service provider;

   (iii) revocation of license for non-compliance of terms and conditions of license:

   (iv) measures to facilitate competition and promote efficiency in the operation of telecommunication services so as to facilitate growth in such services.

   (v) technological improvements in the services provided by the service providers.

   (vi) type of equipment to be used by the service providers after inspection of equipment used in the network.

   (vii) measures for the development of telecommunications technology and any other matter relatable to telecommunications industry in general.

Further, Chapter IV provides that the TDSAT will not have any jurisdiction in matters relating to:

   a. the monopolistic trade practice, restrictive trade practice and unfair trade practice, which are subject to the jurisdiction of the Monopolies and Restrictive Trade Practices Commission established under sub-section (1) of section 5 of the Monopolies and Restrictive Trade Practices Act, 1969;

   (Since the Competition Commission will substitute the MRTPC, this provision will carry forward) and

   b. the complaint of an individual consumer maintainable before a Consumer Disputes Redressal Forum or a Consumer Disputes Redressal Commission or the National Consumer Disputes Redressal Commission established under section 9 of the Consumer Protection Act, 1986.

4. CERC (Electricity Act 2003)

   60. The Appropriate Commission may issue such directions, as it considers appropriate, to a licensee or a generating company, if such

licensee or generating company enters into any agreement or abuses its dominant position or enters into a combination, which is likely to cause or causes an adverse effect on competition in the electricity industry.

5. Competition Act, 2002 Reference by Statutory authority

21. (1) Where in the course of a proceeding before any statutory authority an issue is raised by any party that any decision, which such statutory authority has taken or proposes to take, is or would be, contrary to any of the provisions of this Act, then such Statutory authority may make a reference in respect of such issue to the Commission.

(2) On receipt of a reference under sub-section (1), the Commission shall, after hearing the parties to the proceedings, give its opinion to such Statutory authority, which shall thereafter pass such order on the issues referred to in that sub-section as it deems fit:

Provided that the Commission shall give its opinion under this section within sixty days of receipt of such reference.

6. See the Report on *Relationship Between Regulators and Competition Authorities,* OECD 1999 for details, as well as *Best Practices for Defining Respective Competences and Settling of Cases, Which Involve Joint Action of Competition Authorities and Regulatory Bodies* Study by the UNCTAD secretariat TD/B/COM.2/CLP/44, August 19, 2004.

7. See for instance the discussion in *Framework for Infrastructure Regulation* by S. Sundar and S.K. Sarkar, TERI 2000.

References

Anant, TCA & Jaivir Singh, *Regulation* (2002). *A Constitutional Paradigm,* Draft prepared for Law and Regulation Conference in JNU, November.

Sampson, Cezley and Faye (2003). *Competition and Sectoral Regulation Interface,* CUTS Briefing Paper.

Apurva Sanghi and S.K. Sarkar (2004). "Institutional Approach to Regulation and Competition in South Asian Infrastructure Sectors," *International Journal of Regulation and Governance.*

Relationship Between Regulators and Competition Authorities, OECD 1999.

Best Practices for Defining Respective Competences and Settling of Cases, which Involve Joint Action of Competition Authorities and Regulatory Bodies, Study by the UNCTAD Secretariat TD/B/COM.2/CLP/44, August 19, 2004.

Presentation made by John Vickers, Chairman, Office of Fair Trading, at the Competition Policy Conference of the Regulatory Policy Institute, Oxford, September 15, 2004.

S. Sundar and S.K. Sarkar (2000). *Framework for Infrastructure Regulation,* TERI.

Competition Act, 2002, Ministry of Law and Justice, Government of India.

The Telecom Regulatory Authority of India Act 1997, Ministry of Law and Justice, Government of India.

The Telecom Regulatory Authority of India (Amendment) Act 2000, Ministry of Law and Justice, Government of India.

The Electricity Act 2003, Ministry of Law and Justice, Government of India.

Part II

Competition Policy and Other Government Policies

7 Central Government Policies: Interface with Competition Policy Objectives

T.C.A. Anant • Jaivir Singh

Since this chapter aims to explore the interface between various government policies and competition policy, the professed task of the chapter is to put forward an analytical understanding of both *competition policy* and *government policy*. In the first part of the chapter, we initiate this enterprise by elucidating the assorted dimensions of competition and government policy, to enable us to identify the nature of the dilemmas posed by the simultaneous operation of a competition policy and other government policies. In the second part, we review the broad structures of Central Government policies and competition policy followed in India. This review acts as the background to the third part of the chapter, which seeks to spell out the synergy that is clearly desirable, and should be made possible, across competition and government policies in India.

7.1 Characterising Competition, Competition Policy and Government Policy

7.1.1 Competition as a Process

Popularised by generations of economic textbooks, competition is widely understood with reference to the 'perfect competition' model, where each producer (who is typically one of many similarly placed producers) is a price-taker. The pursuit of self-interest induces the producer to produce up to the point where price is equated to marginal costs. While this model has the pedagogic value of describing the profile of an economy under certain 'ideal' conditions and assumptions, it is not very helpful in serving as an overall guide to competition policy. The model is not universally germane to thinking about a competition policy. This is because the standard against which actual achievement would have to be measured, and mimicked, is hypothetical - a state which can only be achieved by altering the facts of the real world in accordance with the ideal conditions and assumptions of the perfect competition model. Therefore, it is important to view competition more generally, for our purpose, and one way of doing this is to discuss competition, not with reference to an outcome but rather as a *process*, as suggested by Hayek (1979).

The **process** dimension of competition becomes obviously manifest, once it is understood that much of the ongoing economic activity is characterised by situations where it is not known, beforehand, as to who will do the best and by using what means. Thus, competition is the **process** whereby skills and knowledge are acquired and put to the best possible use - the phrase employed by Hayek (1979) is that competition is 'first and foremost a discovery procedure'. From this viewpoint, a crucial element of any competition policy is to secure the process of competition, so that the most favourable conditions are created to induce the discovery of the largest number of opportunities, and such opportunities can be, and are exploited, so as to exhaust their potential. In a liberal economy, if one were to look for such a policy, emanating explicitly from a particular government agency or department, one would look in vain - typically there is little likelihood of a 'Ministry' of Competition. Although, of course, decisions made in each extant ministry would have an impact on competition, and so there may be an impact on competition if an anti-monopoly legislation were in place. This, however, is a matter concerned with the working of law that encourages competition rather than government policy *per se*. Instead, the advancement of competition would be best found in the rights that form the basis of a liberal market economy. For instance, to provide an illustrative example, in the Indian Constitution the 'right to competition' can be read in Article 19(1)(g), which guarantees the fundamental right to "to practice any profession, or to carry on any occupation, trade or business".

Approached from the perspective of rights, the notion of competition can also be thought of as incorporating, within itself, a sense of fairness - fairness in a procedural sense. This is clearly demonstrated by the fact that the presence of free competition is associated with the demand for a level playing field for all protagonists. One need only look into the many accounts, of the demands, of active merchants or entrepreneurs, in almost any historical epoch and geographical location, to drive home this point. Admittedly the demands of merchants and entrepreneurs do not, in themselves, definitively characterise competition – in fact, such demands could be a call to establish entry barriers, but when they are benign they do bring out a very important element of competition. Wherever free competition is privileged, a milieu is created where it is permissible for a protagonist to win on account of some naturally possessed advantage, in terms of skills or technology, but not on grounds of privilege imparted to an individual or a group. To phrase this slightly differently, to advantage free competition is to ensure that the processes of economic activity are fair – every participant stands an equal chance for success, garnering gains only on the basis of some natural advantage.

7.1.2 Government Policy as an Outcome

However, even though the processes associated with competition can be legitimised by the guarantee of certain rights, such rights are typically neither absolute nor unfettered. While the Constitution of India guarantees the right "to practice any profession, or to carry on any occupation, trade or business", subsequent clauses of Article 19 hasten to establish that the State can impose a series of 'reasonable' restrictions on fundamental rights in the interests of the public. Without delving into the exact nature of the term 'public interest' at this juncture, if one associates it with the contents of the *Directive Principles of State Policy*, mentioned in Part IV of the Constitution, a series of ends can be broadly listed. These ends include equitable distribution, equal opportunity, universal access to public goods, and protection of the environment. Rather than entering into the details of specific heads, the reference to the Directive Principles, made here, aims to highlight the point that government policy is obliged to address issues, not only in relation to the processes in the economy, but also pertaining to

the pattern of distribution in society. If competition and its furtherance are understood as a self-sustaining **process**, then concerns about distribution are something quite different in substance – they need to be understood as **outcomes**.

Government policies operate at a variety of levels: the macro, with its concern for the nation/economy as a whole; the meso, with regional or sectoral concerns; and at the micro level, of households and individuals. Further, policies seek to attain a number of complex goals. It is possibly reasonable to say that, by and large, most government policies are oriented to effecting outcomes, rather than processes. The primacy of government policy, being oriented to generating outcomes, rests on the fact that these outcomes can be tangibly demonstrated, and are amenable to being measured. Poverty can be shown to have declined, tax collections to have gone up, erstwhile poor regions can be shown to have become prosperous, etc. Ironically, when it comes to the operation of competition law, in spite of our professing to view competition as a process, it is inevitable that the competition law has to be constructed, and interpreted, with reference to a context. This context is given tangible meaning, with reference to an outcome and thus obliging, what is inherently, a process to be viewed in terms of an outcome.[1] Processes, unlike outcomes, are notoriously hard to measure and monitor. Economic analyses clearly reveal that competition is not determined in terms of the number of firms, in a market, but by their processes and patterns of functioning. Thus, for instance, it is possible for an industry, with even a single firm, to be deemed competitive if the rate of technical progress is sufficiently rapid. Assessing competition is much more a qualitative exercise than is the case with more objective, outcome oriented objectives and therefore, the substance of processes are best seen as being embedded as enabling devices, in the constitutions, that form the structure of the economy.

The variety of outcomes, sought to be effected by government policy, ranges over a number of product and factor outcomes. Thus, for instance, a normative concern of most policy designers is to somehow privilege fairness. Fairness can be understood in either a procedural sense – everyone must have a fair chance, or in a somewhat different way as a fair outcome - individuals x, y and z must have an income that has a present value greater than Rs. 100,000. If fairness is comprehended as a 'fair chance,' this is tantamount to saying that the market determines outcomes. On the other hand if fair outcomes are sought, then the market does not necessarily set outcomes; such outcomes are generally configured at the cost of restricting the domain of the market – thus restricting the play of competition as a process. In other words, it is inevitable that the pursuit of fair outcomes generates a trade-off between furthering competition as a fair process and the impulse to shape fair outcomes. If competition is to be privileged, then it is critical that promoted outcomes are generated in a manner that minimises the trade-off. To argue that one needs to privilege competition does not mean that it cannot be limited. Nevertheless, this must be done, as is also argued, by analysing the process and identifying its limitations. As is argued in another chapter, a number of characteristics, like informational imperfections, and dependencies in technologies/preferences, can lead to process failure. This, then, suggests an alternative process of regulation. This kind of orientation in assessment and analysis has been, and in many senses continues to be, quite alien to the Indian policy discourse, as is evident from an overview of Indian government policies.

7.2 Central Government Policies: An Overview

The constituent document that provides the frame for policy - the Indian Constitution - is both extraordinary and unique, in that in addition to providing for the creation of a democratic secular state, it was also set up with a very clearly envisaged active 'developmental' role for the state in mind. The origin of the economic goals, expressed in the Constitution, can be traced to the prevailing ideology of the Indian National Congress (INC) during the Independence movement. An early indication of this ethos is available in the resolution of the INC presented at its annual session at Karachi in 1931, where it was resolved to adopt a socialistic pattern of development.[2] These expectations were enshrined in Articles 36 to 51 in Part IV of the Constitution, namely the *Directive Principles of State Policy*. It is not, in general, possible to relate specific government policies to specific injunctions (in Part IV of the Constitution). Even so, a broad correspondence with the spirit of the injunctions can be seen, in the laws and policies framed by a series of political regimes, relating to a whole range of economic matters. The laws and policies formulated on this basis have been described, in subsequent critical assessments, as being motivated by a belief in a number of underlying assumptions.

While the list may not be necessarily complete, the key assumptions included:

Export Pessimism - It was believed that demand for Indian exports would not grow fast enough to be a major source of growth.

Savings Pessimism - It was believed that private savings would not be adequate to finance capital accumulation, and would need to be supplemented by public resource mobilisation.

Investment Pessimism - The private sector was considered unable or unwilling to come up with large investments in key basic industries, thus providing the economic rationale for extensive public sector involvement.

Employment Pessimism - It was envisaged that growth of the organised industrial sector, alone, would not create adequate employment, and thus there is a need for direct programmes for employment creation. In addition to this, a legal system was put into place that protected employment in the formal sector.

Market Pessimism - This was probably the most fundamental belief, which permeated almost all aspects of policy formation. It was motivated by both an allergy to "free market" concepts, as part of the rhetoric of the freedom struggle, and on account of the relatively fragmented and primitive nature of most major markets in the country.

The overall consequences of this *weltanschauung* were: a derogation of markets and market forces; a profound distrust of the use of market mechanisms to attain policy goals; and a network of policies and laws, in a wide range of economic spheres, providing a large and explicit role for the state. Till the 1990s, this framework remained essentially untouched, except for two developments that need to be noted. The first development was that it was increasingly realised, starting as early as the 1960s, that the market did form an important dimension of the overall system, and that some of the distorting effects caused by the application of government policies needed to be checked. Among other things, this resulted in the legislation of the MRTP Act and the creation of the MRTP Commission. The second development was initiated, in the 1980s, with the recognition that, at large, incumbent policies did not adequately address the requirements of the environment, which led to a number of legal and judicial developments whose impact is still unfolding. The MRTP Act, once in place, was unable to deliver as expected - in part due to the weaknesses in its own structures and composition of the Commission, but also, in large measures, on account of the *dirigiste* character of policy. Environmental contracts in India continue being administered by the courts, in an *ad-hoc* manner, with little coordinated executive or legislative involvement.

Starting in the early-1990s, a combination of external and internal deficits forced the overall approach to the economy to be revised towards greater market orientation. As a result, it has come to pass that the industrial licensing system has been removed and, bureaucratic control of economic activity has been somewhat diminished. Policy documents released by the Government, often enough, speak about the redefined role of the Government – for example, a 1993 document says :

> "At the Central Government level, priority should be accorded to eliminating remaining barriers to industrial production, investment and import of technology as quickly as possible. The Government's role should shift increasingly to restructuring unviable enterprises, ensuring fair business practices, safeguarding consumer interests and minimising the adverse effect of industrialisation on the environment."[3]

However, in spite of this kind of speak, a large overhang and backlog from the past persist in both attitudes and laws, which prevent the Government from construing and constructing policies that are structured to work in sympathy with market processes. In some cases, this is not just a matter of the persistent past; rather the problem originates from a new source but is approached with a fragmented mindset, which is not appreciative of the nature of market processes. It is important to realise that the argument of privileging competition, or the market, does not mean giving it absolute domain; rather arguments for limiting competition must be based on an assessment of the process and its limitations, rather than on some ex-cathedra justification, based on desirable outcomes.

To illustrate some of these problems, consider some examples:

7.2.1 Trade Policy

- The older regime was marked with quantitative restrictions, tariffs, and an extremely intrusive and restrictive foreign exchange regime. The last decade has seen significant relaxation in quantitative restrictions, reduction in tariffs and an easing of the exchange control regime but even so, the operation of key elements of the trade policy regime have severely anti-competitive dimensions. For example, policies in relation to the operation of anti-dumping measures, intellectual property, etc.[4]

7.2.2 Industrial Policy

- The pre-1991 industrial policy regime used to have explicit entry restrictions through a licensing policy, which to all intents and purposes meant that the state was operating a set of entry barriers. These barriers have been abandoned, yet other barriers remain using a variety of means. These originate in part from zoning restrictions and environmental laws, and in part from the operation of Small Industry protection. The implications of this are that existing large firms are insulated from requirements under grandfather clauses, which act to subsidise their activities; and small industry protection also acts to subsidise inefficient firms.

7.2.3 Public Sector and Privatisation

- The earlier regime had created large public sector monopolies, which are currently being privatised, dis-invested, or converted to independent corporations. The terms of these purchases, however, require that the firms will continue to employ the existing work force and, at times, perform other 'social' obligations. In return, private purchasers often expect the state to ensure that the monopoly status, and/or returns of the concern purchased, will be maintained. Thus, for instance, in telecommunications, the public sector is compensated through Access Deficit Charges; and in power, through regulatory indulgence in tariffs, and protection from "cream skimming"[5]

7.2.4 Tax Policy

- The State has been attempting to introduce transparency and uniformity in rates and structures of taxation, which aim to minimise the effect on specific individuals. However, certain industries/sectors have been lobbying for preferential treatment, and the practice of giving in to such natural political compulsions, by writing specific exemptions and breaks, have vitiated positive developments. There is little attempt at assessing the competitive impact of alternative formulations.

7.2.5 Labour Policy

- The impact of labour policy, on competition, is one of the most interesting and little appreciated dimensions of public policy. The existing regime seeks to protect employment, in the organised sector, through an extensive regime of regulation. Leaving aside the matter of the inability of firms to easily make adjustments to their surplus work force; another facet of this regime is the unwillingness to let units close, on account of poor performance. This implies that, in the event of failure, strenuous efforts are made to revive the enterprise through soft loans, discretionary mergers, etc. This implies that one of the principal pillars of competition 'free exit' is vitiated. Efficient firms face the additional burden of coping with state supported competitors. Quick exit is essential for the freeing up of resources; and voiding unviable contracts, and requiring non-performing units to continue, impacts on the cost and performance of existing firms. A second dimension of labour policy is that the inspection regime, with its known weaknesses and corruption, constitutes a significant barrier to entry.

These brief resumes of the policies followed in India; whether they pertain to product or factor markets – the examples can be almost infinitely multiplied – are all characterised by some element of a maladroit understanding of the market process. This should not be misinterpreted as a suggestion that all issues pertaining to the environment, trade, taxation, industry, labour etc. be 'resolved' by the market. The critique being offered here is quite different. The point is that as policy outcomes are sought to be generated, it is a persistent practice, in India, to do so without bearing in mind that policies need to be framed and implemented in sympathy with the market process, and not in a manner so as to stall the process. To phrase this differently, the *Directive Principles of State Policy* need to be implemented using modes that acknowledge the institution of the market and not by ignoring its presence or being antithetical to it. It is essential to be sensitive to competition, or the market, as a process and therefore, bring in competition assessment as part of policy formulation and reform - an issue to which we turn next.

7.3 Minimising the Trade-off Between Process of Competition and Outcomes

As is argued in the first part of this chapter, if competition is to be privileged, then promoted outcomes should be generated in a manner that minimises the trade-off between furthering competition,

as a fair process, and the impulse to shape fair outcomes. Standard economic analysis often suggests that solutions to policy trade-offs, or conflicts, can be achieved by specifying government preferences. For instance, the government can set 'tolerable' levels of inflation and employment, and seek a solution that satisfies both the constraints. Alternatively, conflict can be resolved by using shadow prices. Whilst normative specification could help in the resolution of choice across outcomes, this is not a very helpful device to negotiate the conflicts between processes and outcomes. In addition, though the notion of shadow pricing is equipped to engage with certain processes, the use of shadow prices is limited only to evaluating public projects.

The trade-off between competition, as a process, and government policy, as an outcome, needs to be analysed by appreciating the link between the robust functioning of the market and government policies. It is essential to realise that both the design, and operation, of policy instruments have an impact on the competitive process by creating barriers to it. To minimise the conflict, it is important to ensure that policy instruments are engineered so that market processes are not thwarted.

This, in turn, requires two broad principles to be followed – transparency and parsimony.

Transparency – Any policy that is pursued with the intent to engineer certain outcomes, in conjunction with the strategy employed to achieve the outcome, will result in a certain configuration of costs and benefits. It is paramount that these costs and benefits are listed openly, so that it is clear as to what extent the suggested policy is, indeed, in the public interest, and to what extent it has been constructed to support some interest group, under the guise of supporting public interest. Thus, the first step is to be aware of the costs and benefits of a policy, and measurements that will clarify the process of policy formulation. Are the benefits going to accrue only to an industry or a social group in society? Who is going to bear the costs? - Apart from shedding light on these kinds of questions, such transparency vitally incorporates the market process in the discourse of policy formulation, since the calculation itself requires one to be mindful of the presence of the market.

Parsimony – If indeed the impacts of policy can be measured, then the policy to be implemented needs to be designed in a manner, which thwarts the competitive process the least – in other words, minimises the trade-off between furthering competition, as a fair process, and the impulse to shape fair outcomes. Such orientation would not only act to further competition *per se*, but would further the objectives of the policy itself, since the policy has been framed, incorporating its impact on the market, and the processes that compose the market.

While such transparency and parsimony in policy formulation and implementation is desirable across the board, it is useful to comment on these issues, in relation to the **Competition Act**, as an illustration in point. Under Section 54[6] of the Act, (the **power to exempt**) and Section 55[7] (**power to issue directions**), the Government has the ability and the right to intervene in the processes of the Competition Commission. These powers imply that government itself is a significant player in the process of competition assessment. It needs to be particularly emphasised, in this context, that the power must be used, in a framework that does not vitiate the entire exercise. The determination of public interest, or sovereign power of the Government, must be based on a coherent, transparent and parsimonious analysis, rather than relying on *ex-cathedra* doctrines of state rights. Within the structure of the **Competition Act**, it can be particularly useful that, under the clauses of Section 49[8], the opinion of the Competition Commission is sought and utilised in a manner so as to provide for an effective competition assessment of any major public policy or reform. Thus, for instance, a prior competition assessment, before privatisation, would lead to a more effective policy. The counter point to this, of course, is the ability of the Commission to undertake such assessments, and make recommendations consistent with market processes, which is, of course, the need across all Government institutions in India.

Notes

1. For further discussion on the importance of the 'context' in the construction and interpretation of competition law see Singh (2000).

2. The emphasis was on State ownership of important resources, protection of workers interests, etc. The session also adopted a charter of Fundamental Rights and economic policy that envisaged 'real' economic freedom for the people. For details, see, A.M. Zaidi and S.G. Zaidi, Encyclopedia of the INC, 1930-35, (1980). These concerns were further reflected in the Avadi resolution in 1955.

3. *Economic Reforms: Two Years After and the Task Ahead (1993) Government of India*, Ministry of Finance, Department of Economic Affairs 33.

4. See the chapter on cross border issues.

5. See Chapters on telecom and energy.

6. Power to exempt:

   54. The Central Government may, by notification, exempt from the application of this Act, or any provision thereof, and for such period as it may specify in such notification—

   (a) any class of enterprises if such exemption is necessary in the interest of security of the State or public interest;

   (c) any enterprise which performs a sovereign function on behalf of the Central Government or a State Government:

7. Power of Central Government to issue directions

   55. (1) Without prejudice to the foregoing provisions of this Act, the Commission shall, in exercise of its Powers or the performance of its functions under this Act, be bound by such directions on questions of policy, other than those relating to technical and administrative matters, as the Central Government may give in writing to it from time to time:

   Provided that the Commission shall, as far as practicable, be given an opportunity to express its views before any direction is given under this sub-section.

   (2) The decision of the Central Government whether a question is one of policy or not shall be final.

8. 49. (1) In formulating a policy on competition (including review of laws related to competition), the Central Government may make a reference to the Commission for its opinion on possible effect of such policy on competition. On receipt of such a reference, the Commission shall, within sixty days of making such reference, give its opinion to the Central Government, which may thereafter formulate the policy, as it deems fit.

References

Economic Reforms: Two Years After and the Task Ahead (1993). Government of India, Ministry of Finance Department of Economic Affairs.

Hayek, F.A. (1979). *Law, Legislation and Liberty. Volume 3: The Political Order of a Free People* London, Routledge & Kegan Paul.

Singh, Jaivir (2000). "Monopolistic Trade Practices and Concentration of Economic Power: Some Conceptual Problems in MRTP Act," *Economic and Political Weekly* December 9, pp. 4437-4444.

8

State Government Policies and Competition

Prabhat Dayal • Manish Agarwal

8.1 Introduction

There are policies/practices of state governments that lead to anti-competitive outcomes and regulatory failures at local level. Unfortunately, these issues are most often ignored, partly because of lack of awareness and partly due to vested interests.

This chapter carries a survey of five such issues, *viz.*, procurement policy, bid rigging in construction contracts, excise policy, truck operations, and retail services. In order to get inputs for the paper, a questionnaire was circulated to various experts and practitioners in the country. Approximately, thirty responses were received.

Indeed, many of our government policies are framed and implemented to promote competition, such as regulatory policies in the utility sector, or using import policy measures to offer competition. One incongruent policy is that on small-scale reservations. Closely linked with it are the state government procurement policies, under which price and/or purchase preferences are given to small-scale as well as other local units in the state.

Overall, these practices affect the competitiveness of local units to a large extent, and tragically remain unaddressed in public discourse. This is coupled with a huge number of regulatory failures at local level.

Similar to happenings at the central level, the construction sector is scandalously infested with collusive bidding at the state level too, without any regulation. The *mafia* appears to dominate in most such businesses in the states and indulge in all types of anti-competitive practices in collusion with politicians. In the area of goods transport, there is a *mafia*-led cartel in various places.

Another area is the state excise policy (revenue generation in liquor and other intoxicants), which is purely under state jurisdiction, and generates the second biggest revenue in the states. Here too, in many states, cartels of liquor traders exist. As a result, bids are suppressed and, state governments lose revenue in the process.

Besides, there are anti-competitive practices in the retail sector as well. Service sectors like auto-rickshaw/taxi operators, barber shops, *pan-biri* shops, etc., form unions and dictate prices.

8.2 Government Procurement Policy

In the federal set-up that we have chosen to adopt, all states vie for the largest slice in the industrial pie. There is competition between states to attract maximum investment. States strive to put up packages for industrial promotion, wherein incentives like sales tax holiday, electricity duty waivers and in various other forms are given. Similar packages are devised to protect local units from outside competition. One such incentive is the preference given by state governments to local units in their procurement policy.

Several states have some government order or regulation, which gives preferential treatment in purchase to units situated within the State (Table 8.1). Under the policy, purchase and/or price preference is given to local units. Most often, the policy is targeted to protect and support small-scale sector units, which are presumed to be less competitive *vis-à-vis* large/medium industries. Even if the products of other units are competitive, they are not purchased. This is evident in the case of Andhra Pradesh, Karnataka, Madhya Pradesh, Rajasthan and West Bengal. The Government of Gujarat gives price preference to cooperatives.

TABLE 8.1

Procurement Policy of Select State Governments

S. No.	State	Policy
1	Andhra Pradesh	• Reservation of 17 products for purchase exclusively from the local SSI units, which are registered with Commissioner of Industries in the Rate Contract System.
2	Gujarat	• Price preference of 15 per cent to cooperatives.
3	Karnataka	• Small-scale industry located within the State given 15 per cent price preference over medium or large-scale industry.
4	Madhya Pradesh	• State Government has established Madhya Pradesh Laghu Udyog Nigam (MPLUN) to promote SSI units and to market the products manufactured by them. • All purchases of state government, state public sector undertakings and local bodies made from units registered with the MPLUN.
5	Rajasthan	• 80 per cent of the stores' requirement by all government departments and public sector undertakings to be met from local units, where the rates are not found competitive, even after grant of price preference and unit from outside the State is adjudged lowest. • 60 per cent of this 80 per cent reserved for local SSI units and remaining 40 per cent requirement to be met from other local industrial units. • Local units given relaxation of 50 per cent in earnest money. • Units within the state have their bids calculated excluding the state sales tax while outside state units have the central sales tax added to their bid.
6	West Bengal	• Small scale industries enjoy a price preference of 15 per cent *vis-à-vis* large and medium industries.

These policies are designed to favour one class of enterprises over others, and distort competition between units producing the same product. In the context of the overall development policy of the state, such policies may be desirable. However, concerns arise, when the policy creates conditions for formation of a cartel of local manufacturers, which is solely dependent on Government's patronage. In such cases, the state government ends up paying higher price for a product, which is often of poor quality. Moreover, with a captive market, where there is no quality control and no threat of competition, the enterprises may become uncompetitive (Box 8.1).

Government at the centre. Accordingly, competition is considered key to survival of small-scale industries (SSIs). It is realised that SSIs cannot survive on government protection and they need to work with a competitive spirit to face the increasingly globalised world.

Another instance of regulatory failure arises from the incapacity of the State government, which results in anti-competitive outcomes. This is highlighted in the case of Orissa (Box 8.2).

BOX 8.1

Barbed-wire Association in Rajasthan

As per an earlier Rajasthan Government policy, a certain quota of barbed-wire was to be procured from local manufacturers. This is supposed to have led to formation of a 'cartel' under the name of Rajasthan Barbed-wire Manufacturers Association in mid-80s. This association hiked the prices, and with an implicit arrangement allocated the total requirement of barbed-wire amongst its members. Consequently, poor quality barbed-wire was procured at a high price, with almost no quality checks at the Government end. Local manufacturers depended solely on Government's patronage rendering them uncompetitive. With the changed Government procurement policy, local units closed down and the association broke up.

(Based on information gathered from personal interviews with reliable sources)

BOX 8.2

Millers' Cartel in Orissa

The State Government of Orissa collects raw paddy from farmers and sells it to millers for further processing, who sell the processed products back to the State Government. The Government of Orissa does not have its own processing industries. The millers capitalise on this and sell the processed products to the state government at a high rate. Ultimately, the Government sells the procured product to the people at a very high cost. The procurement policy has, in this way, become miller-friendly instead of being consumer-friendly.

(Based on information collected through questionnaires)

8.3 Bid Rigging in Construction/Works

An area of government procurement where there are cases of collusion is construction contracts undertaken by the Government.

The point is that whenever such policies are framed, which are designed to protect a class of enterprises, they should be prepared by acknowledging the market process. This is reflected in the policy of the present

As per industry estimates[1], during the last 5 years, all state governments together have spent around Rs. 1,500,000 crore (US$ 300 bn) on civil works. In addition to this, about 800 Members of Parliament (Lok Sabha and Rajya Sabha together) annually receive Rs. 2

crore each, under the MP Local Area Development Fund, for spending on projects/facilities in their respective constituencies, thereby adding Rs. 1,600 crore annually. Add to this kitty, an equal amount that each Member of Legislative Assemby/Council (MLA/MLC) and Corporator receives from the respective state government, or municipal corporation and the figure is around Rs. 4,000 crore annually. The bulk of this amount is spent on civil works, such as bus stands, foot over-bridges, health centres, clinics, hospitals, welfare centres, etc. Considering that the above is only a part estimate, since other infrastructure construction projects have not been taken into account, the total amount spent is simply mind-boggling.

All these projects are generally taken up by government agencies through the medium of contractors. Except in very rare cases, these works are awarded through a system of competitive bidding, which may be international or domestic.

Theoretically, the system of competitive bidding is sound. Notices inviting tenders, for a particular work, are published in international/national/state level newspapers. Depending on the complexity and quantum of the project, bids may be received in single or double envelopes. Bids are opened in front of all bidders, and the lowest bidder is determined through a transparent system and is awarded the work

Be that as it may, this seemingly faultless system may not yield desired results, because of cases where contractors collude and there is a *tender-mafia* at work. As a result of these distortions, competition is subverted and the bidding system fails to produce efficient results, even in cases where rules and procedures are properly followed. Most importantly, corruption in engineering departments is so deep that such practices are encouraged rather than frowned upon. The nexus between contractors and engineers is well established. Rare exceptions do exist, when engineers are not corrupt, but they can hardly fight against the system, which is deeply entrenched.

The extent of the malice can be gauged from the fact that even the Parliamentary Standing Committee on Railways (2004), while discussing the question of procurement of concrete sleepers, observed:

> "*The procurement of concrete sleepers has become a very sensitive matter, because a lot of unscrupulous existing manufacturers have formed a cartel to secure orders by unfair means or tempering with procedure and simultaneously keeping the new competitors out of the race. The Committee is constrained to notice that there exists a regional imbalance in the setting up of concrete sleeper manufacturing units. They also express their unhappiness that new entrants are not encouraged, which ultimately strengthen the cartel of old/existing manufacturers*". In procuring 160 lakhs broad gauge sleepers, the Railways awarded contracts to the existing 71 firms, and ignored the 24 new firms entirely.

As per industry information, there is now a trend towards awarding works in much bigger packages, which effectively rules out most small contractors from bidding, thus restricting competition.[2]

In many cases, large contractors subcontract the work to smaller contractors, mainly because in large projects, it makes sense to subdivide work into smaller lots to make the project management task easier. This subcontracting is taken into account when the large bidders bid, and the profit, of both the sub-contractor and their own is factored in. This leads to an escalation in costs of bigger packages. It is estimated that there can be a 10-15 per cent reduction in cost, if smaller contractors are not excluded from the bidding process. In Chennai, a flyover scam had rocked the state assembly in 2001, where contractors pooled up to share the contract for laying cables at a considerable cost to the taxpayer. But nothing much came of it.

Angered by the malicious process, the Rajasthan Minister for Public Works Department (PWD) announced in the assembly on July 20, 2004, that he would break all cartels, so that smaller contractors can bid for contracts. Subsequently, nothing happened, and it is now business as usual.

Other factors that hamper competition is the pre-qualification criterion, where, for bigger packages, past experience in executing similar works is a must, leaving the contract open for only a few construction companies.

There are good practices as well, which can be adopted to ensure competition in the bidding process. For instance, by selling tender documents through multiple sources. This has been tried in certain contracts and has proved successful. The procedure creates uncertainty among the cartel members, as they are not sure how many bids have been submitted, and by whom. This makes it difficult for the cartel to monitor the number of bids outside the pool, and forces the members to submit reasonable bids.

The Government of Andhra Pradesh's e-procurement scheme is another initiative to tackle the menace of bid rigging, and bring transparency in the entire procedure. It has helped a great deal in eliminating such practices, which were quite rampant earlier. As a result, there has been an increase in the number of average bids received from 3.4 to 6.7,

---

BOX 8.3

Modus Operandi in Bid-Rigging

The entire process of formation of collusion, among contractors while bidding is popularly referred as 'Pooling'.

The process starts with the closing date for purchasing the bid documents. Normally, a meeting is organised of all those who have purchased the bid-documents, and a decision is taken as to whom the contract will be awarded. The popular criteria for this 'selection', among others, include: (i) highest offer made for the 'pool' amount (ii) informal understanding among contenders to maintain rotation and ensure 'equitable' sharing of opportunities.

As per information, the 'pool amount' that the 'winner' has to contribute varies between 2 to 4 per cent of the entire value of the contract. This money is equally distributed among the members of the collusion. That way this parallel system works in quite a 'competitive' and 'democratic' manner!

More often, the departments concerned club smaller assignments together to make it a big one, for unknown reasons, which substantially reduces the chances of competitive bidding.

It is alleged that quite often staff/officials from these construction departments work in tandem with such collusions and receive benefits. Even those who have been part of such collusion admit that 'pooling' cannot successfully be executed, without active support from within the department.

As per the information, such collusion works out in about 30 per cent of cases. Hence, figuring out 30 per cent of the total value of contracts being awarded, in recent years, will offer an indicative estimate of the amount at stake.

(Based on information gathered from personal interviews with reliable sources)

---

besides generating significant cost savings of about 23 per cent. Given the success of this tool, all government departments in the State are expected to switch to the 'e-procurement' mode from January 2005. Encouraged by the success of e-procurement, the Rajasthan Government in its budget for 2005-06 announced following a similar practice.

8.4 Excise Policy

As per Article 246(3) of the Constitution of India, the Legislature of a State has exclusive powers to make laws for any matter enumerated in list II in the 7th Schedule, including production, manufacture, possession, transport, purchase and sale of intoxicating liquors within the state. Item 66 of this list empowers the State Legislature to impose fees in respect of any of the matters enumerated in this list. The excise duty is leviable in respect of alcoholic beverages for human consumption manufactured in the state or produced elsewhere in India.

The key objectives of excise laws are[3]:

8.4.1 Regulation

Under the *Directive Principles of State Policy*, Article 47 lays down that the State shall regard raising the level of nutrition and the standard of its people, and the improvement of the public health as among its primary duties and, in particular, the State shall endeavour to bring about prohibition of the consumption (except for medicinal purposes) of intoxicating drinks and drugs, which is injurious to health. In view of this, some States are pursuing the policy of temperance, such as Gujarat, which has declared complete prohibition, whilst States like Tamil Nadu and Andhra Pradesh, have banned country liquor.

Alcoholic beverage being a state subject, excise policy is in the domain of the state governments. State governments have a plethora of rules and regulations and often at variance with those obtained in other states. Such rules/policies govern licensing and regulations of distilleries/breweries, bottling units, warehousing, wholesale and retail sale, import and export, transport, pricing, labelling and packaging, locational instructions, registration of brands, limit on possession, duties and fees, etc.

8.4.2 State Revenue

Excise revenue from liquor is the second biggest source of revenue, after sales tax, for the state governments. State governments are collecting around Rs. 20,000 crore by levying duties and fees on alcoholic beverages. Governments' policy is largely revenue oriented; the aim is to maximise revenue with minimum effort. All procedures, rules, etc. are determined, considering this objective.

8.4.3 Distribution and Marketing System in Liquor

The various systems adopted by State governments for the distribution and marketing of liquor can be classified as:

- Auction system, wherein group of shops in particular area or individual liquor shops are auctioned for specific period;

- Licensing system, where liquor shops are allotted on fixed fees (through direct selection or draw of lots), renewable on period basis;

- Wholesale trade by the state itself, and retail trade by individuals (Andhra Pradesh, Karnataka);

- Wholesale trade by private parties, and liquor vends managed by the state (Pondicherry);

- Wholesale as well as retail sale by state (Tamil Nadu)

In states, where liquor groups comprising of large geographical areas are auctioned for specific period, a number of malpractices build up over time. In this system, competition is restricted to a few parties who have sufficient money and muscle power to carry out the business. Over time, it encourages cartelisation, resulting in concentration of business in the hands of few licensees. As a result, bids are suppressed and state revenue declines, as is evident in the case of Rajasthan (Table 8.2). The revenue figures show a marginal variation, but in real terms, there is a clear decline.

In its excise policy for 2005-06, the Government of Rajasthan has made significant changes with a view to check the liquor *mafia*. Adopting the model of Karnataka, the government has decided to establish a government-owned agency, Rajasthan State Beverages Corporation Ltd. (RSBCL) to deal exclusively in IMFL, Beer, Wine, and all liquor items (except country liquor). RSBCL will take over the role of purchaser and supplier of liquor, dispensing with middlemen. Furthermore, in a significant departure from its earlier policy of exclusive privilege system, the state government has introduced a two-tier system of licensing for IMFL/Beer - licences for wholesaler as well as retailer, on a fixed licence fees. The process of allotment would be a lottery system. However, country liquor shops will be allotted on the erstwhile group system. The new system aims at devolution of liquor selling rights to larger number of vendors to break the nexus of about a dozen liquor contractors, who informally form a cartel while bidding for selling rights.

Cartelisation has also been witnessed in states where the retail sale is granted by tender-cum-auction system. This system too encourages bidders to collude, resulting in underbidding in the auction, causing loss of revenue to the state government. The state governments of Tamil Nadu, Uttar Pradesh, and Madhya Pradesh followed this system in the past, and faced problems. Later, they replaced the tender-cum-auction system by a system where liquor shops are allotted by a lottery system for a fixed licence fee.

The Government of Madhya Pradesh, in its Excise Policy for 2004-05, replaced the contract auction system, and instead allotted the country-foreign liquor shops on prescribed licence fee, through a lottery system. According to the State Minister for Excise, the change in policy was aimed at subverting the liquor *mafia*, which, through its money and muscle power was building monopolies in the liquor business. Uttar Pradesh also adopted a similar policy from 2002-03 and the state's excise revenue jumped by over 30 per cent as a result.

The Punjab government is also grappling with the problem of monopolies in liquor contracts, and is contemplating to bring changes in the liquor policy. The government is considering to bring the licence system with regard to IMFL, while continuing with open auction for country-made liquor. The fixed fees based licence system, where shops are allotted by lottery has been found to be successful in other states as well, including Jammu and Kashmir, Maharashtra, West Bengal, Andhra Pradesh, Karnataka, and Kerala.

The Tamil Nadu Government too adopted the lottery system in 2001. In the new scheme, uniform licence fee was fixed for all the shops in a given notified area and the privilege was granted to the applicant by direct selection or by drawal of lot, where the number of application was more than one per shop. The new system resulted in an increase in revenue for the state government, by breaking the cartel in liquor business. The state revenue increased by 10 per cent in 2001-02 (Table 8.2). However, the lot system did not last long due to the subversive activities undertaken by those who used to control the retail trade. These people resorted to methods like *benami* applications. Concerned about the attempts of vested groups to subvert one system after another, the state government decided in November 2003, to put an end to private retail trade in IMFL and granted exclusive privilege of retail vending of IMFL to Tamil Nadu Sales and Marketing Corporation (TASMAC), a Government Company.

However, the Tamil Nadu model, of a government company taking over the wholesale and retail trade may not be a good solution. There are already complaints of reduced choice (in brands) and poor quality. Delhi Government experimented with this system, but did not succeed. The liquor trade in the Capital, which was solely run by government corporations till 2002, was thrown open to private sector, due to the inefficiency and corruption that existed in the working of the government corporations. Now the government-owned liquor shops are competing with the private players.

8.5 Truck Operations

Often truck operators, at district level or around major production centres form a cartel, which then leads to increase in freight charges. In most cases,

TABLE 8.2

Excise Policy of Select State Governments and Its Impact

S. No.	State	Excise Policy and its Impact	Annual Revenue (Rs. Cr)			
			2000-01	2001-02	2002-03	2003-04
1.	Andhra Pradesh	• Fixed Licensing System	1243	1652	1856	2276
		• Prohibition fully lifted in 1997				
		• Ban on *arrak* (country liquor), while promotion of Indian Made Foreign Liquor (IMFL)				
		• Marketing done through shops allotted on fixed charges by draw of lots				
		• Sale of toddy permitted only through toddy co-operatives				
		• Wholesale through Government owned AP Beverages Corporation (APBC)				
		Impact of the Policy:				
		• Increased competition at retail level, but restricted competition at the wholesale stage				
		• Significant increase in revenue				
2.	Karnataka	• Country liquor auction system	1550	1977	2094	2346
		• IMFL/Beer Fixed Licensing System				
		• Wholesale through Government owned Company				
		Impact of Policy:				
		• Competition is restricted at the wholesale stage and retail rates are controlled by wholesale prices.				
3.	Rajasthan	• Exclusive Privilege System till 2004-05. Under the system, State divided into groups. Contracts awarded for each group giving the licensee-contractor exclusive right to trade in Liquor in the specified area	1118	1110	1142	1240
		• Until March 2004, RTDC was selling beer through its own shops. This has been discontinued.				
		• Policy changed in 2005-06, with the aim of increasing the number of vendors for IMFL/Beer. Two-tier licensing system introduced – wholesale as well as retail. Selling rights to be granted on a fixed licence fees by draw of lots. Government owned Rajasthan State Beverages Corporation Ltd. established to deal exclusively with IMFL, Beer, Wine, and all liquor items (except country liquor). Manufacturers required to sell liquor only to the Corporation. Wholesalers in a district to get their supplies from the Corporation, while retailers to get their supplies from wholesalers of that district only				
		Impact of Erstwhile Policy:				
		• Small bidders not able to participate in the auctions due to the size of the bid				
		• With restricted number of bidders, only 11-12 liquor operators in the entire state, who have formed a cartel				
		• State Government forced to lower the 'reserve price' repeatedly because bids suppressed by the cartel				
		• Revenue has declined in real terms				
		• No competition in sale of beer after closure of RTDC run liquor shops				
4.	Tamil Nadu	• Exclusive Privilege of wholesale distribution given to state owned Tamil Nadu Sales and Marketing Corporation (TASMAC)	1869	2058	2114	2274
		• Till 2001, retail vends given to private parties through tender-cum-auction system				
		• The auction system replaced by lot system in 2001, to check cartelisation				
		• Though a definite improvement over the auction system, the lot system was discontinued because the persons who controlled the retail trade tried to subvert the system by resorting to methods like *benami* applications				
		• In November 2003, the policy was changed and TASMAC was given the exclusive privilege of retail vending, as well				
		• The policy was changed to eliminate the sale of spurious liquor and widespread violations of Maximum Retail Price (MRP) of liquor fixed by the Government, and to check the cartel, which acted to ensure that applications were not made for a large number of shops, so as to keep them vacant, and thereby to corner the retail vending trade causing loss of revenue to the State Government.				

Contd...

...Contd...

S. No.	State	Excise Policy and its Impact	Annual Revenue (Rs. Cr)			
			2000-01	2001-02	2002-03	2003-04
		Impact of Policy:				
		• Lower prices, as compared to when retail trade was with the private parties				
		• Continuous increase in Government revenue				
5.	Madhya Pradesh	• Wholesale through Government	974	704	890	1100
		• Till March 2004, individual shops auctioned by the government				
		• From April 2004, fixed licence fee to allot individual liquor shops. Under the system, an individual allowed to apply for running one or more country and IMFL shops in the state. In cases where there is more than one applicant, the licensee decided through a draw of lottery				
6.	Uttar Pradesh	• Auction system for retail vends till 2002-03. Since, then fixed licensing system, shops allotted through lottery.	2238	1961	2555	2550

trucks that come in with goods are not allowed to carry freight from the production centre. These unions often have, local or even state level political patronage. There are innumerable numbers of such examples and some of these were also referred to the Monopolies and Restrictive Trade Practices (MRTP) Commission. This section presents various anecdotal cases of the working of these cartels, and highlights their impact on the affected industry, and measures taken, if any, to check such practices.

Truck operators' cartel result in higher transport costs, since trucks bringing in goods charge two-way fare, as they are made to return empty, while transportation costs on out-going goods are about 40 per cent more.

In case of Baddi, Himachal Pradesh, the Baddi Nalagarh Truck Operator Cooperative Transport Society, has monopolised the movement of goods from the state. Controlled by the local MLA, the truck union charges 30 per cent higher on the Baddi-Delhi route and 15-20 per cent on the Baddi-Mumbai route. Trucks coming in with supplies go back empty, because they are not allowed to pick up freight, which only adds to the cost.

The State Government of Himachal Pradesh, has given an excise waiver for investors, and a large number of consumer goods and pharmaceutical companies are setting up manufacturing units in Baddi. However, by controlling the commercial traffic in Baddi, the transport union has reduced the cost advantage, the units would otherwise enjoy. Often, large companies find that cost advantage due to excise waiver is higher than the component of higher transportation costs and are willing to yield to the blackmail of the local transporters. Small companies, however, are facing problems.

As per information collected, Godrej Industries tried to bypass the truck union in Baddi, but this did not last long. Godrej, which has a manufacturing unit in Baddi, established a depot in Chandigarh. They used the Baddi truck union's trucks to transport goods from Baddi to Chandigarh but used other operator's vehicles for rest of the transit. However, this arrangement lasted for only a few days, as the Baddi truck union learnt about this bypass arrangement, and refused to provide trucks to Godrej Industries. Godrej had to give in to their demands.

In the case of Orissa, transport cartels are formed with official backing. For example, the Angul Truck-owners Association, a duly Government registered body operating at the National Aluminium Co. Ltd.'s factory charges as much as 200 per cent more for transportation of ingots under the obliging eyes of the authorities. A complaint was once lodged with the district authorities against the association, but to no avail. Such official cartels are known to exist in other parts of Orissa also such as in Sukinda Mines, Paradeep Port and Balasore.

In a case in Alwar, Rajasthan, in the 1980s, the MRTP Commission had taken action against the local truck union, but with no success. An MLA, who later became a minister in the state, headed the local union. On the cries of the local industry, the issue came up before the district administration. The administration held that the practice followed by the union was not correct and it was stopped only after concerted efforts.

On the other hand, Makrana in Rajasthan was an unfortunate case, as there was no action taken by the district administration, and the stubbornness of the truck operators' union killed the marble business in this one-time capital of marble trade. Makrana had become a '*mandi*', as marble blocks were transported from all parts of Rajasthan and were processed at Makrana. Later, truck operators formed a union and began exploiting the trade-s. The Union was charging tariffs almost 35-40 per cent higher than the prevailing market rates. This led to an increase in transportation costs of marble from Makrana and the usual harassment of dealing with a monopolist union. The harassment grew to such proportions that several marble-sawing plants moved to Kishangarh on the Jaipur-Ajmer National Highway No. 8. Gradually, more and more marble business moved to Kishangarh. As opposed to the 100 trucks, which used to come to Makrana, now hardly 35-40 trucks come. Kishangarh has become a rival *mandi*. Makrana lost its advantage and the town is gradually losing its prosperity!

A similar situation now exists in Bikaner, Rajasthan where the truck operators' union is creating problems in the smooth movement of minerals from the area. Due to obstruction in the supply, the ceramic tile industry, which uses these minerals as raw material are facing hardships, and even closure. The local units have requested the state government to direct the district administration to take necessary action.

The apathy of state government can be observed from the fact that quite often, truck unions come out with open information in news dailies highlighting their restrictive practice. Unfortunately, such notices go unnoticed, and no action is ever taken. In one such instance, the Granite Association of Jalore, Rajasthan and the Jalore Truck Operators' Union, announced a mutually agreed upon decision, that granite factories located in Rajasthan and Gujarat have to use trucks supplied by the union, otherwise it will create obstructions. However, as usual, this went unnoticed, and the union continues with its restrictive practice, imposing a huge transportation cost on factories located in Rajasthan and Gujarat.

In Punjab's Derabassi, truck unions have drafted their own tariffs, increasing costs of production for local units, thus rendering them uncompetitive. A cartel of around 500 truck operators has been troubling the area, since Derabassi's inception as an industrial town in 1987. Most of the state's major industrial towns such as Ludhiana, Jalandhar, Amritsar, and Mandi Gobindgarh, do not have such unions. However, truckers' association flourish in smaller towns. In Sirhind, near Mandi Gobindgarh, such unions stalled industrial growth, resulting in industry to flourish in nearby Khanna and Amloh.

The upshot is that any aberration at a local level can be tackled at the level of district and local administration. It requires willingness on the part of the administration to resolve the problem taking a balanced view after hearing all the parties concerned, as shown in the case of Alwar, Rajasthan.

Additionally, companies can follow practices, which rule out the formation of cartels. For instance, the Birla Cement factory in Chittorgarh, Rajasthan invites bids for transport of goods through the Internet. It provides details of the trucks required on a particular day or week and the destinations where the cement has to go. This helps the factory to get competitive rates, and cartels are thus compromised.

8.6 Other Cases of Regulatory Failures at Local Level

In most towns, taxi and auto drivers demand lump sum payments, even when meters do exist. The charges vary depending on location and also sometime with the category of consumers. The case of Delhi is interesting in this context. Till very recently, a similar situation prevailed in Delhi with respect to auto drivers, who charged lump sum amounts. But now auto drivers in Delhi use meters. The reason for this sudden change: State Government has given clear instructions to the traffic police to *challan* auto drivers, who are found not using meters and cancel their driving licences. The result of this strong stance taken by the state government is easily seen on Delhi roads.

The basic problem is poor enforcement, which in turn is due to lack of political will. Moreover, in many cases, non-compliance costs are lower than compliance costs, as penalties fixed are unrelated to the extent of violations. By taking care of these factors, situations can change in favour of consumers, as shown in the case of Delhi.

BOX 8.4

Taxi Regulation: The Market Reality

Taxi operations is characterised by a potential "market failure" in that some users of taxis (especially those from out-of-town) are unaware of appropriate fares and are unable to assess the maintenance of the taxi before embarking. How should this market failure be addressed?

One possible approach would be to educate taxi users about the need to "shop around" before accepting a ride. However, this might be impractical, especially at those sites (such as major airports) where efficiency of queuing essentially requires that customers take the first cab off the rank. As a result, it might be necessary to licence taxis, to impose standardised meters, and strictly enforce rules that taxis take the shortest route. Even in this case, though, the number of taxi licences need not be restricted. Free entry and exit of taxi drivers will

Contd...

...Contd...

eliminate any rents and will determine the number of taxis available for service at any point in time. The taxi fares should be carefully calibrated to ensure that there is neither a shortage nor a surplus of taxis at both peak and off-peak times. However, at the same time, locals who are highly familiar with routes, distances and fares, and are able to "shop around" may not need such protection. Therefore, it may make sense to develop a "two-tier" taxi system with one tier highly regulated, with the right to service locations mostly used by newcomers to the city (e.g., airports and major hotels) and a second tier, largely unregulated, who can serve all other customers on demand. A two-tier system of this kind operates in the London metropolitan area.

An absence of regulatory control would result in the operation of a large number of taxis. It may also raise concerns that the taxis are over-charging passengers (who are unaware of routes, distances, or appropriate fares), that fights may break out between taxi drivers over potential customers and that the taxis themselves may be poorly maintained, with an unacceptable rate of accidents.

(Adapted from OECD Global Forum on Competition, Background Documentation of the Fifth Meeting, 17-18 February 2005)

Service sectors like barber shops; *pan-biri* shops etc. form unions and dictate selling prices, which are often above the printed price also. For instance, in Mumbai, the *Pan* Merchants Association decides and circulates a price list, which mandates members to sell at prices that are higher than those printed. This is a violation of the Weights and Measures (Packaged Commodities) Rules, but one cannot expect the weights and measures inspector to go around prosecuting every *pan* shop. Such type of practices needs to be dealt with systemically by the state government, but no one bothers! These are local issues and only local solutions will be successful in these cases.

In fact, most often, service providers at the local level resort to these practices because of the need to grease the pockets of enforcement agencies at the local level. For instance, India Gate at New Delhi, where people go out for a stroll etc., is full of ice cream vendors in the evening. All of them charge more than the price printed on the package. Their explanation is that they have to pay *"hafta"* (weekly bribe) to the policemen on duty in order to sell at India Gate, where the business is brisk. Selling at more than what is marked on the package violates the Weights and Measures (Packaged Commodities) Rules, but the Department of Legal Metrology does not haul the ice-cream sellers up, and they continue to overcharge consumers. One wonders, why not use the same police force to enforce rules that favour the consumers. Their power can be used in a positive way to protect consumers rather than harming them.

8.7 Conclusion

The paper follows a case study approach and has taken up five issues for study. At several places, it draws on anecdotal incidents to carry out the analysis. There is a clear need to carry forward this work and do a more comprehensive analysis of various policies/ practices at the state level. For instance, in the context of State Government procurement policy of giving preference to local units, it is worth noting that over time, some states have dispensed with this practice. Examples of such states can be taken to analyse the impact, such as, on quality of products, production level, competitiveness of local units, etc.

The paper highlights that governments at state level, most often, either themselves follow anti-competitive practice or by their policies encourage such practices. Regulatory failures and competition abuses are rampant at the local level, and lack of healthy competition and fair-trading in the marketplace affects the economy and consumers' interest adversely.

There is a clear need for state-level competition and regulatory agencies, backed by appropriate laws, to tackle these practices. There is also a need for state governments to make competition assessment of their policies and practices. In fact, by promoting competition and effective regulation, state governments can protect consumer interest as well as increase their own revenues. In other federal countries, like the USA or Australia, many provinces have their own state competition laws and agencies. Experiences of such countries can be studied, and lessons drawn for India.

Notes

1. "Indian Construction," *Journal of Builders' Association of India*, November 2004.

2. "Awarding contracts in bigger packages for contractors does not necessarily reduce the total cost": Vijaya Raghava Reddy, Chairman, Builder's Association of India, Karnataka Centre, Bangalore, September 1, 2000 (http://www.indiamarkets.com/imo/industry/construction/constructftof1.asp)

3. Galundia, K.S., *Study on Imports of Foreign Liquor* (Post-WTO Scenario), 2000.

References

Galundia, K.S. (2000). *Study on Imports of Foreign Liquor (Post-WTO Scenario).*

Government of Rajasthan, Finance Department (Central Stores Purchase Organisation) Order, Circular No.4/96.

Government of Rajasthan, Finance Department (General Financial and Accounts Rules Division) Order, Circular No.8/2000.

http://www.indiamarkets.com/imo/industry/construction/constructftof1.asp

"Indian Construction," *Journal of Builders' Association of India*, November 2004.

OECD Global Forum on Competition, Background Documentation of the Fifth Meeting, 17-18 February 2005.

Reserve Bank of India, *State Finances: A Study of Budgets of 2002-03, 2003-04 & 2004-05.*

Standing Committee on Railways (2004), Ministry of Railways (Railway Board).

Tamil Nadu, Prohibition & Excise Department, Policy Note 2004-05, Demand No. 36.

www.aponline.gov.in, Government of Andhra Pradesh web portal

www.rajexcise.org, Excise Department, Government of Rajasthan web portal

www.tn.gov.in, Government of Tamil Nadu web portal (Policy Notes of Departments)

www.eprocurement.gov.in, Government of Andhra Pradesh e-procurement web portal

Part III

Competition Policy and Consumers

9 Competition Policy and Consumer Welfare

Pradeep S. Mehta

9.1 Introduction

The economic reforms initiated, since the nineties, through liberalisation, privatisation and globalisation, have brought about momentous changes in the structure of markets, In addition, they have transformed the employment scenario, income generation and consumption patterns of different sections of people. This has also necessitated changes in the legal regime, in the form of scrapping of obsolete laws and enactment of new laws, suited to the economic reforms agenda in the era of globalisation.

One such piece of legislation proposed to be scrapped and replaced, is the Monopolies & Restrictive Trade Practices Act 1969, with the Competition Act 2002. The earlier competition law was plainly out of sync with the emerging economic environment, and thus the new competition law was adopted.

The main objective of competition policy and law, is to preserve and promote competition as a means to ensure efficient allocation of resources in an economy, resulting in:

- the best possible choice of quality,
- the lowest possible prices, and
- adequate supplies to consumers.

To put it differently, the objectives stated above, can be achieved by way of ensuring competition. Obviously, maximising consumer welfare becomes a predominant concern.

Therefore, the need for the Government is to design and implement a competition policy, with the understanding that consumers need the visible hand of the state to protect and promote their interests. Generally, competition policy has two elements:

- A set of policies that enhances competition in local and national markets: a liberal trade policy, relaxed foreign investment and ownership requirements, deregulation and privatisation, etc., and

- Legislation i.e. competition law designed to prevent anti-competitive business practices and unnecessary government intervention.

However, one should bear in mind that competition policy is just one of the tools in the larger context of other overarching public policies, and approaches, that are also needed for promoting consumer welfare. The Indian Consumer Movement was given fresh impetus with the enactment of the Consumer Protection Act, 1986 (COPRA), as it contains provisions for consumer representation as well as simple, speedy, inexpensive and informal justice, to consumers, by means of establishing a separate appeal-and-redressal mechanism. There are forums at the district level, state level, and the apex National Commission at New Delhi. Each has monetary jurisdiction and entertains appeals from the lower fora.

Furthermore, the Act also aims to promote and propagate consumer rights, through consumer education and the establishment of consumer councils at the state and district level, besides the apex Central Consumer Protection Council at New Delhi.

The Monopolies and Restrictive Trade Practices Act (MRTPA) 1969, was amended in 1984 to bring in consumer protection provisions, which dealt with unfair trade practices such as deception, misleading advertising and claims. Thus, the Consumer Protection Act 1986, and the Monopolies and Restrictive Trade Practices Act 1969, have been playing complementary roles in promoting consumer welfare in India.

9.2 Competition and Consumer Welfare

Competition means rivalry in the marketplace, which is regulated by a set of policies and laws to achieve the goals of economic efficiency and consumer welfare, and to check on the concentration of economic power. All these goals have an interactive relationship and, when in harmony, deliver total welfare. Indeed, it is the consumers that are supposedly the biggest beneficiaries of competition. On the other hand, it is the consumers who are the main losers due to anti-competitive activities in a market. The consumers are worse off because of their lack of capacity to deal with such problems.

In this context, it is sometimes believed that competition policy and law are tools for the rich, the urban, and industries alone. However, at the macro level, the design and implementation of a competition policy promotes the advancement and increased welfare of the poor. At the micro level, an effective competition regime or consumer law (covering competition distortions) can prevent consumer abuses, both at industry level as well as in a village or locality where one shopkeeper can cheat the whole community. An appropriate and dynamic competition policy and law are imperative to buttress economic development, curb corruption, reduce wastage and arbitrariness, improve competitiveness and provide succour to the poor.

Before we embark on assessing the consumer welfare implications, it is important to understand the notion of consumer welfare. Unfortunately, there is no agreed definition of consumer welfare. Even so, one can have a fair understanding of the notions surrounding consumer welfare by looking at the United Nations Guidelines for Consumer Protection, adopted by the UN General Assembly in 1985, and amended in 1999. These guidelines represent an international regulatory framework for governments to use, for the development and strengthening of consumer protection policy and legislation, aimed at promoting consumer welfare.

The UN Guidelines call upon governments to develop, strengthen and maintain a strong consumer policy, and provide for enhanced protection of consumers by enunciating various steps and measures around eight themes (UNCTAD, 2001). These eight themes are:

1. Physical safety

2. Economic interests

3. Standards

4. Essential goods and services

5. Redress

6. Education and information

7. Specific areas concerning health

8. Sustainable consumption.

The Guidelines have implicitly recognised eight consumer rights, which were made explicit in the *Charter of Consumers International* as follows:

- Right to basic needs
- Right to safety
- Right to choice
- Right to redress
- Right to information
- Right to consumer education
- Right to representation
- Right to healthy environment.

These eight consumer rights can be used as the touchstones for assessing the consumer welfare implications of competition policy and law, and to see how they help or hinder the promotion of these rights.

9.2.1 Right to Basic Needs

In India, this right is the most crucial, because of high levels of poverty and deprivation. Thus, getting the maximum number of goods, or services, out of a Rupee is more important for those who have less money to spend, than those who have enough of it. By ensuring lower prices, competition can make basic needs more accessible to the poor. Moreover, the poor who are engaged in agriculture, and such other trade, are often unable to get the right prices for their produce, due to anti-competitive practices of the buyers. Hence, if implemented properly, the Competition Act will make a significant contribution in this regard.

In this context, it is worthwhile to quote the World Development Report, 2000-2001:

"Markets work for the poor because poor people rely on formal and informal markets to sell their labour and products, to finance investment, and to insure against risks. Well functioning markets are important in generating growth and expanding opportunities for the poor people".

'Well functioning' implies markets that work efficiently and without distortions i.e. competitive markets, where everyone has the opportunity to participate. However, 'competition' is often less understood and easily distorted by players in the market, even when there are large numbers of them. Competition laws are, therefore, enacted to curb distortions.

The market for agricultural products is very often considered to be an example of a perfectly competitive market. This might be the case for farmers as there is large number of them. Nevertheless, for consumers the experience is different. Products do not directly change hands from farmer to consumer, as there is a chain of intermediaries. These intermediaries abuse their **monopolistic** dominance in the market for final products, whilst in the markets for primary products they abuse their **monopsonistic** dominance. Hence, a huge gap exists between the prices consumers pay, and the prices primary producers receive, implying that the farmers do not get the right price for their products. Of the poor people of the country who live in extreme poverty, approximately 75 per cent live and work in rural areas and, about two-thirds of them draw their livelihood directly from agriculture. Thus, one can hardly overestimate the issue of linkage between market imperfections in agricultural goods, and poverty and, hence, the right to basic needs (Mehta & Nanda, 2004).

An area where competition law could be beneficial to the consumers, specifically the poor, is the mitigation of the adverse effect of a strong intellectual property rights (IPR) regime. Two sectors, namely pharmaceuticals and agriculture, are important in this regard. Coordination between the IPR authorities, such as the patent office and competition authority, is necessary to yield such benefits. By using the compulsory licensing provision, an exploitative situation in life saving drugs can be curbed. This could be an important ingredient in consumers' right to healthcare, one of the basic needs.

Similarly, in the agriculture sector, government interventions, through judicious use of competition law, including cooperation with the competition law authorities in other countries, can help check exploitation by large agribusinesses who control most of the patents in seeds and biotechnology products. A major spin-off of such a coordinated action can culminate in pro-consumer technology development and innovation. This will also help in promoting consumers' right to basic needs.

Sectoral regulatory policies, which are an integral part of competition policy, also play a major role in ensuring the right to basic needs, for example, through mandating universal service obligation on the service providers so that even at a loss, they will have to supply services to the poor and disadvantaged consumers, at a reasonable price.

9.2.2 Right to Safety

Though competition policy and law do not directly deal with safety issues, they can make a significant contribution to promoting safer products and services in markets. In a competitive market, sellers try to attract more customers, not only through cheaper prices but also through better quality, including more safety features wherever relevant. In a cartelised industry, there would be less innovation and less initiative in improving safety standards.

There are, however, complex interconnections between competition, and consumers' right to safety. An integral part of consumer safety is the standard setting process, for different goods and services. Standards perform several important functions in an economy, in which high-tech industries are the drivers of growth and innovation. They provide the information to producers and consumers to enable them to judge the quality of products produced by others, and also to determine the safety levels of those products. In addition, they also ensure the compatibility between complementary products, and even between the various parts of a particular product. This is also important for promoting competition.

However, the standards-setting process often brings competitors together. Any meeting of the minds by horizontal competitors has the potential to harm competition, and standard setting is no different. Moreover, if the process of setting or enforcing the standard is compromised or manipulated, by certain competitors at the expense of others, anti-competitive effects may occur. The existing players can create entry barriers for a potential entrant even with a better product. Even if the process does not appear designed to harm competition, the rules set by a standard-setting organisation could, themselves, have anti-competitive consequences. Due to a lack of awareness, such cases, even if they exist, are not documented in India. However, an example from elsewhere may be worth mentioning (Box 9.1).

9.2.3 Right to Choice

This is probably the most relevant consumer right on which competition policy and law have important bearings. In pure and simple terms, right to choice means that there should be range of varieties/producers available to consumers in each product and services. Looking from this perspective, the 1991 amendment to the MRTP Act that removed the merger review provisions was a setback in this regard. This meant that the number of players would reduce, though this does not necessarily mean higher prices or anti-competitive arrangements. Nonetheless, the Competition Act is a significant improvement in this regard as it has merger review provisions. However, concerns have been expressed that due to high thresholds and voluntary notification requirement, this may not be as effective as it should have been.

BOX 9.1

Anti-Competitive Practice Thwarting Safety Innovation

In the *Allied Tube* (Allied Tube & Conduit Co. *Vs.* Indian Head, Inc., 486 U.S. 492, 1988) case, the US Supreme Court found that a subgroup of the standard setting organisation effectively "captured" the whole group, and harmed competition by excluding an innovative product. In this case, an association that published a code of standards, for electrical equipment, required the use of steel conduits in high-rise buildings, but a new entrant into the market proposed to use plastic conduits. The new product was allegedly cheaper to install, more pliable, and less susceptible to short-circuit.

The incumbent steel conduit manufacturers agreed to use the association's procedures to exclude the plastic product, from the code, by sending new members to the association's annual meeting, whose sole function was to vote against the new product. As a result, the potential entrant's ability to market the plastic conduit was significantly impaired, and consumers were denied the benefit of a potentially significant product innovation.

Source: Joseph J. Simons (2003), *FTC Initiatives in Intellectual Property*, presentation at the American Intellectual Property Law Association Spring Meeting, May 15.

The Right to choice, however, has some other dimensions as well. Any restrictive practice has a bearing on consumers' right to choice. A collusive market sharing arrangement is a prime example of this, where consumers have no choice other than buying from a particular seller. By including explicit provisions, the new Competition Act is likely to tackle such issues in a more effective way than the MRTPA. The inclusion of leniency provisions is another feature that would help identify or expose such practices prevailing in the market.

Certain types of unfair trade practices can also have an important bearing on the right to choice. Misleading advertisements seriously jeopardise consumers' right to choice. According to the MRTPA, offers of gifts could also reduce consumers' right to choice. Gift offering is not necessarily an **offence**. When the cost of the gift is included in the transaction cost, and is against public interest, it is an **offence**. Promotion of a product through contests was also considered to be against the

consumers' right to choice by the Monopolies and Restrictive Trade Practices Commission (MRTPC).

The MRTPC had restrained *Business India* magazine from continuing their sales promotion scheme of contests. A review, conducted by the MRTPC investigating team, revealed that the participants were induced to buy the magazine on considerations other than their choice of participating in the contest. This practice not only distorted competition among publishers of magazines, but also deprived the participants of the benefit of other quality magazines available in the market (CUTS, 2001). Unrestrictive Trade Practices (UTPs) have, however, been put outside the ambit of the new Act.

Another dimension of choice is that, for marginalised consumers, it is restricted due to low purchasing power. From this perspective, lower prices of goods and services imply greater choice for these consumers. As mentioned above, sectoral regulatory policies with universal service obligations promote consumers' choice and increase accessibility.

9.2.4 Right to Redress

The competition authority, with adjudicative power, in any country is an essential component of the grievance redressal system. However, the MRTPC, due to its inefficiency, could not play this role effectively. Over the years, the number of cases pending with the MRTPC kept on growing. There is also a feeling that the MRTPC solved the cases that were less damaging for the consumers and the economy, whilst the relatively more damaging cases remained unattended.

One area where the MRTPC failed miserably is that of dealing with cartels. For example, it is widely believed that there are several cartels that run openly but yet MRTPC hardly did anything to break them. The cases concerning a cement cartel came twice before the MRTPC, but it was hardly equipped to handle the issue. Even in the vitamins cartel case, which was initiated by CUTS, the response of the MRTPC was anything but encouraging.

Nevertheless, it resolved several Restrictive Trade Practices (RTP) and UTP cases successfully. It is expected that the Competition Commission of India (CCI), under the new Act, would be able to do better in this regard. The Act also allows for class action and private action, so that ordinary consumers and consumer groups would be able to use the forum for the redressal of relevant grievances.

Under COPRA, a three-tier, simple, quasi-judicial machinery, at the national, state and district levels, has been established. The COPRA has been recently amended. The amendment, among other things, relates to the rights of complaint, rules of appointment of members, transfer of cases, monetary jurisdiction and enforcement. The amended Act also provides for attachment and subsequent sale of the property of a person not complying with an order. Proceeds from such sales may go to pay the damages of the aggrieved consumer.

Apart from the COPRA and MRTPA/Competition Act, 2002, redress mechanisms are incorporated under the Arbitration and Conciliation Act 1996, and through codes of business ethics. Moreover, some of the sectoral regulators also have redress mechanisms.

9.2.5 Right to Information

In economic theory, the existence of perfect information and its free flow among consumers is one of the basic requirements of perfect competition. A consumer without information about the product or service s/he purchases is as good as deaf and blind. Without information on quality, quantity, potency, purity, standard, and price of goods and services, consumers would not be able to make the right decisions. If consumers cannot make the right decisions, then the process of competition itself gets subverted.

The right to information, about the products and services in the market, is an important component of the MRTP Act as it has provisions for UTPs, including measures against misleading advertisements, which promote the right to information. Unfortunately, the new Act would not deal with such issues. Nevertheless, consumers need not worry as such issues will continue to be dealt with in different forums under COPRA. Voluntary mechanisms, like the Advertising Standards Council of India (ASCI) provide some checks and balances to information that is made available to consumers through advertising.

Simultaneously, consumers also need information on the functioning of government departments and the regulatory bodies that affect competition and consumer welfare. However, they had very little information about the functioning of the MRTPC, except for the occasional press coverage related to particular cases. MRTPC does not even have a website, whereas most competition authorities have well maintained websites. CUTS' experience in the vitamins cartel case is worth mentioning in this regard. CUTS collected some information about the case and passed it on to the Director General (Investigation & Registration) of MRTPC for further action (see Box 9.2).

BOX 9.2
The Vitamins Cartel and the MRTPC

Several leading and sophisticated drug manufacturers, of the world, have been involved in a global conspiracy to fix prices of bulk vitamins, sales volume and allocate markets. This international vitamin cartel continued from 1990 to 1999, and was investigated by the authorities in the US, EU, Australia, Canada, Japan, etc. Heavy fines were levied on the companies found to be guilty.

Subsidiaries of most of these companies are present in developing countries also, including India. The additional cost for developing countries, due to this cartel, is estimated to be US$ 3 bn.[1] Nevertheless, no competition authority from developing countries, except Brazil, has investigated or handled this case. The Indian experience is an example of this.

Keeping in view the international character of this cartel, it was obvious that it must also have had adverse effects in India. These companies, in all probability, would have been engaged in such practices in the country, either through direct sales or by way of exports. The estimated cost imposed by the cartel, on India, was about US $ 25mn, over the 1990s.

To find out more about this, CUTS decided to start a case. As a first step in this direction, all the relevant information on the case, accumulated by several authorities around the world, was collected from the internet and then documented. This information included details of the company, details of the investigation, the judgement and the balance sheets of some of these companies during the relevant period.

Letters were written to the CEOs of these companies in India asking them to give a written undertaking to the effect that they did not engage in any such anti-competitive practice in India. Responses were received from Hoffman La Roche and BASF India Ltd., stating that they have not engaged in such practices but no response came from Rhone Poulenc, which incidentally, was the approver in the US investigation and had escaped punishment.

Being a consumer organisation, CUTS had limited ability and hence it passed the collected information to the Director General Investigation & Registration) with a request for further investigation into the matter. The DG passed on the information to the MRTPC and became the 'complainant'. CUTS was given the status of 'informant'.

On direction of the MRTPC, the DG conducted a preliminary investigation and submitted its Preliminary Investigation Report (PIR). On the basis of the PIR, the MRTPC held that no case can be made and CUTS was informed accordingly. CUTS wanted to get a copy of the PIR in order to see what kind of investigation was done. But the DG said that the copy could be obtained only from the MRTPC, while the Commission said only the DG had the authority to issue it. This clearly showed the lack of awareness about the law in the competition authority. Finally, the case was heard in the court and it was held that the law clearly states that the informant does not have a right to get a copy of the PIR.

To conclude, the way the competition authority worked is very obvious. The kind of investigation done seems rather weak and no body knows what was actually done. The matter has come to an end as far as MRTPC is concerned but CUTS intends to get to the bottom of the matter, so that in future such type of difficulties do not exist.

Source: CUTS (2003), *Pulling Up Our Socks - A Study of Competition Regimes of Seven Developing Countries of Africa and Asia: The 7-Up Project*, CUTS, Jaipur.

Apparently, the Director General made some preliminary investigations on the matter and found that no case could be made. Unconvinced, CUTS wanted to get some details of the investigation, but was denied on the pretext that CUTS was merely an informant and not a complainant. Obviously, whatever its legal status in the case, CUTS was the initiator of the case, the denial of information shows a deprivation of the right to information.

The Parliament recently passed the Freedom of Information Bill, making it an Act. This law is expected to have far-reaching implications for the right to information of the consumer, and is expected to provide transparency, accountability and openness in functioning of the Government and the quasi-governmental bodies. It is expected to correct the curtailing of the consumers right to information, on some pretext or other.

9.2.6 Right to Consumer Education

This is an area that has been neglected in the MRTP Act. However, the new Act is a significant improvement in this regard. It is, indeed, fortunate that the new competition law provides for competition advocacy as one of its core areas of functioning. Under this the CCI will also need to do awareness generation and conduct training programmes for all stakeholders. Awareness on competition issues, amongst the stakeholders, including consumers and consumer organisations, is quite low while prevalence of anti-competitive practices is quite ubiquitous. Without proper education, these cannot be effectively tackled.

The Government of India, through the Consumer Welfare Fund, has the provision to fund consumer education programmes undertaken by consumer groups or the state governments. There is, however, enough scope for improvement in this regard. The media has also been playing an important role. Today, most of the leading Indian periodicals carry regular consumer columns, whilst television channels also have regular consumer programmes.

Some of the sectoral regulators also have consumer education programmes. They provide information to consumers through newspapers as well as electronic media.

9.2.7 Right to Representation

There is no formal mechanism to ensure consumer representation in the implementation of the Act, although consumer representation was done, while drafting of the Act, which had a significant impact in its drafting. Considering that the CCI will advise the Central Government on policy issues, when asked for, lack of a formal mechanism to ensure consumer participation is a considerable deficiency. The CCI has formed an informal advisory committee where consumer organisations, such as CUTS, are represented. Maybe this can be formalised.

The following are some of the mechanisms available in this country, through which individuals and civil society organisations can communicate their concerns to the Government:

- Parliamentary committees
- Committees on petition
- Representation through consumer organisations.

In order to facilitate the process of representation, the Government has set up different Committees of the Union Parliament, as well as representation mechanisms in various Departments. These are known as Standing Committees.

For effective representation by consumers, the Government has set up the Central Consumer Protection Council at the national level. This has legal sanction through COPRA. State Consumer Protection Councils are also required to be set up under COPRA. Some states have district level consumer protection councils as well.

Additionally, some sectoral regulators have arrangements for consumer representation, most notably in telecom and electricity. In electricity, there are state level regulators, as well with consumer representation in some states.

9.2.8 Right to Healthy Environment

Healthy competition promotes innovation. When firms engage in innovative ways of production/service provisions, it often leads to reduced resource consumption, as they have to produce at lower costs to be able to compete. Reduced resource consumption would lead to environmental gains.

The basic premise underlying competition policy, with regard to market-oriented solutions and environmental self-regulation, is that environmental goals will lead to the development of markets for new environmental activities. In that way, a climate of free competition will lead to efficient solutions for environmental problems. In other words, self-regulation may be able to make a better contribution to positive nvironmental performance, if the incentives provided by the market mechanism are ensured. The use of market-oriented instruments, such as levies and tradable emission rights, within environmental policy is the most direct way of interpreting the 'polluter pays' principle (OECD, 1996).

However, the effectiveness of the 'polluter pays' principle will be threatened if the operation of the market mechanism is hampered, or frustrated, through monopolisation or the restrictive practices of cartels. If enterprises can avoid the pressure of competition, they will feel less of a need to make a positive contribution to the environment, due to their ability to shift the costs of their environmental pollution onto others.

.3 Competition Law and Consumer Protection Law

The previous section has already provided a few instances of how the MRTP Act has dealt with anti-consumer practices that are normally dealt with under a Consumer Protection law. This is because MRTPA and COPRA have overlapping jurisdictions, especially in the area of unfair trade practices. There are also several instances where the forums established under the COPRA have dealt with competition or regulatory issues. Here are a few examples (Mehta, 1998):

- Two photo studios in a small village, in north India, were penalised and stopped from exploiting poor and illiterate consumers by cartelising and abusing their dominant position;

- A Bus transport company, in south India, was stopped from charging a higher fare than the government approved tariff rates on a particular route;

- In a class action against a big bank, the bank was ordered not to discriminate between rich and poor consumers, when providing service during a strike, and that it has to maintain a skeleton service at least.

The situation will, however, change once the new Competition Act comes into operation, as it does not have provisions for UTPs, except for situations where businesses are affected by such practices, who cannot seek redressal under the COPRA. A major concern that has been expressed, in this context, is that this will deprive the competition authority of the opportunity to have a good public buy-in, as UTPs are abundantly prevalent in day-to-day life. They also make headlines. Forums under COPRA may, nevertheless, continue dealing with competition and regulatory issues, as many of them have a strong consumer dimension.

9.4 Conclusion

The benefit to the consumers, from competition, depends on the efficient functioning of markets, which implies that markets should function without distortions i.e. competitive markets where everyone has the opportunity to participate. Nonetheless, 'competition' is often distorted by players in the market, even when there are large numbers of them. It is, therefore, important that a competition law is effective to curb distortions at all levels. It is, thus, obvious that the Competition Act may not bring the desired outcomes, if it is implemented only from Delhi or with some regional offices in addition, as there are anti-competitive practices that are prevalent at the grassroots level.

Forums under the COPRA have been dealing with such cases. Even so, this is not being done in a systematic way and, very often, the judgements depend on the subjective views of the chairpersons or the members concerned. One case of restrictive trade practice by a school in Vijaywada (Andhra Pradesh) relating to tied-sales in school uniforms was treated as an unfair trade practice by the District Forum, but it was later dismissed. It only showed the need to build the capacity of district forum members and chairpersons, so as to enhance their appreciation of the law. Such arrangements may be formalised through joint exercises by the Competition Commission of India and the consumer disputes redressal fora. State level competition and regulatory framework should also be considered, as local problems need local solutions. In both Australia and the USA, many provinces have state level competition laws.

As is the case of many other countries, business is well organised and resourced whilst consumers are unorganised and resource-constrained. This asymmetry might pose a challenge for effective implementation of the competition law, which promotes consumer welfare. Thus, it is absolutely essential to create and sustain a consumer movement, which will be well resourced and empowered to advocate consumer interests and competition culture, and spread the same through research, training, lobbying, information dissemination and networking. Moreover, competition advocacy would be more effective if consumer groups are closely involved in the process.

Notes

1. Clarke and Evenett (2002).

References

Clarke, Julian, and Simon J. Evenett (2002). *The Deterrent Effects of the National Anti-Cartel Laws: Evidence from the International Vitamins Cartel*, World Trade Institute.

CUTS (2001). *State of the Indian Consumer: Analyses of the Implementation of the United Nations Guidelines for Consumer Protection in India*, CUTS, Jaipur.

————. (2003). *Pulling Up Our Socks - A Study of Competition Regimes of Seven Developing Countries of Africa and Asia: The 7-Up Project*, CUTS, Jaipur.

Government of India (2003). "The Competition Act, 2002", *The Gazette of India* (Extraordinary), No. 12, January 14, New Delhi.

Mehta, Pradeep S. (1998). *How to Survive as a Consumer*, CUTS, Jaipur.

Mehta, Pradeep S. and Nitya Nanda (2004). "Competition Policy, Growth and Poverty Reduction in Developing Countries", paper presented at a conference on *Competition Policy, Competitiveness and Investment in a Global Economy: The Asian Experience*, May 19-21, Colombo, Sri Lanka.

OECD (1996). *Competition Policy and Environment*, OECD, Paris (OECD/ GD(96)22).

Simons, Joseph J. (2003). *FTC Initiatives in Intellectual Property*, presentation at the American Intellectual Property Law Association, Spring Meeting, May 15.

UNCTAD (2001). *United Nations Guidelines for Consumer Protection*, United Nations, New York & Geneva.

10 Competition Abuses at Consumer Level: Study of Select Sectors

Nitya Nanda • Bharath Jairaj

10.1 Introduction

The main objective of competition policy and law is to preserve and promote competition as a means to ensure efficient allocation of resources in an economy, resulting in the best possible choice of quality, the lowest prices, and adequate supplies to consumers. To put it differently, competition policy and law are used to bring fairness in the market, which finally benefits the consumers. However, consumers come in contact with providers of goods and services at millions of places spread over length and breadth of the country. While there may be adequate competition at the level of manufacturers, this may not be true of the distribution network, through which the goods pass to reach the consumers. Similarly, in several service sectors there are millions of providers operating at local level. Hence, monitoring and maintaining competition or ensuring competitive outcomes in such sectors becomes difficult and competition abuses become rampant at local level.

One such competition abuse is informal collusion at local level. For example, printing of maximum retail price (MRP) is mandatory under the Standards of Weights and Measures (Packaged Commodities) Rules, 1977. MRP includes sales tax and its rate varies across states. Hence, MRP is calculated by considering the highest tax rate charged by any state government. Furthermore, MRP is not necessarily the actual selling price and retailers are expected to sell at prices lower than MRP. However, in practice, retailers do not compete and MRP becomes the reference price for them to collude informally.

Another practice is tied-selling. This normally occurs when there is monopolistic dominance or general scarcity in the market for some goods or services. However, this can also occur even otherwise, if the market players act in collusion and all the players force such tied-selling.

The present study makes an attempt to understand the nature, extent and impact of tied selling in health care and education services. Often schools force the students to buy books, stationeries and uniforms from prescribed shops while the providers of health care services force the patients to buy medicines from prescribed shops or get diagnostic tests done from prescribed laboratories. The issue is, of course, not so simple. Consumers may feel that they are paying higher prices on tied goods and services, while the service providers have their own reasons like maintaining uniformity or quality, especially in health care sector where authenticity of medicines or reliability of diagnostic tests are a concern.

10.2 Methodology

Against this backdrop, CUTS took up a study of tied-selling practices in the provisioning of healthcare services and school education for further exploration. The selection was done on the basis of articulation by several grassroots consumer organisations with whom CUTS maintains a strong network. It was decided to carry out a survey of selected consumers and service providers in a group of cities. Apart from the five big cities of Delhi, Kolkata, Chennai, Bangalore and Mumbai, some smaller cities like Jaipur, Lucknow, Bhopal, Vijaywada and Sambalpur were also selected. Following are the different types of respondents and their numbers (in parentheses):

- Education service consumers (734)
- Education service providers (164)
- Health service consumers (769)
- Health service providers (172).

TABLE 10.1

Distribution of Respondents in Education Services

(As per cent of total respondents)

Type of Schools	Parents/Students going to	Service Providers
Government	27.79	24.39
Local authority	1.50	2.44
Private management	54.77	58.54
Charitable trust	6.13	7.93
Religious mission	9.26	6.71
Others	0.54	0.00
Total (number)	734	164

TABLE 10.2

Distribution of Respondents in Health Services

(As per cent of total respondents)

Type of Service Providers	Consumers Going to	Service Providers
Private allopathic doctor	76.46	63.74
Govt. hospital/health centre/clinic	12.61	15.20
Private hospital/nursing home/clinic	7.67	17.54
Traditional medical practioner (Ayurvedic, homeo, unani or any other system)	3.25	3.51
Total (number)	769	172

10.3 School Education: Tied-Selling of Books, Uniforms and Stationeries

The proportion of schools recommending or instructing the students to buy their books, stationeries and uniforms from a particular place is fairly high as about 31 per cent of the parents of school going children noted. This was more pronounced in Lucknow, Vijaywada and Chennai where the proportions of parents reporting such experience were 70, 56, and 51 per cent respectively. In all other cities the proportion was less than 50 per cent with Sambalpur reporting no such incident and Delhi being least affected among the other cities.

About 38 per cent of the people responded thought that the school authorities resort to such practices due to profit motives, while about 36 per cent thought it was for maintaining uniformity. About 22 per cent even thought, that the schools might be doing so to provide good quality services or making the items easily available to their students.

Regarding the prices charged in the recommended or instructed outlets, about 38 per cent thought that prices were higher than those in open markets and about the same percentage of people (38) thought they were just the same. About seven per cent even thought that the prices could be lower than in the markets.

TABLE 10.3

Motives of School Authorities

	Consumers	Service Providers on Own Motives	Service Providers on Other Service Providers' Motives
Profit motive	38.40	10.53	31.71
Good quality service	21.91	34.21	21.95
Maintaining uniformity	36.08	47.37	36.59
Relationship/friendship with the recommended/instructed place	1.29	2.63	1.63
Don't know	1.55	0	8.13
Other	0.77	5.26	0.00

There was, of course, a high 18 per cent of people who could not give their opinion on this.

TABLE 10.4

Perception on Price Variations

	Consumers	Service Providers on Own Prices	Service Providers on Others' Prices
Same as in the market	37.11	75.76	35.85
Higher than market	37.68	10.61	38.68
Lower than market	6.52	7.58	0.00
Don't know/can't say	18.70	6.06	25.47

When asked about the reasons for buying the items from the recommended outlets, about 36 per cent of the people said that it was compulsory and there was no other option. However, 42 per cent thought that they bought due to easy availability. About 12 per cent thought it was of better quality while the rest 10 per cent thought it was because of reasonable prices.

Interestingly, more than half of the parents (53%) thought that it was unjust and unethical on the part of the school authorities to require the students to buy their books, uniforms and stationeries from any particular outlets. On the other hand, about 23 per cent of the respondents did not find any problem with such practices. About 24 per cent of course could not give their opinion on this. It is also interesting to note that about 12 per cent of the respondents thought that there are laws to prohibit such practices while 34 per cent thought otherwise. Here, as high as 54 per cent of the respondents expressed their ignorance on the issue. As can be seen from the Table 10.5, people with higher income have relatively less problems with such practices from ethics or justice point of view. People with higher income are also less indecisive on this count.

TABLE 10.5

Views on Tied-Selling by Income Groups (Education)

	Lower	Lower Middle	Upper Middle	Higher
Ethical & Justified	12.78	18.22	27.00	36.33
Unethical & Unjust	60.44	54.78	59.11	38.33
Not sure	20.89	20.33	13.89	12.00

Interestingly, when the school authorities were asked about the existence of tied-selling of books, uniforms etc., a higher 38 per cent said that they followed such practices. However, almost half (47 per cent) of them argued that this is done to maintain uniformity, though about 34 per cent talked about quality and 11 per cent thought it was for profit motive. An overwhelming 76 per cent of them thought prices charged at the recommended/instructed places are same as in open market and only about 11 per cent thought they were higher. It is also interesting to note that all government schools claimed that the prices charged by them were same as in the market.

When they were asked about the existence of such practices in other schools, about 66 per cent said such practices do exist, 28 per cent saying they are very common and the rest saying that they exist in some schools. Interestingly, in this context, about 32 per cent think profit is the motive for such practices and for 22 per cent it was good quality, while about 37 per cent thought maintaining uniformity was the reason. Similarly, a significant 39 per cent said prices charged were higher and nobody said that prices were lower, though about 36 per cent said prices were the same. Thus, there are many schools who claim, "We are doing it to maintain quality and uniformity and are not charging higher prices but other schools are doing it for profit motive only". About half of them (52 per cent) also felt that such practice is neither justified nor ethical, while about 44 per cent thought it was not in conformity with the laws of the land.

10.4 Health Services

10.4.1 Tied-Selling of Medicines

Overall tied-selling of medicines was not found to be a major problem as only about 15 per cent of the respondents claimed that they have been asked to buy medicines from a particular shop. However, in some cities the situation seems to be against the trend. In Vijaywada this seems to have happened to about 52 per cent of the consumers. This was on the higher side at

Jaipur as well where about 40 per cent of the people interviewed happened to have such experience. On an average, those visiting private doctors or private hospitals reported a higher incidence of tied-selling of medicine. This was, however, not reflected in the responses of service providers who indicated that such practices may be equally prevalent in both public and private hospitals.

Nearly half of the people who were asked to buy medicines from a particular medicine shop found prices to be reasonable. However, this was not enough a reason to buy medicines from there and people mostly bought from a particular medicine shop to follow doctor's advice or not to annoy him/her. Interestingly, only less than two per cent of the consumers went against the advice of the doctors and bought medicines from some other shop. However, it should also be mentioned here that more than half of these people thought that there was the issue of better or genuine medicines and only about 37 per cent of them thought that doctors do so for profit motive.

TABLE 10.6

Motives Behind Tied-Selling of Medicines

	Consumers	Service Providers on Own Motives	Service Providers on Other Service Providers' Motives
Profit motive	36.98	5.26	35.29
Better/reliable/genuine medicines	52.94	84.21	47.06
Other considerations like friendship/relationship with the chemists' shop etc.	7.56	10.53	11.77
Other	2.52	0	5.88

FIGURE 10.1

Reasons for Accepting Tied-Selling of Medicines

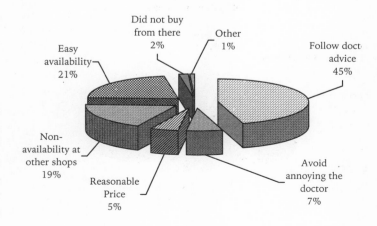

Did not buy from there 2%
Other 1%
Easy availability 21%
Follow doctor advice 45%
Non-availability at other shops 19%
Reasonable Price 5%
Avoid annoying the doctor 7%

When healthcare service providers were asked about tied-selling of medicines, only 11 per cent admitted that they ever resorted to such practices. And among them about 84 per cent argued that they do it to ensure genuine and reliable medicines for their patients. When asked about others resorting to such practices, the response was not much different as only 17 per cent responded in affirmative. However, a much higher, 35 per cent of them thought that the motive behind others resorting to such practice was profit or commission consideration.

10.4.2 Tied-Selling of Diagnostic Tests

In our sample of respondents, slightly more than half of the people were asked to undergo some diagnostic test. Among these people, about half were instructed by the doctors to undergo the test at a particular laboratory. Among those so advised, about 46 per cent were given verbal instruction while about 48 per cent were given written instruction and the rest were advised through nursing or other staff. As with the medicines, people visiting private doctors or private clinics reported higher incidence of tied-selling of diagnostic tests.

Among the people who went to the prescribed laboratory, more than half went simply to follow doctor's advice or not to annoy the doctor. A quarter of them cited better and reliable service as the reason. A section of these people, of course, might have been influenced by their doctors to think so. Slightly more than five per cent said the charge being reasonable was the reason, while for about 11 per cent it was easy accessibility. Just about two per cent of the people went against the advice of the doctor and got the testing done from a different laboratory.

It is, however, interesting to note that though about 35 per cent of people thought that profit motive on the part of the doctors could be the reason for prescribing a particular test centre, an overwhelming 55 per cent thought doctors advised so, to ensure reliable services. It is quite surprising to see that a higher percentage of consumers rather than service providers, think that tied-selling of diagnostic testing is done to ensure reliable testing. By and large people also seem to have confidence in the doctors *vis-à-vis* the desirability of the tests, as only about 16 per cent of them agreed with the view that doctors insist on too many tests.

TABLE 10.7

Motives Behind Tied-Selling of Diagnostic Testing

	Consumers	Service Providers on Own Motives	Service Providers on Other Service Providers' Motives
Profit motive	35.50	35.29	36.45
Better/reliable/genuine testing services	55.00	47.06	51.40
Other considerations like friendship/relationship with diagnostic centre etc.	5.50	11.76	10.28
Other	4.00	5.88	1.87

Interestingly, about 43 per cent of all the people interviewed thought such (tied-selling) practices by doctors are not ethical or justified. A high 30 per cent of course could not give their opinion on this, while about 21 per cent did not have any problem with such practices.

Regarding tied-selling of diagnostic tests, about 36 per cent of service providers admitted that they resort to such practices and 96 per cent of them argued that it was important to do so because of reliable testing services. More than half of them thought that other doctors/clinics do resort to such practices. However, in this context, a much higher, 36 per cent of the respondents thought profit or commission consideration was the main motive, though more than half held the view that reliable service was the main motive. About 40 per cent of the respondents believed that such practice was justified and ethical, while almost equal 42 per cent thought otherwise. About half of them thought it was not in conformity with the laws of the land.

Here also people with higher income have relatively less problems with such practices. This may be due to the fact that price differentials have less significance for rich people and easy availability of the goods and

FIGURE 10.2

Reasons for Accepting Tied-Selling of Diagnostic Tests

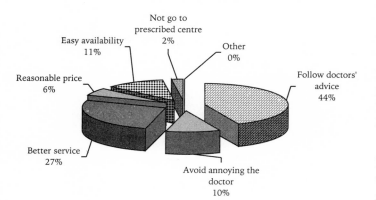

services are important for them. They might also feel that paying slightly more may be worthwhile if the doctors have more confidence in a particular shop or a test laboratory.

TABLE 10.8
Views on Tied-Selling by Income Groups (Health)

	Lower	Lower Middle	Upper Middle	Higher
Ethical & Justified	19.00	18.56	19.89	45.00
Unethical & Unjust	44.67	46.22	53.89	28.50
Not sure	36.00	33.89	26.22	21.50

10.5 Suggestions and Recommendations

Tied-selling is a genuine concern in both education and health services, as it comes out in the survey. However, the issue is far from being a simple one. Concerns of the school authorities of maintaining quality and uniformity cannot be ignored. It is also possible that schools can provide value-added services in this regard, for example, by making all the books and stationeries available under the same roof. School authorities, however, would do it better if they refrain from forcing the students to buy goods that are standardised and easily available in the market. However, it would not be easy for the Competition Commission of India (CCI) to monitor and regulate such practices that operate at micro levels. A way forward could be some guidelines by the state government authorities who regulate the functioning of the schools. The guidelines should ensure that, if at all, schools sell such items they should do that to provide value-added services rather than exploiting the students. Even the consumer forums can be encouraged to take up such cases to ensure that students are not exploited.

The issue is far more serious and complex in the health services sector. Quality of medicines and reliability of testing services are serious issues. Although there is regulatory framework to ensure genuine medicines in the market, there is significant scope for improvement in its enforcement. In the area of diagnostic testing, however, the regulatory framework is almost non-existent. It seems that the regulatory failure in one area can create difficulties in enforcing appropriate regulation in another area. Thus, before any serious attempt is made in removing tied-selling of testing services it would be important to put in place an appropriate regulatory framework to promote and maintain service standards in testing laboratories.

One thing that came out of the survey is that people with relatively lower income are more bothered about the anti-competitive practices that occur at grassroots level. The survey was done at major cities and some smaller ones. There are indications that such practices are more prevalent in smaller cities and towns. It would not be surprising if they were even more prevalent in smaller towns and rural areas. However, it is unlikely that the implementation mechanism envisaged in the Competition Act would be able to deal with such problems. Nevertheless, if the competition policy of the country is to be made pro-poor, such issues cannot be ignored and appropriate alternatives need to be explored.

Part IV

Competition Policy in Agriculture

11

Agriculture Markets in India: Implications For Competition

Ramesh Chand

11.1 Introduction

Markets are a key factor in influencing success/failure of efforts to improve the welfare of producers and consumers. If the marketing system were to be perfectly competitive and efficient, consumers' preferences would be passed on to producers without distortions, and commodities would move from the producer to ultimate consumers without any disruption and with least cost. The allocation of resources in competitive and efficient markets is such that aggregate welfare could not be further improved through reallocation of resources. In reality, this position is seriously compromised because state of perfect competition does not actually exist. This brings into focus the issue of competition and underscores the need to improve competition and efficiency of markets.

Agricultural markets in developing countries are invariably characterised by various imperfections and there is tremendous scope to improve competition and efficiency of such markets, which, in turn, contributes to net social welfare. This requires an in-depth understanding of the functioning of agricultural markets and various factors affecting competition and efficiency. This task is made more difficult by the fact that in developing countries agricultural markets are very complex because of their hierarchy, interlinked transactions, multiple functions and complex ownership.[1]

The present paper looks at the state of competition in agricultural markets. It discusses the functioning of agricultural markets and analyses the role of various factors related to competition, based on the survey of literature. The paper also suggests ways and means to improve market efficiency and welfare of producers and consumers.

11.2 State of Agricultural Marketing

Indian agriculture is dominated by small sized peasant cultivators, who undertake crop and livestock production on their own land, or land partly or wholly leased from other households. Except for cash enterprises, commodities produced on such farms are partly meant for family use, and the remaining part is exchanged. This surplus is disposed off in three ways: (a) direct sales to consumers; (b) sales in the village itself to merchants; and (c) sales in nearby markets. Sales in categories (a) and (b) are termed informal channels of marketing and sales under category (c) are termed as formal channels of marketing.

Markets for agricultural produce have expanded rapidly after Independence. Several factors have contributed to this. These are: increased production and commercialisation, development of communication and transport facilities, and the expansion of the market network. As the distance between market places and production points decreased, sales within villages fell sharply and proportion of the surplus sold in markets followed a sharp increase. This can be seen from the proportion of production that was spared for sale and the absolute magnitude of the marketed surplus of various commodities. Precise information about marketed surplus at country level is not available, but estimates of Marketed Surplus Ratio (MSR) derived from "Cost of Cultivation" data collected from major producing states under the auspices of Directorate of Economics and Statistics, Ministry of Agriculture, Government of India, are used as indicators of surplus. These estimates show that more than half the output of coarse cereals, 63.5 per cent of rice and 73.3 per cent of wheat produced in the country is disposed as marketed surplus by producers (Table 11.1). In the case of pulses, 77-90 per cent produce is meant for sale. The marketed surplus ratio for oilseeds is lowest for sunflower (61 per cent) and highest for soyabean (96 per cent). In the case of cash crops, like potato and sugarcane, more than 90 per cent of production reaches markets, while for jute and onion, almost entire production is sold.

TABLE 11.1

Marketed Surplus (MS) of Various Agricultural Commodities and its Share in Total Production, 1950-51 and 2001-02

Commodity	MS as Per cent of Output 1950-51	MS as Per cent of Output 2001-02	Surplus Quantity 2001-02: Lakh Tonnes
Rice	30.0	63.5	591.0
Wheat	30.0	73.3	526.7
Maize	24.0	51.6	68.7
Jowar	24.0	54.0	42.0
Bajra	27.0	56.9	47.5
Arhar	50.0	77.2	17.8
Gram	35.0	81.3	42.8
Lentil	55.0	89.9	8.4
Groundnut	68.3	68.4	49.3
Rapeseed/mustard	84.3	76.5	38.5
Soyabean	NA	95.8	56.1
Sunflower	NA	61.2	5.0
Sugarcane	100	91.8	2754.9
Cotton	100	86.9	14.9
Jute	100	100.0	21.0
Onion	NA	100.0	48.0
Potato	NA	91.1	219.3

These indicators of the Marketed Surplus Ratio show that the market orientation of Indian agriculture has become extensive in the recent period. Not even half of the production of major crops is retained for farm/household use and consumption. In other words, the share of subsistence production is much lower than the share of commercial production in Indian agriculture.

The size of the market for various commodities can be seen from the quantity of their marketed surplus presented in Table 11.1. The market size for wheat and rice exceeds five crore tonnes. Among coarse cereals, 68 lakh tonnes of maize, 47 lakh tonnes of *bajra* and 42 lakh tonnes of *jowar* are transacted between producers and buyers. Among pulses, gram ranks first with 42.8 lakh tonnes marketed surplus. The quantity of oilseeds sold by farmers during the year 2001-02 was of the order of 38.5 lakh tonnes for rapeseed/mustard, 49.3

lakh tonnes for groundnut and 56.1 lakh tonnes for soyabean. Among all crops, sugarcane comes at the top with marketed surplus of more than 27 crore tonnes. These indicators show the physical enormity of India's agricultural markets and the scope for commercial activity.

A comparison of recent and past estimates of MSR shows that except for cash crops, farmers had very small proportion of produce for sale in the market at the time of Independence (Table 11.1). The reasons included low production, poor infrastructure and the low level of monetisation of the rural economy. Besides poor infrastructure, the other reasons discouraging producers from bringing their produce for sale in the market place was the exploitation of producers in the market by various market functionaries. In order to put a check on such unhealthy practices and to get fair treatment for farmers, the government took steps to bring all agricultural markets under the purview of the Agricultural Produce Market Regulation Act (APMRA). These markets are called regulated markets and their principal objective is to safeguard the interest of producers and to raise the standard of local markets where exchange of agricultural goods takes place. This Act removed several practices that worked against farmers and introduced standard (codes) weights and measures, rationalised market charges; and specified methods for sale transaction; and market conduct to impart competition, efficiency and transparency into market. Further, the Act renders illegal any sale and purchase of agricultural produce outside the regulated (specified) market or market yard except where exemptions are granted. APMRA has been enacted in all the states except the states of Jammu and Kashmir, and Mizoram.

11.3 Role and Functioning of Markets

The main role of agricultural markets is the delivery of product from source to end-consumer and to provide price signals for resource allocation. This requires taking the produce from suppliers (producer farmers) to the ultimate users in the form and quality acceptable and demanded by end-users. This process involves several transactions and logistics in terms of purchase, movement, processing, storage, distribution (supply) and transfer of property rights from farm gate to the consumers. This would also involve price and contract formation. If markets undertake these activities in an efficient and effective way, producers and consumers receive fair treatment, i.e. producers get the worth of their produce and consumers get the worth of their money. However, farmers generally believe that they do not get due share for their produce and that intermediaries corner the share of the consumer's rupee. At the other end, consumers believe that they pay much more than what an efficient and competitive market would require. How can the situation be improved? In order to find an answer to this question, one needs to look at various activities/functions involved in the transfer of produce from the farm gate to consumers. A general illustration of this is given below, though there are several variations on it, depending upon the nature of commodity, the degree of commercialisation, etc.

11.3.1 First Stage

Marketable produce is transported from the farm gate to the market place, which involves cost of packing and transport. The produce is unloaded in the market and then cleaned and sometimes graded. Then an auction takes place, which determines the farm price. After this, the produce is weighed. The producer is paid sale proceeds after deducting (i) labour charges in the market for unloading, cleaning etc.; (ii) market charges like mandi tax etc.; and (iii) brokerage/commission etc. as levied in various states.

11.3.2 Second Stage

The sold produce is then packed, loaded and transported to the next destination. This way, over and above the price paid to producer sellers, the first buyer incurs costs like (i) labour charges in the market for weighing, packing, loading, etc.; (ii) market charges, taxes etc.; (iii) brokerage/commission etc., as levied in various states; and (iv) transport to the next destination, which may be a warehouse, processing mill or wholesaler/trader in another market.

11.3.3 Third Stage

The produce may pass through different market channels after stage two, depending upon whether it is processed, stored for sale in lean months, dispatched to consuming centres or sold locally. So, the costs incurred depend on the form, place and time the produce is taken to consumers. These costs would include cost of processing, storage, transport, packaging and services rendered for the produce. They also involve sales/transfers from one wholesaler to other, among traders etc. Each transaction, function and service adds to the price spread through the costs and margin of various functionaries involved in the movement of produce.

11.3.4 Fourth Stage

The retailer finally purchases the produce from the wholesaler/trader/processor, as the case may be, for sale to ultimate consumers. Again, various types of costs and margins accrue in the transfer of produce and its ownership to retailers. Finally, the retailer incurs some costs, sells the produce to ultimate consumers and retains his/her margin.

These illustrative stages of marketing of farm produce show that the difference between prices paid by consumers or retail price and prices received by producers or farm price, called price spread, consists of following components:

- costs on physical functions, services, material and labour,
- Statutory charges and taxes,
- gross margin of market intermediaries consisting of their cost and net margin,
- transport/storage/processing cost, and
- interest on working capital.

The level and magnitude of various elements of the price spread, in turn, depends upon competitiveness at each transaction, infrastructure, regulations, and institutional arrangements concerning marketing of farm produce. Likewise, the price received/paid to farmers depends upon competition in the market.

An important distinguishing feature of these stages of marketing is that in the beginning of first stage, dealing takes place between producer, having no influence on aggregate market supply, and agro-commercial firm. Similarly, at the end of the last stage of marketing, the small consumer, who exercises no control in the market, deals with an agro-commercial firm. In between these two points, transactions take place among agro-commercial firms who may control supply and price formation – depending on the market structure.

11.4 Price Formation in Primary Markets

The price for farm products for producers is determined in the primary market, where produce shifts hands from the farmer to the agro-commercial entity, like trader, wholesaler, miller etc. These markets satisfy some important conditions of competitive market, particularly on the sellers' side. There are large numbers of sellers. Farm product is produced/supplied by innumerable small producers, who do not have control over aggregate supply and market. This is, generally, not true on the buyer's side. Even if there are large numbers of buyers, competitive markets for farm produce may not exist. This can happen if a single buyer or a group of buyers exercise market power, or, if there is some sort of collusion among the buyers.

The bringing of agricultural markets under the purview of APMRA, and some other institutional interventions by government, have considerably diluted mercantile power in agricultural markets. But, empirical evidence shows that primary markets are still not perfectly competitive. A study based on sound methodology in a regulated market (in Panipat) in the agriculturally advanced state of Haryana found strong evidence of collusion in purchase of *Basmati* paddy/rice from producers (Banerji and Meenakshi, 2001). The authors conclude that relatively small number of buyers in India's grain market lend the price formation process open to manipulation through collusion. Another study in various markets in Coimbatore district observes that entry barriers range from being low (millets) to considerable (cotton), and price information was either secret, imperfectly available or open (Harris-White, 1996 p. 525). The study, however, also observes that structural conditions for competitive behaviour are propitious, as the number of traders was rapidly increasing. Research studies also indicate the common occurrence of excessive charges deducted from producers, and the under cover methods of sale in some markets.

Farmers often take credit from commission agents or traders to meet financial needs of the family and farm (Shepherd, 2004). This binds the farmers to sell their farm produce to or through a particular traders, and takes away the freedom to dispose off farm produce through any other avenue.

Because of the various factors, some of which are mentioned above, markets for sale of farm produce are not perfectly competitive. The situation can be improved by reducing structural concentration of traders and developing countervailing market power. The state has responded to this need in the past by putting in place market regulations and by providing alternative marketing avenues through cooperative marketing agencies and public agencies. The advantage accruing to farmers from the sale of produce through cooperative marketing channels has been revealed by some studies as shown in Table 11.2 and 11.3.

TABLE 11.2

Price Received by Farmers for Cotton in Warangal Market, Andhra Pradesh, from Sale to Various Agencies

Sale Agency	Price: Rupees/quintal
1. Sale to Commission Agent	710
2. Sale to Village Merchant	700
3. Sale to Trader	705
4. Sale to Cotton Corporation of India	792
5. Sale to Miller	785

Source: Krishanaih J. (1998). "An Empirical Analysis of Cotton Marketing in Warangal District of Andhra Pradesh", *Indian Journal of Agricultural Marketing*, 12(1 &3): 6-15.

TABLE 11.3

Price Received by Farmers for Oilseeds in Karnataka from Sale Through Different Market Channels

Oilseed	Coop. Marketing Channel	Private Channels
1. Net Price to Producer Rs./qtl.		
Groundnut	1130	1100 -1102
Sunflower	1183	1130- 1154
2. Producer's Share in Consumer's Rupee (%)		
Groundnut	81.58	79.36-79.56
Sunflower	83.74	79.97-81.45

Source: Mundinamani, S.M., H. Basavaraja and R.S. Poddar (1998). "Role of Farmers' Organisation in Oilseed Economy: A Case Study of Oilseeds Growers Cooperative," *Indian Journal of Agricultural Marketing*, 12(3): 68-80.

Besides providing better prices to producers, the main role of public/cooperative agencies is to improve competitive environment in the market by providing an institutional alternative to the market power of private traders.

11.5 Spatial and Inter-Temporal Market Equilibrium

After its purchase from the farmers, the agro-commercial firm takes the farm produce to consumers. Before reaching the consumers, the produce is transacted among various market functionaries from primary wholesaler to secondary wholesaler, from trader in one market to trader in another market, from wholesaler to processor and back to traders, and in several other ways. In this process the farm produce moves over space, time and form. The only reliable data available for the analysis of efficiency is confined to prices. Accordingly, researchers have examined competitiveness and efficiency in spatial markets over time and form, by analysing relationships between various price time-series and by drawing inference on market integration, independence and segregation. The results vary over commodities. In the case of wheat and paddy/rice, all the important wholesale markets across the country are generally found to be integrated (Jha *et al.*, 1997 and Wilson, 2001). Similarly, markets for rapeseed/mustard seed are becoming increasingly integrated whereas groundnut and *jowar* represent the contrast (Wilson, 2001). The implications of these findings are that in the case of major foodgrains (wheat and rice), markets at wholesale level are working well. In such cases, there should be no barrier to internal trade and government should supplement the operation of market mechanism. Spatial market integration also implies that smooth flow of produce from surplus to deficit region does not require government intervention in terms of procurement and open market sales.

The second approach to find presence or absence of competitive pricing conduct is by analysing the structure, conduct and performance of the markets. The application of this approach is seriously constrained by the complex structure and multiple functions of market functionaries in India (Harris-White 1995). Very large numbers of studies are published in the *"Indian Journal of Agricultural Marketing"*, which reports the marketing costs and net margins of market intermediaries. These studies often conclude that the various market intermediaries take away large and excessive shares of the consumer's rupee. These studies invariably fail to compare the net margin and cost with institutional or structural evaluation of competitive behaviour, which could provide a more sound and scientific evidence of the state of competition.

From the existing evidence about competition in the wholesale agricultural markets, it is concluded that: (a) markets are competitive for major commodities like wheat and rice/paddy, (b) there is lack of enough competition to result in market integration in the case of coarse cereals and some oilseeds, and (c) there is no consistent and authentic evidence for the presence or the absence of competition in large segments of wholesale agricultural markets in India.

11.6 Price Spread

Price spread consists of cost of (i) material and services and net margin of various market functionaries involved in transfer of produce from producers to the ultimate consumers and (ii) taxes and Statutory charges. Wastage and loss of produce during marketing also adds to the price spread. Other things being equal, the price spread varies from commodity to commodity and according to services rendered on the commodity. Over time, the demand for services on produce increases at a faster rate than the demand for the produce itself. Demand for properly cleaned, well packaged products, pre-cooked and ready-made foods results in a higher share for the service components. Because of this, the producer's share in the consumer's rupee is bound to fall. This may not imply a lowering of price for farm produce; rather it may help to improve the price realised by farmers.

Similarly, the farmers' share in the consumer's rupee declines as the produce is sold to distant consumers. This may not necessarily imply that the absolute price received by farmers is lower. This can be seen from the

TABLE 11.4

Price Spread and Farm and Retail Prices of Alphonso Mangoes in Different Market Channels in Maharashtra

Particulars	Producer-Consumer (Local Market): I	Producer-Wholesaler/C.A.-Retailer-Consumer Mumbai: II	Producer-Cooperative-Consumer Mumbai: III
1. Net price received by growers Rs./crate	161.27	182.00	264.00
2. Producer share in consumer rupee (%)	99.25	40.00	74.37
3. Net margin of wholesaler/Commission Agent		92.43	
4. Net margin of retailer		104.79	
5. Net margin of cooperative			37.77
6. Total marketing cost	0.73	75.78	53.23
7. Price spread	0.73	273.00	91.00
8. Price paid by consumer	162.00	455.00	355.00

Source: Wadkar S.S., J. M. Talathi and R.G. Thakare (1994). Price Spread and Market Channels of Alphonso Mango in Ratnagiri and Sindhudurg Districts in Maharashtra, *Indian Journal of Agricultural Marketing*, 8(2): 250-257.

actual experience presented in Table 11.4. When farmers sell mangoes in nearby local markets directly to consumers, they get almost 100 per cent of price paid by consumers as there is hardly any price spread. When the same produce is sold in the market through the wholesaler, who transports it to Mumbai, the growers get a mere 40 per cent of the price paid by the consumers. But this channel gives the growers 13 per cent higher price than that received through direct sale to consumers. Longer marketing channels, which sell produce where it gets a higher price, bring better return to farmers even with a large price spread and a lower share in the consumer's rupee. The third channel represents the evidence in which the price spread is lower than the second channel but both producers and consumers are better off than in the second channel. The reason is that in this channel mango is marketed by a cooperative agency, which retains a very small margin.

Some important inferences follow from Table 11.4. First, the price spread and producer's share in consumer's rupee are very crude indicators of market conduct and performance, price realised by farmers and price paid by consumers. Only when spatial and temporal situations are same, then the price spread can be used to compare the efficiency of various marketing channels and their advantage to producers. Second, in this case, marketing through a cooperative agency, which provides an alternative to private trade, improves competitiveness in the market and benefits both consumers and producers.

The magnitude of the various components of the price spread depends on competition in the market, on regulation and its implementation and on technical efficiency of various market functions like packing, grading, transportation, storage, processing etc. The greater the competition in the market, the lower would be the net margins and mark-ups of market functionaries and lower would be the cost of market services and functions. Several commodities produced in India lose their competitive edge to other countries due to the high cost of marketing, processing and transport (Chand, 2002). There is much scope to improve the technical efficiency of various market functions by modernising market infrastructure, which, in turn, would improve consumers' welfare. There are frequent violations of market regulation to charge excessive rates for various market functions. In some cases in grain market, labour unions dictate produce handling charges and do not permit competitive rates.

India's road transport system, which is the major mode for movement of agricultural commodities for private trade, is far from being competitive and efficient. There are strong unions of truckers and tempo operators in almost all towns and markets, who decide the freight rates and other terms and conditions, with no respect for competition. Then, there are regulations still in operation governing the movement of various goods and multiple checkpoints, which are used less to ensure compliance but more for causing harassment and rent seeking. The net result is that the movement of goods by surface transport turns out to be very costly. Table 11.5 provides some information on domestic and overseas freight charges to demonstrate how poor transport facilities can render imports more attractive than domestic production.

Statutory charges in the market, like purchase tax, commission of agent, *mandi* tax, etc. are an important component of the price spread. In some states, like Punjab and Haryana, these charges add up to a whopping 10-14 per cent of the price paid to producers and substantially raise the cost of produce in the first transaction itself. There is a lot of concern about the desirability and rate of some of these Statutory charges. It is argued that the service provided by agricultural markets does not match the heavy marketing charges and these charges need to be curtailed to reduce the price spread and ultimately the burden on the consumer.

TABLE 11.5

Comparison of Domestic Transport Cost of Grain With Oceanic Freight Charges: Rs./Tonne

Mode/Year	From	To	Rate
Truck/Mid-2000	Punjab	Mumbai	1915
	Punjab	Andhra Pradesh	2610
	Punjab	West Bengal	2470
	Delhi	Mumbai	1210
	Delhi	Andhra Pradesh	2278
	Delhi	West Bengal	1611
Ship/2000	Europe	India	1365
	US Ports	India	1886
	Australia	India	1000
	Bangkok	India	534
Railway/for FCI 1999	Punjab	Mumbai	800
	Punjab	Andhra Pradesh	878
	Punjab	Kerala	1202
	Punjab	West Bengal	792
	Delhi	Mumbai	684
	Delhi	Andhra Pradesh	814
	Delhi	Kerala	1176
	Delhi	West Bengal	675

Source: Chand, Ramesh (2002). *Trade Liberalisation, WTO and Indian Agriculture: Experience and Prospects*, Mittal Publications, New Delhi, Ch.5

11.7 Retail Prices

The formation of retail prices completes the marketing process. Here again, business firm transacts with non-business entity, i.e. consumers. There are a couple of similarities between the first transaction (farmers and agro commercial firm) and the last transaction (transfer of produce from retailers to consumers). In the first transaction, the supply side represents perfect competition, as there are numerous small sellers, each having no influence on market supply. In the last stage, demand-side represents perfect competition, as there are a very large number of consumers, and a single consumer has no influence on total demand. Like producers, consumers are even more unorganised. There is evidence of market power of buyers in the first stage. In the last stage, at retail level, there are also instances of market imperfections, collusion among sellers and exploitation of consumers.

In the case of cereals, pulses and edible oils, retailers do not display quality information about the produce. Consumers are fleeced through various kinds of adulterations. In the case of fruits and vegetables, neither the shops nor the hawkers typically display the price list. These retailers charge prices from each consumer based on his/her willingness to pay, and, in the process, extract as much consumer surplus as they can, rather than charging uniform and competitive prices.

A consequence of poor competitiveness in agricultural markets is that prices are not vertically integrated. When there is industry concentration beyond the farm gate, then middlemen use market power to employ pricing strategies, which result in the complete and rapid transmission of increase in farm prices to retail prices, but slower and less complete transmission of decrease in farm prices (Kinnucan and Forker, 1987), resulting in strong asymmetry between wholesale and retail prices. Such asymmetry generally increases with the number of intermediaries (Peltzman, 2000) and with uncertainty caused by government intervention in farm level or wholesale prices (Kinnucan and Forker, 2000; and Jha and Nagarajan, 2002). It has been empirically found in the case of rice markets in India that the average speed of adjustment is three times slower when the price declines, as opposed to a price increase, and that open market operations at the wholesale level do not reduce significantly the extent of asymmetry at retail level (Jha and Nagarajan, 2002).

In order to improve competition at retail level and to benefit consumers and producers, some innovative marketing mechanisms have been developed in some states. These involve direct sale of farm produce to consumers. They include *Apni Mandi* in Punjab and Haryana, *Rythu Bazaar* in Andhra Pradesh and *Uzavaar Sandies* in Tamil Nadu. Under these arrangements, farmers are allowed to sell their produce as retail to consumers in the towns on selected days and time, without intermediaries. The scale of operation of these marketing arrangements is quite low, as only farmers located in the vicinity of big towns can take an interest in this form of marketing. One such case showing the price benefit to producers and consumers, over commercial marketing channels, is shown in Table 11.6.

TABLE 11.6

Price Received by Producers and Price Paid by Consumers through Commercial Marketing Channels and *Rythu Bazaar*, for Vegetables in Vishakhapattnam

Vegetable	Price Received by Producer in Two Channels: Rs./Kg.		Gain to Producers from Rythu Bazaar Rs./Kg.	Average Price Paid by Consumer: Rs./Kg.		Gain to Consumers from Rythu Bazaar Rs./Kg.
	Wholesaler-Retailer	Rythu Bazaar		Retail Market	Rythu Bazaar	
Potatoes	3.80	5.32	1.52	5.36	5.32	0.04
Onion	3.80	4.50	0.70	5.45	4.50	0.95
Tomatoes	2.80	4.10	1.30	4.25	4.10	0.15
Brinjal white	2.70	5.00	2.30	5.54	5.00	0.54
Brinjal violet	2.60	3.70	1.10	4.70	3.70	1.00
Cabbage	1.25	3.00	1.75	3.40	3.00	0.40
Green chillies	6.80	9.45	2.65	10.20	9.45	0.75
Carrot	5.00	7.09	2.09	8.90	7.09	1.81
Gherkin	2.30	3.82	1.52	4.30	3.82	0.48
Beetroot	2.70	4.78	2.08	6.90	4.78	2.12

Source of Basic Data: Durga C. (1999). "Public Intervention in the Marketing of Vegetables: The Case of Rythu Bazar in Visakhapatnam," *Indian Journal of Agricultural Marketing*, 13(2):137-143.

11.8 Marketing of Livestock Products

Livestock products cover a wide range of products, like milk, meat, wool, eggs etc. Among these, milk is the most important product and dairy accounts for about two-third of the value of total output of livestock. Marketing of milk is totally different from that of crops. There are three major channels in milk marketing. One, milk collected from producers by private vendors who then sell it in the nearby towns to consumer households or to shopkeepers. Two, milk collected by milk producers' cooperatives for further disposal/processing by cooperative milk plants. Three, milk collected by private milk plants or their agents under a contract with milk producers. Both, cooperatives as well as private milk plants, pay the price to farmers based on the fat content in the milk.

Competitiveness in price received for milk by the producers depends mainly on two factors. One, connectivity to motorable road or rail line, which integrates production point to consumption/demand point; and two, competition among the buyers.

Milk Cooperatives, especially the Anand cooperative set up under Operation Flood, have played a laudable role in milk marketing and processing. They have a vast network exceeding 73,000 cooperatives in large parts of the country. Favourable impact of dairy co-operatives on the rural economy and prices received by producers has been documented by several studies (Singh, 1996). Though cooperatives have played an impressive role in milk marketing for a long time, there were several restrictions on the private sector to establish milk plants, particularly in the areas covered by the cooperatives and known as milk sheds. In order to encourage the private sector to enter into dairy production, the Government of India scrapped the Milk and Milk Product Order in April 2002. This would promote competition in milk procurement in the country.

11.9 State Intervention in Agricultural Markets

The state has been intervening in agricultural markets for decades in various ways to improve the efficiency of markets and to ensure remunerative prices to farmers and reasonable prices to consumers. This intervention is of three types. First, framing of rules and regulations for the smooth functioning of markets and the protection of certain interest groups. Second, provisioning of physical and institutional infrastructure. Third, administration of prices.

11.10 Statutory Regulations and Legal Provisions

The most significant of these interventions is bringing agricultural markets under public control by establishing regulated markets in the country and passing of various acts governing movement, storage, processing, sale/purchase of farm produce. All transactions, and conduct of regulated market is guided by provisions of Agricultural Produce Market Regulation Act, which has been amended from time to time. The Act was meant to remove numerous malpractices involving exploitation of producers in the market.

APMRA mandates that the sale/purchase of notified agricultural commodities be carried out in the market area, yards or sub-yards as per the provisions of the Act. Every regulated market has a market committee called the Agricultural Produce Market Committee consisting of representatives of farmers, traders, commission agents, local bodies and the state government. Administrative staff, comprising Market Secretary and auction supervisors, looks after the day-to-day operations of the market committees.

Prices in regulated markets are fixed by open auction in a transparent manner, in the presence of an official of the market committee. Market charges, like commission of the agent, labour charges for cleaning of produce, market fee etc., are clearly defined, and therefore, no other deduction can be made from the sale proceeds of farm producers. Sub-committee of market committee settles any dispute regarding prices or sale transaction. Market charges vary from state to state, and for horticultural and other produce.

Establishment of regulated markets is, in general, found to improve functioning of assembly markets for agricultural produce (Acharya, 1985, 1988; Suryawanshi, 1995). Market regulation is observed to result in an increase in the number of producers bringing their produce to market, reduction in exploitation of weak farmers and higher price for producers (Kahlon and George, 1985, p. 26). However, there are regional differences in the performance of regulated markets. Traditional non-regulatory systems are still found useful and relevant in some states like West Bengal, Bihar and Orissa (Maheshwari, 1998). Of late, some weaknesses of regulated markets have been brought to light. Maheshwari reported the decline in ratio of market arrivals to production in regulated markets in several states during 1983 to 1992, based on which she concluded that market regulation has not brought about any significant change in the marketing channels of rice in various states. The reason for this could be evasion of taxes in the regulated markets. There are also concerns about the use of resources mobilised in regulated markets through market fee from traders and producers for development of market facilities.

Experience in some states, especially in agriculturally less-developed regions, shows that mere regulation does not help to improve market performance if adequate infrastructure is not there. It is reported that one-third of regulated markets in the country do not have a common auction platform. Infrastructure for marketing of perishables like fruits and vegetables, which require special facilities like storage and processing, is awfully inadequate. Based on a survey of studies on agricultural marketing, it is concluded that market regulation is a necessary, but not sufficient, condition for effective competition and for ensuring producer's interest (Rao, 1989 p. 16).

The strongest criticism of APMRA is that it granted marketing monopoly to the state, prevented private investments in agricultural market and restricted the farmer from entering into direct contact with any processor/manufacturer/bulk processor, as the produce is required to be canalised through regulated markets (Inter Ministerial Task Force, 2002). Some provisions of this Act, like purchase rights confined to licensed traders, have prevented new entrants and thus reduced competition. Because of these reasons, the Inter Ministerial Task Force on Agricultural Marketing Reforms (2002) recommended that the APMC Act be amended to allow for direct marketing and for establishment of agricultural markets in the private and cooperative sectors (GoI, 2002). The rationale behind direct marketing is that farmers should be able to sell their produce directly to agribusiness firms, like processors or bulk buyers, at lower transaction cost and in the quality/form as required by the buyers. In response to this, the Ministry of Agriculture, in 2003, prepared a new Model Act for agricultural produce marketing, which can be used by state governments to prepare their individual act. Under the Model Act, the private sector can be licensed to set up market places. The Model Act also allows for contract farming and direct marketing by private trade.

The private sector does not seem to be enthused by the model APMC Act, as it is felt that the Act retains significant government control over agricultural markets. Similarly, the Model Act is said to only generalise the direct buying and contract farming, for which provision is already there under the existing APMC Act.

Anyhow, the Model APMC Act, prepared by the Ministry of Agriculture, GoI, is only a template to persuade various states to change their existing APMC Act. Ultimately it falls on states to frame appropriate APMC acts. Some states in India have taken the initiative in this direction and have amended the regulation to provide for the establishment of agricultural produce markets to be owned and managed by an organisation or corporate body. Accordingly, a national level cooperative agency, the National Dairy Development Board (NDDB), which of late has successfully established forward contract with vegetable and fruit growers, has established an integrated facility for marketing of agricultural produce in Bangalore. This experience is worth emulating at a large scale.

11.10.1 Legal Instruments

Legal instruments are used to regulate market conduct to safeguard the interest of producers and consumers and to raise the standard of agricultural markets. These instruments are put in force and revised from time to time by central and state governments. The most important regulations are the Essential Commodities Act 1955 (ECA), enacted by the Central government, and the Agricultural Produce Market Regulation Act, enacted by the states.

In order to encourage quality and to promote consumers' confidence in agricultural products, another act, known as the Agricultural Produce Grading and Marketing Act (AGMARK), was passed in 1937. It defines standards of quality and prescribes grade specifications with regard to scheduled products. The Act authorises Agricultural Marketing Advisors in each state to grant certificate of authorisation to persons or corporate bodies that agree to grade agricultural produce as prescribed under the Act to use AGMARK grading. The AGMARK grade specifications have been prescribed for about 123 agricultural products, but the use and awareness about AGMARK has remained quite low, despite rising awareness about quality attributes among consumers.

The Essential Commodities Act applies to any commodity declared as essential by the Central Government. Almost all agricultural commodities, like cereals, pulses, edible oilseeds, oilcakes, edible oils, raw cotton, sugar, *gur*, jute are included in the list of essential commodities. The Act provides for instruments like licenses, permits, regulations and orders for price control, storage, stocking limits, the movement of produce, distribution, disposal, sales, compulsory purchase by government and sale (levy) to government. The Central Government and state governments, under the ECA, have put a very large number of control orders into force. Apart from the ECA and the APMRA of various states, several other legal instruments are used to regulate activities of market functionaries.

The main aims of various regulations were (a) to keep a check on exploitation of producers and consumers by private trade through collusion, hoarding etc., (b) price stabilisation, and (c) to raise standards of markets and to improve market performance. Lot of changes have taken place in marketing and trade environment since these regulations were framed. Development of transport and communication network, expansion of marketing and increased competition in economic activities have facilitated the increased role of the private sector in agricultural marketing. A feeling has emerged that numerous regulations have led to an excessive control and intervention by government, which are hampering the participation of private trade in agricultural marketing and are proving counter-productive. In order to increase the participation of the private sector in agricultural marketing, some changes have been made in the ECA to remove the requirement of licensing of dealers and restrictions on storage and movement of foodgrains, sugar, oilseeds and edible oils. Similarly, the Sugar Control Order and the Milk and Milk Product Order have also been amended to allow more freedom and increased participation by the private sector in marketing of these commodities.

11.11 Price Administration

The principal components of price administration during the last four decades have been the following:

- Price support and procurement
- Maintenance of buffer stock and operational stock
- Public distribution system
- Open market operations.

The system of minimum support prices (MSPs) was started in 1965 to provide a remunerative price environment to farmers to encourage them to adopt new high-yield varieties (HYVs) of wheat and paddy and to invest in modern inputs. Over time, the commodities covered under minimum support price have been expanded to include paddy (rice), wheat, sorghum, pearl millet, finger millet, maize, *ragi*, barley, gram, pigeon pea, *moong*, *urad*, *tur*, rapeseed/mustard, *toria*, groundnut, sunflower, soybean, sesame, niger seed, cotton, jute,

copra and tobacco, while sugarcane is covered under Statutory minimum price.

MSPs have been very effectively implemented for some crops, and in some regions through procurement of produce by official agencies. These include procurement of paddy and wheat by Food Corporation of India (FCI) and other official agencies in the states/ regions, which were early adopters of green revolution and offered a sizable marketed surplus, like Punjab, Haryana, Western Uttar Pradesh, Andhra Pradesh, Tamil Nadu, and some parts of Rajasthan and Madhya Pradesh. Guaranteed prices have also been implemented in the case of sugarcane by according statutory status to the MSP, under which sugar factories have to pay the price recommended by government. Besides serving the purpose of MSP, the procurement of rice and wheat is also undertaken to maintain a buffer stock for inter-year price stability and to maintain an operational stock for the public distribution system. While wheat is directly procured by FCI and other public agencies, part of rice is procured through the system of levy, under which rice millers are required to provide a certain per cent of rice from the paddy purchased by them to the government agencies at a levy price derived from MSP.

The state maintains a buffer stock of rice and wheat to guard against the adverse impact of year-to-year fluctuations in domestic output on price stability and food security. Foodgrains procured by government are used in three ways. First, to meet a part of the requirement of the people, through the public distribution system at a subsidised rate. The public granary is also used for social welfare works and schemes. Second, for open market sales to stabilise prices. And third, for exports.

These interventions have served the important purposes of improving food security, maintaining price stability and the creation of favourable pricing environments, particularly for foodgrains in major surplus states. Of late, these interventions have come under severe criticism. MSPs are found to have served only a particular region and most of the crops and states could not benefit from them (Chand, 2003a). Government procurement has created a perverse environment for the private sector to avoid buying from farmers and to prefer buying from government stock, which is causing an excessive burden of stock and food subsidies. MSPs that ignore demand-side factors have also caused adverse impacts on food security (Chand, 2003b). Interventions in recent years have been found to cause an adverse impact on the overall GDP and consumer welfare, particularly of the poor (Parikh, *et al.*

2003). The government's procurement, distribution, and buffer stocking programmes are reported to have had negative impact of repressing private foodgrain marketing, and undercutting its potential contribution to long term food security (World Bank, 1999). This is further said to discourage modernisation of marketing resulting into losses and inefficiencies. Uncertainty about government intervention in grain markets, in terms of procurement and open market sales, in some cases results in hoarding by private trade (Jha and Nagarajan, 1998). The World Bank study (1999) proposes that government should use regulatory mechanisms only when price movements are outside the desired price-band representing width between the ceiling and floor price, which permits reasonable marketing margin for profitable public sector operations.

11.12 Market Infrastructure

Infrastructure is a key factor for performance and in improving the efficiency of any system. Marketing infrastructure involves physical and institutional infrastructure. The foremost marketing infrastructure is a network of well-established and regulated markets. There were around 1000 regulated markets in India at the beginning of the green revolution period, i.e. in 1966. Since then the number of regulated agricultural produce markets has risen to 7161. In total, there are 7293 wholesale assembling markets in India. This expansion of markets has greatly reduced the distance between production points and market places and also resulted in a vast expansion in space for market transactions needed to accommodate the increase in market supply, due to production growth and increase in proportion of marketed output in total output. At present, there is one regulated market per 459 sq. km area on the average.

Proper storage is necessary to maintain quality and to provide protection against losses from moisture ingress, insect-pest infestation and damage by rodents. Storage is of two types. First is warehousing, which is used for keeping the bulk produce of non-perishable commodities like foodgrains, oilseeds, cotton etc. Information about warehouse capacity is available only for public sector agencies like Food Corporation of India, Central Warehousing Corporation (CWC) and State Warehousing Corporation (SWC). These three agencies have the capacity for storing 28, 9 and 20 million tonnes respectively.

The second type is cold storage, meant primarily for perishable and semi-perishable commodities. Cold storage facilities were meagre till mid-1960s – 615 units

with a capacity of 6.82 lakh tonnes. According to recent estimates, there are now about 4200 units in the country, with a capacity for storing 153.85 lakh tonnes of agricultural produce. Out of this, 95 per cent capacity is owned by the private sector.

With rising incomes, standards of living and shifts in tastes and preferences, most of the products are demanded throughout the year, even though the demand is uneven. Per capita demand for perishables like fruits, vegetables and livestock products is also rising. These changes in demand require an accelerated increase in the development of cold storage infrastructure. The National Horticulture Board is providing assistance under a central scheme for the construction/renovation of cold storages in the country.

Road connectivity plays a crucial role in connecting production points with markets, through speedy and efficient movement of produce. Emphasis was placed on constructing good quality roads in the country. Length of surfaced roads has increased from 3.38 lakh km. in 1971 to 13.94 lakh km. in 1997.

Physical infrastructure alone is not adequate to improve marketing performance; it needs to be supported by appropriate institutional infrastructure to meet the desired goals from the agricultural marketing system.

11.13 Forward Trading

Widely divergent views exist on the effects of futures trading in agricultural commodities. Some believe that futures trading reduces price variations and stabilises prices, whereas others vigorously allege that more often than not futures trading aggravates the price trends and increases price variation (Acharya and Agarwal, 1999 p. 156). Till recently, futures trading in India was allowed only in a few commodities, but now it is extended to include almost all oilseeds, oil and cakes, rice, wheat, sugar, *gur*, cotton, *kapas*, gram, potato, *guar* seed, jute and spices. It is expected that forward trading and futures markets would benefit through price discovery and risk management and help in reducing the variation between farm harvest and lean season prices. If futures market helps in achieving this goal, it would benefit both the producers as well as consumers.

11.14 Policy Suggestions and Recommendations

During the last decade the economic and policy environment in India has undergone significant changes, mainly due to new economic policy and reforms started in 1991, and domestic and global liberalisation. This has raised new kinds of issues in agricultural markets and necessitated changes in existing regulations and the system. There is a strong and urgent need to increase private sector participation in agricultural marketing.

There are also serious concerns relating to regional and crop-wise benefits of MSPs. Government intervention, in the form of remunerative prices, needs to be extended to hitherto neglected agriculturally underdeveloped regions, which have a vast unexploited potential for agricultural growth. This would help in transferring technological gains to consumers.

Of late, government intervention in foodgrain markets has been goofed up, which has caused adverse effects on consumers, private trade, regional equity and efficiency, besides increasing the heavy burden of food subsidy on the state exchequer. The level of MSPs should take into account demand-side factors such that prices are not distorted to cause adverse effects on consumers, and there are incentives for private trade to operate in the market. Government intervention should be restricted to regulatory mechanisms only when price movements are outside the desired price-band representing width between the ceiling and floor price, which permits reasonable marketing margin for profitable private sector operations.

Consumer prices are not vertically integrated to wholesale and farm-level prices and there is asymmetric price transmission. Decline in farm prices is passed on to consumers very slowly and to a smaller extent. Lack of competition or concentration of market power and market uncertainty due to factors like government intervention are the main causes for this, despite decades of intervention intended to improve competition.

The functioning of agricultural markets shows that markets for large number of commodities are competitive in the segment where agro commercial firms are involved in transactions with other similar firms. Markets are less competitive where business firms are dealing with consumers and producers. This is reflected in collusive behaviour of the buyers and imperfections at retail level. This calls for improving competition in agricultural markets, particularly at farm and retail level. Alternative avenues for sale and purchase through cooperative marketing agencies are found to dilute market power of private trade to some extent. Besides cooperative agencies, removing all kind of restrictions on entry of private firms at various levels

of agricultural marketing, particularly in purchase of farm produce, would help improving competition.

Legal provisions, like Essential Commodities Act (ECA), restrict the participation of the private sector. Such legal provisions were relevant to check hoardings and other exploitative practices when there were scarcities and markets were segmented. With improved availability of various commodities and the development of communication and transport network, markets are getting spatially and temporally integrated. This environment is conducive for expanding business enterprise and promoting competition. This can be achieved by removing various obstacles in conducting business in agricultural produce.

Under the present Agricultural Produce Market Act in India, state governments alone are empowered to initiate the process of setting up of regulated agricultural markets. This prohibits the private sector from taking any initiative in setting up a modern market infrastructure that requires high investments, entrepreneurial skills, and managerial capacities. The provisions of the APMC Act need modification to facilitate the private sector and cooperatives to establish agricultural markets.

The main reason for high charges and lack of competition in agricultural markets seems to be that small local players dominate the market. Though their number is large, that does not improve market efficiency. Due to the large number and small operations, these players require large margins and cannot take advantage of scale economies. There is a need to attract big businesses to invest and operate in agriculture markets in bulk buying and selling. This would impart scale advantage that would help in getting a better deal for consumers and producers.

Contract farming is being promoted in several parts of the country to raise income of farmers through production of high value crops, better marketing opportunities, and scale advantages. In several cases, the contracting firm wants to directly procure the produce from farmers. Be that as it may, in most of the states and in most agricultural commodities, these direct sales are illegal as the produce is required to be sold only in the notified market area. In such cases, changes in legislation are needed to take full benefit of contract farming. This would reduce market costs and increase returns to farmers.

In some states, taxes and charges on agricultural produce are quite high. There are reports that to avoid these market charges, produce is diverted without entering into regulated markets. These charges need to be rationalised and should commensurate with the services rendered in the market.

There is considerable scope to reduce the price spread by improving transport and processing facilities. Similarly, increased participation of the private sector in agricultural marketing is needed to promote competition. This requires removal of restrictions, like licensing etc. and a favourable regulatory and legal environment for private enterprises in agriculture. Government interventions in influencing market prices that distort demand and supply equilibria or create uncertainties vastly dampen private sector participation in the market, which ultimately hurts consumers.

There is no effective regulation at retail level of agricultural commodities. Quality and price aspects are hardly displayed. Retailers charge prices from each consumer based on his/her willingness to pay and in the process extract as much consumer surplus as they can, rather than charging uniform and competitive prices. There is a need to frame and implement regulations providing complete information about product quality and prices to consumers through visual display. In order to provide more competition at retail level and to benefit consumers and producers alike, innovative marketing mechanisms, like *apni mandi* and producers' sales counters, in consumer centres should be promoted.

Notes

1. According to a study in South India, agro commercial firms can produce, buy, sell, act as a broker, store, transport, finance production and trade (Harris-White, 1996). These nine types of activities can make 362880 combinations. The study observed that 149 sample firms were performing 51 combinations of activities.

References

Acharya, S.S. (1985). "Regulation of Agricultural Produce Markets – Some Observations on the Impact," *Development Policy and Administrative Review*, 11(2), July –December.

————. (1988). *Agricultural Production, Marketing and Price Policy in India*, Mittal Publishers, New Delhi. 317, 320-27.

Acharya, S.S. and N.L. Agarwal (1999). *Agricultural Marketing in India*, Third Edition, Oxford and IBH Publishing Co., New Delhi.

Banerji, A. and J.V. Meenakshi (2001). *Competition and Collusion in Grain Markets: Basmati Auctions in North India*, Working Paper No. 91, Working Paper Series, Centre for Development Economics, Delhi School of Economics, University of Delhi, Delhi.

Chand, Ramesh (2002). *Trade Liberalisation, WTO and Indian Agriculture: Experience and Prospects*, Mittal Publications, New Delhi.

————. (2003a). "Minimum Support Price in Agriculture: Changing Requirements," *Economic and Political Weekly*, Vol. 38 (29): 3027-3028, July 19.

————. (2003b). *Government Intervention in Foodgrain Markets in India in the Changing Context*, Policy Paper 19, National Centre for Agricultural Economics and Policy Research, New Delhi.

Government of India (2002). *Report of Inter Ministerial Task Force on Agricultural Marketing Reforms*, Ministry of Agriculture, New Delhi, May.

Harris-White Barbara (1995). "Efficiency and Complexity: Distributive Margins and the Profits of Market Enterprises," in Gregory J. Scott's (edited) *Prices, Products and People: Analyzing Agricultural Markets in Developing Countries*, Lynne Rienar Publisher, Boulder, London, pp 301-324.

————. (1996). *A Political Economy of Agricultural Markets in South India*, Sage Publications, New Delhi.

Jha, Raghbendra, K.V. Bhanu Murthy, Hari K. Nagarajan and Ashok K. Seth (1997). "Market Integration in Indian Agriculture," *Economic Systems*, 21(3), pp. 217-234.

Jha, Raghbendra and K. Nagarajan (1998). "Wholesale Stocks and Hoarding in Rice Markets in India," *Economic and Political Weekly*, 33(41), October 10.

————. (2002). "Noisy Vertical Markets", *Economic and Political Weekly*, 37(51), December 21.

Kahlon, A.S. and M.V. George (1986). *Agricultural Marketing and Price Policies*, Allied Publishers, New Delhi.

Kinnucan, Henry W. and Olan D. Forker (1987). "Asymmetry in Farm Retail Price Transmission for Major Dairy Products," *American Journal Agricultural Economics*, 69 (2): 285-292. February.

Maheshwari, Asha (1998). "Regulation of Markets, Production and Market Arrivals – A State Wise Analysis of Rice," *Indian Journal of Agricultural Economics*, 53 (3): 351-358, July-September.

Parikh, Kirit S., A. Ganesh Kumar and Gangadhar Darbha (2003). "Growth and Welfare Consequences of Rise in MSP," *Economic and Political Weekly*, 38(9), March 1.

Peltzman, Sam (2000). "Prices Rise Faster Than They Fall," *Journal of Political Economy*, 108 (3): 467-501.

Shepherd, Andrew W. (2004). *Financing Agricultural Marketing: The South Asian Experience*, AGSF Occasional Paper 2, Food and Agriculture Organisation of the United Nations, Rome.

Singh, Katar (1996). "Rapporteur's Report on Cooperatives in Rural Economy," *Indian Journal of Agricultural Economics*, Vol. 51(4) Conf. Number, Oct.-Dec.

Subbarao, K. (1989). "Agricultural Marketing and Credit," Monograph 2, *Research in Economics: Second Survey*, Indian Council of Social Science Research, New Delhi.

Suryawanshi, R.R., B.N. Powar and P.D. Deshmukh (1995). "Marketable Surplus and Marketing Cost of Oilseeds and Pulses in Western Maharashtra," *Bihar Journal of Agricultural Marketing*, 3(2): 201-04, April-June.

Wilson, E.J. (2001). "Testing Integration of Agricultural Markets in India: Conceptual and Empirical Considerations Using Wholesale Prices," in D.P. Chaudhri and S.S. Acharya (edited) *Indian Agricultural Policy at the Crossroads*, Rawat Publications, Jaipur and New Delhi.

World Bank (1999). *India Food Grain Marketing Policies: Reforming to Meet Food Security Needs*, Vol.I and II, Report No. 18329-IN, April 17.

Part V

Competition Policy in Manufacturing Sector

12 State of Competition in the Indian Manufacturing Industry

K.V. Ramaswamy

12.1 Introduction

Industrial and trade policies, in India, have brought into existence particular market structures and the associated degree of competition, which has been changing in recent years. Policy reforms facilitated the entry of both domestic and foreign firms. The liberalisation of imports and FDI (Foreign Direct Investment) are supposed to increase the extent of competition in domestic markets. The focus of this chapter is to make a preliminary assessment of the state of competition in the Indian manufacturing industries.[1] We ask the following key questions: Has there been a definitive change in terms of market structure characteristics? What has happened to the degree of rivalry, and exercise, of market power by incumbents in key product markets? What is the impact of import liberalisation and foreign direct investment (FDI) on market structure and performance?

We attempt to answer these questions by doing an analytical and factual survey of competition in selected manufacturing industries. The empirical literature on market structure in developing countries, including India, was observed to be sparse in 1992.[2] The situation today is not much different. Emerging empirical research has begun to address these questions. Few studies have been conducted on Indian manufacturing.[3] We focus on certain key results of interest in the area of the present study. The aim is to arrive at a broad understanding, and interpretation, of trends in the state of competition in Indian manufacturing in the 1990s.[4] Gaps in our current sphere of knowledge, as well as directions for future research receive greater emphasis.

12.1.1 Meaning of Competition and Competitive Markets

The concept of competition can be defined in many ways.[5] In this chapter, competition refers to rivalry between firms in a market for objects, like market share and profits.[6] Market power is the ability to raise market prices above competitive levels, and exclude competition. Policy intervention requires the prior identification, and assessment, of the intensity of competition in real life product markets. In the case of policy intervention, the standard guiding principles must be determined; as does the difference between competition in a market and competition for a market.[7] Competition **in a market** refers to actions of incumbents in an established market, and those potential entrants who would like to sell the same product. The instruments of competition would be the price or capacity (quantity competition), in addition to other non-price instruments, like new products, advertising etc. This involves erecting entry barriers, product differentiation, research and development, vertical integration, etc.

Competition for a market is defined as a process of creating a **new market**, based on innovative technologies and/or new standards, for example, a new operating system for Microsoft Windows. This involves challenging the sellers of existing products, through the introduction of new products, or creating potential competition, by upfront investment in facilities, to supply a new product. Here, the instrument of competition is neither the price nor the capacity. The measurement of competition for a market is much more difficult than the measurement of competition in a market. In this paper, our focus is on assessing the extent of **competition in markets** in Indian manufacturing. The determinants of intensity of competition in a market are (i) natural barriers to entry (e.g. technology of production that determines the optimal scale and transport cost); (ii) strategic barriers to entry (e.g. R&D, advertising, brand proliferation, distribution networks); (iii) policy induced barriers (e.g.

licensing and import tariffs, etc.); and (iv) the extent of collusion.

12.2 Manufacturing Sector in India: Size and Structure

The manufacturing sector, in India, is still relatively small. The share of the manufacturing sector, in GDP, has remained more or less stagnant in the 1990s (Table 12.1). Other comparable economies have a substantially higher share of manufacturing value-added (MVA) in their GDP. It is exceptionally high in China, with a share of 34 per cent. In South Korea, it is 30 per cent. Brazil and Mexico both have a share of approximately 20 per cent. The relative size of India's manufacturing sector can be assessed by looking at India's MVA as a proportion of MVA in a comparable country. The manufacturing sector in India was less than one-fifth of that of China in 2000.

TABLE 12.1
Share of Manufacturing in GDP*

Industry	1993-94	1996-97	1997-98	1998-99	1999-00	2000-01	2001-02
Manufacturing	16.1	18.2	17.7	17.0	16.7	17.2	16.8
Registered	10.5	12.3	11.6	11.1	10.8	11.2	11.1
Unregistered	5.6	6.0	6.1	6.0	5.9	6.0	5.8

* 1993-94 prices.
Source: National Accounts Statistics, 2003.

The structure of production (or the output mix), in the formal manufacturing sector, did not undergo substantial changes. The share of consumer goods, propelled by consumer durable goods, increased marginally in the 1990s. Basic and intermediate goods sectors, together, share about 40 per cent of formal sector output. The share of the capital good sector declined by 1 percentage point (Table 12.2).

TABLE 12.2
Structure of Manufacturing Output in the Registered Sector: Use-Based Groups

Use-Based Groups	1990-91	1997-98
1. Basic Goods	23.7	23.0
2. Intermediate Goods	16.8	17.0
3. Capital Goods	17.5	16.3
4. Consumer Goods	42.0	43.6
4.1 Consumer Durable Goods	6.8	8.8
4.2 Consumer Non-Durable Goods	35.2	34.8

Source: Nagaraj (2003), Table 6, page 3709.

12.3 Trade and Industrial Policy Liberalisation in the 1990s

The industrial and trade policy reforms (outlined below) initiated in the 1990s have substantially altered the state of competition in Indian manufacturing industries.

12.3.1 Removal of Legal Barriers to Entry

The foremost instrument of industrial policy was the industrial licensing for private entrepreneurs, based on the Industrial Regulation Act of 1956. The new industrial policy of 1991 abolished industrial licensing, in all but 18 industries. In 1993, the passenger car industry was delicensed, followed by the white goods, and the entertainment electronics industry in 1996. The sugar industry was delicensed in 1999. At present, only six industries require compulsory licensing. They are potable alcohol, tobacco products, electronic equipment for aerospace and defence purposes, as well as hazardous chemicals and certain specific bulk drugs.

12.3.2 Removal of Capacity Expansion, Takeovers and Merger Restrictions on Large Firms

There were barriers to entry imposed on large firms, with the Monopolies and Restrictive Trade Practices (MRTP) Act 1969, and the Foreign Exchange Regulation Act (FERA) 1973. The MRTPA restricted capacity expansion; opening of new enterprises; and takeover and merger activity of businesses, with assets of more than Rs. 200 million (later raised to Rs. one billion in the 1984 amendments to the MRTPA), and those of 'dominant undertakings' with assets of more than Rs. 10 million. The definition of dominance refers to a market share of more than 33 per cent (later amended to 25 per cent in 1991). All such restrictions have been removed.

12.3.3 Raising Foreign Equity Participation

Foreign equity participation was made automatic up to 51 per cent stake in 34 high priority industry groups, spread over 160 industries. Equity participation greater than 51 per cent is permitted on case-by-case basis and the nature of production activity. This was later liberalised to enable setting up of 100 per cent subsidiaries in the manufacturing sector, without any restriction on the number of such subsidiaries. FDI (Foreign Direct Investment) of up to 100 per cent under the automatic route in manufacturing activities is allowed in SEZs (Special Economic Zones) except for a small negative list of industries (GoI, Economic Survey 2001-02, Page 155).

12.3.4 *Removal of Protection to Small-Scale Industries*

A number of products (more than 1000) were under small-scale industry (SSI) reservation, like many electronic products, domestic appliances such as irons, mixers, etc. Many of these products were progressively removed from the reservation list, enabling large domestic and foreign firms to enter those product lines. Between 1997 and 2001, 39 items were dereserved (The key items were ice-cream, ready made garments, and toys). An additional 51 items were removed from the list in May 2002. Most recently, 75 items were dereserved in 2002-03. Still a large number of products (more than 600) are currently reserved for exclusive manufacture by SSI enterprises. Large-scale firms can produce these products, provided they meet the 50 per cent export obligation. The 2004-05 budget has sought to remove another 85 items from the reserved list.

12.3.5 *Easing Access to Foreign Technology*

Royalty payments, by all companies with foreign technology collaboration agreements, are permitted without any restriction on the extent of foreign equity participation. Royalty payments up to 5 per cent of domestic sales, and 8 per cent of export sales are permitted without any restriction on the duration of royalty payment. Restrictive clauses, like foreign exchange cost balancing, applicable to consumer goods were removed. Companies are also free to employ foreign personnel. This has been an important step as it improved the technology transfer process. Companies are also free to use foreign brand names and trade marks.

12.4 Trends in Market Concentration Over Time

Market concentration, or seller concentration, is a traditional indicator of the intensity of competition, as it is presumed to facilitate the abuse of market power by the incumbents. It refers to the extent to which sales, in a market, are concentrated in the hands of a few firms. The most widely used index of concentration is the Herfindhal-Hirshchman index (the HH Index). The HH index is defined as the sum of the squares of market shares (percentage share) of all the firms in the industry. This may be regarded as a measure of market power, as there is a direct correspondence between the HHI and the industry average price cost-margin (the Lerner index of Monopoly power).[8]

BOX 12.1
The Herfindhal-Hirshchman Index (The HH Index)

The HH index is defined as sum of the squares of market shares (percentage share) of all the firms in the industry. The HH index declines with increases in the number of firms and increases with rising inequality in market share among a given number of firms. For an industry with only two players with equal market share of 50 per cent the index would be 5000 (the sum of squares of 50). For a monopoly with a hundred per cent of the market the HH index would be 10000 (the square of 100). The US justice department considers an HH value of 1000 as critical in its evaluation of merger proposals. In the context of markets, in India, the application of HH index is not that straightforward due to several factors. First, the presence of unorganised and co-operative firms in many industries leads to under-estimation of industry sales. The market share of unorganised segment in many industries is significant and the organised players face intense competitive pressure from unorganised sector like those in cigarettes, wafer & chips industries, domestic appliances, fans and air-coolers. Second, in some sectors competition from the co-operative sector is significant. This is the case for Amul, in the milk, infant-foods and ice cream industries. Cooperative sector sales are not included in the estimate of total market value of sales due to non-availability of data. Third, estimates of sales of Indian private limited companies and small-scale sector (SSI) firms are often under-estimated. Therefore, the indicated concentration levels are overestimated. Many foreign firms that have entered India recently are not adequately captured in the CMIE database, as many of them are private limited companies. Fourth, unlisted public sector units (PSU) are not covered in the CMIE database. More care is necessary in using the reported HH indices as indicators of competition intensity in this context.

What has happened to concentration levels in different industries, in the post-reform period, in the Indian manufacturing sector? Has the concentration level declined compared to the pre-reform period? A few studies that had examined concentration in Indian manufacturing, during the pre-reform period, reported high levels of average concentration in intermediate, capital goods and the consumer durable goods sector, and had not observed any tendency to decline, at least up to 1994 (Mani, 2000). We have examined the changes in concentration for selected industries in recent years. Three criteria were followed to select these industries. First, the industries should not belong to sectors studied independently in this project (Example, Steel, Cement, Pharmaceuticals, etc.). Second, they should not be subject to any type of price controls (for example, the retention price scheme for Urea in the Fertiliser industry). In such cases, firm conduct cannot be attributed to structure. Third, they should have a fairly large relative market size, or turnover of not less than Rs. 1500 crore (in 2000-01).[9] The choice of this last criterion can be justified since, when one is considering the issue of possible consumer welfare loss, due to market imperfections in the economy, the idea of aggregate welfare loss is more relevant when large markets are found to be imperfect.[10] The selected industries may be grouped under the following four broad categories: (1) Consumer Non-Durable Goods; (2) Consumer Durable Goods; (3) Intermediate Goods; and (4) Capital Goods. The measure of concentration is the Herfindhal-Hirshchman index. The estimates of HH index are taken from the Centre for Monitoring Indian Economy (CMIE) database called Market Size and Market Shares.[11] The reported estimates of HH indices are based on the value of sales of all companies in the domestic market.

Trends observed in four use-based industry groups are summarised below:

12.4.1 Consumer Non-Durable Goods

The consumer non-durable goods sector comprises food, beverages, soaps, and textile products, like apparel, footwear, and certain electrical products, like lamps & tubes. Market concentration has increased in three key consumer goods industries namely, Biscuits, Synthetic Detergents, and Lamps and tubes (See Table 12.3). They are also observed to have one or two dominant firms. For example, Britannia Industries (Market share 32 per cent) in biscuits; Hindustan Lever (42 per cent) and Nirma (21 per cent) in synthetic detergents; and Philips India (29 per cent) and Surya Roshni (14 per cent) in lamps & tubes.[12] Many other products, within the consumer goods sector, were observed to have high levels of concentration, like malted milk foods, ice cream, infant foods, iodised salt, wafers & chips, and cigarettes. Many of these industries are dominated by MNCs (Multi-National Corporations). They have used the route of mergers and acquisitions (M&As) to gain and consolidate their market shares (Kumar, 2000).

TABLE 12.3

Consumer Non-Durable Goods Industry: Changes in HH Index of Concentration in Selected Industries: 1993-94 and 2002-03

	Industry	1993-94	2002-03
1.	Biscuits	500	1660
2.	Soaps	500	370
3.	Synthetic Detergents	1500	2690
4.	Lamps & Tubes	1400*	1850
5.	Infant Foods	3000	3830
6.	Malted Milk Foods	4000	4030

Note: * 1995-96
Source: Market Size and Shares, August 1999 and July 2004, CMIE.

12.4.2 Consumer Durable Goods

'Consumer durables' is a generic term that includes traditional goods, like wooden and steel furniture, bicycles, electric fans, to technologically sophisticated goods like passenger cars, motorcycles/mopeds, colour TVs, washing machines, refrigerators, automobile tyres, and air-conditioners, among others. The market structure in many consumer durables industries is characterised by oligopoly. The estimates of HH index for selected industries, for two years, are shown in Table 12.4. Eight of the fourteen industries show a decline in the levels of concentration. Concentration levels show a marked increase in five industries, namely automobile tires, audio systems, mopeds, motorcycles and bicycles. All five industries have one major firm with a high market share: MRF (Market share 24 per cent) in automobile tires, Hero Honda (Market share 50 per cent) in motorcycles, TVS Motor (Market share 46 per cent) in mopeds, and Hero Cycles (Market share 40 per cent) in bicycles. In the audio-equipment industry, Videocon International Ltd. has emerged as a dominant firm. In the auto-rickshaw industry, Bajaj Auto is a dominant player, with a market share of 75 per cent.

TABLE 12.4

Consumer Durable Goods Industry: Changes in HH Index of Concentration: 1993-94 and 2002-03

		1993-94	2002-03
1.	Automobile Tyres	1090	1900
2.	Air-Coolers	6730	5690
3.	Air Conditioners	2030	950
4.	Electrical Fans	1430	1530
5.	Washing Machines	3610	3190
6.	Refrigerators	3490	1690
7.	Audio Systems	3550	5690
8.	Scooters	3670	3150
9.	3-Wheelers (auto-rickshaws)	8500	5340
10.	Mopeds	2320	3770
11.	Motorcycles	2520	2920
12.	Bicycles	2330	2840
13.	Passenger Cars	4750	2730
14.	Watches & Clocks	2950	2920

Source: CMIE Market Size and Shares, August 1999 and July 2004.

12.4.3 Intermediate Goods

In Table 12.5, estimates of HH index, for a set of selected industries in the intermediate goods sector, are shown. Eight of the fourteen industries show a decline in concentration levels. Two industries belonging to the industry category 'textile fibre intermediates', namely, Polyester Staple Fibre (PSF) and Viscose Staple Fibre (VSF), have a substantial increase in concentration levels. In the PSF industry, Reliance is the dominant player with a market share of 54 per cent. It is reported to be the world's fifth largest producer of PSF. In the VSF industry, Grasim is the dominant player, with a market share of 91 per cent (almost a pure monopoly).

Grasim is reported to have the world's largest plant for producing VSF. Establishing large manufacturing plants, to reap economies of scale, has enabled Reliance and Grasim to achieve the dominant position in the textile fibre intermediates industry. The other two industries that have experienced increased levels of concentration are paints & varnishes and storage batteries. In paints & varnishes, three firms together have more than 63 per cent of the total market. They are Asian Paints, Goodlass Nerolac and Berger Paints. In Storage batteries, the company Exide Batteries has achieved dominance with a market share of 62 per cent. The market share of Exide batteries increased from 53 per cent to 62 per cent, after it acquired the company, Standard Batteries, in 1998. Copper and copper products experienced a remarkable amount of change in market shares. In 1993-94, the state owned company, Hindustan Copper Limited (HCL), was a dominant firm with a market share of 27 per cent. Sterlite Industries had a negligible share in 1993-94. By 2002-03, Sterlite Industries had attained dominance with a market share of 39 per cent. Copper and Copper products are a good example of the emergence of private sector dominance in an industry previously dominated by a public sector unit.

TABLE 12.5

Intermediate Goods: Changes in HH Index of Concentration in Selected Industries

	Industry	1993-94	2002-03
1.	Caustic Soda	700	750
2.	Soda Ash	2900	2040
3.	Paints and Varnishes	1500	1830
4.	Poly Vinyl Chloride (PVC)	2300	2120
5.	Polyester Filament Yarn (PFY)	1200	1060
6.	Polyester Staple Fibre (PSF)	1800	4100
7.	Viscose Staple Fibre (VSF)	7700	9760
8.	Storage Batteries	2900	3560
9.	Television Picture Tubes	1800	2480
10.	Transmission Tower Structure	3300	2940
11.	Copper and Copper Products	780	2310
12.	Primary Aluminium	3020	2790
13.	Aluminium Products	2350	1370
14.	Aluminium Foils	2410	1670

Source: CMIE Market Size and Shares, August 1999 and July 2004.

12.4.4 *Capital Goods*

In Table 12.6, estimates of HH index, for a set of selected industries in the capital goods sector, are shown. Three industries, namely Boilers, Chemical machinery, and Portable Power Generation-Sets (Gensets), have shown an increase in concentration levels. The public sector unit, namely Bharat Heavy Electricals Limited (BHEL), dominates the boiler industry. Larsen & Toubro Limited (L&T), is dominant in the chemical machinery industry. Honda Siel Power Products and Birla Power Solutions, together have 100 per cent of the market for power generation sets. The HH index for the earthmoving machinery industry is also on the higher side, with a dominant public sector unit, namely Bharat Earth Movers Limited, with a market share of 50 per cent in 2002-03.

TABLE 12.6

Capital Goods: HH Index in Selected Industries

	Industry	1993-94	2002-03
1.	Boilers	4540	5670
2.	Tractors	1540	1450
3.	Earth Moving Machinery	3280	2950
4.	Chemical Machinery	2360	2890
5.	Portable Gensets	5090	5720
6.	Textile Machinery	330	300

Source: CMIE Market Size and Shares, August 1999 and July 2004.

12.5 Import Competition, FDI and Profitability in the 1990s

A very important source of pressure upon the behaviour of firms, in a market with entry barriers, is the competition from imports. This can also be termed as the 'imports—as-market-discipline hypothesis'.[13] Domestic industries, enjoying protection and having imperfect market structures, are forced to behave competitively as the intensity of import competition increases. Two approaches have been taken to examine the effect of increased import competition on mark-ups in domestic industries (Harrison, 1994). In one approach, the gross price-average cost margins, defined as the ratio of sales net of expenditure on labour and intermediate inputs over sales, is used as an indicator of mark-up. The behaviour of gross margins, before and after the trade reforms, is compared. In the second alternative approach, output growth rate is regressed on share-weighted growth rate of inputs. The econometric regression exercise yields the mark-up as the slope coefficient. By allowing the mark-up coefficient to vary over time, one can test whether import competition affects mark-up. In brief, the impact of import competition on industry mark-ups is an empirical matter.[14]

The impact of FDI, on domestic market structure and the intensity of competition, is another key empirical issue. MNE (Multinational Enterprise) entry creates competitive pressure for domestic firms. Moreover, large foreign affiliates can pose serious challenges for maintaining effective competition, in host economies, by taking dominant positions and taking control of distribution networks. Foreign affiliates may be established by Greenfield FDI, or created through cross-border M&As. They can have either competition enhancing or competition reducing effects, depending on both country and industry specific situations (UNCTAD, 2000). The evidence from developing countries concerning the impact of FDI on market structure and competitive conduct is mixed (UNCTAD, 2000).

The market for manufactures, in India, was subject to tariff and quota protection for many years. Import liberalisation and the consequent competition from imported manufactures, is another channel that could affect the state of competition. Imports increase the total domestic availability of a goods and reduce the extent of seller concentration in domestic markets. In the 1990s, India liberalised its trade regime by reducing tariff barriers and removing quantitative restrictions on imports. Tariff reduction in particular, in the 1990s, has been dramatic (Table 12.7). The average tariff on manufactures was reduced to 29 per cent, from an average of 70 per cent, in 1990. Import duties collected, as a percentage of value of imports, continuously declined from around 42 per cent in 1990 to 20 per cent in 1999. Imports as a percentage of GDP rose to above 15 per cent at the end of the nineties. More than half of India's merchandise imports consist of manufactures.

The changing incidence of external competition is also measured by the estimates of the effective rate of protection (ERP), in contrast to nominal tariff rates. One of the studies reported that the effective rate of protection, in many industries, has gone up in the 1990s (Pandey, 2004). As the measurement of ERP is subject to several problems, no generalisation can be made with respect to the trends in effective rate of protection. This again forces the policy-making agency to understand the effective external competition by looking at industry specific studies.

TABLE 12.7
Tariff Barriers in India

Year	All Products			Manufactured Products	
	Simple Mean Tariff	Standard Deviation of Tariffs	Weighted Mean Tariff	Simple Mean Tariff	Weighted Mean Tariff
1990	79.0	43.6	56.2	79.9	70.8
2001	39.9	12.4	28.2	30.6	29.0

Source: World Development Indicators 2003 CD-ROM.

12.5.1 Import Penetration Ratios in the 1990s

The reduction of tariffs and the removal of NTBs (Non-Tariff Barriers) are expected to impose import competition pressure on Indian manufacturing. One index to measure such a pressure is to estimate the import penetration ratios. Import penetration ratio is measured as the ratio of value of imports to domestic availability. Domestic availability is measured as the value of production plus imports minus the value of exports. One recent research study[15] has estimated the import penetration ratios for 60 three-digit industries. In a majority of industries the import penetration levels were found to be low and insignificant. A relevant extract from that study is given in Table 12.8. The chemical industry stands out as a singular example of an industry facing severe import competition in the 1990s. More detailed study, at the individual industry level, is necessary to get a clearer picture of import competition. The removal of quotas and the reduction of tariffs have perhaps increased the threat of potential imports as well as the competitive pressure on manufacturing firms in India.

TABLE 12.8
Import Penetration Ratios in Indian Manufacturing: Use-based Classification

Industry Name	1986-90	1991-95	1996-00
Refrigerators & Air-conditioners	0.105	0.028	0.064
Lamps & Domestic Appliances	0.015	0.018	0.035
Motor Vehicles & Parts	0.032	0.032	0.054
Motor Cycles & parts	0.016	0.005	0.027
Radio and TV	0.102	0.080	0.202
Tyres & Tubes	0.003	0.006	0.008
Electronic Valves & Tubes	0.635	0.504	0.438
Cells & Batteries	0.093	0.021	0.058
Paints & Varnishes	0.084	0.070	0.084
Synthetic Rubber and Manmade Fibre	0.156	0.164	0.156
Organic & Inorganic Chemicals	0.234	0.428	0.469

Source: Das (2003).

12.5.2 *FDI and Competition in Indian Manufacturing*

The Indian industrial policy restricted Foreign Direct Investment, and the entry of foreign firms into Indian industries. Liberalisation of policy on FDI is another factor that would have led to greater entry of foreign firms, and increased the extent of competition in Indian markets. FDI in Indian manufacturing is argued to be of the market seeking type. FDI in Greenfield projects signals new entry into an industry. The new entry of firms increases the toughness of competition by bringing in new technology and low costs of production. Incumbent foreign-owned firms might expand capacity, increase promotional expenditure (Advertising), and increase R&D to introduce products in order to protect their market shares. No study appears to have been undertaken to analyse the impact of FDI and competition in Indian manufacturing.

Available data, on industry-wise distribution of FDI, indicates that a major share of FDI inflow has gone into engineering, electrical and electronics, and chemical industry groups (Table 12.9). It is reported that the share of foreign-controlled firms, in total industry sales, varies across industries. Their average share in total sales, of public limited companies, is in the range of 20 per cent to 25 per cent. They are high in cigarettes, dry cells and electric lamps, paints, toiletries, tyres and tubes, pharmaceuticals and industrial gases (Athreye and Kapur, 1999). FDI and the entry of multinational corporations are reported to have increased competitive pressure in a number of industries like beverages, food processing, passenger cars, consumer durables and electrical equipment. At the same time, an analysis of merger and acquisition activities, of multinational enterprises, suggests that most of it was of the non-Greenfield variety, aimed at consolidating the market share position of incumbent MNEs (Kumar, 2000). The focus of MNE acquisition is reported to be marketing and distribution networks of local firms. This would have enhanced the market power of MNEs in their line of business activity. MNE related merger and acquisition deals were concentrated in non-electrical machinery, food & beverages, household appliances, pharma and personal care products (Kumar, 2000). It is important to remember that the lines of activity, in which MNEs are dominant, are relatively small and in a large number of industries, foreign presence is completely missing. Careful studies of the impact of FDI and M&A, on competition, are required to understand the state of competition in India in recent years. In particular, the impact on market structure (Does FDI increase 4-firm concentration ratio in an industry?), non-price competition, sales-distribution network strategies, product differentiation and the complex ways of price discrimination.

12.5.3 *Profitability Trends in Manufacturing in the 1990s*

The behaviour of profit rates (return on capital), over the years, is considered as a key indicator of competitive mechanisms at work. In particular, the effectiveness of competitive pressures in the economy may be measured by the persistence of profit rates.[16] We are unaware of any recent study investigating the persistence of profits in Indian manufacturing, using the data for the 1990s. A few studies, which have examined the average price cost margins, indicate that profit margins have increased in the post-1991 reform period.[17] One study found that market shares of firms were not significant in explaining the gross-profit margins (Kambhampati and Parikh, 2003). This suggests that firm profitability seems to have been driven by factors unrelated to market share. More detailed, industry specific studies, using firm level data, are required to assess the impact of changing structure on profitability and price mark-ups.

12.6 Findings, Conclusions and Suggestions for Future Studies

- Changes in market structure, in manufacturing, show a mixed picture. 21 of the 40 selected industries show an increase in concentration. Concentration levels have declined in the remaining 19 industries.

- One or two large firms are found to dominate the industries that have increased their levels of market concentration. The Public Sector Enterprises (PSEs) are found to be dominant in three industries, namely boilers, primary aluminium, and earth moving machinery.

- In one of the selected industries, a private sector firm has emerged as the dominant firm replacing the public sector enterprise.

- Average nominal tariff rates have substantially declined in the 1990s.

- Import penetration rates were found to be low and negligible across industries, except in the Chemicals industry.

- FDI inflow was concentrated in a few industry groups like machinery, pharmaceuticals and chemicals. MNE related merger and acquisition deals were concentrated in non-electrical

TABLE 12.9

Industry-wise Distribution of FDI Inflow into India: 1991-2001

Categories	Percentage Share								
	1992-93	1993-94	1994-95	1995-96	1996-97	1997-98	1998-99	1999-00	2000-01
Engineering Industries	25	8	15	18	35	20	21	21	14
Electronics and Electrical Equipment	12	14	6	9	7	22	11	11	11
Chemicals & Allied Products	17	18	16	9	15	9	19	8	7
Computers	3	2	1	4	3	5	5	6	16
Pharmaceuticals	1	12	1	4	2	1	1	3	3
Food & Dairy	10	11	7	6	12	4	1	8	4
Total	100	100	100	100	100	100	100	100	100
Value in US$ Million	280	403	872	1419	2058	2956	2000	1581	1910

Source: Table 3.5a and Table 3.5b in Report of the Committee on FDI 2002, GoI, New Delhi.

machinery, food & beverages, household appliances, pharmaceutical and personal care products.

- Average price-cost margins were found to show an increasing trend in the 1990s.

12.6.1 Conclusions

- The structure of market concentration in Indian manufacturing industries is changing. This implies a greater churning of market shares in individual industries, which is a reflection of the ongoing restructuring process, in response to trade, FDI and industrial policy reform of the 1990s.

- Both domestic and foreign-owned firms seem to have taken dominant positions in many industries. Market concentration, measured using data subject to many limitations, has risen in several industries as a consequence. Firms have acquired market power in many industries by establishing large, minimum efficient scale plant and production facilities. The possibility of the emergence of private sector dominance in industries hitherto dominated by PSUs (Public Sector Unit), is real.

- The observed range of concentration levels in Indian manufacturing industries may be high, relative to developed countries. (For example, in the US, in a large majority of industries, the estimated HH index is reported to be less than 1000[18]). This is an outcome of the smaller relative market size of Indian industry and economy. Market size, in many industries in India, is not

large enough to accommodate many efficient firms.

- Market concentration and dominant firms signal the possibility of potential anti-competitive behaviour in many Indian manufacturing industries.

- Trade liberalisation, in terms of the reduction of tariff and non-tariff barriers, has increased the threat of import competition. The evidence on effective rates of protection is mixed. However, the observed low import penetration ratios suggest that the impact of trade liberalisation, on the competitive discipline of domestic firms, is rather limited in a large number of industries.

12.6.2 Gaps in Our Knowledge and Areas of Future Research

- India lacks systematic, industry specific studies on market structure and competitive performance. We know very little about the minimum efficient scale of plants, changes in the size distribution of firms within industries, the number of entry into and exit from individual industries. Impact of imports, FDI and M&A, on the structure, conduct and performance of industries, is not well understood.

- Sources of persistence of dominant firms, in individual industries, and the stability of market shares are other critical areas of research. The challenge of competition policy is to distinguish between cases where market dominance has been achieved due to superior efficiency or competitive skills, from those that were attained due to predatory conduct. Defining what is predatory conduct or practice is complex. Firm and Industry specific case studies are the only option.

- We know very little about the links between the state of competition in input markets and the state of competition in product markets.

- Case studies of industries with new entry, and the response of incumbent firms, would provide further insight on competitive behaviour.

- Competitive conduct of PSU and the impact of privatisation, in some of the industries, on competition would be a useful area of investigation.

- Inter-state trade and tax regulations, and their impact on competition of different industries, deserve serious attention.

- A series of studies defining markets and market boundaries may be initiated.

- Price discrimination practices are likely to become more varied and complex. They require a separate study.

- Tracking price changes at the product level is relevant for understanding competitive behaviour, and this has not been attempted. India needs to develop a database that could help the competition authorities.

- The absence of a reliable and consistent database, linking industry, foreign trade and investment, severely limits research into the issues of market structure and competition. Investing in developing a good database would yield good returns in the years to come.

Notes

1. For an introduction to the analytical framework of structure conduct and performance paradigm see the appendix to this report.

2. Lee (1992).

3. This study does not attempt to be exhaustive in its coverage of studies. Limitations of time and resources have severely restricted the scope of the present study. Detailed referencing to the original extensive literature is minimised in the text to make it reader friendly. Specific details of individual studies are ignored. Industry studies reported in Uchikawa (2002) are the recent additions.

4. Comparison with the structure of competition in the 1980s is useful but not attempted in this study.

5. In economics interpretation of competition differs between schools of thought. We have abstained from attempting a survey of the literature on the meaning of competition and the measurement of the intensity of competition. Several proxies have been used to measure the intensity of competition like industry concentration ratios, markets shares, profitability levels. All are subject to several problems of interpretation. This is not an occasion to discuss all the details.

6. This is a working definition we shall use without getting into technicalities and rigors of economic theory.

7. Geroski (2003).

8. The direct correspondence is established in the model of Cournot-Nash equilibrium. The Lerner Index is equal to $(p-mc)/p$, where p is price and mc is the marginal cost. See Scherer and Ross (1990) for details.

9. Few exceptions are made when the industry in question is considered to be critical to the present study, example, malted milk foods or infant food.

10. One can estimate the deadweight loss to monopoly power in different segments of the economy known as Harberger triangles in applied welfare economics.

11. CMIE estimates the HH index by taking the shares of all companies in the domestic market. It is not adjusted for the market share of imports. Therefore, the degree of concentration is overestimated. The reliable market share data has always been and continue to be scarce. Market share is more subject to errors in industries where large unorganised sector co-exits with the organised segment. For example, in industries like biscuits, lamps & tubes, air-conditioners, steel furniture, air-coolers and domestic electrical appliances. A good discussion of the limitations of the CMIE-PROWESS data base is available in Choudhury (2002).

12. The reported market share throughout in this section is for the year 2001-02 unless stated otherwise.

13. See Levinsohn (1993) for an econometric testing of the hypothesis.

14. Economic theory does not offer unambiguous results in this context. It depends on particular model assumptions. See Helpman and Krugman (1989) for a discussion.

15. Das (2003).

16. For an early application of persistence of profit model to manufacturing firms in India see Vaidya (1995) and Khambampati (1996).

17. See Goldar and Aggrawal (2003) for a summary of such studies.

18. See US Bureau of Census (2001).

References

Athreye Suma and Kapur Sandeep (1999). "Foreign Controlled firms in Indian Manufacturing: Long Term Trends," *Economic and Political Weekly*, Vol. 34, No. 48, pp M149-151.

Choudhury, Mita (2002). "Potential Selectivity Bias in Data: Evaluation of Firm-Level database on Indian Industry," *Economic and Political Weekly*, February 23, pp758-766.

Das, D.K. (2003). "Quantifying Trade Barriers: Has Protection Declined Substantially in Indian Manufacturing Sectors," *Working Paper No. 105*, Indian Council for Research on International Economic Relations, New Delhi.

Geroski, P.A. (2003). "Competition in Markets and Competition For Markets," *Journal of Trade, Competition and Trade*, Vol. 3, No. 3, pp 151-166.

Goldar, G. and S.C. Aggrawal (2003). "Trade Liberalisation and Price Cost Margins in Indian Industries," *Working Paper No. 130*, Indian Council for Research on International Economic Relations, New Delhi.

Government of India (GoI). *Economic Survey 2001-2002*, Ministry of Finance, New Delhi.

Harrison, A. (1994). "Productivity, Trade Reform and Imperfect Competition: Theory and Evidence," *Journal of International Economics*, Vol. 36, March, pp 53-73.

Helpman and Krugman (1989). *Trade Policy and Market Structure*, MIT Press, Cambridge, MA.

Kumar, Nagesh (2000). "Mergers and Acquisitions by MNEs: Patterns and Implications," *Economic and Political Weekly*, August 5, pp 2851-2858.

Kambhapati, S. Uma (1996). *Industrial Concentration and Performance: A Study of the Structure, Conduct and Performance of Indian Industry*, Oxford University Press.

Kambhapati, S. Uma and Ashok Parikh (2003). "Disciplining Firms? The Impact of Trade Liberalisation on Profit Margins in Indian Industry," *Applied Economics*, Vol. 35, No. 4, pp. 461-70.

Lee Norman (1992). "Market Structure and Trade in Developing Countries," in Helleiner. G.K. (Ed), *Trade Policy, Industrialisation, and Development: New Perspectives*, Clarendon Press, and Oxford.

Mani, Sunil (2000). "A Survey of Deregulation in Indian Industry," in Kagami and Tsuji (eds), *Privatisation, Deregulation and Economic Efficiency*, Edward Edgar.

Levinsohn, J. (1993). "Testing the Imports-as-Market-Descipline Hypothesis," *Journal of International Economics*, Vol. 35, pp 1-22.

Nagaraj, R. (2003). "Industrial Policy and Performance Since 1980 Which Way Now?" *Economic and Political Weekly*, Vol. 38, No. 35, August 30-September 5, pp 3707-3715.

Pandey, M. (2004). "Impact of Trade Liberalisation in Indian Manufacturing in the 1980s and 1990s," *Working Paper* No. 140, August, ICRIER, New Delhi.

Ramaswamy, K.V. (2002). "Economic Reforms, Industrial Structure and Performance: The Case of Consumer Durables Goods Industry in India," in Uchikawa Shuji (Ed), *Economic Reforms and Industrial Structure in India*, Manohar, New Delhi.

Uchikawa, Shuji. (Ed.) (2002). *Economic Reforms and Industrial Structure in India*, Manohar, New Delhi.

Scherer, F.M, and D. Ross (1990). *Industrial Market Structure and Economic Performance*, Houghton Mifflin, Boston.

Srivastava, Vivek (2000). *The Impact of India's Economic Reforms on Industrial Productivity, Efficiency and Competitiveness: A Study of Indian Manufacturing Industries 1980-97*, NCAER, New Delhi, Draft.

Sutton, John (1996). *Sunk Costs and Market Structure*, The MIT Press, Cambridge.

UNCTAD (2000). *World Investment Report 2000*, United Nations, New York and Geneva.

US Bureau of Census (2001). *Concentration Ratios in Manufacturing-1997*, US Department of Commerce, Washington D.C

Vaidya, R. (1993). "The Persistence of Profits: The Indian Experience," *Journal of Quantitative Economics*, Vol. 9, No. 2, pp 333-348.

13 Competition Issues in the Indian Cement Industry

Pradeep S. Mehta • Nitya Nanda

13.1 Introduction

From 1914, till 1924, the cement industry in India was in a nascent stage, and the sector had a high import dependence of more than 50 per cent, even though it was not the preferred building material. Lime mortar was the usual adhesive substance used in construction. The industry showed signs of growth, during 1924-41, and the share of imports declined to a mere seven per cent by 1942. Meanwhile, domestic production was growing with severe competition amongst producers, depressing prices and profitability. It was at this juncture that several cement companies came together to create a common identity under the Associated Cement Company (ACC), marking the first move towards consolidation to beat competition in the industry.

Probably to nullify the impact of this consolidation, the British Indian Government brought the production and distribution of cement under its direct control in 1942, citing defence needs in the wake of the Second World War. The control of prices, however, continued even after the war. The Essential Commodities Act, 1955 recognised cement as an essential commodity. Pursuant to this, the Cement Control Order was introduced in 1956 to control both price and distribution of cement (Nath & Bose, 2002).

Such heavy control of the industry resulted in sluggish growth, with the installed capacity reaching only 29 million tonnes (Mt). Also, production was only at 21 Mt in 1981-82, even though the Government declared a 12 per cent post-tax return, on net worth, in 1977 to boost capacity. Realising this, the Government announced partial decontrol in 1982. This resulted in extensive modernisation and an expansion drive and, by 1988-89; the installed capacity had reached 59 Mt, an increase of more than 100 per cent in seven years (Chakravarthy, 1989).

Encouraged by this, the Government introduced total decontrol of cement in 1989. In the next two years, the industry enjoyed a boom in sales and profits. In 1991, the economy pushed for large-scale reforms. However, for the next two years, the industry remained stagnant, without any significant addition in existing capacity, probably due to recession in the economy. The industry, though, picked up thereafter, with the installed capacity crossing the level of 140 Mt in 2002-2003. In addition, there are about 300 mini cement plants in the country with a combined installed capacity of about 11 Mt.

13.2 Current Industry Scenario

The industry has been characterised by a high degree of fragmentation, and is now moving towards consolidation in order to compete with the foreign giants (Mehta, 2003). Since the stock market boom of 1994, there has been hectic activity in the cement industry, in terms of capacity addition. After the boom, when cement prices began to scale new heights, investors rushed in to set up new capacities. In the period from 1993-94 to 1996-97, the annual compounded growth in capacity, at 10.54 per cent, outpaced the consumption growth of 8.8 per cent. Towards the end of the boom-and-bust cycle, cement prices fell, bringing down the companies' profitability in the cement industry.

Of late, cement companies have been doing well. In the year 2003-04, production in the country surpassed 117 Mt, with the capacity utilisation level reaching almost 85 per cent. Most of the companies have posted a healthy bottomline growth, during the financial year 2003-04, piggybacking on higher sales, improved price realisation and lower interest costs. This trend is expected to continue in the future as well, considering the Governments' commitment to boost infrastructure and economic reforms. The efforts here are to help expansion in GDP that has been growing at a fast pace, second only to China.

According to a CRIS-INFAC (2003) study, cement demand will grow by 8-9 per cent over the next five years, strong enough to support capacity addition of up to 50 Mt. This optimism is based on the continuous boom in the housing sector, in addition to the government thrust on roads and other infrastructure. It is also observed that only about 8-10 Mt of the required increase in capacity may come from the improved efficiency of existing capacity, whilst the remaining gap of about 40 Mt, needs to be covered by Greenfield/ Brownfield ventures.

TABLE 13.1
Indian Cement Industry – Demand and Supply (in Million Tonnes, MT)

	2002-03	2003-04	2004-05P	2005-06P
Net Functional Cement Capacity	132	137	141	148
All-India Consumption	108	113	122	132
Exports	3	3	4	4
All-India Production	111	117	126	137
Surplus/Deficit	0.3	0.9	0.7	0.7
Cap Utilisation (%)	84.4	85.7	89.7	92.1
All India Consumption Growth (%)	9.0	5.2	7.2	8.0

Source: UTI Sec estimates.

India is already the second biggest market for cement in the world, only after China. Nevertheless, the per capita consumption of cement, in India, is at 82 kgs as opposed to the world average of 255 kgs, and the Asian average of 200 kgs. With easy availability of raw materials and cheap labour, the country also has great potential for exporting to the nearby markets. The long-term potential of the cement industry in India, therefore, seems to be quite bright.

It is, however, likely that mini cement plants are on the death row. Mini cement plants are operated by local players, typically based on the Vertical Shaft Kiln (VSK) technology, and are dependent on fiscal incentives for their survival. These plants have a capacity of less than 20,000 tonnes. Conceived at a time when small was considered good, they are now fast losing the *raison d'être* of their very existence. Though they enjoy some cost benefits, these are neutralised by the quality of the cement produced and transportation costs incurred. This is quite apparent from the fact that, whilst the

average capacity utilisation level of large plants stands at 85 per cent, for the mini plants, the level is below 50 per cent.

TABLE 13.2
Indian Cement Industry – Some Key Figures

Large Plants	
Companies (Nos.)	54
Cement Plants (Nos.)	125
Installed Capacity (MT)	140.07
Cement Production (MT) 2002-03	111.35
Manpower Employed (Nos.) Approx.	1,35,000
Turnover in 2001-02 (US$mn) around	6,000
Mini Plants	
Cement Plants (Nos.)	300
Installed Capacity (MT)	11.10
Cement Production (MT)	5.00(P)

Note: 1. Large Plants means capacity more than 0.198 MT per annum.
2. Mini Plants means capacity less than 0.198 MT per annum.
3. (P): Provisional.
Source: CMA (2004).

13.3 Nature of the Industry

The cement industry in India is spread across the length and breadth of the country, with 125 large plants owned by 54 companies. However, the cement factories are clustered in a few locations depending on the availability of raw materials, namely coal and limestone, as both are bulky items that make transportation difficult and uneconomical. Proximity to sizeable markets also plays an important role, in this regard, as the final product is bulky as well. Most of the limestone deposits in India are located in the states of Andhra Pradesh, Chhattisgarh, Gujarat, Madhya Pradesh, Maharashtra and Rajasthan, leading to the concentration of cement units in these states.

13.3.1 Market Structure

As cement is a low value commodity, freight costs assume a significant proportion of the final cost. Due to the very nature of cement, being very bulky and incurring huge transportation costs, manufacturers tend to sell cement in the nearest market first, and then sell in distant markets only if additional realisation is greater than freight costs incurred. This highlights the regional nature of the cement industry. The Indian cement industry is normally viewed in terms of five regions:

North: Punjab, Delhi, Haryana, Himachal Pradesh, Rajasthan, Chandigarh, J&K and Uttranchal;

TABLE 13.3

Region-wise Capacity, Production and Consumption

Region	Number of Plants	Installed Capacity (MT)	Percentage of Total Capacity	Cement Production (MT) 2002-03	Percentage to Total Production 2002-03	Total Consumption 2003-04	Percentage to Total Consumption 2003-04
Northern	23	25.20	18	23.88	22	22.60	20
Eastern	24	21.71	16	16.73	15	16.95	15
Southern	43	44.30	32	32.67	30	31.65	29
Western	18	25.33	19	18.86	17	22.60	20
Central	17	20.99	15	17.45	16	16.95	15
Total	125	137.53	100	109.59	100	110.75	100

Source: CMA (2004).

West: Maharashtra and Gujarat;

South: Tamil Nadu, Andhra Pradesh, Karnataka, Kerala, Pondicherry, Andaman & Nicobar and Goa;

East: Bihar, Orissa, West Bengal, North-Eastern States, Jharkhand and Chhattisgarh; and

Central: Uttar Pradesh and Madhya Pradesh

As can be seen from the above Table, the Southern region is the largest market, both in terms of consumption and installed capacity. The southern market is also quite insulated from competition, from other markets, due to its geographical location and transport costs. The Eastern market is also quite insulated. Most of the plants in this region are concentrated in the states of Chattisgarh and Jharkhand, which are located in the extreme West of the region, whilst they serve markets in far off places like the Northeastern states. Thus, it is quite difficult for plants, located in other regions, to serve this particular region. The Western region is the most open to competition, from other regions, as it can be served by some plants in the Southern, Northern and Central regions. The remaining regions are served from their neighbouring regions to some extent.

This kind of scenario is reflected in the prevailing average prices, as well their movements. The prices are relatively higher in Southern and Eastern regions, which also had reasonably higher growth in prices. The Northern region also had a higher growth in prices, probably due to a surge in demand. However, the Western region is the only market where prices actually fell.

Traditionally, the Indian cement industry has been characterised by a large number of small manufacturers. However, the consolidation process over the last few years has led to the emergence of a couple of big

TABLE 13.4

Region-wise Scenario in Average Cement Prices

(in Rs.)

	Price (2002-03)	Price (2003-04)	% Change
Northern	136	142	4.0
Eastern	141	146	3.4
Southern	139	145	4.6
Western	133	132	-0.9
Central	127	128	1.2

Source: CMA (2004).

players. The top six[1] players hold about 60 per cent of the total capacity, whereas some 46 odd players, together, hold the rest. The median installed capacity of these players is just 0.86 of the total capacity. From regional perspective, the size distribution is even more skewed. For example, Lafarge, the sixth largest player in India, is the largest player in the Eastern market.

TABLE 13.5

The Major Players in Indian Cement Industry

Producer	Capacity in 2002-03 (Mt)	Share of Total Capacity (Per cent)
Grasim-L&T	29.9	21.51
GACL-ACC	28.2	20.32
India Cements	8.8	6.34
Madras Cements	5.0	3.58
Century Textiles	4.7	3.24
Lafarge	4.5	3.24
Top 6 players	81.1	58.37
Remaining capacity	57.8	41.63
Median capacity	1.2	0.86

Source: CRIS:INFAC (2003).

13.3.2 Exports

The cement sector is relatively insulated from international markets. This is largely due to inadequate infrastructure, such as lack of bulk handling arrangements in our ports to carry out international trade. Being a very bulky item, international trade of cement is very limited, and only between neighbouring states. This is amply borne out by the fact that cement accounts for no more than 0.20 per cent of total world exports. Although India has been consistently exporting cement in the past, the volume of exports took a beating after the Southeast Asian crisis. From a peak of 2.68mn tonnes in 1997-98, cement exports from India have slid down to 2.06mn tonnes in 1998-99. Nevertheless, the situation has improved gradually, though it remained around at approximately three million tonnes, even in 2003-04.

Having a long coastline, India is well positioned to export cement to the Middle East and Sri Lanka. Unfortunately, congestion in the Indian ports and the lack of cement handling facilities restrict the free movement of cement out of India. Hence, only those companies who have their own jetties are able to export. Moreover, prices in the international market too are currently at non-remunerative levels. Nevertheless, companies like Gujarat Ambuja and L&T are major exporters, exporting mainly to benefit from incentives, like the duty-free import of high-grade coal and oil. Notwithstanding, large-scale cement exports are possible, only when cement prices in the international market look up.

13.3.3 Imports

Cement imports are negligible due to the very nature of the product. Moreover, it is unviable for any Asian supplier to compete in the Indian market unless they resort to dumping, which would inevitably result in anti-dumping measures being imposed on them. The Union Budget 2002-2003 brought down the cement import duty to 20 per cent, from the previous 25 per cent. This decrease is not so attractive to international players, as the cost of freight to carry the material inland would make the imports unfeasible. The price of cement in India is low compared to the international market, making India an unattractive country, for cement export by the international players.

13.4 Competition Concerns

As highlighted above, cement does not have any substitutes, which makes its demand inelastic. Also, since transportation costs constitute a major portion of the costs, the firms serve regional markets and do not operate out of their region. This typical nature of the industry has allegedly driven the firms to form cartels

and indulge in other collusive activities to reduce competition. The following are the activities that have significantly highlighted competition concerns:

13.4.1 Mergers and Acquisitions

Consolidation is not an entirely new phenomenon to the domestic cement industry. Even so, in the financial year 2001-2002, consolidation in the sector gained pace. Big players have taken over smaller ones, and the cumulative cement capacity in the country is now under the effective control of a small number of large and financially strong players. It is well known that the likelihood of attempted collusion, as well as its success, increases as the number of players involved becomes smaller, and as each one's leverage in the market share increases. Both these conditions appear to prevail in the Indian cement industry today and, hence, the authorities need to be vigilant to prevent anti-competitive practices in the market.

International players find India's expanding cement market a lucrative playing field, as the current demand in the Indian market is set to exceed its installed capacity very soon. Whilst a few multinationals have been eyeing the Indian market, Lafarge and Italcementi have already made their foray. Of the two ways of entering, viz. Greenfield venture and acquisition, foreign companies have resorted to the latter. This is mainly because of the long gestation period (24 months) and a high unit capital cost of approximately Rs. 3,500 per tonne, associated with the setting up of a new venture. Moreover, unit acquisition costs range from US$ 75 and US$ 80, per tonne capacity, and the MNCs are ready to offer a price range of between US$ 85 and US$ 90.

The trend towards consolidation is often viewed as a positive development for several reasons. First, the concentration of cement companies, in the hands of financially strong cement manufacturers, is often favourable for focussing on long-term vision, and allows for improved operating conditions in the entire industry. Second, the financial strength of these cement giants would help in rescuing assets that are on the verge of becoming, or have already become, non-performing assets in the books of Indian financial institutions.

Nonetheless, consolidation has negative aspects as well. Since the majority of the market share is in the hands of a few large companies, they can come together and collude, leading to a decline in competition. The industry has witnessed more than a dozen take-overs, both domestic and international, in the last few years.

TABLE 13.6

Recent Acquisitions in Indian Cement Industry

Year	Acquirer	Acquired	Consideration
Late-1990's	Lafarge	TISCO and Raymond	Rs. 5.5 billion and Rs. 7.85 billion respectively
1998	Gujarat Ambuja Cements (GACL)	Modi Cement	Rs. 313 crore
2001	Italcementi	India Cement which had earlier acquired the following in 1998-99:	
		Sri Vishnu Cement	Rs. 385 crore
		Raasi Cement	Rs. 445 crore
		Cement Corporation of India	Rs. 200 crore
1999	Grasim	Sri Digvijay Cements and Dharani Cements	Rs. 290 crore each
1999	Grasim	Indian Rayon's Cement Plant	Rs. 750 crore
2001	Grasim*	10 per cent stake in Larsen and Toubro (L&T) from the Reliance Infocom Project*	Rs. 2.5 crore
1998	GACL**	14.4 per cent stake in ACC	Rs. 1000 crore
1998	GACL**	DLF Cements	Rs. 131 crore

Note: * Larsen and Toubro had proposed a de-merger last year, attracting three foreign suitors -Lafarge, Holderbank and Cemex. By the end of 2003, Grasim's stake in CemCo (L&T's demerged cement business) reached 51 per cent.

** Lafarge was also eyeing the two companies, but GACL overtook them by acquiring the same.

The takeover of L&T by Grasim, and the strategic alliance between GACL (Gujarat Ambuja Cements Ltd.) and ACC (Associated Cement Companies Ltd.) have resulted in two major blocks controlling over 42 per cent of the domestic market share. Before this major restructuring, the top 5 cement majors in the domestic industry accounted for 30 per cent of total capacity. Post restructuring, the top 5 companies account for more than 55 per cent of total cement capacity in the country. This has shut down the possibility of any foreign major gaining a strong foothold in the Indian cement market. Nevertheless, the foreign players are holding discussions with willing Indian players; the strategy being to get a foothold in the Indian market first and consolidate later. For this, foreign players are not averse to offering a price tag higher than the market value of the acquisition.

A KK Birla Group company, Zuari Cement had a huge cash reserve after the European major Italcementi took a 50 per cent stake in the company for Rs. 370 crore. According to senior company officials, Zuari Cement was to step up capacity from two million tonnes to eight million tonnes by 2005. This was to be achieved mainly through acquisitions. Even the two largest players, Grasim-L&T and GACL-ACC, have adequate cash surplus for acquisitions.

There are views that indeed these cement giants should grow further, as cement business is capital-intensive and, therefore, a business of scale. Whilst the largest Indian player, Grasim-L&T, has a capacity of about 30Mt, the largest global player is Lafarge, with a capacity of 150Mt. However, Lafarge's market as well as production capacity are spread over different countries of the world. Grasim-L&T is an Indian company, with a very small share of its production going to export markets. It is also more concentrated in the Southern and Western regions of India. Moreover, it is also questionable if such a structure gives Lafarge any cost or efficiency advantage, or market advantage only.

GACL is expected to increase its capacity by 5-6 Mt within the next three years. Furthermore, it is also exploring opportunities to set up operations in the Middle East and even Europe, preferably through acquisitions. Overseas expansion might give the Indian giant the opportunity to grow bigger, without creating competition problems in the Indian market.[2] GACL is also likely to consolidate its holding over ACC, which is still vulnerable to hostile bids. Lafarge is another company, which is sitting on a huge cash reserve. Part of the reserve is likely to be used to expand its business in India, possibly through the acquisition route.

Despite significant consolidation in the cement industry, over the last few years, the size distribution remains highly skewed. As a matter of fact, it has increased due to consolidation. Thus, even as the largest player boasts an installed capacity of 30Mt, the median size of the remaining cement companies stands at 1.2 Mt (0.86 per cent of market share). Obviously, a large number of companies are operating far below the efficient scale (Dhawan, 2003). From the point of view of market competition, it would have been far better if, for example, Grasim took over a dozen smaller companies rather than L&T's cement business. It has been found that, in the Indian context, the relatively larger firms, with a market share of more than one per cent, performed distinctly better than the smaller ones (Vaidya, 2002).

13.4.2 Cartels and Price Rigging

It is widely believed that the cement manufacturers have been engaged in collusive price fixing since the beginning of the decontrol of cement prices in 1989. Indeed, price fixing could be a legacy of the erstwhile control regime. In this regime, the price was essentially determined by the Government. However, the cement manufacturers came together under the Cement Manufacturers Association (CMA) to lobby for higher prices. Thus, discussing prices has always been an important part of their collective lobbying activities. It would not be surprising if they continued to be engaged in similar activities even as the government withdrew from price determination.

The Cement industry is known to be prone to cartelisation worldwide. Cement being a low value bulky good is more or less immune from export competition in major relevant markets as the transportation cost is very high. The product being nearly homogeneous, fixing price does not pose any major problem. Moreover, as at least two years are required for a cement plant to commence production, from the time orders for plant and machinery are placed, and then another six months to stabilise production, the entry of a new player into a particular market is quite restricted. All these conditions make the cement industry ideal for cartelisation (*See Box 13.1*). In line with this, cement cartels were detected and busted in most major jurisdictions throughout the world. The possibility of cartelisation in India gets strengthened as the market is fragmented, and few sellers dominate each of the fragmented markets.

In 1991, the Indian cement industry was formally accused of price rigging, for the first time. The Monopolies and Restrictive Trade Practices Commission (MRTPC), was asked to adjudicate on a matter of collusive price setting in the Delhi market. The decision, however, went in favour of the industry. The industry had argued that the existence of bottlenecks in the movement of cement, from the plants to the major markets, was responsible for the surge in prices. These bottlenecks did not allow the natural forces of arbitrage to operate in the sense that, even if a producer had

excess capacity, the cost of shipping to the market experiencing a shortage was prohibitive.

BOX 13.1

Cement Cartelisation Around the World

The world's largest cement company was fined by the EC, in 2003, for participating in a cartel in the German cement market. Lafarge's plasterboard unit was fined € 250mn, and it was one of three companies hit by a € 478mn charge, after being found guilty of a six-year conspiracy to fix the price of the widely used product.

. . . .

In December 2002, the price of cement had fallen to an exceptionally low LE (Egyptian Pound) 125 per tonne in Egypt. The drop had caused serious worries among the cement producers. In response, almost all the local cement producers met, and set a price range for cement between LE167 and LE176 a tonne. However, no action could be taken, as Egypt did not have a competition law.

. . . .

In October 1998, the Monopoly Control Authority (MCA) of Pakistan noticed a simultaneous and uniform price increase, to the tune of Rs. 100 (from Rs. 135 to Rs. 235) per bag, by the cement manufacturers. The All Pakistan Cement Manufacturing Association (APCMA) attributed this to the increase in the costs of inputs, and higher taxes. Upon inquiry, the MCA found that there was no substantial increase in input costs, and that the taxes had been lowered sometime before. The MCA ordered the APCMA to deposit a sum of Rs. 4.25bn, earned by the industry as additional revenue between mid-October 1998 and February 1999. The MCA further imposed a fine of Rs. 100,000 on each individual unit, and in the case of non-compliance, another Rs. 10,000 per day. The cement manufacturers went to the provincial High Court and obtained a stay order. Finally, the Government intervened and negotiated with the companies, to set the price at Rs. 200 per bag and also to lower the taxes.

. . . .

In Japan, cement firms' consistent pattern of selling cheaply overseas, and dearly at home, is widely believed to be due to the discipline of the domestic price cartels. Cement firms allegedly threaten to cut off sales to construction companies that buy imports.

After economic liberalisation in 1991, cement manufacturers, in India, enhanced their installed capacities in the hope of mammoth sales. The expected demand hike did not materialise, due to the slowdown that followed and, hence, manufacturers were left with excess supply, which they dealt with by collusive practices such as price-fixing and market sharing. Over the past two decades, cement production in India has increased five fold, whilst its demand has slackened in several parts of the country, creating a surplus production capacity. To meet this glut in the market, cement manufacturers formed a cartel and stopped despatches all over India, from November 27, 2000, to December 3, 2000. Despatches resumed from December 4, but with a uniform price hike all over the country.

The weak demand was met with a supply squeeze. Cement manufacturers in India were accused of creating an artificial cement crisis. Leading cement manufacturers: GACL, ACC, L&T and Grasim, were perceived to be acting as a cartel. The Builders' Association of India (BAI) reacted by demanding government intervention to initiate action, under the MRTP Act for "unfair trade practices," resorted to by the cement industry. The BAI approached the Central Government, and petitioned it to reduce the import duty of cement, from 38 per cent to 10 per cent, to encourage the import of cement. The association also demanded the withdrawal of additional special duty and countervailing duty on cement, since this would hamper imports from possible cement suppliers in countries, such as Thailand, Indonesia, China and South Korea.

The MRTPC initiated a *suo moto* enquiry into the cement price hike, between November 27, 2000 and December 3, 2000. The commission issued notices to the five major cement companies to respond to the complaints against them, before the Commission. The companies were also directed to submit details of the total turnover of the cement despatched, to the distributors and the market, from January 2000 to December 2000, on a monthly basis.

The notice of enquiry was issued after hearing the submissions and, *prima facie* being satisfied about cartelisation. The Commission also issued a short notice for February 28, 2001 on an injunction application. The injunction application prayed for restraining the cement companies from forming a cartel, in price quantity and/or market control, and raising the prices to an artificial level and, consequently, directing them to roll down the prices to the level prevailing on November 15, 2000. The application also prayed for restraining the cement companies from withholding the supplies and manipulating the output, by stopping production or despatches.

The complainant (the BAI) also submitted that the cement manufacturers had taken undue advantage of the Government notification, wherein it has been made mandatory for importers/manufacturers to register themselves with the Bureau of Indian Standards (BIS). This is because the artificial scarcity created by the domestic suppliers cannot be met by imports, in the short run.

Cement manufacturers, on the other hand, denied any cartel type arrangements. They claimed that the price hike was the result of an increase in the cost of manufacturing cement. The cost of raw materials and inputs escalated, due to royalty charges and a hike in coal prices, thus, justifying the cement price hike. Cement manufacturers further claimed that, even after the price hike, the price was still not attractive when the return on investment was considered. This claim was countered by the Builders' Association of India (BAI) saying that the cement manufacturers, asking for a fair return on investment, was like the consumers being told to virtually underwrite the losses of the cement industry. In a decontrolled price arena, this amounted to inviting price control. The industry must bear the burden of wrong commercial decisions, and not pass on the burden to the consumers, claimed the BAI.

The BAI, on their part resorted to the selective boycott of cement manufacturers. The Government also responded to the demands of the BAI by slashing the import duty in the 2001-02 budget. Furthermore, the BAI arranged to import 800,000 bags of cement, at a landed cost of around Rs. 140 per bag at a time, when the ruling prices in Mumbai were at around Rs. 185 per bag. The prices of cement started falling throughout the country. In fact, in the Western market, prices fell even below the previous level (See Box 13.2).

Allegations of price-collusive behaviour, by the cement industry, continue to be raised time and again. So much so, that *www.indiainfoline.com*, a leading business information website, starts its page on "Cement Industry – Cost Structure and Pricing" with the statement, "In India, cement prices are purely a function of cartels (except in Western India where cartels don't survive for long)". It goes on to add: "The cartel decides the floor price and the sales volume by the individual members in a region. Obviously, the biggest beneficiary is the largest player. Southern states feed themselves and are impossibly hard to penetrate. This is the reason why cartel is strongest here. In the North, Punjab, Delhi, Haryana, cannot have strong cartels because of despatches from Rajasthan. Because of very limited limestone, UP does not have many plants but the consumption is taken care of by states enjoying excess surplus—MP and Rajasthan. Hence, cartel in these states (MP, UP and Rajasthan) is impossible."

BOX 13.2

Builders' Boycott to Break the Cartel!

It has been a long-standing allegation that cement prices in India are not determined by market forces, but by collusive price-fixing of the manufacturers. In 2001, the cement cartel, after showing signs of weakness for a few months, once again became active. The said cartel stopped despatches all over India from November 27, 2000, to December 3, 2000. Dispatch resumed from December 4, but with a uniform price hike all over the country. The price hike was about Rs. 50 per bag, a rise of almost 50 per cent.

This was too much to digest for the major construction companies, who consumed about 60 per cent of the total cement consumption in the country. These companies, under the banner of Builders Association of India (BAI) urged the Cement Manufacturers Association (CMA) to roll back the prices. However, the CMA turned down their demand. The BAI decided to stop purchasing of cement from January 15, 2001, and their construction activities came to a grinding halt in many projects, even though they had strict deadlines. After a few days, the builders realised that civil work could not be stalled indefinitely, as they were also losing over Rs. 5 crore daily.

BAI, thus, decided to change its strategy. Instead of boycotting all the manufacturers, they targeted two major companies, Grasim and GACL, who were also believed to be leading the cartel. The idea was to create an incentive problem amongst the players, which could lead to a rift among them.

Meanwhile, BAI also lobbied the Government for a 10 per cent reduction in basic customs duty, from the then existing 38 per cent, as well as for the removal of the surcharge of 10 per cent, anti-dumping duty of Rs. 10 per metric tonne, and the countervailing duty of Rs. 350 per metric tonne. The BAI even allied itself with the then Chief Minister of Maharashtra, Vilasrao Deshmukh, who had a series of meetings with the Union Finance Minister, Yashwant Sinha. In the 2001-02 budget, the Government reduced the import duty, and removed the surcharge, as well.

Taking full advantage of this, the BAI arranged to import 800,000 bags of cement from the Far-East, at a landed cost of around Rs. 140 per bag at a time, when the ruling prices in Mumbai were at around Rs. 185 per bag. Consequently, cement prices started falling.

It is not known if good sense prevailed upon the cement majors; if Lafarge triggered disunity, by refusing to play ball with the domestic players, especially in the Eastern market, where it is the biggest player; or if it was because of the actions of the BAI and the Government. The dealers felt that the prices were falling because of renewed competition among the manufacturers.

There are, of course, good reasons for making such observations. As can be seen from the Table 13.7, the Southern region has huge excess capacity, both in absolute as well as in relative terms, and yet the average prices, prevailing in the region, are higher compared to other regions. The South also had the highest increase in average prices in the year 2003-04,

over 2002-03. In the Western region, the average prices had a fall, even though they were quite low compared to other regions.

TABLE 13.7

Region-wise Excess Capacity and Price Movement

Region	Installed Capacity (MTs)	Total Consumption 2003-04	Excess Capacity	Relative Excess Capacity	Average Price (2003-04) per bag of 50 Kgs. (in Rs.)	Price Rise Over 2002-03 and 2003-04
Northern	25.20	22.60	2.60	11.50	142	4.0%
Eastern	21.71	16.95	4.76	28.08	146	3.4%
Southern	44.30	31.65	12.65	39.97	145	4.6%
Western	25.33	22.60	2.73	12.08	132	-0.9%
Central	20.99	16.95	4.04	23.83	128	3.4%
Total	137.53	112.75	24.78	—	—	—

Source: CMA (2004).

In the meantime, the MRTPC lost its vigour due to the adoption of the new Competition Act. It is not known if any case was lodged with the MRTPC or if there has been any progress in the case initiated by the MRTPC, as noted above.

In a significant move, the Gujarat Government asked the cement manufacturers to bring down prices, alleging that the prevailing high prices were artificially created through cartelisation. The manufacturers were, of course, not bound to oblige as the State Government did to have any legal instrument to force them to do so. Any action, on the alleged collusive behaviour of the cement manufacturers, can be initiated only after the new Competition Commission of India starts operating.

13.4.3 Other Issues

Recent events in the industry have shown that it is not difficult for new players to enter the market. However, entry can only be made through the acquisition route in the short run. The gestation period of installing a cement plan is fairly lengthy and, hence, entry through Greenfield route takes time. Coupled with this, is the fact that, competition from imports is extremely limited, making a "hit and run" entry extremely difficult. Thus, the market is contestable in a limited sense.

The Indian cement market has had a reasonably good number of players. Despite the recent trend towards consolidation, dominance by a single firm is not yet perceived to be an important issue. Hence, no case of predatory pricing or other such anti-competitive behaviour, arising from dominance, has been reported so far.

One important aspect of the Indian cement market is that nearly 30 per cent of total cement consumption in the country is in the government sector, with the Central Public Works Department (CPWD) or State PWDs. The Governments (both Central and States) buy cement in bulk, through competitive bidding. However, there are good reasons to believe that such a bidding procedure may be subverted by bid rigging.

As the number of sellers willing to deliver, at a particular location, would be rather small, there would be enough mutual understanding amongst the players to facilitate collusion. It is also unlikely that a surprise player would shock the conspiring parties, as the high transportation costs make that difficult. Moreover, the product being nearly homogeneous, the price becomes the sole determinant and, hence, rigging a bid becomes easier, as the calculations made by the players are unlikely to be upset by non-price considerations.

13.5 Concluding Observations

The cement industry in India has immense growth potential, which is waiting to be tapped, by either domestic cement giants or international majors. Nonetheless, the increasingly concentrated industry faces larger and larger risks of firms resorting to collusive practices and uncompetitive behaviour, as the market share of few companies becomes significantly large when compared to other firms. The cement companies have allegedly tried to increase prices through forming informal cartels. As mentioned before, cartelisation in cement industry is a global phenomenon and, hence, there is enough scope for learning, in this regard, from other countries.

Recent consolidation, leading to the emergence of a handful of dominant players, has changed this, increasing the likelihood of cartels becoming more successful in future. In that sense, big foreign players are welcome, as a large number of strong players would make cartelisation that much more difficult. However, it has been observed that consolidation in domestic industries also takes place, in order to face the challenges from foreign competitors. In order to protect the economy and consumers, from collusive behaviour and other anti-competitive practices, the new competition law is required to be implemented vigorously.

The Monopolies and Restrictive Trade Practices (MRTP) Act 1969, the outgoing competition law of the country, does not have merger review provisions. The Act earlier had provisions relating to Mergers and Acquisitions (M&As), under which no M&A activity could take place, prior to the consent of the Central Government. The related sections were however, omitted in 1991. Though the provision for demerger still exists, it has never been used by the MRTPC or the Government.

The new Competition Act has merger review provisions, and such activities will be subject to surveillance and regulation for any possible adverse effect on competition. The M&As will not be a taboo in the eyes of competition law. The litmus test will be whether the benefits of the merger or acquisition outweigh the adverse effects on competition. Merger review notification is subject to certain thresholds and is not mandatory. If the merger consideration exceeds a certain limit, only then it is subject to voluntary notification to the Competition Commission.[3]

The Competition Act directs the Competition Commission of India to take into account many factors for the purpose of determining whether there would be an appreciable adverse effect on competition. Among the listed factors are the:

- level of competition through imports in the market,

- extent of barriers to market entry,

- extent of effective competition in the market,

- extent to which substitutes are available, and

- nature and extent of innovation.

It is also mandated to adjudicate on M&A by weighing potential efficiency losses against potential gains.

As has been noted before, there is sufficient scope for further consolidation in the industry, as there are many small players. Consolidation amongst them should be encouraged to improve efficiency. Even so, further consolidation among the bigger players should be carefully watched, and may not be allowed. In this era of globalisation, they should rather be encouraged to start overseas operations instead of acquiring further dominance in the domestic market, if the potential for abuse of dominance is very high.

On the issue of cartelisation, no credible action has been taken, despite repeated allegations to this effect. As a matter of fact, the record of the MRTPC, in handling cartels as such, has been rather hopeless. The underlying problem is that the scope of provisions relating to cartels in the MRTPA is very limited and weak. This, along with weak investigation capacity due to resource constraints, amongst other extraneous factors, is the primary reason for cartel formation going unchecked for years. The new law is a significant improvement, in this regard, with clearer provisions and a leniency programme.

Clearly, cement is one of the sectors that will need the careful attention of the Competition Commission, once it starts functioning on a reasonable scale. The cement industry has been trying to underplay the issue by claiming that the Government, or the regulators, should leave the industry alone, as it is already supplying cement at one of the lowest possible prices in the world. Nevertheless, this does not necessarily mean that there is no cartelisation, or that they are very efficient. This may also be due to the fact that the price of key raw materials of cement are still regulated in India, and the manufacturers might be getting them at low prices.[4]

The technology in the cement industry is more or less standardised,[5] with little scope for the firms collaborating on R&D activities. It is, therefore, likely that if they are hobnobbing with each other, it is probably for mutual understanding on price fixing or market sharing. Admittedly, proving collusive behaviour would be an uphill task for the new competition authority. Although, there is one important source of information, that may be explored. Careful analysis of the documents, related to bid offers by different companies in Central and State Government bids, can give important clues to any possible patterns of the systematic rotation of winning bids, stable shares of companies in overall procurement, etc., if bid-rigging has taken place. This information would also be helpful in detecting collusive behaviour in the market as well (Vaidya, 2004).

Cement is one of the basic goods, extremely important for economic development. This is more so in India, as the country needs huge investment in infrastructure development, requiring the growth of cement consumption. The availability of cement at competitive prices is, therefore, of utmost importance. The Competition Commission of India, thus, needs to take the business, of maintaining competition in the cement market, very seriously.

BOX 13.3
Issues for Further Research

- Careful analysis of the bid offers by different companies in Central and state government contracts can give important clues to the occurrence of any collusive behaviour.
- A Rolling programme on the analysis of cement price movements, in regional markets.
- Comparative analyses of cement markets, in countries where cement cartels have been successfully busted, with that of India.

Notes

1. Considering that the combinations of Grasim-L&T as well GACL-ACC are to be treated as one player, though legally each are different companies.

2. GACL and L&T have already developed facilities in Sri Lanka. However, no manufacturing is done there. They import cement powder or clinker from India, and only packing and grounding (in case of clinker) are done in Sri Lanka.

3. Competition Act 2002, Section 6 (2). Section 5 (a) of the CA 2003 states that the acquisition of one or more enterprises by one or more persons or merger or amalgamation of enterprises shall be a combination of such enterprises if (i) the parties to the acquisition jointly have - either in India, the assets of the value of more than Rs. 1000 crore (US$ 208 mn) or turnover more than Rs. 3000 crore (US$ 625 mn) or - in India or outside India, in aggregate, the assets of the value of more than US$ 500 mn or turnover more than US$ 1500 mn; (ii) or the group to which the enterprise whose control, shares, assets or voting rights have been acquired or are being acquired, would belong after the acquisition, jointly - have or would jointly have either in India, the assets of the value of more than Rs. 4000crore (US$ 833 mn) or turnover more than Rs. 12000 crore (US$ 2500 mn) or - in India or outside India, in aggregate, the assets of the value of more than US$ 2 bn or turnover more than US$ 6 bn.

4. The two major inputs for cement are coal and limestone. Whilst coal prices are regulated by the Government, limestone costs are also *de facto* regulated, as the royalty is determined by the Government.

5. There are two major types of cement: Ordinary Portland Cement (OPC) or blended cement (known as Pozolana Portland Cement or PPC). However, in terms of technology used, they are not substantially different. There are some special quality cements as well, but they are rather small in terms of market share. In blended cement, fly ash and blast furnace slag are mixed. Fly ash and slag are almost freely available and causes environmental problems as well and, hence, the environmental policy discourages their use. However, government procurement policy tends to negate as CPWD and state PWDs refuse to buy blended cement.

References

Chakravarthy, S.M. (1989). *Indian Cement Industry: From Control to Decontrol*, Wadhera Publications, Bombay.

CRIS-INFAC (2003). *Cement Annual Review*, October.

Dhawan, Radhika (2003). "Mergers in the Air," *Businessworld*, July 14 (http://www.businessworldindia.com).

Mehta, Pradeep S. (2003). "Mergers & Acquisitions – Cementing the Industry," (*mimeo*), CUTS, Jaipur.

Nath, P. and P.R. Bose (2002). "Leveraging Liberalisation: The Case of Indian Cement Industry" in *Economic and Political Weekly*, July 27.

Vaidya, R.R. (2002). "Intermediate Goods Industries: Case Studies of the Cement and Steel Industries" in S. Uchikawa (ed.) *Economic Reforms and Industrial Structure in India*, Manohar Books, New Delhi.

————. (2004). "Competition Policy and the Indian Cement Industry" (*mimeo*), Indira Gandhi Institute of Development Research (IGIDR), Mumbai.

CMA (2004) http://www.cmaindia.org

http://www.indiainfoline.com/nevi/ceme2.html

http://www.indiainfoline.com/nevi/ceup.html

http://www.indiainfoline.com/nevi/fiup.html

http://www.utisel.com/reports/cement%20valuation%20report.pdf

14 Competition Scenario in Indian Steel Industry

A.S. Firoz

14.1 Introduction

Competition issues are to be seen in general, in the context of the market power of a firm or a segment of the industry, and the growth and investment opportunities of individual firms or specific segments of the industry. Some of the issues are hinged on market competition, including market share, and the ability of the firm to control market price from the favourable nature of the market itself. The matters related to pricing are subject to imperfect market structures at one level as well as some 'ethical' issues the society gets used to by expecting the industry or firms to act in the larger interest of the society and not as a pure individual profit seeker. Therefore, while the outcomes of competition are desired in 'consumer interest', 'public interest' at times takes precedence over the former. In such cases, drawing a balance between public and consumer interests becomes the core of any competition policy objective.

Again, in the context of measuring the level of distortion in price that may have resulted from an imperfect market structure, one has to have a benchmark. Following the market theory, the best option will be to take the perfectly competitive price level. It may be an altogether different matter that such a price reference may not at all be found in the real market. The issue of pricing and the market structures are relevant to competition issues also, in the context of entry barriers, self created, historically developed or naturally found, effects of which are again reflected in price distortion.

Market price distortion can arise out of abuse of dominance as well. Here the major concerns are the size of the firms, market shares, mergers and acquisitions, etc.; in effect, the degree of concentration of market power through ownership. There is another important issue attached to it. The larger firms, with the advantages they derive from the system, purely due to their domination through ownership, become unduly more competitive in the capital market. They thereby create for themselves favourable conditions for growth at the expense of smaller firms (which could be even more efficient), leading to further concentration of market power, and help themselves with higher than the industry average growth rates. Although such conditions may not affect the consumer interest directly, they certainly work against other segment of the industry or other players in the market.

Trade and other government policies have significant bearing on the competition issues. The matter of subsidies, and non-tariff barriers to trade, etc., may bring in significant distortions in the domestic market, and in the process alter the competitive positioning of individual players in the market. The specific role of the state in creating market distortion, and thereby the competitive conditions in the market, is a well-known issue in this country. However, the trade related issues have drawn far greater attention in the context of international trade.

Are competition issues relevant in the context of the Indian steel industry?

In fact, one does not need to go very far to convince that steel, being a manufactured and globally tradable product with no inherent shortages, and the market being almost free from any significant policy restriction, is not expected to throw up any substantive competition policy issues, compared to say sectors like telecom, electricity, oil, etc. The issues can, however, be identified, depending on the understanding one has on competition itself. The industry, therefore, can at best, be expected to throw up problems of very specific nature only. It may not really be possible to bring these under a larger generalised framework. However, there are issues that make one concerned about the competition issues in the industry from the point of public policy. These arise from the growing oligopolistic nature of the market, and relatively higher growth rates for individual large entities, made possible by active support of the financial system and the state, and intra-industry competition tilting in favour of the big.

The basic character of the steel industry is almost the same worldwide. Therefore, one can expect the competition issues in this country to have extensive similarities with those elsewhere. It will make sense, therefore, to look at the industry also from a global perspective and try to place the Indian context in it. In many ways, what is being witnessed today globally may be the trend for tomorrow in this country. This paper, however, does not dwell on these issues, fearing loss of focus on the more immediate concerns in the Indian context.

This paper examines the structure of the steel industry in India. It seeks to identify the structurally inherent and also the market determined positioning of various steel firms, specifically to see their market power, *vis-à-vis* both their final consumers as well as those within the steel industry. The issues emerging out of the size and market shares, specifically taking into consideration the investment aspects, will be taken up subsequently.

14.2 Deregulation in the 90s and the Emerging Policy Framework

Steel was a regulated industry sector till 1992, and the erstwhile policy was to allocate scarce investment and infrastructure resources for optimum and planned development of the industry, and to make available this scarce industrial intermediate to the users at reasonable prices. The basic purpose of the past policy was to manage a scarcity driven market for its fair and equitable distribution.

The pre-reform steel market in India was controlled in all relevant areas. Competition was limited in this shortage-infested market, with the market having no real role to play in the growth or performance of individual firms, and the allocative efficiency of investible resources. The prices set by the government were more on political consideration than on the basis of costs of production or market demand and supply balance.[1] Although one can expect such a system of controlled prices to be favourable to the consumers, in the absence of an elaborate and extra-efficient distribution mechanism, the trading intermediaries,

with whatever role they were allowed to play, could gobble up the margin between the market and the administered prices, with little benefits left for the thousands of small consumers.

Various economic reforms, introduced since 1991, started changing the contours of regulation in this important industry. In 1991, the government lifted the provisions that reserved investment in the integrated steel plants only for the public sector. The sector was opened up further by the removal of the erstwhile licensing system. In January 1992, the regulations on pricing and distribution of steel were lifted. Along with this, the levy towards Engineering Goods Export Assistance Fund (EGEAF) was also abolished. The levy towards Steel Development Fund (SDF) was also subsequently done away with retrospective effect.

The government, however, decided to continue with priority allocation of steel to defence, small-scale industries, atomic energy and the north-eastern states of the country. These changes were brought in by bringing necessary modifications in the Iron and Steel Control Order, under the Essential Commodities Act. The Freight Equalisation Scheme, which was created to ensure delivery of iron and steel at the same rail freight to a customer located anywhere in the country, was substituted by a system of freight ceiling subsequently. The government then, in steps, opened up the sector for foreign direct investment, and now permits 100 per cent equity holding in any steel company by foreign companies. The steel industry's trading environment changed with the abolition of regulations related to external trade, and significant lowering of import duties on steel and related raw materials.

14.3 Structure of Industry

Steel is a heterogeneous industry with widely differentiated products, varying technology and economics. The steel industry in India, in particular, exhibits a larger degree of heterogeneity and differentiation than in other countries. The structure of the industry is complex and with an equally intricate interplay of forces of dependency and integration, the competition scenario has turned fairly interesting, more so in recent times, with dynamic changes in the structure of the industry.

Steel is produced in India, using a variety of technologies, in plants with extensive variation in size, vintage and levels of process integration.

The differential competitive positioning on this count has been derived historically as a result of the government policies in the past that gave rise to significant market distortions.[2] To some extent, this disparity continues even today, not necessarily as a conscious policy of the government, but more as a necessity for convenience to move along the already laid out tracks and the difficulties perceived in any attempt to change past policies. To elaborate, although the choice of technology has become increasingly market determined, it is based on pure commercial considerations. The policies related to ownership and leasing of mines and specific government interventions do significantly influence the technology choice and investment decisions. The policy related to leasing and operation of iron ore, and even coal mines, has been significantly liberalised, allowing for substantial captive ownership by steel plants.[3] The mushrooming of inefficient small units of steel has been the outcome of the government's restrictive and regulatory policies of the past, especially the erstwhile licensing system. Technology choice, even in the deregulated era, has been fashioned by the residual impact of the restrictive mining policies, and the erstwhile price and distribution controls in a segment of the industry.

14.4 Competition Structure of the Steel Industry

The first step to understand the nature of competition in the Indian steel industry will be to examine the position of major steel producing companies and industry segments in terms of production capacity. For that, one of the more convenient ways to go about will be to examine the crude steel production capacities of various steel companies (major ones), and the groups of small companies with distinct technology characters and the changes in their respective shares over time.

It is interesting to observe from Table 14.1 that the share of crude steel capacity of SAIL has fallen from about 38 per cent in 1997-98 to about 31 per cent in 2003-04. At the time when the economy was opened up in the early-90s, SAIL accounted for a significant share in the total crude steel production and nearly 100 per cent of the wide Hot Rolled Coils (HRCs) production capacity. The company has 23 per cent share in long products at present. Further, with their sales of semi-finished products to smaller mills, they literally controlled the steel market in the country. TISCO, the other dominant player, gradually raised their steel production capacity, as also the market share. What is interesting to note is that the market share of very small units, producing steel using induction furnaces or small electric arc furnaces, increased over the years, as is evident from Table 14.1.

TABLE 14.1

Crude Steel Capacity

('000 tonnes)

Unit	1997-98	1998-99	1999-2000	2000-01	2001-02	2002-03	2003-04 (Prov)
SAIL							
Bokaro	4000 (12.64)	4000 (12.36)	4360 (12.98)	4360 (12.78)	4360 (12.76)	4360 (12.43)	3820 (9.73)
Bhilai	3925 (12.40)	3925 (12.13)	3925 (11.69)	3925 (11.51)	3925 (11.49)	3925 (11.19)	4150 (10.57)
Rourkela	1550 (4.90)	1900 (5.87)	1900 (5.66)	1900 (5.57)	1900 (5.56)	1900 (5.41)	1642 (4.18)
Durgapur	1802 (5.69)	1802 (5.57)	1802 (5.37)	1802 (5.28)	1802 (5.27)	1802 (5.14)	1785 (4.54)
IISCO	360 (1.14)	325 (1.00)	300 (0.89)	380 (1.11)	380 (1.11)	380 (1.08)	423 (1.08)
Alloy Steels Plant (ASP)	234 (0.74)	234 (0.72)	234 (0.70)	234 (0.69)	234 (0.68)	234 (0.67)	123 (0.31)
Visvesvaraya Iron and Steel Plant (VISL)	95 (0.30)	95 (0.29)	95 (0.28)	95 (0.28)	95 (0.28)	95 (0.27)	108 (0.27)
TOTAL (SAIL Group)	11966 (37.81)	12281 (37.94)	12616 (37.57)	12696 (37.23)	12696 (37.15)	12696 (36.18)	12051 (30.68)
TISCO	3050 (9.64)	3050 (9.42)	3280 (9.77)	3500 (10.26)	3500 (10.24)	3500 (9.97)	4000 (10.18)
Rashtriya Ispat Nigam Ltd. (RINL)	2700 (8.53)	2700 (8.34)	2910 (8.67)	2910 (8.53)	2910 (8.52)	2910 (8.29)	3476 (8.85)
Essar	2200 (6.95)	2200 (6.80)	2200 (6.55)	2200 (6.45)	2200 (6.44)	2400 (6.84)	2400 (6.11)
Jindal Vijaynagar Steel Ltd. (JVSL)	1570 (4.96)	1570 (4.85)	1570 (4.68)	1570 (4.60)	1570 (4.59)	1570 (4.47)	1570 (4.00)
Ispat	1200 (3.79)	1200 (3.71)	1200 (3.57)	1500 (4.40)	1500 (4.39)	1800 (5.13)	1800 (4.58)
Lloyds	450 (1.42)	450 (1.39)	450 (1.34)	450 (1.32)	450 (1.32)	450 (1.28)	450 (1.15)
Other Electric Arc Furnaces (EAF)/Mini Blast Furnaces (MBF)	1230 (3.89)	1230 (3.80)	1634 (4.87)	1722 (5.05)	2168 (6.34)	2561 (7.30)	3562 (9.07)
Induction Furnaces (IF)	7280 (23.00)	7690 (23.76)	7720 (22.99)	7556 (22.16)	7178 (21.01)	7203 (20.53)	9970 (25.38)
GRAND TOTAL	**31646**	**32371**	**33580**	**34104**	**34172**	**35090**	**39279**

Source: Joint Plant Committee. The figures have been in certain places changed from what the JPC has published for correction considering data obtained from other sources.

Note: Percentage share of grand total given in parentheses.

The nature of competition in the steel market will not be significantly different if the actual output is considered against production capacity. Actual output criterion is being adopted at a later stage, when specific products are being considered.

14.5 Competition Structure by Product Category

In general, the structure of competition in the Indian steel industry can be summarised as shown in Table 14.2. The Table shows the major players in the market, as also the dominant players in it for each respective product category. By a dominant player, one means here a large individual producer, or a group of small producers, who have a significant market share and can lead the market price.

From the above table, it can be seen that the nature of competition in the steel market is extremely complex, especially when seen for each product separately. Steel products vary by size, shape, chemistry and physical properties, and the steel going into higher end industrial or critical construction applications has to satisfy a large number of physical and chemical properties. Since a given steel plant has limitations, on account of diseconomies of scale and technical constraints, in producing all the grades and shapes, competition for each gets confined to only a smaller number of players. It, therefore, makes little sense to talk of the industry as a whole to understand the nature of competition in the market.

14.6 Competitive Structure for Relevant Products

Before one proceeds with the analysis further, it may be important in the light of the above to identify some 'relevant' products in the industry to assess the nature of competition in the industry as a representative case. It may not be possible or desirable to study the market of each individual product to come to some broad conclusions on competition issues for the industry as a whole.

Among the flat products, HRCs occupy the most critical position in the chain of products in the industry. It is one product that requires extensive investment and economies of scale for profitable production, and with its position as the **'mother flat product'**, controls the prices of the downstream and even the upstream products. This position of strength has also been due to the fact that this is the largest traded product in steel. Therefore, while dealing with flat steel products, focus will be on the HRCs.

In the case of long (non-flat) products, the choice of a 'relevant product' is more complex. While a semi-finished product, like billet, can be seen as the mother of most long products, the volume traded is not significant and the price of billets may not necessarily decide the price of long products. Although there are significant differences, once the pencil ingots are also taken into account and placed along billets, the volume traded becomes large.

TABLE 14.2

Product-Wise Dominant Players and Market Character

Product	Players	Dominant Players	Market Character
Bars and Rods	Re-rolling mills, SAIL, TISCO, RINL	Varies along products and product characteristics	Wide range of products and the number of products involving competition among the major players or industry groups is small. Strong competition among the re-rolling mills.
Light Structurals	Re-rolling Mills, SAIL and RINL	Re-rolling mills	Competition is among the re-rolling mills.
Medium Structurals	RINL, SAIL	RINL	Limited competition.
Heavy Structurals	SAIL, fabrication units, JSPL (small quantities in production)	SAIL	Expected limited competition with JSPL in place, Oligopoly.
Railway Materials	SAIL, JSPL (yet to supply to Indian Railways)	SAIL	Limited competition expected with JSPL in place. Bilateral monopoly till now.
Cut to Length Plates (products of plate mills)	SAIL	SAIL	Monopoly.
HR Coils	SAIL, TISCO, JVSL, Essar Steel, Ispat Industries		Potentially a competitive market, but, with strong global and domestic demand, cartelisation can be expected.
HR Sheets	SAIL, TISCO, JVSL, Essar Steel, Ispat Industries	SAIL	Small volume product sold mostly to the end users directly.
CR Coils/Sheets	SAIL, TISCO, Ispat Industries, merchant CR producers, importantly Bhushan Steel	SAIL, TISCO and merchant producers	Competitive market with differentiated products.
Galvanised Sheets/Coils	SAIL, TISCO, Ispat Industries, merchant producers, importantly Bhushan, JISCO.	SAIL, TISCO, JISCO	Highly competitive market.
Electrical Sheets	SAIL and EBG	SAIL	Small domestic production base and substantially imported.
Tinplates	SAIL, TCIL	SAIL, TCIL (Tata Group)	Oligopoly.
Large Diameter Pipes	SAIL, Saw Pipes, Others	SAIL, Saw Pipes	Oligopoly.
Stainless Steel Flat Products	SAIL, Jindal Stainless, small players	SAIL, Jindal Stainless	Highly competitive.

The other alternative is to take bars and rods. Still, given the difficulties arising out of the heterogeneous character of the bars and rods and the widely divergent prices of these products, it makes more sense to consider billets/pencil ingots together – for our analysis. These two are substitutable in most cases, which is not the case when various bars and rods are considered.

The character of competition in the steel market is understood better once the nature of integration within the industry is taken into account. For example, the merchant producers of CR coils/sheets (CRCs) and also of galvanised sheets and coils (GP/GCs), have to depend on the companies producing their required inputs of HRCs. Let us try to look at this scenario in detail.

14.7 Hot Rolled Coils (HRCs)

SAIL and TISCO produce HRCs as well as downstream products like CRCs and GP/GCs. Given the capacity of their downstream mills, they are forced to sell significant quantities of HRCs on merchant basis. They do so also because it makes more business sense to have a diversified mix of saleable products. These companies have their downstream facilities in the same complex. Ispat Industries and Jindal Vijaynagar Steel Ltd. (JVSL) have downstream units separately, either as sister entities or part of the same company. Although a significant part of the HRCs they produce go to the downstream units, given the fact that their plants are separated, it may make more sense for them not to make a distinction between captive sales and outside sales, if the terms are comparable. Also, as in

the case of SAIL and TISCO, each of these two companies has more HRC capacity than what they have for the downstream products. The case of Essar Steel is different, as they do not have downstream capacities directly owned by them. The market structure for wide HRCs can be seen from Table 14.3 below.

It is evident from Table 14.3 that out of about 13 million tonnes of HRCs produced for the year 2003-04, the five major producers, SAIL, TISCO, Essar Steel, Ispat Industries and JVSL together have a share of about 93 per cent, and nearly 100 per cent of the production on a merchant basis. This is after considering the sales of JVSL and Ispat to their downstream units, located elsewhere, as merchant sales, as the companies indicated that these are strictly on commercial terms. The merchant sales include exports and in 2003-04, exports of HRCs reached 1.716 million tonnes. That is, the actual supplies to the domestic market were somewhere around 6.638 million tonnes.

This accounted for about 90.6 per cent of the total size of the market on actual trade basis, after imports and outputs from other medium sized plants [small quantities of HRCs, less than a million tonnes, are produced by companies like Jindal Iron and Steel Company (JISCO) – from purchased slabs] were taken into account.

This shows that the five companies have significant market share, and, if cartelised, could easily influence the market prices to conform to their interests.

But, the question arises; does this level of concentration give the HRC producers sufficient degree

TABLE 14.3
Market Structure for Wide Hot Rolled Coils (2003-04)

Name of Company	Estimated Capacity (Million Tonnes)	Merchant Production (Million Tonnes)	Estimated Captive Consumption (Million Tonnes)	Total Production (Million Tonnes)	Percentage of Merchant Sales	Share of Company in Total Industry Production	Share of Company's Merchant Production in Total Industry Production
SAIL	5.3	2.548	2.1	4.648	54.8	35.8	19.6
TISCO	2.0	1.306	1.54	2.846	45.9	21.9	10.1
Essar Steel	2.2	1.7	0	1.7	100	13.1	13.1
Ispat Industries$	1.8	1.5	0	1.5	100	11.6	11.6
JVSL$	1.6	1.3	0	1.3	100	10.0	10.0
Others#	1.0	0	0.985	0.985		7.6	0.0
Total	13.9	8.354		12.979		100	64.4

Source: The base data for the table has been collected from various sources, including directly from the companies concerned.

$: Captive sales not considered as these are market based and units separated.

#: No reliable data could be available on the division between merchant and captive sales. These are being, therefore, put in the captive sales category, as plants producing them have downstream processing facilities.

of pricing power? This may not be so, because of the following factors:

1. Imports at six per cent of the total consumption of HRCs (for the year 2003-04) in the market is not significant, though not negligible either. In the past, the import duty rates were significant and provided reasonably high protection to the domestic industry. The conditions today have changed considerably with the reduction of the rate to five per cent. Also, with the rupee gaining strength, especially against the US dollar, the protection to the industry has also fallen to some extent. Naturally, with this, one would expect a drop in the pricing power of the domestic industry. It may further be noted that even if the duty rates are high, the HRC customer industry can always procure their entire material, to the extent needed for production of downstream products meant for exports, through duty free imports. This quantity being limited, the customer industries can manipulate their way through the system of Duty Entitlement Pass Book Scheme (DEPB) and Advance Licenses and bargain hard to have the prices in their favour.

2. Even if actual imports are not significant, the import option can itself be a major competitive threat. Even a cartelised industry may not be able to dictate terms to its customers when the reference import price is low. At best, they may all merely agree to the price corresponding to the import price. It has been observed generally that domestic prices have dropped below the import price when the market is weak and are at par with, or even higher, when the market is strong and the pricing power is with the seller. But, with indirect, yet strong government interventions, steel producers may not have fully exploited the conditions in the market to their full advantage. It may be seen from Table 14.4, that domestic retail market prices, somewhat based on the prices at which the main steel producers sell to the traders, have been lower than both the landed costs of imports (with full duty paid) and their export price equalisation rate. While major steel producers may have specific constraints or strategic reasons for doing so, this shows the role that government intervention can play in the market. This itself is a derivative of the political pressure that can be exerted by any interest group or customer body on the government to act that way.

3. How much the merchant user industry will pay for HRCs depends on how much will it earn by converting the HRCs into downstream products, like CRCs, GP/GC, etc. If the downstream market

TABLE 14.4

Assessment of Pricing Power: Comparison of Actual Prices and Theoretical Possibilities HR Coils

Non-China Destination	Mar-04	Apr-04	May-04	Jun-04	Aug-04	Aug-04 Post-Duty Change	Sept. 2004
Global Export Price (fob) US$/tonne	500	520	530.0	550	600	600	650
Export Realisation Rs/tonne	22625	23530	24115	25163	31248	31248	33706
Duty Free Import (C&F) Rs/tonne	24888	25793	25935	26993	29760	29760	32410
Landed Costs of Import (Rs/tonne)	30910	32034	32211	33525	36664	34998	38114
Export based Domestic Price Ex-plant (Rs/tonne) (a) with DEPB	25412	26429	27086	28263	36398	36398	39261
Export based Dom Price Ex-plant (Rs/tonne) without DEPB (b)	25412	26429	27086	28263	32498	32498	35206
Export based Mumbai Price (Rs/tonne) For Outsourced Material	27210	28226	28883	30060	36895	36895	39656
Export based Mumbai Price (Rs/tonne) For Local Material	28515	29532	29692	30880	33988	33988	36965
Difference (a)-(b) Rs/tonne	0	0	0	0	3900	3900	4055
Domestic Price (Mumbai) Rs/tonne	32600	30500	29875	30500	32250	32250	31750
Difference: Export based Dom price minus actual Dom price Mumbai Rs/tonne with DEPB	-7188	-4071	-2789	-2237	4148	4148	7511
Difference: LCI minus Dom Price Rs/tonne	-1690	1534	2336	3025	4414	2748	6364
Ratio Export Realisation/Dom Price	0.69	0.77	0.81	0.83	0.97	0.97	1.06
Ratio: LCI/Dom Price	0.95	1.05	1.08	1.10	1.14	1.09	1.20
Ratio: Export Based Price/Dom Price	**0.83**	**0.93**	**0.97**	**0.99**	**1.14**	**1.14**	**1.25**

Source: Economic Research Unit, JPC and Metal Bulletin.

is weak and the buyers stick to lower prices, the producers of HRCs will have the option either to sell at a lower price, or export, considering that production stoppage is not a rational decision.

4. Most of the users of HRCs are medium sized firms, but together they make a big clout in the political system, forcing the government to intervene strongly in their favour whenever the pricing scenario turns against them. In fact, public opinion seems to favour the consumer when steel prices rise fairly often, and given the public perception about criticality of steel in the nation's life, the government remains sensitive to public outcry in a significant way. This is evident from the developments in the recent past. Only a few months ago the government literally forced the steel majors to maintain stability of steel prices at a relatively low level. The fact is that the global conditions of the market and the domestic demand and supply conditions provided room for them to raise prices. The government intervened so strongly that a spurt of voluntary (?) price cut announcements followed, led by a private sector steel major.

It may be noted that downstream CRC and GP/GC production in the secondary sector accounted for nearly 5.5 million tonnes of HRC consumption. This includes imports of HRC as also those purchased from narrower HR strips produced by medium sized plants. This scenario shows the magnitude of the business involving merchant HRC sales to downstream product manufacturing. While none of the parties involved can be expected to be price takers in the market, the competitive position can turn largely favourable to the HRC manufacturers, if favourable alternatives like imports at reasonable import duty are not made available to the buyers.

The producers of HRCs, who also make downstream products like CRCs and GP/GCs etc., may resort to discriminating pricing, maintaining a low differential between HRC and CRC (or other downstream products). If the price differential between these products is lower than the cost of conversion of HRC to downstream products for a merchant mill, the entire economics of merchant production falls apart. This is a common and tactical pricing policy, followed normally by integrated mills to prevent excess competition in their downstream products' market and also excessive capacity build up on merchant basis.[4] However, merchant production may still flourish for niche products and market segments, where they can extract higher revenue.

The intra-industry issues of this kind have drawn more attention in recent times. The government has been sensitive to the ultimate consumers of steel in India by taking proactive action to arrest steel price rise. In the past also, the government had taken highly protective measures to protect the interests of the steel makers. For example, the merchant mills producing CRC, GP/GC and even steel tubes had, in fact, been hurt by what they describe as undue protection provided to the HRC manufacturers by high import duty, and non-tariff import barriers like floor prices etc. The government position was based on the need to prevent a financial catastrophe for the HRC producers in the face of a global crisis in the industry. Considering the fact that these firms involved huge capital investment and employed large numbers of workers, the users of HRC considered the same as against their interests, as they also faced the same global downturn in their product market.[5]

As mentioned earlier, the HRC downstream market is more competitive, especially in the case of GP/GC sheets and in specific segments of CRCs. Even then, by maintaining a price differential unfavourable to the merchant mills, the integrated mills can keep the downstream product prices sufficiently competitive, taking the advantage of integrated operation and lower conversion costs at their own plants, absence of transportation costs and certain non-refundable/non-adjustable taxes, reduced material loss, and, to some extent, economies of scale. Secondly, they have significant individual and collective market share, and, at times, can turn price makers. Therefore, control over HRC makes the integrated mills stronger in the market for downstream products as well.

14.8 Billets/Pencil Ingots

It may be seen here that SAIL (plus Indian Iron and Steel Company, IISCO), TISCO and RINL put together account for 23.2 per cent of the total production of billets/pencil ingots. The share of the secondary producers (electric arc furnaces and induction furnaces) is 76.8 per cent. But, considering the fact that the main producers export substantial quantities of their semis and then semis are imported and are also available from ship breaking and other sources, the share of the main steel producers in the market comes down to 21.1 per cent and that of the secondary producers to 69.7 per cent, with re-rollables from shipbreaking etc. taking a significant 13.1 per cent share (Table 14.5).

TAELE 14.5

Market Structure for Billets/Pencil Ingots (2003-04)

	Production	Production Share (%)	Market Share (%)
SAIL+IISCO	1.532	14.8	13.4
TISCO	0.548	5.3	4.8
RINL	0.334	3.2	2.9
Total Main	**2.414**	23.2	21.1
Secondary	**7.972**	76.8	69.7
Total Production	10.386	100.0	90.8
Shipbreaking and other Re-rollable scrap	1.5		13.1
Imports	0.15		1.3
Exports	0.6		
Total Supply of Billets for rolling	11.436		
Estimated Main Producer Domestic Sales	1.814		

Source: Estimated from the base data collected from The Joint Plant Committee and Shipbreakers' Association.

The market share of the main steel producers does not look to be large enough for total business control. Even though, considering the fact that the secondary producers are about 750 in number and the main producers only three, one can appreciate the individual position of each producer in the market. There are, however, divergent opinions on whether with such high market shares the main producers can command prices. Who follows whom in the market is difficult to establish. Further, with significant quantities of billets of the main producers going to contract sales, spot prices are more likely to be determined by localised conditions and primarily by the players in the secondary sector.

14.9 Cartelisation

Definitely, it appears from the above that under normal conditions, the steel majors cannot really dictate terms with their CRC and GP/GC customers (downstream). Yet, there has been a lot of talk about cartelisation in the steel industry, especially involving large HRC producers.

The near simultaneous announcements of steel price increases several times in the past have brought in strong accusations of cartelisation and price manipulations on the part of the major steel makers. The situation has changed significantly, and, in the very recent past, the prices of HR Coils have not only differed from one another, but also their timing of the decisions to change price has been different. Given the fact that any such collective pricing decision may be purely a response to external pricing alternatives available to their customers, these actions may not conform to the pure textbook cases of cartelisation to maximise joint profits. Further, even if there may be some agreement on the base price, the actual transaction prices will depend on the discounts offered by the producers, which vary across them, over regions, time and specific situations. At the end of the day, the producers end up competing in a limited way among themselves, despite having some broad understanding over prices.

Interestingly, while the private producers seem to have had closer relationship, the public sector undertakings' (PSUs) pricing did not totally conform to the levels adopted by the private companies. While this is taken to some extent as a lethargic response of the PSUs to change, and the subsequent delay in decision, the PSUs do come under certain political pressure to remain range bound in their actions. For example, the compulsory declaration of prices of major products in newspapers every month, on a government order, although makes the PSU transactions more transparent, their ability to rule the market will be substantially lowered due to the inherent inflexibility in the system, notwithstanding the fact that the prices publicly announced by the PSUs may become benchmarks for the rest. Also, if SAIL, for example, is out of the cartel, with 30 per cent market share only, with the remaining 70 per cent lying with the other four major producers, it will not make any difference to them, if they decide to fix prices among themselves. In such a case, SAIL will be a mere follower in the market, except in situations when the company, under external non-economic compulsions, is forced to drop prices against the market trends to meet altogether different objectives.

As far as semi-finished steel products are concerned, although the secondary sector has a large share of the market, the main producers can still hold sway in certain specific situations with their share in the market. However, in general, and under normal conditions of the market, especially with import options wide open through traders, the pricing power of the main producers is largely restricted. Here also, whether the major steel producers act as a cartel remains questionable, given the localised nature of the markets and specific locations of the mills.

The question of greater importance is whether the players act as a cartel at all. We have said above that a cartel (formal or informal) among the domestic producers can work only when the market is strong and the supply line is choked due to capacity constraint. While one would tend to point to the recent developments in the market where evidently the producers worked in unison, no trace of cartelisation was evident when the prices crashed prior to 2002. The domestic producers were undercutting each other at prices below even the import price. A detailed examination of this aspect will be required to understand the market, whether it provided conditions for formation of cartels, whether the cartel prices (even if assumed to be so) were globally competitive, etc.

Since the prices are divorced from costs and are based on the best alternative cost principle and that an efficient mill cannot continuously increase capacity to grab a larger market share by sheer dint of its low cost, there is no compulsion on the competitive firm to reduce price to grab a larger share of the market. Further, as firms with low efficiency do not die (soft budget constraints), any move to reduce prices will be counterproductive, as the inefficient firm will also do so as there is no fear of death for it. Therefore, it will always make more sense for the mills to work out a common pricing strategy.

What has been observed here is that although the dominant steel makers show enough market power by sheer size, the abuse of dominance has been restricted by non-market interventions by the state at one level and by public pressure created by the unified campaign and action of the consumer groups at the other. While the ideal conditions for the competitive growth of the industry would have been to allow the market forces to operate, the state has been forced to intervene in public or political interests. Most such interventions correct one problem, but generate several other market distortions and corresponding competition issues.

While it is evident that the steel producers were not together all the time, certain externalities were created in such a way that the industry gained as a whole *vis-à-vis* the steel consuming industries. Most of these had come from direct state interventions and have been protective in nature.

For example, even when the current import duty rates were dropped to levels comparable to several developing countries, the same remained at very high levels for a long time, as high as 25 per cent till January 2004. Also, till recently, the industry benefited from the floor prices imposed on prime steel products, not only when the global prices dropped to abysmal levels, but also when they started rising to reasonable levels. These have, nevertheless, been abolished. The

industry also gained from certain procedure related non-tariff barriers, like mandatory certification requirement for quality of imported products by the Bureau of Indian Standards (BIS). This involved a lengthy and cumbersome procedure entailing high transactions costs for the importers. The government also designated ports for imports of certain categories of steel with a clear intention to curb their imports. These measures although were, at times, against the interests of certain segments of the steel industry itself (for example, the merchant CRC and GP/GC producers), they served the major steel producers when it came to competition with the user industry. The continuation of anti-dumping duty on non-alloy steel at the time has been questioned widely by the consumer industry. Further, a prohibitive import duty on seconds and defectives also goes against genuine consumers, forcing them to buy these at high costs.

The differential competitive positioning of the steel firms on this count has been derived historically as a result of the market distorting regulatory government policies in the past.[6] To some extent, this disparity continues even today. This may not have been due to any conscious policy of the government to favour any individual group or segment of the industry, but the slow process of change has resulted in continuation of such differentiating competitive conditions. Although the choice of technology has become increasingly market determined and is based increasingly on pure commercial considerations, the policies related to ownership and leasing of mines and specific government interventions do significantly influence the technology choice. The policy related to leasing, captive ownership and operation of iron ore, and even coal mines, has been significantly liberalised, allowing for substantial captive ownership by the steel plants.[7] After all, the new conditions too do not favour every player equally. The mushrooming of inefficient small units of steel has been the outcome of the government's restrictive and regulatory policies of the past, especially the erstwhile licensing system. Technology choice, even in the deregulated era, has been shaped by the residual impact of the restrictive mining policies and price and distribution controls in a segment of the industry in the past.

14.10 Mergers and Acquisitions

Interestingly, while consolidation in the steel industry is one of the most prominent trends at the global level, development in India has not been that significant.

The consolidation in the steel industry worldwide has been driven by several factors. The most important of them obviously is the interest of the steel firms to reduce competition within the industry, control prices and reduce costs to enlarge profits further. The most important M&As have taken place during the period when the steel industry globally went through an unprecedented crisis and many found survival difficult without restructuring. In many cases, there were other strategic considerations related to the market and operations. The need for consolidation was also shaped by the general perception and also the real time experience that a fragmented industry was not in position to draw sufficient sympathy of the capital market, especially when the industry's fortunes were in the doldrums.

But, there are other compulsions too. The iron ore and coking coal industry, on which the steel industry is heavily dependent, have been consolidated at a rapid pace. Some of the major steel user industries, like automobiles, have been consolidated through a series of mergers and acquisitions. Even steel equipment manufacturers and technology firms have gone into the same mode. Therefore, unless consolidated, steel firms would be disadvantageously placed both in the input and the output markets.

In India, however, M&As in steel have been insignificant affairs. Most of the consolidation has, in fact, taken place involving restructuring of family businesses. The reason for that seems to be the fact that the Indian steel market itself is not large enough, and the competitive position of the individual players has not yet been fully established, with each seeing growth for itself in the future. Also, the prospects of growth have been such that all the current players seem to be accommodated comfortably in the set up. Only when the big challenges emerge and the competition gets tough, the consolidation in the industry will probably gain pace. Also, with a fragmented or captive input market and differentiated and divided output market, there is no pressure on the industry immediately to get into the M&A mode for its own survival.

4.11 Competition Issues in the Context of Investment and Growth

Steel is a huge infrastructure and raw materials' dependent industry. Capacity creation involves substantial direct capital costs on plants and machinery, as also on developing infrastructure for raw materials, transport logistics, storage etc. While some of these infrastructure related costs may be taken care of by the state, there are still substantial costs to meet when it comes to setting up steel capacity. The government policy in regards to selective area-based infrastructure development will have a significant implication on investment in the industry, and also change the relative competitive position within the industry, as a plant where infrastructure is better developed gets an edge over the rest. The point remains valid in the case of plants losing out to others because of the failure of the state or deliberate neglect of the same in and around their location. The policy adopted by states where iron ore is located, *viz*, Orissa, to lease out iron ore mines only to those steel firms that set up their plants in that state, raises a serious competition issue. Also, the differential pricing policy of the state-owned iron ore companies – one price for private companies and another (lower) for government-owned companies – raise major competition concerns in the market.

A major area of competition within the steel industry is in the capital market. There are two major implications of the nature of competition, in the financial resource market on steel, as also the steel user industries. If flow of liberal funds creates excess capacity in the steel industry, the steel market will turn hugely competitive and the steel customers will reap the benefits from it. However, if the resource market is not competitive and funds flow into only a select few, growth of oligopoly or monopoly may be expected in due course.

The behaviour of the banks and their discriminating policy can become an entry barrier for large steel units, as given the sheer size of their investment requirement, nothing can proceed further unless they are assured of funds from the banking sector. While the banking institutions can be expected to work on market determined commercial basis, keeping their own interests ahead, one will not be surprised if their decisions are systematically manipulated to provide advantage to the existing players. This is where competition is hit directly.

As discussed above, the 90s involved mainly a transition from a regulated and controlled economy to an open one. With economic reforms, capacity expansion took place in the private sector at a brisk pace, making the market more competitive with larger number of players in it, along with more effective external trade options. On the other hand, the possibility of monopoly behemoths taking over the steel market with their sheer size and scale advantages cannot be ruled out, if the investment policy, and, in particular, the capital market, remains in favour of a few against competitive norms of the market.

The recent announcements of various steel companies, of their plans to expand capacity in the coming years, show that if their plans materialise, the steel market will see significant increases in concentration and the emergence of strong oligopolies in most product categories. The Tables (Table 14.6 and Table 14.7) below show the likely scenario in the year 2011-12, compared to the existing position.

14.12 Regulatory Authority

There has been a talk about the need and feasibility of having a regulatory authority for steel. Since the steel industry in India has had a long history of price and distribution control, the first issue that comes to anybody's mind is whether it is at all possible, desirable or practical to have an authority, within or outside the government, to set or functionally monitor steel prices.

Given the heterogeneity in steel, it may be, in the first place, extremely impractical to bring in price regulation. Given the globalised nature of business today and the emerging competition within the industry as discussed above, it may also not be desirable to have a government or a non-government authority to set steel prices.

If this is the case, then is there still a role for the government to play in the business of the steel industry?

There are two major ways in which the government may intervene in the affairs of the steel industry. One, by fiscal policy measures, and two, by having a powerful watchdog (say, a competition authority) to set terms for the industry whenever the overall consumer interests are adversely and unreasonably affected. Such a body may be empowered further to keep a watch on the supply side of the market and examine investments, mergers, acquisitions, etc. Having a watch on the growth of monopolies or oligopolies and taking preventive measures, the government, through such an authority, can curb the pricing power of the firms and protect the consumers, generally large in numbers and dispersed regionally. Such an authority can also curb occasionally observed conditions of differentiated and discriminatory pricing, applied over the consumers either on criteria of location or size. The authority can also work on commercial disputes involving bilateral monopoly cases. The body can also remove distortions that may crop up in the fiscal regime, which may provide undue benefits to one segment of the industry at the cost of another.

TABLE 14.6

Capacity of Plants: Crude for Carbon, Stainless and Alloy Steel

(Million Tonnes)

	2002-03	2003-04	2004-05	2008-09	2009-10	2010-11	2011-12
TISCO (Jamshedpur)	3.5	4.1	4.1	5.0	5.0	5.0	7.5
TISCO (Duburi)							3.0
SAIL+IISCO+ASP	12.7	12.1	12.7	15.0	15.0	15.0	15.0
RINL (VSP)	2.9	3.5	3.5	5.0	5.0	7.5	6.8
Essar	2.2	2.4	2.4	4.0	4.0	4.0	4.0
JVSL	1.6	1.6	2.4	4.0	4.0	4.0	4.0
Ispat	1.8	2.4	2.4	3.6	3.6	3.6	3.6
Mini Mills	13.5	14.0	14.6	17.5	17.8	18.2	19.3
Small EAF+ Small BOF	3.5	4.0	4.4	5.9	5.9	5.9	6.7
Small IF	10.0	10.0	10.3	11.6	11.9	12.3	12.6
Total Crude Steel Capacity	38.2	40.0	42.1	54.1	54.4	57.3	**63.2**

Note: Estimated from various announcements made by the respective companies and assessment made on the basis of the same. Several other projects have been announced recently involving major global companies. Since there are conflicting reports about their intentions, the same have not been included.

While the government already has institutional arrangements to deal with such cases, either in the respective administrative ministries or at the Tariff Commission, such a body may examine disputes of continuous nature, where repeated government interventions have failed,. A competition authority is a must to monitor the action of the major banks and the financial sector to prevent differential treatment to prospective investors. All these, after all, can be well accommodated within the purview of the already established competition authority and no separate regulatory body is needed for steel.

14.13 Conclusion

Competition issues in the steel industry are fewer and are not as significant as in industries like telecom, electricity and petroleum products, primarily because of the basic character of the product and its market, high level of global trading and continuous reduction in barriers to trade. Given the high degree of differentiation and heterogeneity of steel products and the commodity character in each such differentiated product segment, the issues related to dominance and abuse of dominance are not found to be significant despite the increasing level of concentration in the industry. With relative low price elasticity of demand, the steel market resists price manoeuvrability by dominant players. There are, however, complex intra-industry competition issues arising out of merchant

TABLE 14.7

Capacity Expansion Projection

	Capacity (Million Tonnes)							
	2002-03	%age share	2003-04	%age share	2004-05	%age share	2011-12	%age share
TISCO (Jamshedpur)	3.5	9.2	4.1	10.25	4.1	9.7	7.5	11.9
TISCO (Elsewhere)							3.0	4.7
SAIL+IISCO+ASP	12.7	33.2	12.1	30.25	12.7	30.2	15.0	23.7
RINL (VSP)	2.9	7.6	3.5	8.75	3.5	8.3	6.8	10.8
Essar	2.2	5.8	2.4	6.0	2.4	5.7	4.0	6.3
JVSL	1.6	4.2	1.6	4.0	2.4	5.7	4.0	6.3
Ispat	1.8	4.7	2.4	6.0	2.4	5.7	3.6	5.7
Mini Mills	13.5	35.3	14.0	35.0	14.6	34.7	19.3	30.5
Small EAF+Small BOF	3.5	9.2	4.0	10.0	4.4	10.5	6.7	10.6
Small IF	10.0	26.2	10.0	25.0	10.3	24.5	12.6	19.9
Total Crude Steel Capacity	38.2	100.0	40.0	100.0	42.1	100.0	63.2	100.0

operations, where a buyer of an intermediate product can compete with the mill producing that in the finished product market. The pricing issues relating to the intermediate product have been a major controversy, where the producers of the same are being accused of adopting unfair means to squeeze the merchant mills.

In the past, SAIL was the only producer of wide HR coils and had the bulk of the flat products' markets under its fold. After liberalisation, with several new entrants in the market and with external reforms and the coming of the small merchant mills, the finished flat products' market in the country has become extremely competitive.

By and large, the steel market is competitive in India and the competition issues are more likely to be witnessed in the areas of investment and growth and in the government policy related to minerals. The competition scenario for the steel market in the market for investment funds, mainly loans from the banks and financial institutions, has been biased in favour of the larger players. While this need not be specific to the steel industry, where such biases are common globally, what is important is that the basic criteria of sanctioning loans, which remain the most important factor for any firm to be able to invest for growth, have not been necessarily performance or efficiency based. This creates distortion in the competitive growth of the industry.

Abuse of dominance is difficult to establish both logically as also statistically. The years ahead will see ownership concentration to rise in the steel sector. The industry will have to be watched carefully.

State interventions have been an important contributor to distortions in the market, despite the fact that some of the interventions have been in favour of the consumers. The high retail prices of steel, much above the producers' prices, have clearly shown that while large steel customers, procuring their requirements directly from the producers on a contract basis, have taken advantage of the state interventions and public outcry, the small consumers have suffered.

Notes

1. Although on paper, the steel prices were to be based on an elaborate model developed by the Bureau of Industrial Costs and Prices, in practice, the same was rarely followed.

2. The erstwhile licensing policy of the government in the first place prohibited private entry into the integrated route and then gradually allowed private investment only in small EAF based mini steel plants before deregulating the sector completely in 1991-92. Further, price and distribution control for steel produced in the integrated sector, till 1992, did not allow for sufficient growth for the players already in the industry.

3. At present, coal blocks can be allotted to even private parties in the steel production, but there are still some technical and procedural hurdles, to be removed, nevertheless, in due course. It may be interesting to note that the new integrated steel projects, most of them located in the state of Orissa, under various stages of implementation or conception are all being planned with captive iron ore.

4. This is a worldwide phenomenon and conflicts between the integrated and the merchant producers on such grounds are common. With many of the steel companies on both sides entering into stable contractual relationship, the conflicts have been significantly reduced. However, problems of this nature are inherent in the very basic structure of the industry and therefore cannot be got rid of easily, unless, of course, there are external interventions.

5. This argument was used more specifically to counter imposition of floor prices on HR coils at an artificially high level of US$ 302 per tonne, when the global prices of HRC went down to US$ 210 per tonne C&F, and those of CRC to US$ 280 per tonne. It may be noted that even after the government had withdrawn the floor prices, the same had to be maintained for years following a court verdict on it.

6. The erstwhile licensing policy of the government in the first place prohibited private entry into the integrated route and then gradually allowed private investment only in small EAF based mini steel plants before deregulating the sector completely in 1991-92. Further, price and

distribution control for steel produced in the integrated sector did not allow for sufficient growth for the players already in the industry.

7. At present, coal blocks have not been allotted to private steel companies. It is learnt that the policy is being further liberalised to accommodate the same in the near future. It may be interesting to note that the new integrated steel projects, most of them located in the state of Orissa, under various stages of implementation or conception, are all being planned with captive iron ore.

References

1. Statistics released by the Joint Plant Committee through their bulletins and other publications (selectively used).

2. Data collected directly from the industry.

3. Government Notifications related to Iron and Steel Control Order.

4. Newspaper reports.

15 Competition Policy for the Pharmaceuticals Sector in India

Nitya Nanda • Amirullah Khan

15.1 Introduction

The Indian pharmaceutical sector has come a long way, from being almost non-existent before 1970, to becoming a prominent producer of healthcare products, meeting almost 95 per cent of the country's pharmaceutical needs, today. Till the year 2002, the Indian pharmaceutical market (domestic market only) was valued at over US$4bn and grew by 8-9 per cent. The growth rate would have been even lower, had it not been for the new products launched in the last two years. The total Indian production constitutes about 1.3 per cent of the world market in value terms and 8 per cent in volume terms. Almost 3000 new products were launched in the last two years with sales estimated at US$280mn.

The domestic industry has evolved substantially and is transforming itself from a reverse-engineering led industry, focussed on the domestic market, to a research-driven, export-oriented industry with global ambitions. As per an estimate by McKinsey & Co, the pharmaceutical industry in India has a unique and exciting opportunity to grow, from about US$5.5bn in 2000 to US$25bn in 2020.

The Indian pharmaceutical industry is highly fragmented, with over 20,000 producers. The organised sector comprises 250-300 players, with the largest player having a market share of approximately 6 per cent. Indian pharmaceutical companies are now tapping into the large opportunities that exist in the global market.

The industry is today being recognised globally for its strengths in:

- Availability of a large pool of low-cost and highly skilled pool of scientists and medical professionals
- Chemistry and synthesis skills
- Successful scaling up of laboratory processes to plant scale
- Cost effective and commercially viable non-infringing processes
- Manufacturing facilities of international standards
- Quicker adoption of new technology

The Indian pharmaceutical industry attracted global attention during the global controversy on TRIPs and public health, prior to the Doha Ministerial Conference of the WTO, when it came with a promise of providing affordable medicines to the global poor. However, today, there are doubts in some quarters if the industry can provide affordable medicines even to the people in India, in the changed scenario of a new patent regime and a deregulated environment (Malhotra and Lofgren, 2004). Since 1970, the prices of essential drugs have been regulated by the Drug Prices Control Order (DPCO)[1] with the National Pharmaceutical Pricing Authority (NPPA) fixing the prices of a range of drugs since its establishment, in 1997. However, over the last few years, substantial decontrol of prices has taken place, with the number of drugs under price control coming down from 370 in 1979, to just 38 in 2002.

15.2 The Global Scenario

The global pharmaceutical industry is presently valued at approximately US$400bn. Growth rates differ across nations, with developing countries like South Korea, Taiwan, India, etc., notching high growth in the range of 12-15 per cent p.a. Pharmaceutical is a continuous growth industry, immune to economic recession and commodity cycles. Rising population, new disease incidence, or the resurgence of certain diseases, spurs the growth.

Countries can be classified into five categories, according to the stage of development of their pharmaceutical sector. These categories are outlined in Table 15.1.

TABLE 15.1
The Structure of the Global Pharmaceutical Industry

Stage of Development	Number of Countries		
	Industrial	Developing	Total
Sophisticated pharmaceutical industry with a significant research base	10	Nil	10
Innovative capabilities	12	6 (Argentina, Brazil, China, India, Korea and Mexico)	18
Those producing both therapeutic ingredients and finished products	6	7	13
Those producing finished products only	2	87	89
No pharmaceutical industry	1	59	60
Total	31	159	190

Source: R. Ballance, J. Progany & H. Forstener, UNIDO, The World's Pharmaceutical Industries: An International Perspective on Innovation, Competition & Policy (1992), in K. Balusubramaniam, Access to Medicines: Patents, Prices and Public Policy – Consumer Perspectives (2001) (paper presented at Oxfam International Seminar on Intellectual Property and Development: What Future for the WTO TRIPS Agreement?, Brussels, March 20, 2001).

The sophisticated, research-based part of the global pharmaceutical industry, is highly concentrated in a handful of countries, notably the USA, the UK, Germany, and Switzerland, and is composed of just a few companies. Part of the reason for this is the high cost and high risk of R&D activities. The average cost of developing a drug is estimated at $500 million, including the costs of developing drugs that never reach the market.

Currently, there are fewer than 40 firms, under patent protection, competing in highly lucrative drug markets. According to the pharmaceutical industry, long-term patent protection is essential because otherwise drug companies cannot afford to develop new medicines. These companies derive most of their profits from a small number of drugs. In fact, 75 per cent of drug company profits come from 10 per cent of drugs. Profitable markets are also highly skewed, geographically. Most of their profits are earned in the US market, where drug prices are not regulated, and therefore are much higher than in the other rich country markets, such as the EU and Japan (Nanda and Lodha, 2002).

15.3 Nature of the Pharmaceutical Industry

The usage of pharmaceuticals, in India, is governed by four primary medical sciences: Allopathy (modern science), Ayurveda (an ancient Indian Science mainly using herbal remedies), Unani (Chinese origin), and Homeopathy, of which allopathy is the most popular. This paper focuses on allopathic medicines only. In fact, much of the production, distribution and consumption, of the other three types, of medicines takes place in the informal sector and hence, remains unregulated. Moreover, it is only allopathic medicines that are subject to price regulation in India.

The pharmaceuticals market is broadly divided into bulk drugs[2] (20 per cent) and formulations[3] (80 per cent). The pharmaceutical sector is a high technology and knowledge-intensive industry. The industry has a two-tier structure. The largest firms account for the majority of the R&D investment, in the industry, and hold majority of the patents. A large number of smaller firms manufacture off-patent products; or under licence, to a patent-holder.

The Indian pharmaceutical industry (domestic and overseas markets) was valued at approximately US$ 5.5 bn in 2000. The industry has grown substantially over the last three decades. The industry's export performance is steadily rising. Aggregate numbers, for about 50 of India's top pharmaceutical companies, show that they get over a third of their sales from overseas markets.

The organised sector accounts for 70 per cent of the industry, in terms of value. The top ten companies account for 30 per cent of total sales. Six of the top ten companies are: Ranbaxy, Dr Reddy's Laboratories, Cipla, Sun Pharma, Zydus Cadila and Nicholas Piramal. The transnational companies (TNCs), in the list of top ten pharmaceutical companies, in India are Glaxo, Smithkline, Pfizer, Aventis and Novartis. The individual market shares of companies are small. However, this does not mean that there is intense competition in the market. This is because pharmaceutical products are not single homogenous goods, and there are a large number of several "relevant markets" within the industry. Roughly, they can be looked at as different therapeutic segments. In fact, as can be seen from the Table 15.3, in some of the segments there are high levels of concentration.

TABLE 15.2
Key Statistics of the Indian Pharmaceutical Industry

	Growth Indicators		
	US$ mn		Growth CAGR
	1965-66	*1999-2000*	
Capital Investment	31	549	9%
Production			
Formularies	33	3508	14%
Bulk Drugs	4	830	17%
Import	2	756	19%
Export	1	1457	25%
R&D Expenditure	1	70	14%

Source: Pharmaceuticals and Drug Manufacturers website; IDF analysis.

Table 15.3 gives an overview of the major therapeutic segments in the Indian pharmaceuticals sector. These segments account for nearly 80 per cent of the domestic formulation market.

15.4 Regulations in the Pharmaceutical Industry

In a normal product market, firms try to boost sales and, consequently, profits, by reducing prices. Competition between firms, to provide the highest quality product for the lowest price, ensures efficient allocation of resources in the economy. It also means that the benefits of increased efficiency are shared between consumers, in the form of lower prices and higher quality; and firms, in the form of profits. However, the drugs market has special characteristics. Drug consumers in developed countries are usually covered, by either private or public insurance, and so do not pay directly for medicines. Consumption patterns are not affected by prices, therefore, firms do not have any incentive to keep prices low.

In many countries, it is the government that bears most, or all, of the costs of medicines. As a monopsonist (single buyer), the government may be able to control drug prices, and prevent drug companies from exploiting the market. However, in developing countries, the situation is quite different. Generally, people are covered neither by public nor private insurance. The coverage of public provisioning of healthcare services, and medicines, is also limited.

However, this does not imply that pharmaceutical companies compete with each other through prices in developing countries. Instead, they compete through innovation. Product markets for drugs – defined by 'therapeutic classes' (medicines with the same therapeutic purpose) tend to be highly concentrated, with one or two firms accounting for the bulk of sales in each sector. Moreover, consumers are very often not the decision-makers. The doctors and the pharmacists have a significant role to play and the companies often try to influence them, sometimes via huge incentives. Recently, there has been a growing tendency, amongst developing country consumers, to bypass doctors, but of course, that does not improve the situation. The consumers fall prey to company advertisements or to local pharmacists. This very often leads to the purchase of more expensive medicines, or use of irrational (or combinations of) drugs, which may lead to medical complications, sometimes even causing death (Nanda and Lodha, 2002).

It is precisely because of this phenomenon that practically all countries in the world have mechanisms to regulate the pharmaceuticals industry, in general, and drug prices, in particular. In Australia, since 1993, new drugs, with no advantage over existing products, are offered at the same price. Where clinical trials show superiority, incremental cost effectiveness is assessed to determine whether a product represents value for money at the price sought. In the UK, there exists the pharmaceutical price regulation scheme - a voluntary agreement between UK's Department of Health and the Association of the British Pharmaceutical Industry, in which companies negotiate profit rates from sales of drugs to the National Health Service (NHS) (Sen Gupta, 2002).

Globally, drug companies are being forced to reduce the cost of medicines. Pressure is being mounted by Health Insurance Companies, Health Management Organisations (HMOs) and Governments (in countries like the UK and Canada, where the State provides Health Insurance cover) all over Europe and North America. These pressures have become stronger in recent years, with the realisation that spiralling drug costs are making health insurance cover (whether state funded or privately managed) unsustainable.

In all these countries, there is a significant move to insist on generic prescription in most cases, thus opening up a huge generics market. Large TNCs are forced to compete on, more or less, equal terms with a large number of lesser-known companies, and also sell drugs at relatively cheaper rates. In the US, for example, from 1995 through 1997, generic drug prices showed a double-digit rate of decrease. In the US, this change was facilitated by the Hatch-Waxman Act, which made the approval process of generic drugs much easier. Since 1984, this has resulted in a dramatic increase in competition from generic drugs, leading to an estimated

TABLE 15.3

The Nature of Competition in Different Therapeutic Segments

Product Category	Patent Coverage	DPCO Coverage	Market Size and Growth	Players	Comments
Analgesics & anti-pyretics	Most of the popular drugs like Aspirin, Analgin and Paracetamol are off-patent.	High	Rs. 4bn and growing at 17-18% yoy (year-on-year)	Major players in formulations are Burroughs Wellcome, SmithKline Beecham, Hoechst and Wockhardt. A large number of local players.	Margins are low.
Antacids and Anti-ulcerants	Large number of new under-patent molecules, due to ongoing R&D on developing more effective ways to combat acidity/ulcers.	High	Antacids: Rs. 1.8bn, growing 8-9% yoy. Anti-ulcerants: Rs. 2.3bn growing at 17-18% yoy	Antacids: Knoll and Parke Davis.Anti-ulcerants: Glaxo, Cadila, Ranbaxy, Dr. Reddy's Labs etc.	
Antibiotics	The earlier generation drug groups such as Penicillins (e.g. Amoxycillin) and Macrolides (e.g. Erythromycin) have mostly gone off-patent. Newer generation groups like Quinolones (e.g. Ciprofloxacin) and Cephalosporins (e.g. Ceftriaxone) are still largely under patent.	The latest generation drugs	Rs. 21.6bn and is growing at 13.5% yoy.	Glaxo, Ranbaxy, Cipla, Hoechst, Alembic, Burroughs Wellcome, Ambalal Sarabhai etc.	A vast range of drugs.
Anti-tuberculosis products	All popularly used drugs are off-patent.	Only Rifampicin is covered.	Rs. 2.9bn, growing at 11% yoy.	Lupin (dominant), Hind. Ciba., Cadila, Glaxo and Hoechst.	
Anti-parasitic & Anti-fungal products	Most of the popular drugs are off-patent.	Relatively low.	Rs. 3.9bn and growing at 19-20% yoy	Anti-protozoal: Nicholas Piramal[4], SmithKline Beecham Pharma, Ranbaxy, and Cipla.Anti-fungal: Bayer, Fulford, Glaxo etc.	Presence of a multitude of players keeps margins low.
Cardiac Therapy	New drugs are continually introduced by TNCs abroad. However, most of the drugs popularly used in India are off-patent.	Low	Rs. 5.6bn and is growing at 17-18% yoy	Sun Pharma, Torrent, Cadila, ICI etc.	The world's top therapeutic segment. Share of TNCs is relatively low.
Corticosteroids	All drugs popularly used in India are off-patent.	Key drugs Betamethasone and Dexamethasone.	Rs. 3.6bn, growing 16.5% at yoy.	Glaxo, Crosslands, Wyeth, Fulford, Merind. etc.	TNCs have been dominating but now local players are increasing their presence.
NSAIDs, Anti-rheumatic products	All major drugs used in India are off-patent.	High, due to inclusion of major drug, Ibuprofen.	Rs. 5.2bn, growing at 15% yoy.	Knoll, Roussel, Hind Ciba, Pfizer etc.	Local players have higher presence in topical formulations.
Respiratory System ailments	Very low.	Very low.	Cough & cold formulations market: Rs. 5.6bn (75% are anti-cough preparations), growing at 24.5% yoy Anti-asthmatics: Rs. 2bn, growing at 15.5% yoy.	Anti-cough: Pfizer, Parke Davis, Nicholas Piramal. Anti-cold: Burroughs, Alembic etc. Anti-asthmatics: Cipla (dominant)	
Vitamins	All drugs are off-patent.	Very high.	Rs. 5.7bn growing at 14% yoy.	E-Merck, Pfizer, Glaxo, Abbott etc.	Local players have poor presence in the segment.

Source: Confederation of Indian Industry (2000), "Report on the Pharmaceutical Sector in India", Presented to International Trade Centre, Geneva.

saving of $8-$10 billion in 1994 alone (Sen Gupta, 2002).

It is well recognised that medicines are not like any other product. Access to medicines is a matter of life and death for people. It also involves peoples' rights to health care, one of the basic needs. Ironically, it is also a unique example of market failure. This occurs due to the fact that consumers are not empowered to make their own choices. Thus, any regulatory mechanism, for pharmaceutical products, must take into account this peculiarity of the market. Apart from the manufacturers, the regulatory framework must include sufficient mechanisms to regulate the behaviour of doctors as well as the distributors of medicines, including those at the retail level - the pharmacists.

15.4.1 *Regulating Prescribing Doctors*

For most pharmaceuticals, it is not the consumer who decides which medicines to consume – a prescribing physician typically makes this choice. The pharmaceutical companies spend large sums in an attempt to influence the prescribing practices of doctors. To address this problem, a few countries have evolved a regulatory framework to regulate doctors' prescribing practices. Prescription audit is another method to make a post-facto analysis, which creates an incentive for doctors to be careful. Some countries have sought to create financial incentives for doctors to maintain a high level of rationality and cost-effectiveness in their prescribing behaviour.

15.4.2 *Regulating Pharmacists*

Most countries have separated the role of physicians and pharmacists to ensure that physicians do not have a financial interest in the pharmaceuticals they prescribe. Japan and Korea are exceptions. Japan has a very high rate of pharmaceutical consumption per capita, even taking into account the high average income. Korea is currently in the process of separating the roles of physician and pharmacist. In some countries, the pharmacist also has some degree of control over the drugs actually consumed. For example, one US study found that 77 per cent of physicians asked by a pharmacist, to switch prescriptions, consented to do so.

15.4.3 *Regulating Prices*

The question of setting the efficient price is significantly more difficult in therapeutic classes, dominated by a single manufacturer or, in which there are two or more manufacturers producing imperfect substitutes. The alternative mechanisms to control the prices of drugs are:

1) International benchmarking – Establishing the price of a pharmaceutical according to the prices in other reference countries.

2) Control on the evolution of prices over time.

3) Control of prices relative to cost.

15.5 Pharmaceuticals Regulation in India

At the time of independence in 1947, the bulk drug industry in India was in the infancy stage, with a meagre investment of Rs. 10 crore and production worth just Rs. 26 crore. Most of the bulk drugs and formulations were imported. Since then, the Indian pharmaceuticals industry has evolved through the opportunities presented by the regulated environment. Initially, the TNCs had a near monopoly. They imported and marketed formulations in India, mainly low cost generics for the masses, and also a few specialised, life saving, high priced products. With the Government increasing pressure against imports of finished products, TNCs set up formulating units, and continued importing bulk drugs.

In the early fifties, the Indian Government took steps that created the current pharmaceutical industry. These steps included the introduction of compulsory manufacturing of finished products and later, of raw materials of new drugs, in India. The resultant investments in plants, and transfer of technology, led to the training and employment of a large number of people in the drug industry. In the 60s, the Indian Government laid the foundation of the domestic pharmaceuticals industry by promoting two public sector companies, Hindustan Antibiotics Ltd. (HAL) and Indian Drugs and Pharmaceuticals Ltd. (IDPL), for the manufacture of bulk drugs. However, TNCs maintained a lead due to the backing of their global R&D. The high cost of basic research deterred local players in the private sector.

Till 1962, the drug industry was bereft of any price control. In 1962, there was Chinese aggression on India and Emergency was declared. The Government feared that, as a result, drug prices might rise. Accordingly, for the first time, under the Defence of India Act, 1915, statutory control was imposed on the prices of drugs and pharmaceuticals. The Drugs (Display of Prices) Order, 1962, and the Drugs (Control of Prices) Order, 1963, were promulgated. Under the Drugs Prices (Display and Control) Order of 1966, it was made obligatory for the manufacturers to obtain prior approval, from the Government, before increasing the prices of any formulation.

During 1970, the Indian Patents Act (IPA), and the Drug Prices Control Order (DPCO) were passed. Under the IPA, substances used in foods and pharmaceuticals could not be granted product patents. Only process patents were allowed for a period of five years from the date of the grant of patent, or seven years from the date of filing for patent, whichever was earlier. The introduction of the IPA provided a major thrust to the Indian pharmaceuticals industry; and Indian companies, who through the process of reverse engineering and synthesis, began to produce bulk drugs and formulations at lower costs.

The DPCO is an order issued by the Government, under Section 3 of the Essential Commodities Act, 1955[5], empowering it to fix and regulate the prices of essential bulk drugs and their formulations. The order incorporates a list of bulk drugs whose prices are to be controlled, the procedure for fixation and revision of prices, the procedure for implementation, the procedure for recovery of dues, the penalties for contravention, and various other guidelines and directions. The order is subject to the guidelines of Drug Policy and supposedly aims to ensure equitable distribution, increased supply, and cheap availability of bulk drugs.

The DPCO, which aims towards the availability of essential drugs at affordable prices, has played a vital role in directing the pharmaceutical industry's fortunes. The DPCO, of 1970, effectively put a ceiling on prices of all mass-usage bulk drugs and their formulations. Its primary objective was to protect the interests of consumers, and ensure a restricted but reasonable return to producers. The order was a landmark regulation and has had several implications in shaping the Indian pharmaceuticals industry.

The Drugs and Cosmetics Act, 1940, governs the import, manufacture, distribution and sale of drugs, in India. The Drug Controller General of India (DCGI), an authority established under the Drugs and Cosmetics Act, 1940, oversees the conduct of clinical trials. The DCGI is also responsible for the approval and registration of drugs, and issues manufacturing and marketing licences for the same. However, this paper will not discuss the functioning of the DCGI, as it is beyond the scope.

15.5.1 DPCO, 1970

The DPCO was first passed in 1970 and then revised in 1979, 1987 and 1995. In its introductory form, DPCO was a direct control on the profitability of a pharmaceutical business, and an indirect control on the prices of pharmaceuticals. It stipulated that a company's pre-tax profit from its pharma business should not exceed 15 per cent of its pharma sales (net of excise duty and sales tax). In case profits exceeded this sum, the surplus was deposited with the Government. So, a pharma company had the freedom to decide the prices

of its products. Product-wise margins were also flexible, so long as the overall margin did not exceed the stipulated norm. Since individual product prices did not require approval from the Government, bureaucratic hurdles were low.

15.5.2 DPCO, 1979

In 1974, the Government of India (GoI) appointed a committee under the chairmanship of Rajya Sabha MP, Mr. Jaisukhlal Hathi, to inquire into the conditions prevailing in the sphere of pharmaceuticals in the country. The DPCO, 1979 was loosely based on the recommendations of the Hathi Committee. The revised DPCO stipulated ceiling prices for controlled categories of bulk drugs and their formulations. The retail prices of controlled formulations were decided by applying the concept of MAPE (Maximum Allowable Post-manufacturing Expenses).

The pricing formula was retail price[6] = (MC+CC+PM+PC) × (1+MAPE/100) + excise duty. MC was the material cost, including cost of bulk drugs/excipients; CC was the conversion cost as per the dosage form; PM was the cost of packing material suitable to dosage form; and PC was the packaging charge calculated in accordance with established costing procedures. The DPCO, 1979, put 370 drugs under price control. These drugs were segregated into three categories, having different MAPE. The most important drugs, including life-saving drugs were put in Category I, which had the least MAPE. Through this DPCO, around 80 per cent of the Indian pharma industry (in value terms) was brought under strict price control. However, 13 TNCs challenged the order and succeeded (see Box 15.1).

BOX 15.1

Diabolical Profiteering: Supreme Court

Indian consumers were cheated of over Rs.400 crore, which the Supreme Court defined as diabolical profiteering. 13 TNC drug manufacturers, after obtaining a stay on the DPCO, 1979, from our 'convenient' High Courts, had ignored the prices fixed under this. Ultimately the Government of India had to appeal to the Supreme Court, which upheld the validity of its action and directed the Government to assess and recover the amounts.

In its judgement on April 10, 1987, the Supreme Court made a shocking observation. It discovered that Hoechst India Ltd. had fraudulently priced Baralgan Ketone, a non-essential drug.

While Hoechst had applied for a price level of Rs. 3,500 per kg. The Government, after analysing the cost, fixed it as Rs.

Contd...

...Contd...

1,810.20 per kg. Before the DPCO, Hoechst was charging a price of Rs. 24,735.38 per kg. But instead of reducing it to Rs. 1,810.20 per kg., or even Rs. 3,500 per kg., as requested of them, they continued to sell the drug for Rs. 24,735.38 per kg., under the protection of the High Court's stay order.

The angered Supreme Court observed thus:

"We see that the price, of Rs. 24,735 per kg; at which the manufacturer was previously selling the drug, and at which he continues to market the drug to this day because of the quashing of the order fixing the price, by the high court; is so unconscionably high, even compared with the price claimed by itself, that it appears to justify the charge that some manufacturers do indulge in 'profiteering'".

Little money was recovered, and in spite of various parliamentary interventions, the matter languished in our courts. Whatever the little that was recovered, was put into the Drug Price Equalisation Fund to subsidise public sector manufacturers. The money was not refunded to consumers through an appropriate mechanism.

Source: All About GATT-A Consumers Perspective, CUTS, February 1996.

15.5.3 DPCO, 1987

In 1984, the Kelkar Committee released its Report, in which it recommended the exclusion of a number of drugs from the purview of price control. Various suggestions were made for determining the criteria for inclusion and exclusion. The DPCO, 1987, was based on the Drug Policy of 1986, and the Kelkar Committee Report. In the DPCO, 1987, the number of bulk drugs under price control was significantly reduced from 370 to 142. In addition, the categories of control were reduced to two, and higher MAPE was provided for each category of controlled drugs (75 per cent and 100 per cent respectively). However, around 75 per cent of the pharmaceutical industry was still under price control.

15.5.4 The Drug Policy of 1994

In September 1994, the New Drug Policy was announced. The New Drug Policy liberalised the criteria for selecting bulk drugs, or formulations, for price control. In addition, industrial licensing was abolished for all bulk drugs. All hindrances to capacity expansions were removed, and it was expected that, as a result, supply would rise, resulting in higher competitive pressures. Foreign investment up to 51 per cent was also permitted in the case of all bulk drugs, their intermediates and formulations. FDI above 51 per cent could also be considered on a case-to-case basis. Nevertheless, five bulk drugs; Vitamin B1, Vitamin B2, Folic Acid, Tetracycline and Oxy-tetracycline were reserved for the public sector till 1998.

15.5.5 DPCO, 1995

The latest Drug Price Control Order was passed in 1995. The basic structure of this DPCO is the same as that of the earlier orders, except that a uniform MAPE of 100 per cent was granted to all controlled formulations. Nevertheless, the span of price control, under DPCO 1995, was liberalised considerably from 142 drugs to just 76.

The Pricing of Bulk Drugs: The methodology, through which prices of DPCO-controlled bulk drugs are fixed, is as follows. While fixing the maximum sale price of a bulk drug, the Government has to provide either a post-tax return of 14 per cent on net worth, or a return of 22 per cent on capital employed.[7] Each company can choose one of the two methods, mentioned above, as per its own volition. So, the choice of method is company-specific and not product-specific. Based on the chosen method, each company submits to the Government, a detailed working of the prices of various bulk drugs that it requires. The Government subsequently studies the applications made, by the major players for every bulk drug, and cost audit reports of manufacturers, before arriving at the final price. The price so decided will be binding on all manufacturers, irrespective of their actual cost of production.

The Pricing of Formulations: The methodology, through which prices of formulations are fixed, is as follows. In the new system, the retail price of a DPCO formulation is fixed equal to $(MC+CC+PM+PC) \times 2 +$ excise duty. In order for the Government to decide the price of a controlled formulation, each manufacturer is supposed to submit to the Government, details of material cost, manufacturing process, etc. For imported drugs and formulations, the landed cost, including customs duty and clearing charges, is the benchmark to fix prices. A margin of 50 per cent is allowed to the importer to cover the selling and distribution expenses, including interest and profit.

15.5.6 Pharmaceutical Policy, 2002

The new Indian Pharmaceutical Policy, 2002, has focused on liberalisation by further reducing the number of drugs, subject to price control, and opening up the market to foreign investment. The new Pharmaceutical Policy, 2002, further reduced the number of drugs under price control to just 38. The key features of the Pharmaceutical Policy, 2002 are:

- Reduction in the number of drugs under price control to 38 (19 per cent of the market) from 74 drugs (over 40 per cent of the market) under the 1995 policy.

- A Drug Development Promotion Foundation (DDPF), and a Pharmaceutical Research & Development Support Fund (PRDSF), to be established to boost research and development.

- Foreign investment up to 100 per cent to be permitted, subject to stipulations laid down from time to time in the industrial policy.

- Abolition of industrial licensing for all bulk drugs, intermediates and Formulations.

TABLE 15.4

Market Share of Drugs Under the DPCO, 1979–2004

Year	Number of Drugs	Approximate Market Share (%)
1979	347	80
1987	142	60
1995	74	> 40
2004	38	20

Source: Malhotra and Lofgren (2004).

15.6 Decontrol and Pharmaceuticals Prices

Drugs and formulations have been subjected to price control for more than three decades now, though significant decontrol was introduced in 1995. Drug prices vary from country to country, for a number of reasons, including patent regulations, government controls, purchasing power, currency exchange fluctuations, etc. Due to the price control and patent regime, drug prices fell considerably, in India, and were among the lowest in the world. However, some studies have shown that prices of drugs started rising as soon as controls were removed. Furthermore, in almost all segments, the brand leader for a particular drug (i.e. the brand with the highest turnover) is usually one of the most expensive (in some cases twice as expensive!). If an expensive brand sells more in the market than cheaper alternatives, it should be evident that the price of a drug does not determine its volume of sales (Rane, 2002).

It may no longer be true that drug prices, in India, are among the cheapest in the world. Drugs that are still patent protected are much cheaper in India due to India's earlier Patent Act of 1970. Off-patent drugs (which account for 80-85 per cent of current sales in the country) are not necessarily cheaper in India. In fact, generally drug prices are higher in India than those in neighbouring Sri Lanka and Bangladesh. Even more disturbing is the fact that prices of some top selling drugs are higher, in India, than of those in Canada and the UK. This comparison is on the official foreign exchange conversion rate. If we take the purchasing power parity (PPP), then the difference goes through the roof. One US$ is approximately Rs. 8 on a PPP basis, while Rs. 43 on the official exchange rate.

TABLE 15.5

International Cost Comparison of Select Drugs

Drug	Dose	Canada	UK	India
Amoxycillin	250 mg	1.75	2.59	2.89
Ampicillin	250 mg	1.75	2.42	3.18
Erythromycin	250 mg	1.25	2.87	3.28 - 4.17
Cephalexin	250 mg	3.00	7.74	4.46
Propanolol	40 mg	1.25	0.25	1.39
Atenolol	50 mg	—	2.65	1.29
Prednisolone	10 mg	1.50	1.09	1.32
Paracetamol	500 mg	1.25	0.32	0.49
Haloperidol	0.25 mg	0.13	1.60	0.55
Phenobarbitone	30 mg	0.25	0.28	0.50

Note: Single units, tab/cap/vial, has been taken for all drugs. Prices are in Indian Rupees. Conversion rate is $1=Rs. 42.52, 1 Canadian dollar = Rs. 25, 1 Pound = Rs. 70. Based on the figures available in British Columbia Children's Hospital Formulary, British National Formulary, No. 35, March 1998, MIMS India, March 1998. (Source: Sen Gupta, 2002).

The price difference exists because market mechanisms are ineffective in stabilising prices of drugs, as there is no direct interaction between the consumer and the drug market. Companies are able to sell over-priced drugs through aggressive promotional strategies aimed at doctors, and by providing lucrative margins to chemists. Incentives to buy large quantities of prescription drugs have become commonplace in India, where thousands of drug manufacturers compete for shelf space, and the country's half-million pharmacists wield an unusual amount of clout. Hence, often there is a huge gap between the wholesale price and the retail price.

Pharmacists in developed countries have little influence over the volume of prescription-drug sales. There, the marketing push usually targets doctors, the main legal conduit for prescription drugs. In India, many patients are too poor or too busy to see a doctor and often rely on local pharmacists for medical advice. As a result, powerful drugs are routinely, and illegally, sold over the counter.

A study by the Mumbai-based market-research firm, Interlink Healthcare Consultancy, found that all but one of the top 25 drug companies, in India, offered heavy discounting deals at least once a month. A letter to pharmacists from Blue Cross Laboratories Ltd., a Mumbai company, outlined a deal that offered pharmacists up to a 103 per cent profit margin on a variety of prescription drugs (Pearl and Stecklow, 2001). Some pharmaceutical companies argue that such huge incentives are not meant to boost sales without a prescription. They are required to defend their own prescriptions, as the Glaxo India's Director of Pharmaceuticals, said: "...for every two Glaxo prescriptions written, only one Glaxo drug ends up being sold, because druggists often substitute a competing medication".

In effect, pharmacy-owners banded together to form a huge cartel in the guise of a trade association, All India Organisation of Chemists and Druggists (AIOCD). The AIOCD launched boycotts against drug companies to grab higher profit margins. The associations also began demanding that drug companies obtain a "no-objection letter" from each state trade association, before a new drug could be sold there. Otherwise it would be excluded from the pharmacists' stock lists. For each new drug, the trade groups usually solicit a cash donation. AIOCD has also forced some drug companies to sign "memorandums of understanding" in which they agree to increase profit margins of pharmacies (Pearl and Stecklow, 2001).

BOX 15.2

Rent-seeking by Pharmacists: A Few Cases

Strong-arm tactics of the pharmacists' associations (at state level as well as national level) are nothing new. In 1984, a case came before the MRTP Commission as the Retail and Dispensing Chemists Association, Bombay, directed all the wholesalers and retailers to boycott a Nestle product, till its demands were met by the company.

The Commission observed that the boycott represents an attempt to deny the consumers certain products, which they are used to and, therefore, the hardship to such consumers is indisputable. The Commission accordingly passed a 'cease and desist' order (RTP Enquiry No. 10/1984).

Even before that, in 1982, the All India Organisation of Chemists & Druggists, had to face a similar stricture in a similar case (RTP Enquiry No. 14/1982, order dated 25-9-1984).

AIOCD was brought before the Commission once again, in 1983. It issued a circular to various pharmaceutical companies, threatening that if they dealt with the State cooperative

Contd...

...Contd...

organisations and appointed them as Stockists, granting them sale rights, it would expose the companies to a boycott by its members. The case was decided in 1993, and the Commission observed this to be the restrictive trade practice of refusal to deal (RTP Enquiry No. 37/1983, decided on 25-6-1993).

Nevertheless, undeterred, AIOCD decided to boycott the "Septran" range of products, manufactured by Burroughs Wellcome (India) Ltd. When the case came up before the Commission, AIOCD pleaded that it did not issue any such circular to the dealers, threatening to boycott the products. However, the Commission observed that a boycott could be conducted by way of an understanding among those perpetrating it, or by word of mouth among them. Merely because of the absence of a circular, calling upon the sellers to boycott, it could not be said that there was no boycott (1996, 21 CLA 322).

15.7 Major Competition Issues

For many pharmaceutical products, which face few rivals in their therapeutic class, the primary, competitive threat is that the rival firms will develop substitutes. But, the barriers to entry are substantial as it would require huge expenditure on R&D. However, as the Indian patent regime did not recognise product patents (until 2004), such entry barriers were not very high, as a rival could produce the same product, using a different process developed through reverse engineering. The situation will, however, change in the new patent regime. Let us now take a glimpse at the three major types of competition problems, *vis-à-vis* the pharmaceutical industry in India:

1) Collusion.

2) Mergers and acquisitions (horizontal or vertical).

3) Abuse of dominance (including IPR related).

15.7.1 Collusion

Collusive activities among the Indian manufacturers of pharmaceuticals have not yet been discovered. However, existence of such a tendency in certain segments, where there are just a few manufacturers, cannot be ruled out, particularly when an international cartel in bulk vitamins was in existence for quite a long time. In any case, even the international cartel inflicted heavy damage on Indian consumers and businesses. According to one estimate (Clarke & Evenett, 2002), the vitamins cartel, alone, cost India about US$25mn, in the 1990s, due to overcharging.

Collusive behaviour of the pharmacies in India is a matter of grave concern. The benefits of price decontrol, of several drugs, are probably going to the pharmacists disproportionately, more than the manufacturers. This defeats the very purpose of deregulation that is meant to provide manufacturers with the ability to spend more on R&D. By giving extra profits to the pharmacist, instead of reducing the retail price, manufacturers are keeping medicine prices higher than necessary for Indian patients. This would also mean that the market for medicines would be smaller than it would have been otherwise. Hence, this is harmful for the long-term growth of the industry.

This issue has engaged the attention of the Government. In December 2004, the Ministry of Fertilisers & Chemicals tried to bring in curbs on trade margins of pharmacists, by amending the DPCO. This move was strongly resisted by AIOCD. On the contrary, they demanded for the lowering of Maximum Retail Prices, which are under the control of manufacturers. The AIOCD added that it would be impossible for them to survive on a maximum gross margin of 20 per cent, excluding excise duty.

BOX 15.3

Pharmacy Regulation in France

The pharmacy sector is highly regulated in France. There is hardly any aspect of this activity (licensing, installation, cleanliness, compensation, commercial practices, etc. that are not subjected to regulation. Despite strict limitations on entry, new pharmacies are created at the rate of 50-60 per year, down from 250 per year, between 1962 and 1991.

Source: "Competition and Regulation Issues in the Pharmaceutical Industry", OECD, DAFFE/CLP(2000)29.

As per the provisions of the new Competition Act 2002, only trade unions are allowed to engage in collective bargaining. Hence, the activities of the pharmacists' association to extract higher margins would stand illegal. However, it is not going to be easy to take strong action when more than 500,000 pharmacists are involved. Should the manufacturers be also allowed to engage in collective bargaining with the pharmacists; Or should there be a negotiated settlement in the short run? - may be the questions that will dog the regulators. In any case, such collusive behaviour must be done away with, in the long run, to ensure growth of the industry, and a fair deal for the consumers. Dealing with such a situation is going to be one of the biggest challenges for the competition authority.

15.7.2 Mergers & Acquisitions

As of now, the Indian pharmaceuticals industry is highly fragmented. Hence, it is expected that the coming years will see intense consolidation activities. In fact, most of the top global pharmaceutical companies are consolidating their market positions, either through product rationalisation, brand acquisitions, or company acquisitions. Companies are re-evaluating their strengths and emphasising product segments that are profitable.

Whilst many domestic companies are enhancing their product portfolios by expanding therapeutic reach through product launches in new high margin segments, several others are trimming their portfolios to focus on particular therapeutic segments. Aventis, Glaxo SmithKline, Wockhardt and Ranbaxy have cut down their product portfolios in order to be more focussed. Sun Pharma, Nicholas Piramal and Dr. Reddy's Labs. have opted for brand/company acquisitions to increase their therapeutic reach and market penetration. Large Indian pharmaceutical companies are also expanding their reach overseas through acquisitions abroad. Examples include Ranbaxy's acquisition of RPG Aventis, and Wockhardt's acquisition of CP Pharmaceuticals.

Pressure on drug prices has made global pharmaceutical TNCs resort to mergers and alliances, in a bid to reduce R&D duplication and costs, combine product portfolios and increase reach. The total number of alliances increased from 120, in the mid-1980s, to nearly 400 in the mid-1990s. These alliances often allow pharmaceutical companies to draw upon each other's research expertise, and bring products to market more rapidly and more effectively. The mega-mergers in the global pharmaceuticals industry, in the last few years, have been Glaxo-Wellcome-SmithKline Beecham; Hoechst-Marion-Merrell Dow-Roussel; Pfizer-Warner Lambert; Ciba-Sandoz (to form Novartis); and Hoechst Marion Roussel-Rhone Poulenc (to form Aventis). The trend is expected to continue, and such mega-mergers in the global market are likely to raise competition concerns in several markets, including India.

The new Competition Act provides for merger review beyond a threshold level. As the threshold level is reasonably high, only the big deals will come under the scrutiny of the competition authority. This does not necessarily mean that all such deals need to be blocked. The deals will require complex analysis to examine the impact of the deal on different therapeutic segments. For example, Glaxo-Wellcome-SmithKline Beecham was allowed to merge by the EU, on the condition that they divested product categories where competition concerns could arise. The deal went unchallenged in most developing countries. However, South Africa, who closely cooperates with the EU, imposed similar conditions before it allowed the merger of their local subsidiaries. This shows how India can deal with merger and acquisition cases, not only of domestic companies but also of global companies, with local presence in India.

BOX 15.4

Mega-Merger – Glaxo-Wellcome and SmithKline Beecham

Two large pharmaceutical giants, Glaxo Wellcome and SmithKline and Beecham merged to become GlaxoSmithKline (or GSK). This merger created a leading global pharmaceutical company with sales of £18.1bn in the year 2000. Headquartered in the United Kingdom, GSK supplies products to 140 markets in the world. Obviously, the merger created competition concerns in several countries, yet it went unchallenged in most of them. India did not have a merger review provision in its extant competition law, the MRTPA, so the merger was not investigated. In Sri Lanka, the competition authority did not even take up the case of merger between Glaxo Wellcome and SmithKline Beecham, saying that it did not have jurisdiction, even though both the companies had commercial presence in the country!

In an earlier instance, during the merger of Glaxo Laboratories Pakistan Limited and Wellcome Pakistan Limited, the Monopoly Control Authority (MCA) of Pakistan took initiative to investigate. But MCA failed to take any action and the case was abandoned halfway. The reason provided by the MCA for this abandonment was that calculating market shares of individual products with the identification of their substitutes as required in the case was a complicated and the MCA did not have qualified and trained staff for this exercise.

The handling of the merger case by South Africa is quite illustrative. Upon investigation and evaluation of the merger the Competition Commission reached the conclusion that the transaction should be prohibited on competition and public interest grounds. In particular the Commission was concerned that the merger would result in the merging parties having high market shares in two therapeutic categories. The Commission stipulated that there would be unacceptable level of concentration in respect of Bactroban, Zelitrex and Famir and there were no appropriate substitutes to counter any price gouging, or ease of entry to offset the concern.

Upon prohibition of the merger by the Commission, the merging parties volunteered to license out some of their products identified by the Commission to be the cause of competition concern. The merging parties and the Commission reached an agreement and the merger was allowed conditionally. Interestingly the conclusion of the Commission in making its recommendations to the Competition Tribunal was substantially the same as the conclusions of the EC in so far as the overlap of products was concerned. This may partly be due to the fact that the Commission sought and received extensive cooperation from both the US and EC. However, it may be noted that the Commission completed its investigation before the case was decided by the EC.

CUTS (2003), *Pulling Up Our Socks: A Study of Competition Regimes of Seven Developing Countries of Africa and Asia* - Final Report of the 7-Up Project, CUTS, Jaipur, India.

15.7.3 *Abuse of Dominance*

The pharmaceutical industry, in India, has been a very interesting case study on competition issues, on account of its growth pattern. Much of the growth is attributed to the Patents Act, 1970, which did not allow product patents, and restricted the life of drug and chemical patents to seven years. This, also, has significant implications for abuse of dominance in the Indian pharmaceuticals market. Since pharmaceuticals is a knowledge-based industry, intellectual property rights play a crucial role, which mandate monopoly status to companies. Often, such monopoly status is abused to the detriment of consumers. However, as India did not allow product patent, it was difficult for a company to sustain such monopoly status for long, as rival companies came out with the same product, with a different process through reverse engineering. Thus, India did not bother much about abuse of dominance in the pharmaceuticals market.

However, the WTO TRIPS agreement has committed India to honour the WTO mandated product patent regime from 2005. Hence, from the beginning of 1995, any products entering the market would essentially be marketed by a monopolist. This means that in the new patent regime, abuse of dominance, which was almost non-existent earlier, is likely to become quite frequent. India, thus, needs to learn the art of dealing with abuse of dominance, in which its experience is almost non-existent. Moreover, the related provisions in the Competition Act (2002) are not strong enough. In this context, the example of the Patented Medicine Prices Review Board (PMPRB), of Canada, may well be worth looking into.

BOX 15.5

Patented Medicine Prices Review Board (PMPRB) of Canada

Created in 1987, under the Patent Act, as an independent quasi-judicial tribunal, the PMPRB limits the prices set by manufacturers for all patented medicines, new and existing, sold in Canada, under prescription or over the counter, to ensure they are not excessive.

As an independent quasi-judicial body, the PMPRB carries out its mandate independently of other organisations, such as Health Canada, which approves drugs for safety and efficacy; and public drug plans, which approve the listing of drugs on their respective formularies for reimbursement purposes.

The PMPRB has a dual role:

Regulatory: To protect consumers, and contribute to Canadian health care, by ensuring that prices charged by manufacturers for patented medicines are not excessive.

Contd...

15.8 In Lieu of Conclusion

The pharmaceutical industry, which till now has been characterised by its complexity, intense competition, low prices, and high level of fragmentation, is on the verge of a major shift as it prepares to meet the challenges of the forthcoming product patent regime. Post-2005, we will see a major shakeout, with a lesser number of players, and an increasing focus on higher value areas like drug discovery, drug delivery systems and technology licensing. The top bracket companies, having a strong R&D focus to deliver better value to the consumer, and innovate cost-efficiency, will survive and become even stronger. According to pharmaceutical industry estimates, a new drug costs Rs. 200 to Rs. 1000 crore to develop in India. However, as of now, India's top ten pharmaceutical companies spend only 3.3 per cent of their revenues on research, compared with 10-11 per cent spent by the Western companies.

It is estimated that in the next five years, over US$50bn worth of drugs will go off-patent. This will enable Indian companies to launch their generic equivalents in these markets. The global generics market is widely expected to grow faster than the global pharmaceutical market, in the next few years. The major challenge to face the Indian Pharmaceuticals market is the new patent regime. The prices of vital medicines, under patent, are bound to go manifold. The Government should be careful and must take all the precautions to protect the rights of the third party, and the party affected i.e. the public at large.

The pharmaceutical manufacturers are demanding more liberalisation, arguing that competition, and not price control, will improve availability and affordability of essential drugs.[8] Several arguments have been advanced as to why price controls would hurt, not help, consumers. For example, it is the profit on new, successful drugs that prompt the intensive research and development needed to find the next generation of miracle cures. A successful drug must pay for its own research, as well as the research on the unsuccessful ones, on which the company also risked money.

However, despite Finance Minister P. Chidambaram's indication that the Government will reduce the rigours of price control, where it has become counter-effective, reducing the number of essential drugs on the DPCO will not be easy. Firstly, the United Progressive Alliance Government's National Common Minimum Programme has promised to "take all steps to ensure the availability of life-saving drugs at reasonable prices". Secondly, any move to reduce the number of drugs in the DPCO may be considered to be in contravention of the Supreme Court order. This is relating to the K.S. Gopinath case ruling on March 10, 2003, in which the Government was directed to ensure that "... essential and life-saving drugs do not fall out of price control" (Narain, 2004).

In any case, given the peculiarity of the market, ensuring competition is easier said than done. The Indian pharmaceutical regulatory regime has been quite hard on the manufacturers, but has been extremely soft on the two other groups of important players: the doctors and the pharmacists. Indian Medical Council (Professional Conduct, Etiquette and Ethics) Regulations, 2002, have sufficient provisions to ensure good behaviour on the part of the doctors. However, it is more of a good endeavour rather than binding rules. Moreover, there is no mechanism to monitor if the doctors are following them.

One way to check rent-seeking behaviour of the doctors, as has been successfully experimented, even in neighbouring Bangladesh, is to mandate doctors to prescribe drugs with generic names. Even the Indian Medical Council (Professional Conduct, Etiquette and Ethics) Regulations, 2002 state that, "Every physician should, as far as possible, prescribe drugs with generic names." However, given the enormous clout of the pharmacists in India, this mandate may not work, and could even make the situation worse. What is, thus, desperately required in India, is an effective mechanism to contain the rent-seeking behaviour of the pharmacists.

If it is difficult to promote and maintain competition because of the peculiarity of the market, in the sense that consumers do not decide their purchases, then the same may not be true for bulk drugs. The purchasers of bulk drugs are informed producers, rather than helpless consumers. Thus, there is a need to study the behaviour of the bulk drug market and, if desirable, to further decontrol the sector.

If we are talking about promoting competition in the Indian pharmaceutical market, we also need to look at import competition. Currently, only a few specified life-saving products can be imported at zero duty. For most other pharmaceuticals, the duty rate is quite high as they attract a basic duty of 30 per cent; a countervailing duty of 16 per cent; a surcharge equivalent to the rate of excise duty, if the item was made in India; and special additional duty. The effective duty rate thus works out to be more than 56 per cent. For the scheduled (regulated) drugs, the protection is much higher as the MAPE is 100 per cent, for domestically manufactured drugs; and 50 per cent for imported drugs. The issue needs a closer look.

It is essential for the pharmaceutical sector, in India, to operate under a law that curbs anti-competitive activities. Despite ubiquitous regulations, competition is not entirely excluded from this industry. Competition is the key driving force behind the development of new innovative drugs, and a significant factor in keeping down the prices and production costs of off-patent drugs. Few aspects of the pharmaceutical industry, even though highly regulated, are unaffected by regulatory controls. The MRTP Act, 1969, did not have adequate provisions to deal with a large number of anti-competitive practices, like collusion or cartelisation, mergers and acquisitions, and abuse of intellectual property rights, which is a very common practice in the pharmaceutical industry, if viewed globally. The new Competition Act, 2002, is a much improved law, and has the required provisions, including extra territorial jurisdiction, though the provisions on IPRs is rather weak. This needs to be buttressed.

Notes

1. See section, "Pharmaceuticals Regulation in India" for details on DPCO.

2. A bulk drug is any pharmaceutical, chemical or biological product including its salts, esters, stereoisomers and derivatives, conforming to pharmacopoeia or other standards and which is used as such or as an ingredient in a formulation. (Source: The Drugs Prices Control Order, 1995).

3. A formulation is a medicine processed out of bulk drug/s for internal or external use for or in the diagnosis, treatment, mitigation or prevention of disease in human beings or animals, but shall not include any medicine included in the Ayurvedic, Homeopathic or Unani system of medicines. (Source: The Drugs Prices Control Order, 1995).

4. Nicholas Piramal took over Rhone Poulenc in 2000.

5. The Essential Commodities Act, 1955 was enacted for the control of production, supply, distribution, trade and commerce in certain commodities that were declared essential by the Central Government. The Act defines "Essential Commodities" to include drugs since they are considered essential for the health of society.

6. This retail price is different from the Maximum Retail Price (MRP) as applicable to all other packaged goods. While MRP for other goods are inclusive of all taxes, in case of medicines local taxes are not included in MRP.

7. In respect of a new plant, an IRR of 12 per cent based on long-term marginal costing is allowed and where production is from basic stage, a post-tax return of 18 per cent on net worth or a return of 26 per cent on capital employed is allowed.

8. The Indian Pharmaceutical Alliance (IPA), comprising 11 big companies, said that they would oppose any restriction on the prices of 'branded' drugs manufactured by them. The pharma industry has assured the Government of a price-freeze till March 31, 2005. This has been echoed by the Indian drug manufacturers' association (IDMA), as well as the Organisation of Pharmaceutical Producers of India (OPPI). The IDMA is a premier association of the Indian pharmaceutical industry and has come to be regarded, in different circles, as the 'Voice of the National Sector.' IDMA members comprise large, medium and small companies from all over India, manufacturing bulk drugs and formulations. The OPPI is another premier organisation of pharmaceutical manufacturers in India. Its membership consists of companies with international collaboration, and large Indian companies. It represents primarily research-based companies in India.

References

Balusubramaniam, K. (2001). "Access to Medicines: Patents, Prices and Public Policy – Consumer Perspectives", Paper presented at Oxfam International Seminar on *Intellectual Property and Development: What Future for the WTO TRIPS Agreement?*, Brussels, Mar. 20, 2001).

Clarke, J.L. and S.J. Evenett (2002). "The Deterrent Effects of National Anti-Cartel Laws: Evidence from the International Vitamins Cartel," AEI-Brookings Joint Centre for Regulatory Studies, *Working Paper 02-13*, Washington DC.

Confederation of Indian Industry (2000). "Report on the Pharmaceutical Sector in India," Presented to International Trade Centre, Geneva.

Ernst & Young (2004). *Global Pharma Report 2004*.

Government of India (2002), *Pharmaceutical Policy – 2002*, viewed 24 December 2004, <http://pib.nic.in/archieve/lreleng/lyr2002/rfeb2002/15022002/r1502200212.html>.

Government of India (2002a). *The Tenth Five Year Plan: 2002-2007*, Planning Commission, New Delhi, viewed 24 December 2004, <http://planningcommission.nic.in/plans/planrel/fiveyr/welcome.html>.

India Infoline, *Sector Study on the Pharmaceutical Industry*.

Keayla, B.K. (1994). "Patent Protection and the Pharmaceutical Industry," in K.R.G. Nair and Ashok Kumar, eds., *Intellectual Property Rights*, Allied Publishers, Delhi.

Lalitha, N. (2002). "Indian Pharmaceutical Industry in WTO Regime-A SWOT Analysis," *EPW* August 24, Pp 3542-3555.

Malhotra, Prabodh and Hans Lofgren (2004). "India's Pharmaceutical Industry: Hype or High Tech Take-off?," *Australian Health Review*, 28 (2): 182-193.

McKinsey & Co, *Vision 2010 for the Pharmaceutical Industry in India*.

Nanda, Nitya and Ritu Lodha (2002). "Making Essential Medicine Affordable to the Poor," *Wisconsin International Law Journal*, Vol 20, No 3.

Narrain, Siddarth (2004). "A Life-saving Order," *Frontline*, Vol 21, Issue 15 (July 17-30).

OECD (2001). *Competition and Regulation Issues in the Pharmaceutical Industry*, DAFFE/CLP(2000)29.

Pearl, Daniel and Steve Stecklow (2001). "Drug Firms' Incentives Fuel Abuse by Pharmacists in India," *The Wall Street Journal*, August 16, 2001.

Rane, Wishvas (2002). "Prices of Prescription Drugs: Marginal Rise in Cardiovascular Products," *EPW* August 17.

Sen Gupta, Amit (2002). "New Pharmaceutical Policy: A Savage Attack on Healthcare and a Licence to Profiteer," PHARMABIZ.com.

Part VI

Competition Policy in Infrastructure Sector

16 Competition Issues in Telecommunication Sector

Mahesh Uppal

16.1 An Overview of the Sector

India's telecommunications network is one of the ten largest in the world with revenues of roughly US$20bn. The Government is the main player in the sector and employs more than 4,00,000 persons. The network has grown to almost ten times its size in the last ten years. This network, though large, is also sparse, since on the average, only 1.5 per cent of India's majority rural population has a telephone connection. Of the 607,509 villages in India, a sixth are still without a phone.

India is divided into telecom circles, which are roughly co-terminus with the states of India. The major services, fixed and mobile, are licensed on a circle basis. However, there are some differences, both in the definition as well as the scope of services on offer in each circle. This is captured in Table 16.1 at the end of the chapter.

In recent years, the sector has seen significant private sector participation after the government's decision to review the policy framework and setting up a regulatory body.

There has been substantial growth and dramatic expansion in the range of services available, as well as a fall in their prices. Figures (16.1 to 16.9) show various parameters for India's telecom sector. The figures show that the growth has been most dramatic for mobile users. Urban subscriber numbers have risen faster than rural, hinting that benefits of competition, such as choice, quality and lower prices may yet not have reached all to the same extent. The data indicates greater efficiencies as well as significantly higher revenues.

The link between these parameters and the nature and scope of competition in the telecommunications market is one of the purposes of this paper.

A Series of Figures Highlighting Telecommunication Evolution in India from 1999 to 2004:

FIGURE 16.1

Change in Size of Telecommunication Work Force from March 1999 to March 2003

Staff Number in Incumbent Telecommunications Operators are Stagnant

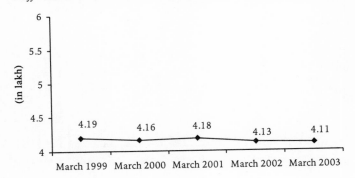

FIGURE 16.2

Growth of Total Telephones, Fixed Lines and Mobile Phones from March 1999 to 2004 (All India)

Mobile Phones Surge as Fixed Line Growth Tapers Off

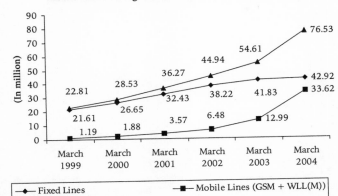

FIGURE 16.3

Growth of Urban Lines and Rural Lines from March 1999 to 2004 (All India)

Rural Telephones Lines Fail to Keep Pace with Urban Lines

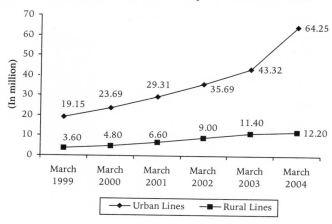

FIGURE 16.4

Growth of Rural Lines based on Circle Type from March 1999 to 2004 (Circle wise)

Growth of Rural Lines in Poorer States is Lower

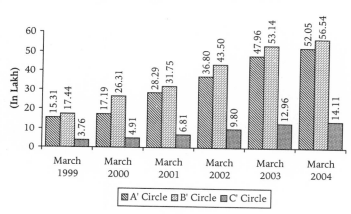

FIGURE 16.5

Growth of Village Public Telephones (VPTs) from March 1999 to 2004 (All India)

Growth of Village Public Telephones (VPT's) is Slowing Down

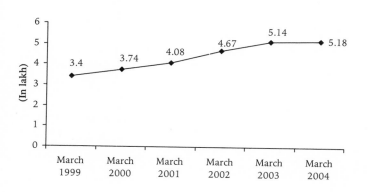

FIGURE 16.6

Growth of Village Public Telephones (VPTs) Based on Circle Type from March 1999 to 2004 (Circle-wise)

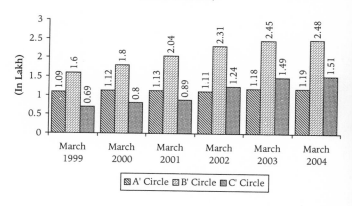

FIGURE 16.7

Telephone Access (Measured by Tele-density: Number of Telephones by Population) According to Economic Status of States—March 1999 to 2004

Telephone Access is Still Low in Poorer States

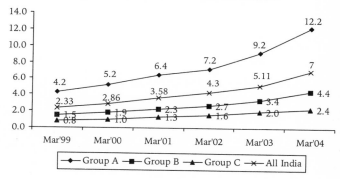

Note: Group A – Metros, Maharashtra, Tamil Nadu, Karnataka, Andhra Pradesh, and Gujarat.

Group B – Kerala, Punjab, Haryana, Uttar Pradesh, West Bengal, Madhya Pradesh, and Rajasthan.

Group C – Himachal Pradesh, Jammu & Kashmir, Bihar, Assam, Orissa, Andaman & Nicobar, and the North East.

16.2 Indian Telecom Policy Changes

Till the 1980s, India's telecommunications industry was almost entirely controlled by the government, which performed all roles including equipment manufacture, licensing, policy-making, regulations and operation of services.

Progressive easing of monopoly began with the opening of manufacturing to competition from the private sector. The early-90s saw the introduction of several new electronic communication services, besides voice telecommunications. In 1992, the Government of India took the view that the new "value-added services"

FIGURE 16.8

Telephone Access: Rural and Urban Telephone Lines March 2000 to March 2004

Difference in Urban and Rural Teledensity is More Marked

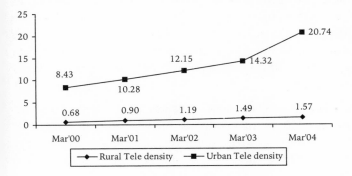

FIGURE 16.9

Telephone Access: Fixed Lines and Mobile Phones March 1999 to March 2004

Number for Fixed and Mobile Phones is Almost the Same

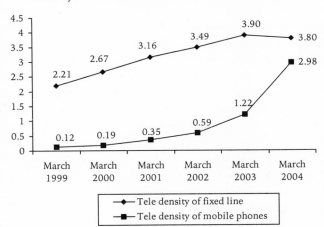

could be left for private sector entrepreneurs to provide. The investments required were relatively low and the commercial threat to the main telecommunications service provided by the Department of Telecommunications (DoT), was not significant.

Rather unusually, cellular mobile services, which require the building of substantial infrastructure, like towers, were classified as value added services. In effect, the opening in 1992 of cellular services, first in metros to private sector operators, heralded the beginning of network creation by private entrepreneurs.

The entry of the private sector in other telecommunications services, besides the so-called value-added services all over India, was finally cleared in May 1994 when the National Telecom Policy (NTP) was announced.

NTP-94 outlined the basic policy framework for the development of the telecommunication sector in the country. Briefly, the policy aimed at:

- Providing telephone connections on demand.

- Connecting every village to the telephone network.

- Enabling access to world class services.

- Allowing Indian companies to provide basic telephone services.

- Using private initiative to complement government efforts to raise additional resources through innovative financing schemes like leasing, deferred payments, 'Build, Operate and Transfer', and 'Build, Lease and Transfer'.

- Ensuring the protection of customer interests and allowing fair competition.

It was significant that the NTP-94 allowed the private sector, including foreign companies, as long as their equity was between 10 per cent and 49 per cent in the operating company that was awarded the licence, to provide *all* services. It was also interesting that the proposal to do so referred to the large investment (Rupees 230 billion) required to meet the telephony targets of the policy as the main reason to invite private sector participation. There was no acknowledgement *per se* of the benefits of, or need for, competition in bringing down prices, improving quality or market expansion. Consequently, it was not surprising that the need for independent regulation in a multiple operator environment, where the Government of India itself was a player, was reduced to "arrangements for allowing fair competition".

16.3 Experience with Telecom Regulation in India

India's telecom sector saw competition in the provision of telecom services for the first time with the entry of private sector players in the cellular market. The private companies were not competing head-on with the incumbent DoT, which provided almost all types of services throughout India, except in Delhi and Mumbai where the Mahanagar Telephone Nigam Ltd. (MTNL), also majority-owned by Government of India, was the service provider. In the event, the government players had opted out of the mobile market, since they felt fixed line demand needed to be addressed first, as well as the fact that they did not think the highly-priced mobile services had a role in a poor country like India.

The Telecom Regulatory Authority of India (TRAI) was set up in 1997, well after mobile services had begun in 1995.

Mobile services were expensive at Rs. 16/per minute to be paid to make or receive calls using a mobile, a price cap ironically specified in the licence issued to mobile operators. The operators were to pay fixed line operator DoT access charges to connect to the fixed line network. The mobile operators were to retain airtime charges. Both the charges were passed on to the user.

With the rapid growth world-wide of mobile telephones, DoT and MTNL were quick to realise that they had probably erred in choosing to stay out of the lucrative mobile market and attempted to play spoilsport. The DoT soon responded with a tariff hike for calls from fixed lines to mobile phones, thus making it more expensive. MTNL announced plans to enter the mobile market soon after.

Mobile operators were soon knocking the doors of the newly created TRAI. The TRAI provided them quick relief and quashed the DoT's tariff proposals. Later, it also disallowed MTNL from entering the mobile market on grounds that the terms and conditions of its licences were unavailable and the government had not sought TRAI's prior approval when it licensed MTNL to provide mobile services.

The DoT appealed to the High Court against this decision of the TRAI, as well as a later decision of the body, which sought to move the mobile operators to a calling-party-pays regime where the mobile user, like the fixed one, would pay only to make outgoing calls. The Government of India, i.e. DoT, won its appeals against the TRAI. The Government, according to the High Court, did not need to consult the TRAI on any licensing decisions. The TRAI did not also have the right to alter revenue sharing arrangements, i.e. interconnection terms of operators, since this function stemmed out of the operators licences and the TRAI's role in licensing was only limited.

By 1998 private businesses were running mobile services throughout India, although a small element of fixed line services too had begun, on a modest scale, in Madhya Pradesh and Andhra Pradesh. Maharashtra, Gujarat, Punjab and Rajasthan too had one fixed line licensee each, who had not yet started providing services in any significant numbers.

The private businesses soon found themselves in financial trouble and unable to pay the huge amounts committed in licence fees. This resulted in defaults, and disputes between operators and DoT – as to who was responsible for the failure of new operators to pay their dues. The operators claimed government had made business unviable because of expensive delays in providing clearances, especially for frequencies. The High Court ruled against the operators when they sought to prevent government from taking action against defaulters and en-cashing guarantees given by operators.

The private operators lost all their cases. They had also failed to persuade the courts on powers of the TRAI on licensing and interconnection. There were several representations to the government from both Indian and foreign operators to allay the fears that private investors felt both commercially and also with respect to a virtually powerless regulator. They felt that the regulatory regime, like its counterparts in the Western developed countries, did not provide sufficient incentive or security to new investors competing with a government. This was particularly worrying since the government was compromised because of the obvious conflict of interest in its roles as licensor, policymaker, regulator and operator. In its latter role, it enjoyed, contrary to all principles of fair play or economic regulation, a licence which allowed it to provide all services across India, while its competitors (private players) needed service-wise and region-wise licences. The view was further strengthened by the conspicuously feeble commitment to a robust competitive regime in telecommunications, as evidenced by its stand in the WTO's "Regulatory Reference Paper" discussed below.

The government then faced the dilemma of allowing the private telecommunications sector players, which included the "who's who" of Indian and foreign players, to die and face the resulting bad publicity and possibly more pressure or to change its approach. It chose the latter. It announced a change in policy through the formulation of New Telecom Policy 1999 (NTP-99). From the operators' perspective, the most important part of the NTP-99 proposals was the move from a licence fee regime to a revenue sharing one and the statement in it that DoT and Mahanagar Telephone Nigam Ltd. (MTNL) would be allowed entry into the mobile business. The warring groups were placated.

In some respects the policy objectives were familiar. They prioritised on access, especially in rural and remote areas. The emphasis on a modern world-class infrastructure remained. But, NTP-99 differed in its focus, in that now the creation of a competitive telecommunications sector was recognised as an objective, as was the need for a level playing field. As an implicit recognition, that the government's multiple roles as licensor, policymaker, regulator and operator were untenable if competition was to survive, the NTP-99 document also acknowledged the importance of achieving efficiency and transparency in spectrum management in the increasingly competitive wireless sector.

16.3.1 Provisions of NTP 99

NTP-99 stipulated the following:

- Operators could move to a revenue sharing regime from the one where they pay fees bid by them.

- DoT/MTNL would enter the mobile service market.

- Telecom Regulatory Authority of India would be strengthened.

- The Department of Telecommunications would be restructured.

- Cable operators would be allowed to provide and use their infrastructure for telecommunications services, if they obtained a licence.

- Convergence between services would be encouraged.

16.3.2 TRAI Act (1997) Amended

NTP-99 was followed, in 2000, by the amendment of TRAI Act (1997). The amendment gave the TRAI an exclusive mandate to fix and regulate tariffs and interconnection and removed all government interventions in these two functions. It also mandated the government to seek advice from the TRAI before it licensed a new operator, although such advice would not be binding. Interestingly, the amendment envisaged reconstitution of the TRAI and the creation, in addition, of the Telecom Dispute Settlement and Appellate Tribunal (TDSAT), to which inter-operator disputes, operator-government disputes, and appeals against the TRAI decisions could be made. All but one member of the erstwhile TRAI were removed and replaced by a team, which in the new dispensation enjoyed no legal protection, beyond a right of being heard, if the government wished to remove them from office. The earlier TRAI members could only be sacked after a successful reference to the Chief Justice of India. Almost all newly appointed full-time members were former government bureaucrats with little demonstrated expertise in the sector.

The message in all this was mixed. The TRAI had been considerably empowered to carry out its task of economic regulation and competition management. However, the body's members knew how easy it was for the government to remove them. The government controlled, through its operators, the overwhelming share of revenues of the sector and had considerable powers related to hiring and firing.

16.3.3 Creation of Bharat Sanchar Nigam Limited (BSNL)

The operating company, Bharat Sanchar Nigam Limited (BSNL), was carved out of the Department of Telecommunications in 2000, leaving a dramatically smaller DoT to deal with policy-making and related government functions, including licensing and spectrum management.

16.3.4 Unification of Fixed and Mobile Licences

The new TRAI would grapple with a new competition issue almost as soon as the body was formed. The fixed line players brought to the attention of Government of India, as well as the TRAI, the fact that CDMA technologies, being used by fixed line players, could also be used to provide mobile services. They demanded to be allowed to offer mobile services as a part of their fixed line licence. The TRAI was persuaded, as was the Government of India. Limited mobility services, much to the consternation of cellular mobile operators, began in 2002. Virtually all fixed line operators, except Bharti, who already had a national presence in mobile business through its GSM service and fixed line business in several states, sought to use this option to provide mobile services in competition with existing mobile players. The result was aggressive litigation by cellular mobile service providers who alleged foul play and back door entry into their mobile business, for which they had paid huge licence fees.

The case went through several ups and downs, as well as controversies, on its way to the Supreme Court. Before the merits of the case could be fully pronounced upon by the Supreme Court, the TRAI made a proposal to the government to merge or unify fixed and mobile licences. The Government of India accepted this unorthodox proposal. An important consequence was that Reliance, which had not been a significant player in the mobile business, soon became a formidable one through the conversion of its numerous fixed line licences.

The unification of licences has successfully ended crippling litigation in the sector. However, it would seem that this is a policy (of unification) response to address a regulatory or competition issue.

Draft recommendations of the TRAI on the unified licensing regime have been released in recent weeks. While the recommendations have yet to be accepted, they could have far-reaching implications for competition. The document proposes a new licensing category of niche operators for providing access in rural areas. It also proposes a unified licence containing virtually all major services, including fixed, mobile, national and international long distance, Internet telephony, etc. Nevertheless, in its effort to provide a level playing field to erstwhile long distance operators, it recommends high entry barriers for new players in the unified licence. This will serve to protect incumbent long distance providers, besides BSNL, from future competition. The proposals, if accepted, will hurt small players in particular, since even services like Internet telephony will require huge upfront payments for entry, unlike in most other countries.

16.4 Evolution of BSNL and MTNL in the Last Decade

The changes following NTP-99 and the TRAI Amendment Act (2000) have reduced operators' commercial burden considerably and resulted in extraordinary growth of private sector businesses, especially mobile. The competitive pressure following the entry of two more mobile players in 2001 has led to a considerable fall in prices and expansion of services.

There is very little serious competition in the fixed line business. BSNL and MTNL, between them, control almost 95 per cent of the fixed line subscribers. The other major player in this market is Bharti Touchtel (See Figure 16.12) with about 1.5 per cent market share. In March 2003, BSNL's & MTNL's share was 86.53 and 11.16 per cent respectively, but in March 2004, it reduced to 84.29 and 10.18 per cent respectively.

Private sector companies Reliance and Bharti lead the market share stakes in the mobile business. However, BSNL is a close third. (See Figure 16.13) It is interesting, however, that MTNL in lucrative metros of Delhi and Mumbai has failed to prove itself in the mobile business. Today, as Figure 16.13 shows, it is behind several other operators, like Idea, which entered the mobile market much later.

FIGURE 16.10

Subscriber Base of Fixed Services for March 2003 and March 2004

Incumbents Still Dominate Fixed Services

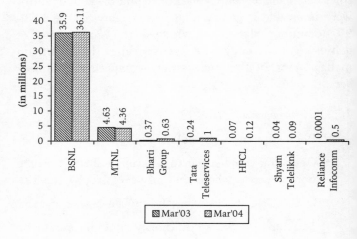

FIGURE 16.11

Market Shares of Fixed Services for March 2003 and March 2004

Most Private Players Shunning Fixed Services

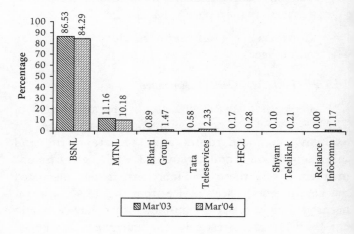

The last one year (2003-2004) has seen a dramatic improvement in the share of Reliance in the mobile segment. This is due to its extremely competitive prices, which have enabled it to add on large numbers of first-time users. The company has sought to exploit its economies of scale in view of its virtually national presence. It also had an advantage in that it started providing de facto mobile services – for which it later paid a penalty of Rs 1500 crores – even when its licence had not been revised to include such services and when its legality was still being challenged. This gave it an edge over competitors. Tatas provided limited mobile service, but much later.

FIGURE 16.12

Subscriber Base of Cellular Services for March 2003 and March 2004

Reliance has Made Spectacular Gains in Mobile Market

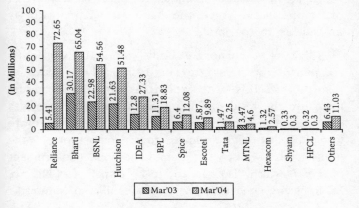

FIGURE 16.13

Market Share Cellular Services for March 2003 and March 2004

Smaller Players Struggle to Retain Market Shares

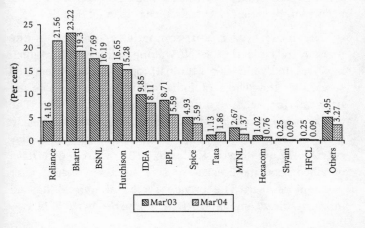

The long distance market too has seen interesting market dynamics. Competition in the market has led to over 75 per cent fall in long distance rates both nationally and internationally. The competition by newcomers Bharti and Reliance has been formidable. Anyhow, BSNL has been quick to respond and has shown itself to be as aggressively competitive by reducing tariffs.

Videsh Sanchar Nigam Limited (VSNL) had a monopoly to provide international telecom services till 2002, though the government had said, in its WTO commitments, that this monopoly would continue till 2004. The company was partly privatised in 2002 and its management passed on to the Tatas, after they were successful in an auction to acquire a major share in the

company. The Government of India currently owns 25 per cent stake in the company. Following its privatisation, there have been three more entrants in the international long distance (ILD) business, *viz.* Reliance, Bharti and Data Access. BSNL has recently been given a licence to provide ILD services.

The Internet market too has begun to show the fixed line incumbents as the most likely winners. Starting from a scratch, today they are way ahead of seemingly more nimble-footed operators, such as Sify and VSNL, who started services much before BSNL or MTNL.

16.5 M&A Trends

The unification of the fixed and mobile licences in the country has forced operators to consider their long-term role in the telecommunications market. Several parts of the country, especially metros and the high revenue A-type circles, often have as many as seven mobile operators serving the region. This number is higher than the number of operators in almost all major regions of the world.

The risk of an overheated market is real. Consequently, the telecommunications sector has seen the exit of several smaller players from the market. These have included Shyam in Rajasthan, Escotel in Kerala, Haryana, and UP (west), and Aircell (Tamilnadu).

Before this overheated stage too, post the NTP-99 stage freeing up operators from huge licence fee commitments, the market saw the exit of several smaller operators, such as Usha (Calcutta), Fascel (Gujarat) and the dilution of holdings of Essar group in its circles by selling out to Hutch.

Unusually for India, the Tatas and the Birlas (in partnership with AT&T) had merged their operations in 2000, creating a much larger footprint in the mobile market. Idea, in its earlier *avatar* as Birla Tata AT&T, had also earlier bought out RPG in Madhya Pradesh. Tatas acquired Hughes' fixed line business in Maharashtra. Bharti bought out Skycell in Chennai and Spice in Kolkata, about a year ago.

Hutch bought out Max in the earliest acquisition in the mobile market that happened in 1998.

Observers believe that Spice will soon exit its mobile business in Karnataka and Punjab.

There are indications that India's telecom market will be serviced by four or five operators who are currently engaged in extending their presence to most parts of the country. The likely "winners" or "survivors" are believed to be Reliance, Bharti, Tata

Teleservices, Idea and Hutch, besides the state-owned incumbent BSNL. Of these, Idea and Hutch seem to be focused on the mobile access business, while the others have a presence in virtually all telecom services being provided to Indian subscribers.

It is useful to assess the impact of this market consolidation on subscribers. In larger markets of mobile services, especially those in metros and A-type Circles, it is unlikely that consumers will suffer as a consequence of this seemingly lowering competition. In effect, though, the four operators that are likely to remain in most circles are quite adequate.

In the case of fixed line services, which are still the mainstay of most rural people, the situation is likely to be problematic. In most cases, only one operator, BSNL, serves rural people. Most rural people in India still do not have access to competition and its consequent benefits through more attractive prices, quality, as well as actual choice. TRAI's draft recommendations for Unified Licensing Regime (ULR) envisage the role of niche operators in providing telecom services in rural areas. Even though, it is unlikely that they will provide any significant competition, since the business proposition on offer to them is not attractive enough to invest in a potentially loss-making service. Indeed, it is seen that subscribers are fewer in the poorer C circles and they pay higher call charges. Therefore, any consolidation is likely to result in reduced competition in poorer areas, where competition may not survive or thrive to any significant extent.

The Government of India issued guidelines for merger and acquisitions (M&As) in the telecom sector in India. The guidelines allow companies to takeover others in their own areas of operation (circles), as well as in other regions. The former (M&A in own circle), is subject to a requirement that the merged company shall not have a market share greater than 67 per cent as a consequence of the merger, and that the number of companies that will remain in the market, post merger, will not be less than three.

16.6 Existence of Anti-competitive Practices

The rapid growth in the telecommunications sector in recent years tempts one to view the progress as a consequence of increasing competition. This is unfortunately true to a limited extent only. The sector is currently witnessing a great deal of anti-competitive practices. It is also ironic that these emanate from, or concern, the government-owned BSNL, because of the government's role in licensing, policy-making and operations.

To recapitulate, anti-competitive practices provide the practitioners the ability to raise prices independently of competition. These are also those activities or actions of a major player in the market, which provide market advantage to a player at the cost of competitors, since the same activity option is unavailable to the latter.

BSNL is a corporate body. Some of the anti-competitive practices are not, technically speaking, a result of BSNL's own explicit action. For example, many are the results of terms on which BSNL provides services in the market, which are manifestly more favourable than those allowed to its competitors by the licensor, viz. Ministry for Communications (Government of India), which also happens to be owner of BSNL. So, BSNL is the chief beneficiary of a conflict of interests.

This conflict is further exacerbated by the fact that the regulator, TRAI, also reports to the same Ministry. In addition, TRAI has staff from the DoT at virtually all levels. In its seven-year old history, TRAI always had a Member on its Board, who was a part of telecommunications operations of DoT or BSNL. Indeed, a current Member is the first chairman of BSNL.

The most brazen anti-competitive practice in the market today is that BSNL (along with MTNL, which operates in Delhi and Mumbai) operates an integrated service for the whole of India, while its competitors are licensed for each region and service separately. The latter's licenses came on payment of substantial fees, in most cases. BSNL has paid no licence fee to provide any service. Thus Bharti, Reliance, BPL, Hutch etc. have obtained separate licences to serve different states, after payment of fees. The private sector, therefore, has an inherent disadvantage when it competes with BSNL.

Further, to make matters worse, the fixed and mobile access providers, who, even after the unification of licences, hold the Unified Access Service Licence (UASL), may provide services in a state of choice, but may not interconnect across service areas. Thus, even if they hold licences for contiguous areas, operators must reach their customers in the other area only by connecting to long distance service providers, amongst which BSNL is the most ubiquitous and the largest.

Regulations today allow BSNL to receive an Access Deficit Charge (ADC), which seeks to compensate BSNL whose fixed line rentals and call charges are considered loss-making operations that must be continued in public interest. The ADC is currently a surcharge on all calls to the fixed line network. Importantly, operators of mobile users pay it even if the calls themselves do not reach the fixed network at all. The amount of ADC has been calculated as close to Rs. 40 billion. (It was Rs. 130 billion before and is being currently reviewed). As things stand, against all norms of fair competition, BSNL receives ADC payments from its competitors, even though it refuses to undertake tariff revision that the current TRAI regulations have allowed it to carry out for several years. Thus, the local call charges, supposedly run at a loss by BSNL, are being held at Rs. 1.20 for 3 minutes, while the rules allow BSNL to charge the same amount for 2 minutes. The perverse incentive to BSNL to adopt this approach is easy to see since the losses so incurred can be directly recovered from payments from its competitors. The latter often claim BSNL uses these revenues to undercut them in the more lucrative mobile market. BSNL thus does not face the risk of customer displeasure or of losing customers to competition in such an environment. There is no transparency in the use of ADC amount, as BSNL has not effected account separation to justify the amount it is receiving. Moreover, the basis of calculating ADC is questionable, since it uses BSNL's own accounting data to ascertain the ADC amount. Another concern is that the ADC fails to separate calls made to profitable and non-profitable fixed lines. By lumping all fixed calls under one category, the ADC essentially becomes a tax on BSNL's competitors. These are some of the key factors that have led to a lot of debate on the issue of ADC.

What's more, the objectives of providing ADC are no different from USO and there is a strong case for their merger. TRAI has stated this will happen in about five years. But, this may be much too late for those who will face the consequences of the current provisions. The provisions are patently not "competitively neutral" as most enlightened regulatory regimes would normally strive towards.

BSNL has successfully resisted sharing its infrastructure, acquired since the days of its being a public owned monopoly, with its competitors, even though regulations demand it. Its ubiquity enables it, for example, to roll out lucrative mobile networks in places where its competitors will require considerable resources to reach. While this may sound strange at first, the fact that BSNL has a large fixed line infrastructure in place means that it has physical presence, towers, buildings, offices, qualified staff etc. all over the country, which can be easily redeployed to provide or augment mobile services.

BSNL has successfully fought or stayed economic regulation of itself as a manifestly major player in the market, with over 60 per cent of all access customers and more than that proportion of revenues. It has foiled TRAI's attempts to impose modest asymmetric regulation, which required it to report tariffs a week earlier than its competition. This is in spite of such asymmetric regulation being based on international best practices and sound economic regulatory principles.

BSNL is yet to come up with its Reference Interconnect Offer (RIO) mandated by TRAI. Such an RIO would provide the much needed transparency and predictability to seekers of interconnection for whom this is the lifeline. BSNL has frequently used the threat to cancel interconnection agreements if competitors will not accept its terms and conditions in their totality.

A phenomenon that has now acquired considerable importance is the fact that BSNL is now India's largest Internet Service Provider (ISP), even though it was one of the last to enter the business. A closer look at the picture demonstrates that unlike its competitors, who have usually one business, i.e. of ISP, BSNL has two when it comes to Internet services. It provides dialup access to the public telephony network that its own users, as well as most of the customers of its competitors, need and the ISPs (e.g. Sify) cannot provide. This anomaly gives BSNL two revenue streams, viz. call charges for access to the telephone network as well as charges for providing Internet access. The opportunity for cross-subsidising – the competitive ISP business with the less competitive dial-up business is obvious. BSNL subscribers pay much less for Internet access, which is frequently bundled at a token price (1 paise per minute) with dial-up charges, which are considerably higher than this rate.

The rapid growth of BSNL's ISP business is therefore not too surprising. Indeed, BSNL's advantages are multiplied when we see that it is currently able to offer a single bill service to access the Internet, which reduces customer anxiety about multiple bills considerably. This bundling is not an option for competitors who are fast losing market share.

BSNL has successfully thwarted the attempts of competing ISPs by making it difficult to access the net through use of competing network providers (e.g. Bharti), who would have an incentive to offer more attractive pricing to ISPs. The Internet Service Providers Association of India has often alleged/complained to the TRAI that numbers of competitors are frequently unavailable when users need to dial them. Since the numbers are being accessed from BSNL phones in most cases, BSNL can control access to the numbers of its competitors who are interconnected to BSNL's network.

The TRAI has had virtually no success in ensuring transparent accounting from BSNL, which, if available, would have enabled it and BSNL's competitor to identify cross-subsidies more readily. However, accounting separation, though a regulatory requirement in India, as elsewhere, has not been carried out by BSNL, even as its claims for subsidy continue to be processed.

The above practices, may, in some cases, be described by the orthodox as BSNL taking advantage of what rules – *albeit* biased in its favour – allow it do in the market place. Though, in view of the government's conflict of interest in framing these rules, these practices cannot but be seen as anti-competitive.

16.7   WTO Agreement on Basic Telecommunications Services: Insight into Government Approach to Competition in the Telecom Market

An important event in 1997 gave important clues about Government of India's thinking on competition in the telecommunications sector.

In 1997, India, along with nearly hundred other countries, became a signatory to the WTO agreement on basic telecommunication services. The agreement seeks to facilitate the opening of telecommunications markets across the world and to promote market access through removal of entry barriers. It also proposes independent economic regulation in the sector, traditionally controlled by governments and/or monopoly companies owned by them.

The agreement, predictably, was promoted by countries with the largest telecommunications markets. Still, it should be seen in the context of the rapid advance in communications technologies, which have changed the economics of this sector. Recent developments have rendered untenable the need for state-run monopolies to provide services on grounds that telecommunications was a sector with economies of scale that made competition a luxury, which poor countries, especially, could not afford.

On 24 April 1996, the WTO Negotiating Group on Basic Telecommunications brought out its Regulatory Reference Paper. The Paper addresses the main entry and competition issues in the regulatory framework for what it called basic telecommunication services, which, unlike in the terminology used for India, do include both fixed and mobile services.

Competition in the telecommunications market depends critically on the ability of new entrants to interconnect to the existing network. A new competitor starting from scratch cannot survive if its subscribers cannot reach the large numbers already using the existing network that they are in competition with. Thus, the absence of effective interconnection can be a major barrier to entry in the telecommunications market.

The WTO reference paper therefore concentrates on ensuring access of newcomers to "essential facilities" controlled by "major suppliers". We give a brief overview of the Paper to highlight what the critical competition issues in the telecommunications sector typically are and how the government, or more specifically its Department of Telecommunications, saw them.

Essential facilities are defined in the WTO Regulatory Reference Paper as "facilities of a public telecommunications transport network or services that

(a) are exclusively or predominantly provided by a single or limited number of suppliers; and

(b) cannot feasibly be economically or technically substituted in order to provide a service."

A major supplier is defined in the Paper as a supplier that has the ability to materially affect the terms of participation (having regard to price and supply) in the relevant market for basic telecommunications services as a result of:

(a) control over essential facilities; or

(b) use of its position in the market.

16.7.1 *Competitive Safeguards*

The WTO reference paper envisages competitive safeguards for prevention of anti-competitive practices in telecommunications, which include:

"(a) engaging in anti-competitive cross-subsidisation;

(b) using information obtained from competitors, with anti-competitive results; and

(c) not making available to other services suppliers, on a timely basis, technical information about essential facilities and commercially relevant information, which are necessary for them to provide services."

16.7.2 *Interconnection*

The reference paper also envisages that signatories will ensure interconnection with a major supplier at any technically feasible point in the network

"(a) under non-discriminatory terms, conditions (including technical standards and specifications) and rates, of a quality no less favourable than that provided for its own like services or for like services of non-affiliated service suppliers or for its subsidiaries or other affiliates;

(b) in a timely fashion, on terms, conditions (including technical standards and specifications) and cost-oriented rates that are transparent, reasonable, having regard to economic feasibility, and sufficiently unbundled so that the supplier need not pay for network components or facilities that it does not require for the service to be provided; and

(c) upon request, at points in addition to the network termination points offered to the majority of users, subject to charges that reflect the cost of construction of necessary additional facilities."

16.7.3 Universal Service

The reference paper, while giving a signatory the right to define the kind of universal service obligation, prevents such obligations from being imposed selectively to hurt competition, "provided they are administered in a transparent, non-discriminatory and competitively neutral manner"

16.7.4 Licensing

The document stipulates that where a licence is required

(a) all the licensing criteria and the period of time normally required to reach a decision concerning an application for a licence, and

(b) the terms and conditions of individual licences.

The reasons for the denial of a licence will be made known to the applicant upon request.

16.7.5 Independent Regulators

According to the reference paper "The regulatory body is separate from, and not accountable to, any supplier of basic telecommunications services. The decisions of and the procedures used by regulators shall be impartial with respect to all market participants."

16.7.6 Allocation and Use of Scarce Resources

The document says, "Any procedures for the allocation and use of scarce resources, including frequencies, numbers and rights of way, will be carried out in an objective, timely, transparent and non-discriminatory manner."

India's version of the WTO Regulatory Reference Paper (hereinafter the "Paper") says a lot about its approach to competition in the telecommunications sector. We will illustrate this with some examples.

In section 1.1 of Competitive Safeguards, the Paper envisages that for the prevention of anti-competitive practices in telecommunications,

"Appropriate measures shall be maintained for the purpose of *preventing suppliers who, alone or together, are a major supplier, from engaging* in or continuing anti-competitive practices"

However, the highlighted words are missing from India's version of the Paper. Government of India, it would imply, does not see the need for any special measures for regulating "major suppliers" and sees new entrants as no different.

In section 1.2 on Safeguards, the document says that anti-competitive practices referred to above shall include, in particular, engaging in anti-competitive cross-subsidisation.

However, India's version excludes this reference to cross-subsidy.

On interconnection, the document stipulates that "Interconnection with a major supplier will be ensured at any *technically feasible* point in the network." and that "Such interconnection is provided *under non-discriminatory terms and conditions, including technical standards and specification, and rates". In India's version, the word technically feasible point becomes specified point and the reference to "non-discriminatory terms"* is absent.

The Indian version ignores the provision in the Paper, which requires that interconnection is ensured in a timely fashion, on terms, conditions (including technical standards and specifications) and cost-oriented rates that are transparent, reasonable, having regard to economic feasibility, and sufficiently unbundled so that the supplier need not pay for network components or facilities that it does not require for the service to be provided."

For settlement of all too familiar disputes relating to Interconnection, the original Paper envisages an "independent body, which may be a domestic body". The Indian version commits to a *domestic regulatory authority*.

In section 3, relating to Universal Service Obligation (USO), India conspicuously excluded reference to the obligations being applied in a "competitively neutral manner".

In the section on Public availability of licensing criteria too, India did not commit to making public anything more than the criteria themselves, although the original Paper requires that time to take decisions and reasons for denial of a licence too would be known publicly.

In the section on Independent Regulator, while the Paper required the creation of "a body, separate from, and not accountable to, any supplier of basic telecommunications services", India's version chose to remain silent, even though, as it happened, the setting of Telecom Regulatory Authority of India was in fact just weeks away.

In the important section 6, Allocation and use of scarce resources, the Government of India removed reference in the allocation process being carried out in a *"transparent and non-discriminatory"* or *"in an objective and timely manner"*.

16.8   Entry and Exit in the Telecommunications Sector in India

India's telecommunications sector is one of the most open in the world today – with no limits on the number of players in any service in the sector. A barrier to entry might be the unavailability of radio frequencies that are required to run mobile services. Otherwise, a player may seek any licence and expect to receive it in a reasonable time of a few weeks. Leaving the sector is not as easy but still relatively straightforward.

On the other hand, for easy entry to perform its economic role in ensuring robust competition, much more than "low entry barriers" is required. Unless the distortions in the market due to a patently anomalous licensing regime are removed, the role of free entry will be limited.

Still, the relatively low barriers in most parts of the telecommunications business in India have not, in fact, resulted in much new entry. Rather, it has catalysed consolidation through Mergers and Acquisition.

16.9   Relationship and Coordination between Regulatory Agencies

The biggest threat to competition in the telecommunications market today is the distortions in the market caused by government policy rules and regulations set by different government agencies. While this is not entirely due to lack of coordination between these agencies, the role of such coordination cannot be underestimated.

There are two levels at which coordination is necessary. One is between the TRAI and the Competition Commission of India (CCI). The other is between the TRAI and the Wireless Planning Co-ordination (WPC) wing.

The role of the TRAI in issues relating to competition is limited by Section 14 of its legislation, the Telecom Regulatory Authority of India Act 1997, which denies it jurisdiction in all matters that would go to the Monopolies and Restrictive Trade Practices Commission (MRTPC). The MRTPC was India's only competition regulator. The CCI has of course now superseded the MRTPC on grounds that the MRTPC was no longer adequate to carry out the competition mandate. The CCI therefore replaces reference to the MRTPC in the TRAI Act 1997. There has been no change in the TRAI's mandate with respect to competition since its inception.

The above separation between the roles of the CCI and the TRAI is a major concern. The lack of a significant and robust competition mandate for the TRAI – even if it was to run concurrently with the CCI's – means that a function like competition management, which is perhaps the single most important task carried out by telecommunications regulators world-wide, is not under purview of the TRAI. It is also not surprising therefore that as seen in the previous section, some of the areas in which the TRAI has been least effective has been in ensuring a level playing field for all the players in the field.

There may be a risk of so-called "forum shopping" in two agencies with an overlapping mandate, since it might be an incentive for people to approach agencies which seem to them to be likely to promise their kind of relief. To avoid this, there may well be need for hierarchy between the TRAI and the CCI with respect to their role in regulating competition in the telecom market. There may also be a need to establish norms for agencies when dealing with issues raised with them. For instance, the CCI could be the last port of call after sector regulators like the TRAI have disposed off the matters raised with either of the two agencies.

The case of South Africa is interesting: The Competition Commission and the Independent Communication Authority of South Africa (ICASA) have entered into a memorandum of agreement, under which both bodies can act pursuant to their authorising statutes, while allocating a lead role to one or the other in a particular case. The Commission would take a lead if the issue was access to an essential facility, and

ICASA would take the lead if it were breach of a tariff or licensing condition. The agencies have also established a joint working committee to coordinate responsibilities for particular investigations.

The coordination between the TRAI and the WPC wing is also critical in the new environment, where wireless communications is increasingly the most convenient and inexpensive method of connecting people and places. The TRAI currently does not involve itself in the fees to be paid by operators for use of wireless frequencies. This means that a critical component of telecommunications costs is today being dealt with two agencies that do not seem to co-ordinate with each other on a regular basis.

16.10 Role of Foreign Players in India's Telecommunications Sector

The Department of Telecommunications had mandated that Indian companies seeking to enter the fixed or mobile services market have foreign partners with prior experience of providing telecommunications services. This was presumably to ensure that Indian companies, with no experience in providing telecommunications services in a monopoly market, had access to the requisite experience. The foreign investors were expected to bring in at least 10 per cent equity, but in no case more than 49 per cent. Most Indian operators are today owned in part by international investors.

The rules for foreign direct investment (FDI) have now been changed. Foreign investors can own up to 49 per cent of operating companies directly. Since the remaining 51 per cent can also be owned by a joint venture between Indian and foreign companies, foreign investors can own up to 74 per cent of Indian operators. This is the case with Hutch and possibly with some other operators.

Given that we are dealing with a service industry like telecommunications, rules for FDI have a slightly different import, since unlike other types of businesses created in partnership with other investors, the infrastructure created by service industries is virtually impossible to relocate out of the country. The risk of easy flight of foreign capital is much less in the telecommunications sector.

Consequently, all other things being equal, foreign investment in the telecommunications sector may, in fact, offer an opportunity to raise funds for an important and extremely expensive undertaking. Foreign ownership has raised concerns about security issues in critical sectors of India's economy. These risks will have to be addressed in a robust but creative way, which may or may not include limits on the extent of foreign ownership.

The treatment of FDI in most countries is based on national priorities. Thus, US maintain controls on foreign ownership of its broadcast facilities. On the other hand, Canada, fearful of being swamped by culture, and US interests, maintains controls on ownership of both telecom as well as broadcasting. However, the implications of replicating these controls may be different for each country, depending on whether or not it has the ability to generate the high investments required for sectors like telecom from within the country.

16.11 Conclusions

The number of telephone lines per person has grown almost tenfold in the last decade. This is partly due to the advent of private players in the market. These players have tended to target the more lucrative parts of the market, especially mobile services, which seem to display a fair degree of competition in the market place. Nevertheless, competition and investment, though present, is yet to be seen in fixed line services, which are used by the majority of households, even as mobile phones now outstrip fixed lines in number. There are several barriers to entry in these latter services, where benefits of incumbency are largest. It is here that BSNL rules the roost. Its importance also lies in being the sole operator in most parts of rural India and in many smaller towns where the majority in India lives. The existing regulatory regime has been largely unsuccessful in controlling BSNL's market power and regulating it effectively. The fact that BSNL is wholly government-owned also provides important hints that the reason for the failure to regulate BSNL effectively is the conflict of interest that government and regulators face in taking decisions that will impact its position in the market place.

TABLE 16.1

Areas Included Under Telecom Circles in India

Name of Telecom Circle/ Metro Service Area	Areas Covered	Category
01. West Bengal	Entire area falling within the Union Territory of Andaman & Nicobar Islands and the area falling within the State of West Bengal and the State of Sikkim. For GSM cellular, Kolkata is a separate Circle.	B
02. Andhra Pradesh	Entire area falling within the State of Andhra Pradesh.	A
03. Assam	Entire area falling within the State of Assam.	C
04. Bihar	Entire area falling within the reorganised State of Bihar and the newly created State of Jharkhand.	C
05. Gujarat	Entire area falling within the State of Gujarat and the Union Territory of Daman and Diu, and Silvassa (Dadra & Nagar Haveli).	A
06. Haryana	Entire area falling within the State of Haryana, except the local areas served by Faridabad and Gurgaon Telephone Exchanges.	B
07. Himachal Pradesh	Entire area falling within the State of Himachal Pradesh.	C
08. Jammu & Kashmir	Entire area falling within the State of Jammu & Kashmir, including the autonomous council of Ladakh.	C
09. Karnataka	Entire area falling within the State of Karnataka.	A
10. Kerala	Entire area falling within the State of Kerala and the Union Territory of Lakshadeep and Minicoy.	B
11. Madhya Pradesh	Entire area falling within the reorganised State of Madhya Pradesh, as well as the newly created State of Chhattisgarh.	B
12. Maharashtra	Entire area falling within the State of Maharashtra and the Union Territory of Goa. For GSM cellular, Mumbai is a separate Circle, which includes Mumbai, New Mumbai and Kalyan Telephone Exchanges.	A
13. North-East	Entire area falling within the States of Arunachal Pradesh, Meghalaya, Mizoram, Nagaland, Manipur and Tripura.	C
14. Orissa	Entire area falling within the State of Orissa.	C
15. Punjab	Entire area falling within the State of Punjab and the Union Territory of Chandigarh.	B
16. Rajasthan	Entire area falling within the State of Rajasthan.	B
17. Tamilnadu	Entire area falling within the State of Tamilnadu and the Union Territory of Pondichery. For GSM cellular, Chennai is a separate Circle, which includes Chennai Telephones, Maraimalai Nagar Export Promotion Zone (MPEZ), Minzur and Mahabalipuram Exchanges.	A
18. Uttar Pradesh-West	Entire area covered by Western Uttar Pradesh with the following as its boundary districts towards Eastern Uttar Pradesh: Pilibhit, Bareilly, Badaun, Etah, Mainpuri and Etawah. It will exclude the local telephone areas of Ghaziabad and Noida.	B
19. Uttar Pradesh - East	Entire area covered by Eastern Uttar Pradesh with the following as its boundary districts towards Western Uttar Pradesh: Shahjahanpur, Farrukhabad, Kanpur and Jalaun.	B
20. Delhi	Local Areas served by Delhi. Ghaziabad (Uttar Pradesh), Faridabad (Haryana), Noida (Uttar Pradesh), and Gurgaon (Haryana) are included in it for GSM cellular.	Metro

17 Competition and Regulation in Energy Sector in India

Devendra Kodwani

17.1 Introduction

Energy fuels the economy. The efficient use of energy has a critical effect on overall development and the standard of living, as the cost and availability of energy determines the cost structures for several other sectors as well.

The energy sector comprises of primary sources, including petroleum, natural gas, coal, hydropower, wind power, and atomic energy. Electricity is the secondary form of energy that is produced from the primary sources. Looking at the massive inefficiencies, perceived to be prevailing in the entire energy sector, the lack of an appropriate framework to address sectoral competition issues, is one of the major concerns. A framework is needed in order to attain competitiveness and efficiency across the value chain.

For that, the entire energy sector needs to be looked at, comprehensively, vis-à-vis competition and regulatory concerns. India has the opportunity to learn from international experience in designing regulatory regimes.[1]

The Competition Act is the major instrument that prevails to achieve economy-wide competitiveness. In India, the Competition Act was enacted, in 2002, to replace the extant Monopolies and Restrictive Trade Practices (MRTP) Act 1969. The Electricity Act 2003 governs the electricity sector. There is a central electricity regulator at the Federal level, and a state-level regulator created in several states. An independent regulatory authority is on the anvil in the oil and gas sector. The coal sector is governed by the relevant ministry.

Whilst analysing the competition issues in specific sectors, the important issue arising is that of jurisdiction between the sectoral regulators and the economy-wide competition authority. Whether the economy-wide competition authority should deal with competition issues, or whether it should be left to the sectoral regulators. The other possible way out is defining specific roles for both the authorities, without any overlaps. However, in such a case, defining the role of respective authorities, as well as formalising the interface between them, becomes crucial. It is desirable to reach a workable arrangement, to ensure that the mandate of the economy-wide competition authority does not conflict with that of sectoral regulatory bodies. Nevertheless, one must bear in mind that neither competition nor the regulation per se can be the policy goal, rather these are the instruments to realise the desirable outcomes, through creating a competitive policy environment.

This chapter examines how sectoral competition policy may be used to facilitate the evolution of competitive energy markets to attain desirable outcomes. The next section gives a brief overview of the energy sector in India, followed by subsequent sections, dealing with the issues of competition and regulation in Coal, Petroleum, and Power sectors respectively. The concluding section integrates the complete discussion on competition in the entire energy sector.

17.2 Energy Markets in India and Government Policy Orientation

In 2001, India accounted for 3.5 per cent of the world's demand for commercial energy, which is the sixth highest consumption in the world. With an annual GDP growth rate target of 8 per cent for the Tenth Five Year Plan, the energy demand is expected to grow at 5.2 per cent.[2] However, per capita consumption of energy, at 479 kilograms of oil equivalent (kgoe), is hardly one fifth of the world average, and compares poorly with developing countries like Brazil (1051 kgoe), China (907 kgoe) and Thailand (1319 kgoe).[3] The Planning Commission of India estimates that the demand for energy is likely to grow at 6.6 per cent and 6.1 per cent respectively, during the 10th and 11th Five Year plans. For the period, 1954-55 to 2001-02, the supply of primary energy grew at an annual compound growth rate of about 3.5 per cent.[4] Projecting the future demand, on the basis of the past trends, might prove unrealistic as the large proportion of demand comes from subsidised agricultural and household consumers. Even when the subsidy support in electricity, gas, petrol and diesel sectors, is reduced to reveal more reliable demand patterns, the demand is likely to go up as the Indian economy will continue to grow for the next few decades.

Filling up the expected demand supply gap would need fresh investments for exploration and exploitation of primary energy sources, like coal, oil and natural gas, and renewable resource based power generation. Investments would also be required for improving the productivity in all energy sectors. The experience of State-led capital investment, in energy sectors, shows that it has not kept pace with the requirements. The petroleum sector outlay for the Ninth Plan was Rs. 74,014.18 crore. The estimated expenditure up to 2001-02 was Rs. 49,407.77 crore, representing about 67 per cent utilisation. In the electricity sector too, there is huge investment required in generation, transmission, and distribution.

The Planning Commission indicates the way the Central Government intends to reform the energy sector, as it says, *"the Government has been endeavouring to provide a policy environment that encourages free and fair competition, in each element of the energy value chain, and attracts capital from all sources—public and private, domestic and foreign[5]."* The 10th Plan document suggests that the Government would set up coal and petroleum authorities, and examine the possibility of setting up a single regulatory authority for energy to work in association with sub-sector regulatory authorities.[6] Competition policy on energy requires an integrated view on all sectors, and an Apex Committee on Energy, as proposed in the 10th Plan, will be a welcome step in that direction. There may not be a need for a separate regulatory authority for coal, as is argued in the following section.

Apart from the deregulation and restructuring implied by the above policy initiatives, the Government also proposes to introduce significant changes in the overall regulatory, institutional, and legislative environment, and to reduce subsidies. The stated policy goals concern economic efficiency, energy security, access, and the environment.

In the upcoming three sections, competition and regulatory issues are discussed for coal, petroleum and power sectors, before concluding the issues with regards to the entire energy sector.

17.3 Coal

Coal contributes to nearly 50 per cent of the total indigenous primary energy supply. Therefore, the energy sector in India cannot become competitive till this important part of the energy supply chain remains entirely in the public sector and faces no competition. The potential indigenous supply of coal, in India, is given by the geological estimates. As of January 2001, coal reserves for the country were estimated to be at 245.69 billion tonnes (bt). Out of this, proven reserves are 91.63 bt, the remaining are indicated and inferred reserves.[7] The coal supply has increased from 70 million tonnes per annum, at the time of nationalisation, to 355 million tonnes in 2003-04.

At present, coal production and distribution is completely dominated by Public Sector Units (PSUs). Nearly 85 per cent of total production, in India, comes from the collieries of Coal India Ltd. (CIL), and its subsidiaries, owned and managed by the Central Government. About 10 per cent of the supply comes from another PSU, Singareni Collieries Company Limited (SCCL).

In addition to the indigenous supply of coal, around 5-6 per cent of the total consumption is imported. Coal is freely importable (it is in Open General List), however, there is an import duty, from 5 to 15 per cent, applicable to different grades of the imported coal.

Almost 75 per cent of the entire consumption is used as fuel by power generating plants. The other major coal users include steel, cement, fertilisers, chemicals, paper, and thousands of medium and small-scale industries. Railways have been reducing their direct consumption of coal as steam locomotives are being phased out. Even so, the increased electrification of the railways is likely to further boost the derived demand for coal from power generators.

17.3.1 Nationalisation to Deregulation: An Incomplete Journey

The coal sector was nationalised in the early-seventies, with the stated reason of *"dissatisfactory mining conditions, e.g. slaughter mining, violation of mine safety laws, industrial unrest, failure to make investments in mine-development, reluctance to mechanise, etc., and in order to meet the long range coal requirements of the country*[8]. It was done in two phases with the enactment of the Coal Mines (Nationalisation) Act, 1973. In the first phase, coking coalmines were nationalised, followed by the non-coking coalmines. However, there were several loopholes in the 1973 Act, as the property rights were challenged in the court of law.

The situation forced the Government to pass the Coal India (Regulation of Transfers and Validation) Act in 2000. This empowered the Central Government to direct the transfer/allocation of property rights and mining rights, through Coal India Ltd, to a subsidiary company or to another subsidiary company, where this subsidiary is vested with such land or mine rights. This was done with the stated objective of ensuring better utilisation of the coal reserves.

Meanwhile, the 1973 Act was amended, in 1976, to allow captive mining by the private sector, producing iron and steel, and also to sub-lease mining to private parties where rail transport was not required. In 1993, the Act was further amended to allow captive mining by the private sector for power generation, as well as value addition in terms of the washing of coal. Later, the private sector cement producers were also allowed to carry out captive mining.

The Government has attempted to introduce the private sector in non-captive mining, which could have introduced competition in the sector. The union cabinet approved the presentation of the bill, in Parliament, to this effect in 1997. However, before the bill could be introduced, trade unions became agitated and threatened to strike. Since then, there have been several attempts by the Government to consult with trade unions and introduce the bill. Unfortunately, the Government has not succeeded so far. The latest version, the Coal Mines (Nationalisation) Amendment Bill 2000, is lying with a group of Ministers for discussion. Legislative clearance appears to be the biggest hurdle for the introduction of the private sector in coal mining, marketing, and exposing the sector to competition. The reasons are not a secret. Coal being a labour intensive industry, political commitment and courage are required to take the trade unions on board and initiate reforms through liberalisation and privatisation.

17.3.2 Deregulation of Pricing: But No Price Competition

Pricing is one of the tools normally used in competing markets. Till 2000, the Central Government had powers to fix prices of coal under section 4 of the Collieries Control Order (1945) and the Essential Commodities Act, 1955. In the nineties, the gradual deregulation of pricing was initiated. In March 1996, the Government deregulated the prices of coking coal, and grades A, B and C of non-coking coal. Subsequently, in March 1997, on recommendation of the Committee on Integrated Coal Policy, the prices of soft coke, hard coke and the D grade of non-coking coal, were also deregulated. CIL and SCCL were allowed to fix the prices of E, F and G grades of non-coking coal, once every six months, by updating the cost indices, as per the escalation formula contained in the 1987 Report of the Bureau of Industrial Cost and Prices (BICP).

The Colliery Control Order 2000, replacing the earlier order of 1945, paved the way for full deregulation of coal pricing in India, leaving no power with the Central Government in this regard. However, effective competition, around differential pricing, is unlikely to arise as almost the entire supply side, in the non-captive segment is dominated by public sector enterprises, with CIL having nearly 85 per cent of the market share.

Consumers still have little choice when choosing a supplier that can offer competitive prices. The choice is further restricted due to the continuation of the administered allocation system, which is discussed in the following sub-section.[9]

17.3.3 Canalised Distribution: Hurdle to Introduction of Effective Competition

Although pricing freedom has been given to the coal producing companies, through the Colliery Control Order of 2000, the distribution of coal is still managed or mediated by government agencies. Distribution to core sectors (defined by the Government for this purpose, include Power, Steel, Cement, Defence, Fertiliser and Railways) is done through two committees within the Ministry of Coal.

The Standing Linkage Committee (Long term), considers the potential requirement of coal, at the planning stage and links the requirement with the long-term perspective, from a rational source, after examining the factors like quantity and quality required, time frame, location of the consuming plants, transport logistics, development plans for coal mines, etc. The long-term committee is headed by the Additional Secretary in the Ministry of Coal, and has members from different Ministries, including Railways, Power, Surface Transport, and the Planning Commission, Central Electricity Authority, Coal India

Limited, Central Mine Planning & Design Institute Ltd. (CMPDIL) and SCCL.

The SLC (Short term), for the power and cement sectors, is similarly structured and allocates the supplies to these two sectors on a quarterly basis. Till recently, the supply to the steel sector was also regulated through some linkage committee.

The distribution of coal, to consumers in non-core sectors, is regulated by CIL, through the non-core sector Linkage Committee that was set up in 1982. In the emerging new policy framework for the sale of coal to the non-core sector, emphasis is being given on having bilateral agreements, between supplying subsidiary companies and the consumer, for well-defined commitment on the part of both. This should remove the intermediating role for the Linkage Committee.

17.3.4 Conclusion: Issue is Competition and Not Regulation

Foregoing description of mining, pricing and distribution systems in the coal sector explains that the coal sector is not operating in a competitive manner. Since the whole sector is owned by the Government, there is no competition among the suppliers of coal. There appears to be no economic compulsion to maintain the nearly monopolistic status of Coal India Ltd, and its subsidiaries in coal mining and selling.

Given the fact that coal constitutes about 50 per cent of the primary energy consumption in India, competitiveness of the entire energy sector critically depends upon the competitiveness in the coal sector. The demand to make the coal sector competitive can be the immediate issue for the CCI to advocate competition. The major prerequisite to promote competition, in the coal industry, is the removal of entry barriers, for the private sector, in mining and selling for non-captive purposes. Allowing private investors, only in mining, without allowing them to sell directly to consumers, is least likely to attract private miners, as they virtually face single buyer, i.e. Coal India, who would then, in turn, allocate to consumers. Such a market structure does not help to promote competition. Even in the case where private mining companies are allowed to compete with public sector units to supply to consumers, directly, there is another hiccup as the bulk consumers of coal are power generation plants.

Most of the state owned power generators face precarious financial situations, due to the poor financial condition of the State Electricity Boards (SEBs), who are largely unable to pay their dues on time. The distribution wings of SEBs are sick due to the accumulated financial loss that continues to accumulate. This state-dominated, interdependence cycle, of energy supply, highlights the need to liberalise the energy sector and introduce competition at different stages of the supply chain, starting from coal and petroleum, all the way till the end-user markets.

Regulated allocation of coal also limits price competition, as allocation is not guided by the price, bid by buyers, but by other considerations, like balancing the requirements of different sectors (many of them working under other ministries of the Government).

Another issue that will facilitate competition in the coal sector is the restructuring of Coal India Ltd., and making the subsidiaries of CIL, independent companies who could be corporatised and privatised. Even before making any case for restructuring the coal industry, it is rational to examine the performance of the coal sector and find out whether there are efficiency gains to be achieved from competition. The productivity of various companies needs to be analysed. The reported output productivity figures for Coal India Ltd., and Singareni Collieries Co. Ltd., show substantial improvements over the last decade.[10] There is a need to examine several other aspects of coal production and supplies, in order to better understand the scope for improvements.

Given that the scope of economic regulation, in terms of price controls or investments, in the coal sector is negligible, no need arises to reflect upon the issues of economic regulation in the sector. Both the prices as well as the investments, in the sector, should be market-determined variables. The fear that open markets for coal would result in other sectors, particularly electricity, being deprived of the required coal due to the poor creditworthiness, appears to be real. The only way forward is to make electricity distribution an economically viable business. This requires major reforms in the electricity sector, discussed, below, in section 5.

17.4 Petroleum Sector

The contribution of hydrocarbons (oil and natural gas) in India's total energy supply is approximately 45 per cent (nearly 36 per cent from oil and 9 per cent from natural gas). The demand for petroleum products during 2001-02 was 100.43 million tonnes, growing at about 4.9 per cent during the period 1997-2002. The supply of oil and natural gas depends on the exploration and developments of oil fields, on and off shore. The successful exploration and efficient refining and logistics determine the overall cost of this primary source of energy.

17.4.1 Steps in Market Development, Undertaken and Envisaged

A policy group of Government, Hydrocarbon Vision – 2025, has recommended that the oil PSUs be restructured for competitiveness. Wide ranging policy measures, including price decontrol, opening up the hitherto state controlled exploration segment, and marketing of petroleum products, restructuring oil and natural gas PSUs, and privatising some of the oil PSUs, were all proposed to achieve oil security, capacity addition in oil accretion, refining and marketing infrastructure. The key objectives to guide framing of hydrocarbon policy are economic efficiency of the sector and concern for the environment. The steps taken so far, in this context, are discussed below.

17.4.1.1 Consolidation of Oil PSUs

In 2001, state-owned PSUs were consolidated through mergers and buyouts of other PSUs, with the view to make them stronger and capable of withstanding the likely increase in competition from other PSUs, as well as private players in the sector. This decision is expected to strengthen the competitive position of PSUs as the economies of scale, in refining and distribution, would reduce the operating costs for the consolidated units. The global experience of the oil industry suggests that the market structure should evolve with a few large corporations emerging in oligopolistic competition. In India, before the nationalisation of oil companies, the markets were dominated by Shell and Exxon multinationals. Post-liberalisation, these companies are back in Indian markets to compete with PSUs and newer players, like Reliance Industries and Essar, in retailing.

17.4.1.2 Opening Up Exploration for Private Sector

The exploration of new oil fields was allowed through the New Exploration Licensing Policy (NELP) that provided incentives and a level playing field to private parties who could bid for exploration blocks. In January 1999, 48 blocks were offered for bidding and, out of these, 25 blocks were awarded. Subsequently, the Government signed contracts for production sharing for 4 out of 25 blocks, with the nationalised and private oil companies. In December 2000, a further 25 blocks were offered, on bid, followed by another 27 blocks in March 2002. This measure has created incentives for private

sector enterprises to bring capital into the high-risk exploration activity.

17.4.1.3 Refining Opened Up to Private Sector

Private sector companies were allowed to set up oil refineries, the largest project among them being that of Reliance Industries, at Jamnagar in Gujarat.

17.4.1.4 Dismantling of Administrative Pricing Mechanism (APM): An Aborted Attempt

A major oil sector reform has been the abolition of APM with effect from 31 March 2002. This step must go a long way in both demand and supply management, though it does not give market forces the complete freedom to fix the price. The price revision has to be discussed with the Government, each time. Recently, the Oil and Natural Gas Corporation (ONGC) chairperson, commented that "*Domestic pricing of petro-products and their derivatives has been the key factor in holding back investment in the Oil & Gas business... if we continue to throw the issue of energy pricing below the carpet, we will face a situation where the economy, which is highly-dependant on energy, will not be sustainable*[11]".

Additionally, there is the thorny issue of subsidies on kerosene and LPG that needs to be addressed. The oil companies have been arguing with the Government to directly subsidise the target beneficiary population rather than doing so through the oil companies. However, little political will, so far, has been demonstrated to deal with the subsidy issue objectively.

17.4.1.5 Marketing of Kerosene (SKO), LPG and LSHS Opened for Private Sector

A significant step towards introducing competition in the down stream value chain, in the Indian petroleum sector, was the decanalisation of SKO, LPG and LSHS products. From 1993 onwards, private parties have been allowed to import, as well as market, these products at the prices determined by the market forces, in parallel to the PSU dominated marketing system. The new entrants are expected to develop infrastructure for imports of these products, tankers for storage, LPG Bottling plants, in addition to setting up their own distribution and marketing network including, transportation arrangements. The parallel suppliers are not required to obtain any prior approval from the Ministry of Petroleum & Natural Gas to undertake the parallel marketing of these products. The entry into the business is, however, subject to approval from various other government agencies, before private parties can start the operations. The various requirements to be complied by non-PSU suppliers are as follows:

- Required to obtain a 'rating' from the notified agencies, before starting any activity relating to Kerosene and LPG, under the parallel marketing scheme.

- Required to obtain necessary clearance from Statutory authorities, like the Chief Controller of Explosives, Pollution Control Boards, local bodies, etc., as applicable.

- Required to intimate their intention and capabilities to import, bottle, market, distribute and sell such products, before commencing these activities under the Kerosene (Restriction of use and Fixation of Ceiling Price) Order 1993, and LPG (Regulation of Supply and Distribution) Order 2000 [earlier, as per the LPG (Regulation of Supply and Distribution) Order 1993].

- Required to submit a monthly return to the Government, before the 15th day of the following month, giving the details of the LPG and Kerosene imported port-wise.

- The LPG Control Order 2000 (earlier 1993) specifies that the cylinders, regulators and valves, to be used by the parallel marketers, have to be distinctively different from those used by the public sector oil companies.

Whilst regulations to ensure safety and regularity of supply are desirable, the last condition mentioned above, which requires the suppliers to use cylinders, regulators and valves to be distinctly different from those used by PSUs, is an anti-competitive requirement. It reduces the freedom of LPG end-users in switching from one supplier to the other. Similar arrangements were present in telecom industry before the sector was liberalised, as the state-owned incumbent service provider, the Department of Telecommunication (DoT), used to insist on buying telephone instruments as well. Such tie-in sale arrangements force the customers to spend on two different types of cylinders, and other equipment required in case they want to change the gas supplier.

Under the parallel marketing scheme, a gross amount of 6184 TMT, of kerosene, was imported by 115 different firms. Similarly, 24 parties have imported 974 TMT of LPG, by July 2001. Even though the volumes are limited, this has introduced some degree of competition in the distribution segment of the petroleum sector. Undoubtedly, far more scope exists to make the sector more competitive.

17.4.1.6 Restructuring and Disinvestment

Though the State and Central Governments have been trying to restructure and disinvest in oil companies, since 1991, the employees of these companies and the opposition parties have resisted the move. However, government control of Indian Petrochemical Corporation Ltd. was taken over by Reliance Industries and part of the government ownership was transferred to individuals through an initial public offer (IPO). Given the fact that presently the Central Government relies on the support of Communist parties, it looks like a long shot to talk about privatisation of oil companies in immediate years. In such a case, this bottleneck will continue to severely limit the scope for developing a competitive market in the petroleum sector.

17.4.2 Regulating Petroleum Sector

The complete supply chain of oil and natural gas includes:

1. Exploration,
2. Well development and production of oil and gas,
3. Bulk transport of crude oil and gas,
4. Refining and value addition,
5. Bulk transport of petrol, diesel, and gases,
6. Retailing through petrol and gas stations.

It is worth reflecting on the economic features of each of these activities, from the competition policy perspective. The initial two activities, which are better known as the upstream chain in the oil sector, are regulated by the Directorate General of Hydrocarbons, which implements the New Exploration Licensing Policy (NELP) of the Ministry of Petroleum and Natural Gas. Private sector companies, including foreign companies, are allowed to bid for the exploration and exploitation of oil and gas fields. In a way, the upstream markets have been de-regulated. Exploration is perceived as high risk and capital-intensive business, with property rights for exploration solely resting with the Central Government for all oil and gas fields in Indian Territory. The effective development and extraction of oil and gas are also capital-intensive activities. However, with inadequate domestic production and substantial import dependence, the producers of crude oil and natural gas do not face much competition in domestic markets. Therefore, the introduction of private sector is desirable for the development of competition in this segment. The CCI will have to watch out for dominance, by any of the market players, as the market is now in evolution mode. Since the mining and oil production licences are given for longer periods, it will be desirable to monitor the developments, from the bidding stage itself, as this would ensure that no anti-competitive practice thwarts the emergence of effective competition.

The Petroleum Regulatory Board Bill, 2002, waiting to be passed by the Parliament, is not concerned with the upstream petroleum industry. The major proposed functions of the Petroleum Regulatory Board are envisaged to be:[12] *fostering competition, licensing, and regulating* the down stream activities, like bulk transport of petroleum products and retail distribution.

Licensing will be for the marketing of petroleum products; setting up and managing LNG terminals; and laying and operating a common carrier pipeline network. The proposed board will *regulate* the access to the common carrier, as well as the transportation cost through the common carrier. The board would *secure equitable distribution*, by detailing and monitoring the retail service obligations for the retail and marketing segment of the industry. The proposed Bill is silent on the issue of subsidies. There is one ambiguous objective inserted, to prevent consumer exploitation through the Regulatory Board, to *"prevent profiteering by the entities"*. Such an abstract objective would give discretionary powers to the Board to interfere in the working of firms, in the name of public interest. Aside from the discretionary regulatory risk this provision has brought in, it would be challenging to actually prove what particular type of behaviour, of the regulated entity, is profiteering. This ambiguity and difficulty of proof is especially due to the word 'profiteering', which remains undefined in the Bill.. The cost structure in some segments, like distribution and retail, might be measurable rationally; though the estimate of costs of the refinery and value addition process would seriously suffer from asymmetric information, provided by the regulated entities. This would make the task of regulation quite difficult. Therefore, it is desirable to debate and reconsider the referred provision in the Bill, lest the main objective, of the Regulatory board, of enhancing competition in the sector, might get defeated.

In the down stream chain, only transportation pipelines for oil and gas will exhibit natural monopoly characteristics. They, therefore, need to be regulated for access and price. No other segment of the oil and gas production and supply industry needs to have price regulation. Yet, competition concerns, including the abuse of market power and/or other anti-competitive practices, might require monitoring and pro-active action/advocacy on competition authorities' part.

17.5 Power Sector

There is no doubt that inadequate power supply is the biggest bottleneck that the Indian economy is facing. The average per capita consumption of electricity, in India, has nearly doubled in the last fifteen years, from 178 kWh in 1985 to 355 kWh per annum, in 2000. Nevertheless, it compares poorly with 719 kWh per capita consumption in China, 1783 kWh in Brazil, 787 kWh in Egypt, 5843 kWh in UK and 8747 kWh in the USA.[13]

The power sector in India is in the Concurrent List of the Constitution. Consequently, the Central as well as the State Governments are both empowered to engage in the generation and supply of power. Despite witnessing some progressive policy initiatives, to promote private sector during the early-nineties, the outcome so far has been far from satisfactory. The much discussed Independent Power Producers (IPPs), became disillusioned when Power Purchase Agreements (PPAs) proved less than effective contracts to supply to State Electricity Boards, the sole buyers allowed to purchase electricity. There remains huge, unmet demand for fresh investments in the electricity generation, transmission and distribution sectors. Yet, non-viability of electricity distribution as a business, and the fragile financial position of government owned SEBs, do not offer attractive propositions for private investments.

Much debated reforms in the power sector have achieved very little, so far, in terms of meeting their stated objectives. Investments in generation have fallen short of the expectations in the Ninth Plan. The Ninth Plan envisaged the addition of 40,245.2 MW generation capacity, however, the actual addition is less than half of the expected figure, at 19,015 MW. The states were to add 22,656.7 MW during that period, against which they managed to add only 13,954.1 MW. The bigger disappointment, and rather a policy failure was that of inadequate private investment flow to the sector. Investors could add just 5061 MWs of generation capacity, against the expected 17588.5 MWs.

This is factual commentary on the implementation difficulties of the restructuring of the electricity industry. In 2002, total private generation capacity stood at 10 per cent and the remaining 90 per cent was owned and managed by the state suppliers (SEBs, Electricity Departments, and Central Government-owned utilities). Interstate transmission and distribution, within states, still remain subject to state monopolies, except in a few urban areas such as Mumbai, Delhi, Ahmedabad, Surat and Kolkata. In India, thermal and hydro-based plants contribute to nearly 85 per cent of installed generation capacity whilst gas based plants account for 10 per cent. The remaining plants use diesel, wind, and nuclear power as primary energy sources.

17.5.1 Poor Financial Performance of SEBs

The investment in the power sector, during Five Year plans, has exceeded the planned outlay but almost two-thirds of the investment flowed into generation, with a mere quarter in Transmission and Distribution (T&D). As a result, the T&D system has not been upgraded and, therefore, operates inefficiently, with high losses close to 40 per cent, intermittent supplies and poor quality of electricity. The financial performance of SEBs and other EDs (Electricity Distributors) has also been unsustainable. High losses; leakage in transmission and distribution; non-targeted subsidies to farmers and domestic sectors; and poor recovery, remain amongst the major reasons responsible for the unsustainable financial performance. For instance, the net subsidy, offered to electricity consumers in 2001-02, was Rs. 32,381.97 crore. Since price distortions are acute, the tariff for agricultural consumers recovers barely 15 per cent of the cost of supply, in states like Punjab. Recently, the power is provided, free of cost to the farmers in Andhra Pradesh.

Besides high T&D losses and untargeted subsidies, the SEBs have been incurring operating losses (commercial losses), which were estimated to be Rs. 24837.22 crore, in 2001-02. The differential pricing, charged to different consumer groups, has affected the allocation of resources, and the demand and supply side management of the electricity sector. Currently, the subsidies to target consumer groups are being directly passed on to the consumers, through SEBs, in the form of supplies on lower prices. SEBs are supposed to be reimbursed by the respective state governments. However, in practice, this reimbursement is quite cumbersome, and subject to the position of state government finances. Given that the financial position of most of the state governments in India are stressed, the amount of unrecovered subsidies has been increasingly bleeding the SEBs to financial sickness,

and resulting in negative rates of returns in the range from 12 per cent to 40 per cent. Unless, a serious stance on subsidies and reimbursement mechanism is taken, the SEBs are bound to be headed for financial disaster.

17.5.2 Issues in Competition and Economic Regulation

17.5.2.1 Market Structure and Restructuring

The electricity supply industry is a series of vertical activities. The sequence is generation, transmission, supplies at high voltage (bulk buyers), and finally, distribution (to low voltage consumers). Vertically integrated State Electricity Boards (SEBs) currently dominate the industry. They generate, transmit, supply and distribute electricity. Restructuring the industry and separating these activities (unbundling) was felt necessary for bringing about efficiency and improved accountability in each segment, and also to potentially privatise the separated activities. Nevertheless, competition and regulation issues still remain complex, even after restructuring.

17.5.2.2 Generation of Electricity: Challenges in Creating Competition

Neither the technology nor the economics of power generation, support or justify the existence of natural monopoly characteristics. Therefore, generation could easily be visualised as a competitive industry with multiple suppliers. The Electricity Act 2003 has created a liberal policy environment to facilitate the entry of new players into the generation business. In fact, no licensing is required to undertake power generation activity. The only clearances required are those relating to various technical standards. Regulations for captive generation have also been liberalised, and access to the transmission lines has been provided in order to wheel the electricity from one point to the other.

However, the extent to which these initiatives would help, in the development of a competitive market structure, in the generation segment of electricity industry would depend on the following factors:

1. Freedom, for the generation companies, to price the electricity sold to SEBs and other consumers.

2. Evolution of a trading system to facilitate the buying, and selling, of electricity by the distribution companies and bulk consumers (discussed in sub-section 5.2.4).

3. Access to transmission grids in order to transmit electricity, both inter- and intrastate, at reasonable costs (discussed in sub-section 5.2.4).

4. Markets for corporate control for private generating companies.

The Act does not provide for the first condition of freedom to price. Section 62 of the Act says that the, *"Appropriate commission shall determine the tariff, in accordance with the provisions of this Act, for the supply of electricity by a generating company to a distribution licensee."* This provision is likely to limit the possibility of competition in generation markets.

To facilitate price competition in the electricity generation market, the suppliers (generators) should not, alone, have the freedom to compete on prices, but the buyers (bulk consumers and distribution licensees) should also be provided with cost effective access to transmission grids. In the absence of that, competition in generation markets is less likely to develop.

Competition can only be scaled up, provided new players enter the generation market. The Electricity Act 2003 allows relatively simplified procedures to set up new power generation plants. However, the private sector is likely to invest in generation, in a big way, provided the thorny issue of tariff fixation is solved satisfactorily and it is left up to the market to determine the tariffs for generation units. Other than that, there is the matter of honouring the sale contracts between generators and buyers (SEBs). The earlier efforts made by the Government to build the confidence of investors, through signing PPAs, has not worked as most of them plough into difficulties, despite the fact that respective governments provided the escrow account guarantees. The Dhabol Power Project, in Maharashtra, is the classic example of how state governments and SEBs can weaken the prospective market development in the electricity supply industry. Broadly, the weaker institutional and legislative framework was primarily responsible for the ineffectiveness of the first phase of reforms. Unfortunately, political convictions, particularly at the state level, do not seem to have changed much in this regard. Even so, in 2004, a major, national political party promised free power to farmers, during the elections in Andhra Pradesh, and has subsequently taken steps in that direction, after coming into power in the state. Similar developments are taking place in other states as well, including Tamil Nadu and Punjab. The commitment of most state governments, however, on reducing the subsidies is hardly encouraging.

The revenue generation of SEBs, and their successors, is contingent upon the Government reimbursing the subsidies offered to various consumer groups. Thus, their financial position is in bad shape. The Electricity Act 2003 clearly mandates the state electricity regulatory commissions to phase out cross subsidisation in a time bound manner. The Act also says that in case the Government decides to subsidise any section of consumer, it has to pay the required amount up front to the distribution utilities. Given that most distribution utilities still remain state-owned and managed bodies, the implementation of such provisions, both in letter and spirit, remains a matter of concern. In the last few years, it has been observed that state governments have not disbursed the promised support to the distribution utilities, and have forced the utilities to incur excessive market borrowings, hence, the increased interest liability.

So, it appears that competition in the generation segment of the electricity industry is unlikely to develop, in the short term, even though the Act has laid down the rules of the game.

Competition for corporate control, through mergers and takeovers, provides new impetus for economic efficiency. This is an important dimension of managing competition in any sector. The competition commission is bound to face the cases concerning takeovers by, or of, generating companies. In case the combinations involve another regulated utility, the cross subsidisation, or separation, of regulated segments will pose additional challenge.

The jurisdiction of the Electricity Regulatory Commission (ERC), and that of Competition Commission of India (CCI), needs to be clearly established lest it would lead to confusion and litigation. The Electricity Act 2003 does not confer any possible role to the CCI, even in cases of market dominance. The Competition Act 2002 does not empower the CCI to adjudicate whilst the Central Electricity Regulatory Commission (CERC) has been vested with the same powers, in case of disputes arising between government-owned generating companies and transmission licensees, on tariffs and interstate transmission issues. State Electricity Regulatory Commissions (SERCs) are empowered to deal with similar matters involving generating companies and licensees, within the state. Even though the issues related to competition, amongst generating companies or other anti-competitive behaviour having an impact on the competitive functioning of the generating companies, are still not clarified. Although, the Electricity Act 2003 envisages that an important function of the CERC and SERCs would be to promote competition in the electricity sector. As things stand now, the roles of the regulatory and competition authorities are likely to overlap in this regard.

Evidently, with restructuring and the increased participation of private players in energy markets, the economics of related network industries, such as gas and electricity distribution, would lead to convergence of these industries. It is therefore desirable that, rather than following piecemeal approach, a comprehensive competition policy framework for the network industries, is adopted.

17.5.2.3 Transmission of Electricity: Regulation Versus Managed (indirect) Competition

As per the Electricity Act 2003, the Central Transmission Utility and State Transmission Utilities were to be created to co-ordinate the inter- as well as intrastate transmission of electricity. This would involve technical arrangements, like the creation and management of National and State Load Despatch Centres, to facilitate wheeling of electricity.

Transmission of electricity shows signs of natural monopoly. Consequently, market competition is unlikely to develop in this segment, which necessitates economic regulation to secure economic efficiency in this activity. Yet, it is possible to exert market pressure on the transmission monopoly, indirectly, in case the monopoly is privately held by a licensee. For example, the transmission utility can be owned by all the distribution companies (who could be private or public) that use the transmission grids, for wheeling of their energy. A licensee can be in charge of transmission lines at the national level. Whilst there have to be mandatory obligations, on all parties involved, so that the continuity and quality of supply is ensured, such arrangements shall provide appropriate incentives for the holding companies to promote efficient transmission operations, as inefficiency in transmission would have to be borne by the competing distribution companies.[14] Such a structure presents a better case compared to the existing arrangements, which provide for only regulated pricing mechanisms in transmission activity.

At present, transmission grids are mainly owned and managed by the government-owned utilities. The transmission charges are regulated, and are proving to be a difficult regulatory decision in the current transitional phase, as the system is still evolving. Recently, it became controversial when the Regional Load Despatch Centres and State Load Despatch Centre both insisted on payment of wheeling charges that would effectively mean increased cost of transmission. In response to a petition filed by a trader, the CERC had to come out with explanatory order to clarify the issue in May 2004.[15] The incentive structure, for owner-managers of the Load Despatch Centres, still needs to be clarified. It appears that the owner-managers would be expected to work on a no-profit-no-loss basis. This highlights the complexity of regulatory and competition issues, specifically those that the Indian electricity market is bound to encounter, during the next few years.

17.5.2.4 Infrastructure for Wholesale Trading of Power: A Technical and Regulatory Challenge

The Power Trading Corporation has been created to perform an extremely complex function of facilitating trade in electricity markets. Generators, the Central Transmission Utility, SEBs and other bulk buyers, constitute the market place for electricity. Currently, the wholesale market for electricity is regulated by the CERC. The experience of open access, for interstate transmission since May 2004, has highlighted some of the regulatory challenges in managing competition. For instance, the CERC has realised the need for amending the regulations pertaining to charging the interstate, short-term and long-term customers. Real time pricing, in wholesale markets would require stringent monitoring of the behaviour of generators, as well transmission utilities. The regulatory authorities are required to remain equipped with the necessary capabilities to examine the pricing movements and the potential abuse of the market power by the players, including incumbent producers.

17.5.2.5 Distribution of Electricity: Need to Empower the Consumers

It will take some time before the reliable, state-wise estimates, of the actual cost of generation, can be developed, separately. Nonetheless, the total cost of supply normally includes the cost of generation of electricity, which accounts for around 60-65 per cent; about 10 per cent is the transmission cost and the remaining 25 per cent, or so, accounts for the distribution. It is evident that effective competition in generation, that improves the efficiency in the generation segment, can result in lower costs of electricity supply. In addition, distribution companies, which are mostly state monopolies at present, provide substantial scope for efficiency improvement. The issues pertaining to competition, and regulation in the electricity distribution segment, are as follows:

1. Regulation of tariffs.

2. Scope of competition for retail investors.

3. Privatisation of distribution companies.

Distribution companies would normally be local monopolies in their respective areas, although it is difficult to suggest the optimum size of a distribution company. The tricky question being faced, while restructuring the state electricity board, was to decide on the appropriate number of distribution companies in a state. Some states cover large areas, whilst others have smaller areas but with high consumer density. In such situations, the determinant should be exposing the distribution companies to the pressures of markets, i.e. decisions of consumers and investors. This requires a long-term approach, whereby the SEBs are restructured and privatised; and the provisions of the Electricity Act 2003, with regard to Open Access, are implemented.

As things stand, the SERCs are expected to regulate the prices, of electricity supply to final consumers, and also to foster competition. The SERC's success on tariff determination, and getting it implemented for different consumer groups, has been quite limited. Rao (2004) provides a comprehensive commentary on the short regulatory experience that India has acquired so far. He concludes that, till recently, the state regulatory bodies were mostly headed by those who earlier have worked in government. Given the fact that the regulated entities are mostly state owned and managed, he observed that effective regulation is yet to be found. The intentions of lately conceived institutions of independent regulation, might come to a not, if the Government's tendency to accommodate sinecures is not arrested at the earliest. It should be emphasised that regulators have to have the required capacity, as well as to maintain an arm's length relation with the Government. There is a need to revamp the appointments systems of regulatory bodies, to infuse professionalism into the working of these institutions, which could play a vital role in inducing competition and achieving a sound regulatory environment.

So far, the state regulators have been concentrating more on tariff determination. However, the acceptance of tariff determination by the state governments, particularly in case of the heavily subsidised agricultural sector, has been less. This has rendered much of the regulatory exercise of little consequence, in terms of either enhancing efficiency or improving the availability of electricity by creating a better atmosphere to attract investment in generation.

Privatisation of distribution has been attempted only in the cases of Orissa and Delhi. Therefore, drawing a conclusion about regulatory efficacy, in regulating private utilities, and enabling competition, is not yet possible. It would be too early to pass a value judgement on the effectiveness of regulation. Nevertheless, the biggest lesson, to be learnt from the 90s, is that the state ownership of utilities has created perverted political payoffs from the electricity sector; non-targeted subsidies and the narrow, short-term view of the politicians has only worsened the situation.

Subsidies pose the largest political hurdle in creating real competition in the distribution segment. Unless efficient delivery mechanisms, to extend the Government support in a targeted manner, are evolved to rescue the distribution utilities from unsustainable financial burdens, the successful privatisation of these utilities and the emergence of competition would be difficult to achieve. Otherwise, it is possible from the economic and technical perspectives, to introduce competition in the distribution segment. International experience, particularly in Britain, suggests that doing so would be quite feasible.

The Electricity Act 2003 mandates open access in a time bound manner, and, in fact, some of the states have started moving in that direction. For instance, the Rajasthan Commission has framed the regulation to allow open access from April 2005 onwards, to start with allowing bulk consumers, of above 15 MW load, in the first phase. For the CCI, demanding the state regulatory commissions to facilitate competition, in electricity distribution, by providing for effective open access, could be one of the topics in its advocacy agenda.

17.5.3 Conclusion on Power Sector

Some significant initiatives have been taken up in the power sector. There has been a sustained attempt at designing appropriate policies to create competitive markets in the electricity supply chain. Unfortunately, the complexity, as well as political significance, of the sector has made it difficult for most states to effectively and wholeheartedly structure the markets in electricity supply. A great deal of commitment is needed to address the competition and regulatory concerns of this key sector, which fuels the economy.

Rao (2003) argues that, perhaps within the next 10 years, major reforms in the electricity sector will take place and we would be able to consider, *"a simulation of the British system where the consumer chooses which electricity supplier he want: to buy from. For bulk consumers, this choice can be given much earlier."* This may be so, but it generally takes time for effective policies to evolve in network industries, particularly when they have to go through restructuring and the transfer of ownership in a politically sensitive environment such as the power sector in India[16]. Wood & Kodwani (1997) argued, in context of Indian power sector, *"...that private ownership, competition and constructive regulation create an incentive structure that results in more consumer satisfaction in the long run. The transition phase from public to private sector can be difficult and politically hazardous but the evidence of agency costs in the present system is substantial...However, it should be recognised that the British approach may not be entirely relevant here, as the Indian and British power sectors are in different stages of development. The British electricity market has stable demand, with slow growth, but in India demand for electricity is likely to continue rising rapidly over the coming decades."* The regulatory implication of this is that, whilst fixing the rates for monopolistic segments, such as transmission and local distribution, allowances will have to be made for the capital expenditures required for the upgrade and expansion of networks.

Sea changes have been legislated in the power sector, in the last decade, and the introduction of the Electricity Act 2003 is the most significant amongst them. Even so, any effective change will take time and painstaking efforts to push forward the reform agenda, towards the creation of competitive electricity markets.

As far as the overlap in the mandates of the two regulatory authorities is concerned, the Electricity Act 2003 does not envisage any role for the CCI. Therefore, it is advisable to clarify whether the CCI will have any role to play in the sector.

17.6 Conclusion

Competition and independent regulation should be viewed as instrumental to achieve sectoral efficiency and competitiveness. The immense task, before the regulators, is to facilitate the creation of competitive markets in all possible segments of this vertically integrated industry. To start with, the restructuring of coal, petroleum, and the electricity sectors is desirable, so that natural monopoly segments could be easily distinguishable from the rest that need not be regulated.

Given that the coal sector is virtually a state monopoly, restructuring to introduce competition at the mining and distribution level is considered necessary. Making coal pricing competitive would bring down the cost of power generation, steel, and cement production, amongst others. There is no case for economic regulation of coal prices, but since the domestic supply of coal is less than the demand, this situation is likely to hood the fact that the introduction of competition (on prices) may crowd out the core sector PSUs. To tackle the situation, Government should take the required measures to make such PSUs pay their coal bills rather than unduly protecting them at the cost of the coal sector. Otherwise, it will effectively kill the incentive for the private sector to enter mining operations.

The upstream petroleum sector, comprised of the exploration and exploitation of oil and gas, is moving towards more competition, and there does not appear to be any form of price control. Control on prices, and subsidies, continues to bleed dry the public sector marketing companies. These are major competition concerns that need response, possibly with the framing of a sectoral competition policy for the energy sector.

Subsidising kerosene, LPG, and diesel is a tricky issue to deal with. While there may be some genuine, social concerns that Government has to take care of, the non-targeted subsidies, offered in terms of concessional pricing, distort the market, making it difficult for private firms to cater to these segments. The concerns, with regard to subsidised electricity supplies to the farm and domestic consumers, are of a similar nature. The only possible way out of this complex situation is for the Government to target subsidies, objectively, to the well-identified deserving people. In fact, there is a strong case for the Government to directly support the needy people in one go, rather than canalising through a range of services, which is often not so efficient.

Present gas (LPG) prices are determined by the Central Government. While electricity is predominately in the purview of the states, the interstate wheeling charges for electricity are determined by the CERC. Given that the gas distribution networks are set to expand in due course need shall arise to examine the gas transmission prices more closely. The effectiveness of the CERC's approach, in fixing interstate transmission charges, can be scrutinised in order to draw some lessons for gas and oil transmission pricing.

As far as the electricity sector is concerned, there is no need to regulate prices in the electricity generation business. Nevertheless, competition in the generation segment is critically dependent on the availability of power trading systems, and open access to the transmission grids at reasonable costs, which require regulatory intervention.

It is highly recommended to have an integrated and comprehensive approach towards the competition and regulatory concerns of the entire energy sector, which, so far, is lacking in India. Any piecemeal approach would adversely affect not only the competitiveness of the sector, but that of the entire economy, given that energy is a major input for almost all economic activities. Importantly, only the pipeline network for oil and gas transmission, and the transmission and distribution grid for electricity, exhibit the characteristics of a natural monopoly. Hence, these may require regulatory intervention.

The extent to which the different primary sources of energy (i.e. coals, gas, oil, nuclear) can compete with each other also needs to be examined. This will be more important; particularly as price competition is allowed into the electricity generation market.

Corporate control issues (M&A/combinations) in energy markets should be strictly viewed in the light of likely consequences on the level of competition, rather than based on the size of the combined entity. As long as the competition process is not adversely affected by the size of the combined entity, the competition authorities' intervention need not be triggered.

It is desirable to research the referred dimensions of competition and regulation, in energy markets, elsewhere in the world, including New Zealand[17], the UK, Chile and several others.

Finally, a proactive approach on competition, and other concerns require considerable expertise and skills. Therefore, institutional capacities need to be enhanced and upgraded on a continuous basis. In this context, the training of regulators, and their staff, needs to be measured and addressed appropriately. Universities and other well-positioned institutions are required to fine tune their existing programmes and/or initiate new courses in industrial and regulatory economics.

Notes

1. In UK separate regulatory bodies for gas and electricity markets were created at the time of privatisation of these industries in late-1980s and early-1990s, which were then merged in Office of Gas and Electricity Markets.

2. Planning Commission, (2003).

3. *Ibid.*

4. Calculated by author from the data given in Five Year Plan Document, Planning Commission, Govt. of India.

5. Source: http://www.planningcommission.nic.in/plans/planrel/fiveyr/10th/volume2/v2_ch7_3.pdf.

6. *Ibid.* p.66.

7. Source: http://www.coal.nic.in

8. http://www.coal.nic.in

9. There is some move towards competition among the buyers for free bidding for coal through e-auctions for purchase of coal from Coal India Ltd., and its subsidiaries.

10. http://www.coal.nic.in/cpdanx.htm#ANNEXURE-IV

11. Address by Mr. Subir Raha at the Conference on 'Business Opportunities in Down Stream Oil and Gas Sector', organised by the PHD Chamber of Commerce and Industry (PHDCCI) at New Delhi on January 4, 2005.

12. Source: http://petroleum.nic.in/prbill.htm

13. It should be noted here that per capita consumption in countries like UK and USA is affected by the local climatic conditions significantly. Therefore, inferences based on the per capita consumption about the economic development or other issues need to be understood in proper context.

14. Although it is bold to venture into thinking that the unbundling of SEBs, followed by disinvestments of distributing entities and open access for consumers, would become reality in the foreseeable future, the author remains optimistic. This is not because of some wisdom that would prevail in political leaders, but because most SEBs would run themselves into the ground and privatisation would become inevitable. Such a scenario does not appear to be too far off in future.

15. See CERC order in matter of Interstate Open Access regarding petition 48/2003 filed with CERC.

16. What is interesting to note is that, along with electricity, even telephony and water industries are perceived to be somewhat different. They are known as public utilities. As a result, the general perception of people, in most of the countries, is that the utilities need to be either provided or regulated by the Government. This has been mostly because of the natural monopoly conditions that prevail in some segments of these industries.

17. See for example Bollard and Pickford, 1997.

References

Bollard, A. and M. Pickford (1997). "Utility Regulation in New Zealand, in *Regulating Utilities: Broadening the Debate*", (ed. M E Beesley), Institute of Economic Affairs, London.

Cook, Paul (2001). "Competition and its Regulation: Key Issues," *Paper No. 2, Working Paper Series*, Centre on Regulation and Competition, IDPM, Uni. of Manchester.

Hayek, F.W. (1948). *Individualism and Economic Order*, Chicago University Press, Chicago.

Hoekman, B., P. Holmes (1998). *Competition Policy, Developing Countries, and the World Trade Organisation*, Workshop on Trade and Competition, WTO and Beyond, Venice, Dec 4-5, 1998.

Kodwani, D.G. (1997). *Efficiency Gains in Regulated Utilities: Post Privatisation Experience in England and Wales*, University of Manchester, UK, 1997.

McNulty. Paul, J. (1968). "Economic Theory and the Meaning of Competition," *The Quarterly Journal of Economics*, Vol. 82, No. 4, 639-656.

Ministry of Law and Justice (2002). *Competition Act*, Government of India, New Delhi.

Parker, David (2001). "Economic Regulation: A Preliminary Literature Review and Summary of Research Questions Arising," *Paper No. 6, Working Paper Series*, Centre on Regulation and Competition, IDPM, Uni. of Manchester.

Planning Commission, *Tenth Five-Year Plan*, Government of India, New Delhi, 2003.

Posner (1974). "Theories of Economic Regulation," *Bell Journal of Economics* 5:335-358.

Rao, S.L. (2003). "Competition in Electricity," *Maharashtra Economic Development Council Journal.*

———. (2004). *Governing Power*, The Energy Research Institute, New Delhi.

Schumpeter, Joseph, A. (1954). *History of Economic Analysis*, Oxford University Press, New York.

Smith, Adam (1937). *The Wealth of Nations*, Modern Library, New York.

Wood D., and D.G. Kodwani (1997). "Privatisation Policy and Power Sector Reforms: Lessons from British Experience for India," *Economic and Political Weekly*, Vol. 32, No. 37 p. 2350-2358, 13 September.

18

Competition Issues in Transportation Sectors

Sunil Jain

18.1 Introduction

Serving a land area of 3.3 million square km and a population of one billion, India's transport system is one of the largest in the world. It consists mainly of roads, railways, and air services. In a few states, inland water transport plays a small supplementary role. And with its long coastline, India has over 150 seaports.

In most developing countries, transport demand (usually measured in tonne-km. and passenger-km.) increases somewhat faster than the gross domestic product (GDP). India is no exception. During the 1990s, India's economy has grown by 6 to 7 per cent a year, and its total transport demand has grown by about 10 per cent a year. The road sector, which already enjoys an 80 per cent share of land transport demand, has witnessed a 12 per cent annual growth in freight demand and 8 per cent in passenger demand. Meanwhile, both air and sea transports have enjoyed healthy growth. But the demand for rail transport has grown at a slower pace, at just 1.4 per cent a year for freight and 3.6 per cent a year for passenger.

While the transport sector has grown at a healthy rate of 10 per cent a year, this is the sector that has the greatest possibility to hold back India's GDP growth target of 8 per cent.

For instance, due to severe congestion of the main arterial highways, trucks and buses travel at just around 25-30 km. an hour, a clear indication of just how much extra time and money is being wasted. In fact, the Rakesh Mohan Report on infrastructure (1996) estimated the economic losses from bad roads at anywhere upto Rs. 30,000 crore a year, or around 1 to 2 per cent of GDP each year.

In case of sea transportation, shipping goods from South-east Asian countries to the East coast of the United States, for instance, is much cheaper than that from India, despite the longer route that has to be covered.

Since the early-1990s, the government has made efforts to fix things. It passed a Multi-Modal Transport Act to facilitate door-to-door shipments and in 1993, the government amended the Merchant Shipping Act to allow Indian vessel owners and operators access to the capital markets. The ports sector has been opened up for private sector participation. In just the last decade, the share of minor ports, many of them developed by the private sector, is up from around 6 per cent to 25 per cent[1] in total ports traffic.

Similarly, repealing the Air Corporation Act of 1953 and replacing this with an Act, in 1994, that allowed competition and private participation in the scheduled domestic air transport services has led to a dramatic surge in traffic.

Yet, the transport sector remains very inefficient. While airport charges in India are on an average 80 per cent higher than the international average, air travel within India costs a lot more. In the case of seaports, while Indian ports charge less than global rates for cargo-related services, the vessel-related charges are four times higher, as a result of which the total costs in India are around a sixth higher.

The reason for this sorry state of affairs eventually boils down to policies that inhibit competition in the sectors and poor regulation.

In the case of ports sector, for instance, despite allowing the private sector to invest in major ports, there are few instances of this happening, as it is up to the port authority (the government) to decide to allow competition. In the Jawaharlal Nehru Port Trust (JNPT) where this was done in 1999-00, there has been a dramatic surge in productivity. Despite the government's talk of corporatising ports, there has not been any action on this so far. The Tariff Authority for Major Ports (TAMP) has been established, but it has limited role and just functions as a cost-plus pricing centre.

It is worse in the case of the railways. They are the primary medium for transporting containers across the country's vast hinterland and enjoy a monopoly over this, through the Container Corporation of India (Concor). Apart from raising charges, Concor has only 3,000 wagons as against the demand of over 5,000 wagons at present.

Similarly, in the aviation sector the government has recently allowed private airlines to fly abroad, but the barriers to entry are still high, and all types of levies are put on aviation fuel. Goods transport by road is often at the mercy of cartels of transport firms, who dictate freight rates.

18.2 Civil Aviation

The importance of civil aviation sector to the economy is well recognised. According to estimates of the International Civil Aviation Organisation (ICAO),[2] $100 spent on air transport produce benefits worth $325 for the economy; a hundred additional jobs in air transport results in 610 new economy-wide jobs.

In case of India, it is estimated that foreign exchange transactions worth $22.5 billion are directly facilitated by the civil aviation sector, and another $96 billion indirectly through civil aviation services.[3] Indeed, 95 per cent of tourist arrivals into the country are by air, and 40 per cent of country's exports/imports by value take the aerial route.

India has an eminent position in the civil aviation sector with a large fleet of aircrafts. In all, 56 airlines are operating scheduled air services to and through India and 22 foreign airlines are flying over Indian territory. There are over 400 airports and 1091 registered aircrafts in the country. In addition to the three public sector airlines Air India, Indian Airlines, Alliance Air - there are two main private operators - Jet Airways and Sahara India Airlines. There are also 41 non-scheduled air transport operators.

The aviation sector in India can be broadly classified into three distinct functional segments:

(i) Operations, including the activities of Indian Airlines (IA) and its wholly owned subsidiary Alliance Air (AA), Air India (AI), Pawan Hans Helicopter and other private operators;

(ii) Infrastructure, under the purview of the Airports Authority of India (AAI); and

(iii) Regulation and development, the responsibility of the Directorate General of Civil Aviation (DGCA) and the Bureau of Civil Aviation Security (BCAS).

18.2.1 Operations

The airlines industry was nationalised in 1953 with the enactment of the Air Corporation Act, and assets of nine existing air companies were transferred to the two new corporations - Air India International and the Indian Airlines. Thus, the operation of scheduled air transport services was made a monopoly of the two government-owned corporations.

In 1994, the wheel turned a full circle as the Air Corporation Act, 1953 was repealed to pave the way for private participation in scheduled domestic air transport services. With that, the monopoly of the government-owned Corporations on scheduled air transport services ended.

Following the entry of private operators, the number of aircraft kilometres flown grew by 155 per cent and the passenger kilometres by 76 per cent, between 1994-95 and 2001-02.[4] By 2000-01, private operators carried 48.2 per cent of the passengers in the country, and now, Jet Airways has a higher market share than Indian Airlines.

The government-owned Indian Airlines and the private operators, Jet Airways and Air Sahara, provide regular domestic services. Air Deccan, 'a low-cost no-frills carrier' has recently started operations. Air India – the national carrier – carries domestic travellers between metro cities, from where it operates international flights. Indian Airlines also flies to a few international destinations in the neighbouring countries in South and South-east Asia, as well as to the Gulf. In early-2004, government allowed the domestic private airlines to fly to international destinations, though restricting them to the SAARC region. Later during the year, in December 2004, private airlines were allowed to fly to all international destinations except the Gulf.

With the entry of private operators, competition has increased, particularly in the domestic sector where private operators are there for over a decade now. There has been an improvement in the quality of services. Airlines are cutting fares and offering other freebies to expand their market share. With the entry of no-frills airlines, competition in the civil aviation sector has entered a new phase.

TABLE 18.1

Passengers Carried since 1992 on Domestic Sector (in lakh)

Year	Indian Airlines (Domestic)	Private Air Carriers	Total Domestic	Growth of Domestic Air Transport (%)	Private Air Carriers (market share)	Indian Airlines (market share)
1992	80.58	4.11	84.7	5.14	4.85	95.15
1993	67.46	20.92	88.38	4.32	23.67	76.33
1994	68.94	36.10	105.05	18.86	34.36	65.64
1995	70.82	48.93	119.75	13.99	40.86	59.14
1996	69.99	49.08	110.07	-8.08	44.59	55.41
1997	73.79	41.35	115.14	4.61	35.91	64.09
1998	69.46	49.14	118.6	3.01	41.43	58.57
1999	65.38	56.92	122.3	3.12	46.54	53.46

Source: http://civilaviation.nic.in/moca/acvl.htm

Till a few years back, Indian Airlines, by virtue of being the dominant player with a market share of over 60 per cent used to set the trend – be it in additional services, discounted fares or special rates and incentives. But now, with new players coming into the market, the situation has changed. Air Sahara and Jet Airways often take the lead in special packages. Now even Air Deccan and other budget airlines are offering new schemes, such as dynamic fares.

Till 2003, the fare war among domestic airlines, especially Indian Airlines, Jet and Sahara was on domestic flights. But now, with the opening of international routes to domestic private operators, competition has spread there as well.

18.2.2 Infrastructure and Regulation

India has over 400 airports out of which the Airports Authority of India (AAI) manages 122 airports, of which 94 are civil airports (including 11 international airports) and 28 are civil enclaves in defence airfields.

In India, though the number of airports is more than in some of the neighbouring countries, such as China, most are underutilised and underdeveloped. Presently, various airlines are operating only through 61 airports. The remaining airports are lying unutilised – handling at best occasional aircraft operations. Additionally, over 40 per cent of the passenger traffic is concentrated in the two main international airports at Delhi and Mumbai, and as a result, the limited terminal capacity at these airports has led to increased congestion, bunching of flights and delays in passenger clearances. This situation is exacerbated by outdated infrastructure, inadequate ground handling systems and night landing facilities, and poor passenger amenities. The poor utilisation of existing capacity has impeded development and growth of the sector, and today only 10 airports are profitable.[5]

Even though airport charges are among the highest in the world, only ten airports in the country make profits. The others remain poorly equipped, with mounting losses.

The Airports Authority of India, which was formed in 1995 by merging International Airports Authority of India and National Airports Authority, is responsible for regulating, operating and managing airports and providing air traffic services. These multiple roles obviously create serious conflicts of interest.

The key concerns in the airports sector are inadequate management of existing facilities and the need for additional capital for augmenting capacity. The latter calls for private participation in the airports and, where feasible, introducing elements of competition. Given the limitations in India's airport infrastructure, a more suitable method of introducing competition could be to introduce "competition for the market" in airport services,[6] where an existing airport is given on a concession, through a competitive bidding process. However, this essentially represents a case of a public monopoly being turned over to the private sector, and regulation becomes important to ensure that the private sector does not gouge airlines and passengers.[7]

In order to improve the performance of airports, the Naresh Chandra Committee on Civil Aviation has recommended unbundling of the AAI, along with corporatisation of airport managements. The committee has suggested that each of the larger airports should be managed by an independent corporate entity, while the smaller airports could be grouped together on a regional basis and corporatised. This would help these secondary airports to get the attention they deserve. The unbundling of AAI would ensure that conflicting functions, most importantly the regulatory function, are hived off to independent entities.

Among other things, an independent regulator is required to keep a watch on pricing, because airport services are usually a monopoly.

The Cabinet Committee on Infrastructure has recently decided to establish a regulator for the civil aviation sector. The regulator will be concerned with all economic activities including landing, tariff, freight and user charges. The proposed regulator will be different from the Director General of Civil Aviation (DGCA), who will only look after air traffic control and safety.

The government has recently cleared the privatisation proposal of the two major airports, Delhi and Mumbai, but only after considerable delays. Unfortunately, while the two airports have been crying for expansion and upgradation for years, several proposals from the AAI in the past were turned down on the pretext that the two airports are going to privatised, which did not take place until the government's recent action.

18.3 Competition Concerns in Civil Aviation

Despite the various initiatives taken by the Government of India, there are certain concerns relating to competition in the civil aviation sector. Most of these concerns emerge from the government's distortionary policy.

18.3.1 Route Dispersal Guidelines Creating a Non-level Playing Field

Route dispersal guideline is an administrative mechanism aimed at extending air transport services to regions/routes that are not necessarily commercially viable. This is one of the policy measures where government intervention has affected the competitiveness of state-owned carriers and their ability to compete effectively with the private operators.

The guidelines stipulate that all scheduled carriers fly at least 10 per cent of their capacity on trunk routes in the North-eastern sector, Jammu & Kashmir, Andaman & Nicobar Islands and Lakshadweep (category-II routes). Since load factors in these routes are poor, it is a loss-making proposition. Anyhow, due to political pressures, Indian Airlines is forced to fly 17 per cent of its flights on these routes, incurring an extra annual loss of Rs. 62 crore. This lowers Indian Airlines' competitiveness and restricts inter-airline competition.

Besides, 50 per cent of trunk route flights have to be flown on Category III routes (that is, on non-trunk and non-category-II routes). On these routes too, IA is forced to fly a greater share of flights in comparison with private airlines. According to figures provided by airline officials, IA flies 74 per cent of flights servicing these smaller towns and loses Rs. 134 crore a year, in the process.

Normally, routes that are not found to be commercially viable by major airlines can still be serviced by niche airlines with appropriate aircraft. Of late, Air Deccan – a private "no-frills" airline – is providing air travel to category III routes in a big way. In such a scenario, the route dispersal guidelines may need to be reviewed to ensure that they facilitate the emergence of specialised airlines.

18.3.2 Procedural Delays Affecting Competitiveness of Public Sector Carriers

For the past three years, the public sector airlines have been trying to procure aircrafts to expand their fleet. Unfortunately, their proposals are still doing the rounds of the government departments in search for a final approval.

The delay over aircraft acquisition has resulted in foreign airlines utilising 70 per cent of their entitlements, whereas Indian carriers are utilising only 30 per cent. It has been suggested that the private airlines be allowed to use the bilateral traffic rights, not utilised by the public sector carriers. However, the argument is not as simple as allocating unused bilateral traffic rights to private airlines. Had the state-owned airlines been allowed to acquire more aircrafts, there would have been no unused bilaterals in the first place. The state-owned airlines appear to be deliberately kept down to allow the private sector to consolidate.

There is clearly a need to establish a fair playing field and a policy on the role of the public sector airlines. Instead of ad-hoc allocation, a clear policy is needed on the distribution of bilaterals between the public carriers and the various private airlines, existing and forthcoming. This may be done by way of competitive bidding.

With the opening up of the skies, full autonomy needs to be given to the public sector airlines so that they can take decision in accordance with the market process and also implement the same without loss of time. Top managers of the public sector airlines say that there is no dearth of ideas or plans to chart out a course of action, but it involves government clearance at every stage.

18.3.3 Facilities and Preferences Given to Public Sector Carriers Distort Market Process

In the Delhi and Mumbai airports,[8] the state-owned Indian Airlines has a full terminal to itself, while the private-sector competitors are all cramped in one. This is despite the fact that Jet Airways alone has a higher market share than Indian Airlines. This has been possible because the government-run Airports Authority of India controls all terminals, and only Indian Airlines is allowed to provide third-party ground handling services.

Besides, private airlines are not allowed to establish hangars for major maintenance overhauls at airports and consequently have to outsource maintenance activity to high cost locations abroad.[9]

Another anti-competitive practice followed is that Government staff and employees of public sector undertakings are permitted domestic air travel only by IA. This is clearly restrictive.

18.3.4 Cost of Fuel Affects Inter-Airline Competition

Due to state taxes and charges on fuel, airlines flying in India pay around 75-80 per cent more for having to buy fuel in the country. So, on average while the average price of aviation fuel for domestic airlines is Rs.19,811 per Kilolitre (KL), international average is of Rs.10,192 per KL.[10] Even within India, domestic operators pay 51 per cent more for the fuel than international operators.

Apart from lowering the viability of airlines, this impacts inter-airline competition, as any airline that is able to fly overseas and pick up fuel there is better placed. This explains the rush by private airlines to fly abroad. The issue of high taxes is likely to hit budget airlines, especially since they are not going to fly on overseas routes (till the time they have an experience of 5 years) and will not be able to pick up cheap fuel.

The government is planning to allow private players to supply aviation turbine fuel (ATF), which is currently a monopoly of the three state-owned firms, Indian Oil Corporation (IOC), Bharat Petroleum Corporation Ltd. (BPCL), and Hindustan Petroleum Corporation Ltd. (HPCL). The entry of private operators and the consequent competition in the supply of ATF in the country is expected to reduce the operating costs of airlines subject to the constraint of state taxes. This might lead to further reduction in airfares, which are presently constrained by costs, such as ATF, on which the airlines do not have any control.

18.3.5 Other Policy Created Distortions

The government has allowed experienced (5 years' operation) private sector airlines to fly to foreign destinations. However, giving permission to only experienced airlines will restrict entry of other less-experienced operators, mainly the no-frills airlines, for a certain period. This would, in turn, limit competition on international routes. It is not surprising that the two beneficiaries, Jet Airways and Air Sahara, had made this demand some time back. While, on one hand, the two airlines have been pleading with the government to allow them to fly to all overseas destinations (till now the exclusive preserve of state-owned airlines), on the other hand they have been demanding for such restrictive provisions.

Other policy measures that restrict competition include not allowing foreign airlines to hold a stake in Indian airlines. Since those most interested in the airline business have to be other airlines, this means there will be less foreign players setting up airline firms in India. In addition, the government decides the minimum number of aircrafts that airlines own/operate as well as the minimum capital that an airline should have. These barriers relating to licensing requirements artificially limit competition.[11]

18.3.6 Allocation of Slots and Role of Competition Authority

An area of airport operations that requires regulation is the allocation of slots for airlines. While slot allocation is carried out differently across countries, the key is to ensure that the dominant airline, typically the national or incumbent airline does not hold undue sway over the process and hoard otherwise under-utilised slots.

Regardless of the approach adopted for allocation of slots, there is strong possibility for anti-competitive behaviour, since a dominant operator would be willing to pay more than a competitor for acquiring valuable slots. In due recognition of this reality, many countries rely primarily on competition law to prevent airlines from attaining a dominant position in slots.[12]

Furthermore, given the dynamic and complex nature of the industry, competition authorities are typically given significant discretion in imposing conditions while approving mergers and alliances. For instance, as part of the pre-conditions for British Airways/American Airlines alliance, the European Commission required the merging airlines to give up a large number of slots to competitors wishing to provide U.S.-London services, but could not obtain slots through normal allocation mechanism. In view of this, in India too, competition laws (and the Competition Commission of India) would be required to play an active role to regulate restrictive trade practices by airlines.

18.4 Ports

Indian ports are the gateways to India's international trade by sea and are handling over 90 per cent of foreign trade by volume and 60 per cent by value.

There are 12 major ports and 185 minor ports. Ports in India are divided into "major ports" (ports where the central government plays policy and regulatory functions) and "minor ports" (which are guided by state governments). As of today, the 12 major ports of the country handle about 75 per cent of the traffic. They are Chennai, Cochin, Ennore, Jawaharlal Nehru (Mumbai), Kandla, Kolkata, Mormugao, Mumbai, New Mangalore, Paradip, Tuticorin and Visakhapatnam.

The minor ports, which are under the jurisdiction of the respective State Governments, constitute an important competitive alternative to the major ports. Cargo handling operations are undertaken in about 61 ports while the remaining are restricted to fishing and passenger traffic. The latter half of the 1990s has witnessed the emergence of these minor ports as major players in cargo handling. Their share in maritime traffic has gone up from 10 per cent in 1996-97 to 25 per cent in 2003-04.

18.4.1 Private Sector Participation

In keeping with the general policy of economic liberalisation, the port sector has been thrown open to private sector participation. A number of existing facilities have been taken over by private players and many new facilities have also been set up at existing ports. As of now, container terminals at Jawaharlal Nehru, Chennai, Tuticorin and Visakhapatnam Ports are managed by private operators. Two new ports (Mundra and Pipavav in Gujarat) have also been constructed in the private sector.

In addition, recently JNPT has signed a concession agreement with Maersk-Concor consortium for operation of third terminal in the port. Cochin Port is also in the process of signing a concession agreement with Dubai Port Authority for international container trans-shipment terminal.

Private sector participation in operations and infrastructure activities of seaports has resulted in a radical change in the organisational model of ports, converting from service port model to landlord port model, where the port authority retains the port infrastructure and regulatory functions, whereas private operators provide the port services. With privatisation, the role of Indian ports too is changing from a service port model to a landlord port model. Ennore Port is one such example.

P&O (Peninsular & Oriental) Ports of Australia and Port of Singapore Authority International (PSA International) are among the largest investors in the port sector in India. P&O received the first container terminal (at Jawaharlal Nehru Port) in the country to be offered to private participation. The project is called the Nhava Sheva International Container Terminal.

18.4.2 Establishment of Tariff Authority for Major Ports

By amending the Major Port Trust Act of 1963 in 1997, the Government of India established the Tariff Authority for Major Ports (TAMP), an independent authority. However, its authority is limited only to determination of tariffs at major ports. It doesn't have any authority to take other measures to introduce competition, such as the telecom and electricity regulators have. Till very recently, TAMP used to set floor prices below which the ports were not allowed to compete. Now, the government has asked TAMP to fix tariff ceilings instead. In any case, under the 1997 amendment, the government allowed the major ports as well as itself the right to establish their own rates irrespective of what the TAMP said!

With limited powers, inadequate definition of its role and functions, and limited professional and industry specific resources, TAMP is facing significant challenges in discharging its primary responsibility of ensuring fair prices and a level playing field for all users and service providers at the major ports. For example, although terminal handling charges by private operators may constitute a significant proportion of the total cost of moving cargo through the ports, there is no explicit provision in law, empowering TAMP to regulate tariffs for terminal handling charged by private operators. TAMP is also not empowered to requisition records, summon and cross-examine witnesses, enforce orders and impose penalties for non-compliance.

18.4.3 Performance Trends

The growth in the cargo handled at Indian ports has increased from a level of 19.38 million tonnes in 1950-51 to around 457.96 million tonnes by 2003-04.

About 80 per cent of total volume of port traffic handled is in the form of dry and liquid bulk, while the remaining 20 per cent consists of general cargo including containers. There has been an impressive growth of container traffic in the last few years with growth of over 15 per cent per annum during the five years up to 2003-04.[13]

While container traffic has grown well in India, there is still a considerable lag when compared with the larger international ports. The largest port in the world in 2003, Hong Kong, processed 20.1 million TEUs (20-foot equivalent units). The tenth largest port, Antwerp, processed 5.4 million TEUs. In contrast, JNPT, India's largest container port, handled around 2.3 million TEUs in 2003-04.[14]

With infusion of new technology and capacity building, the congestion at Indian Ports witnessed in the 1990s has reduced in some places and operational efficiency has also improved leading to capacities being marginally ahead of demand.

The average turnaround time for vessels in India's ports has improved from 8.1 days in 1990-91 to 3.7 in 2001-02. Anyhow, this is still very high compared to just a few hours in ports like Colombo. What makes things worse is that, except for the JNPT (where there are already two operators and a third has recently been introduced), handling costs have gone up by around 15 per cent on an average in the period 1995-96 to 2001-02 – this at a time when India's costs are already higher than those in other countries.

The crux of the problem is that despite all the changes over the past decade, efficiency levels remain very poor by global standards, and port capacities are around just 50-60 per cent of those in comparable ports in Asia.

While India's ports suffer disadvantages like lower drafts, the policy of loading the ports inefficiencies onto prices makes things even worse. According to a presentation made by JNPT Chairman Ravi Budhiraja at a conference,[15] on a per TEU basis, JNPT is competitive with other ports when it comes to cargo related charges – while JNPT charges $42.7, Singapore charges 59.1, Dubai 90.4 and Colombo 105.3. This advantage, however, is frittered away by the much higher vessel related charges (for berthing, pilotage and towing). JNPT's vessel related charges are 37.9 *versus* 7.2 for Colombo, 6.4 for Dubai and 9.7 for Singapore.

The reason for the higher vessel charges is the inefficiency and extra manpower at government-run ports that is loaded onto the charges. On an average, the employee productivity at a typical Indian port is in the range of 200-440 TEUs as compared to 1,080 in the West Port of Malaysia and 2,300 in Singapore. As a result, while Singapore turns around ships in under 12 hours, JNPT and Cochin take around 37-50, and Chennai takes 145 hours.

In the few ports where there has been some competition, like the JNPT, the difference is discernible. When there was just one operator at JNPT, the container traffic grew steadily from 0.34 lakh TEUs in 1989-90 to 6.69 lakh TEUs in 1998-99. The introduction of a new player the next year resulted in a major change, and by 2002-03, the port's container traffic leapt up to 19.3 lakh TEUs – of this 12 lakh TEUs came from the new Nhava Sheva terminal. The P&O Australia run Nhava Sheva Terminal's productivity levels are at least two-thirds higher than those of JNPT, and not surprisingly its turnaround time is also around a third less and traffic volumes around two-thirds more.

To meet the demands of trade and industry, ports have been expanding their infrastructure in a big way. Despite these efforts, ports are unable to handle additional traffic. The problem now is not that of handling capacity in the major ports but of evacuation from these ports. This problem is also reflected in a decline in JNPT's performance, which has experienced a worsening of both average pre-berthing time and average turnaround time over the years. The pre-berthing waiting time at JNPT is a particularly important problem, given the fact that JNPT accounts for over half of India's container traffic. These difficulties have been primarily caused by the poor road and rail container evacuation infrastructure from the port to its hinterland.

18.5 Competition Concerns in Ports

In terms of technical parameters, the rate of progress in India's ports sector appears to be impressive. Anyhow, maximisation of intra-port and inter-port competition still remains an area of concern.

To foster intra-port competition, the Government of India decided in 1996 that major ports would become landlord ports and cargo-handling services would be privatised. Still, not much has happened. Neither the Government of India nor the ports are conscious of the need to promote competition. In fact, more than once the government has lost the opportunity to create intra-port competition. For instance, in Chennai, the government put out all the (six) container berths in one bid instead of dividing them among two or more operators, which resulted in one party getting the facility for all six berths. In the process, the government lost the opportunity to introduce intra-port competition.

It has also to be pointed out that in the present dispensation, where Port Trusts are the owners and also service providers, they are called upon to introduce competition or put out some of their facilities for private handling and face competition from them. This, in fact, gives ports, as owners as well as service providers, an opportunity to discriminate against competing service providers.

Monopolies elsewhere also influence pricing and competition within the country. For example, P&O Australia runs the container terminal facility in Kalang (Malaysia), Colombo, Karachi, Nhava Sheva (JNPT), and Chennai. They had also bid for Cochin, but looking at their monopoly in the region, the government did not allow them to bid. Nonetheless, by operating facilities in and around India they are still in a position to hike up rates in India or make operations in India difficult for others.

The government, while inviting bids, should look at the existing operations of the bidder to ensure that a monopoly does not emerge. The European Commission does this on a regular basis. In one such case, the European Commission did not allow Hutchinson Whampoa of Hong Kong to enter into the Rotterdam Port because they were already controlling about 35 per cent of container handling facilities in Europe.

There are moves towards business consolidation, as shipping firms want to enter port operations. While this may be termed as vertical integration, there are fears that this would lead to extension of monopoly power.

Recently, the JNPT granted the third container terminal operation to a consortium of Maersk and Concor. While Maersk is the world's biggest shipping company, Concor is India's monopoly rail service provider for container movement. As of now, Maersk vessels carry about 30 per cent of India's containerised export-import cargo and contribute to about 60 per cent share of the total box traffic handled by JNPT and Nhava Sheva Terminal. This development has raised fears that the terminal facility may turn into a captive facility instead of functioning as a common user facility.

And while there is a great private sector initiative (theoretically the private sector can invest in all existing ports as well), the fact is that most major ports have just one operator, and that is the port authority itself.

The Tenth Five Year Plan assumes that, of the Rs. 16,311 crore that will be invested in the sector, Rs. 11,256 crore will come from the private sector, but it is difficult to see how efficiency levels can be hiked unless genuine competition is allowed and more private sector participation is allowed in the major ports. The way forward is to corporatise ports, but this too has been limited. According to the plan, JNPT was to be corporatised first, followed by the Haldia Dock Complex which would be delinked from the Calcutta Port Trust. Kandla, Tuticorin and Mangalore were to be done after two years; Mumbai, Paradip, Vizag and Chennai a year afterwards, and so on.

Another concern arises in the area of dredging. Presently most of the dredging requirements of major ports, particularly maintenance dredging is met by the Dredging Corporation of India. Measures need to be taken to promote Indian dredging industry including the private sector so as to provide competitive dredging at the least cost.

18.6 Railways

Introduced as early as 1853, Indian Railways has grown into the second largest railway network in the world under a single management. The network spread and expanded rapidly and has now become the principal mode of transport in the country. The Railways has also been modernised in terms of technology, ticketing, computerisation and overall management. This effort has been in tune with the requirement of moving large volumes of passenger and freight traffic.

Besides, the Railways have created focused business organisations to cater to some of its main activities, which were earlier given only peripheral attention. Thus, the Container Corporation of India (CONCOR) was established in 1991 to handle domestic and international container traffic. Besides, Indian Railways Catering and Tourism Corporation (IRCTC) has been set up to take over the catering and tourism establishments of the Railways. RailTel Corporation of India Ltd. has been formed for creation of optic fibre cable network to meet Railways' communication requirements.

Railways' experience has shown that corporatisation of its many activities, which only enjoyed peripheral attention within the Railways, have immensely contributed to the process of building expertise in these spheres. One unique and distinguishing feature of these corporations is that they have been consistently making profits since their inception.

18.6.1 *Performance in Freight Traffic: Railways Versus Road Transportation*

Eight major commodities, which constitute the core sector of the economy contribute eighty-nine per cent of railway's freight traffic. These are coal, fertiliser, cement, petroleum products, foodgrains, finished steel, iron ore and raw material to steel plants. The balance is 'other' commodity moving in bulk and in containers.

The world over, long distance freight is carried by railways, but in India the share of the railways in traffic is declining with each passing year (Figure 18.1). In 1950-51, railways carried 89 per cent of total goods traffic and roads carried only 11 per cent. As per current estimates, Indian roads carry 70 per cent of the freight traffic of the country. The highways, even though they make up only 2 per cent of the road network by length, carry 40 per cent of this traffic. While road traffic has grown by 12 per cent annually in the 1990's, rail traffic has gone up only 1.4 per cent. The shift in freight movement from railways to roads has taken place despite rail's advantages in terms of bulk freight movement, carrying potential, and economical land (Box 18.1).

FIGURE 18.1

Rail Versus Road Freight Traffic in Per cent

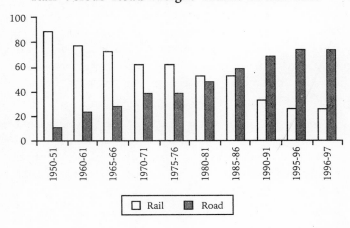

traffic, freight trains in India run at average speed of 23 km an hour as compared to an ideal speed of 40-50 km which is possible with the modern locomotives and electrification.

According to estimates made by the railways, with even declining share in freight traffic, a fourth of 'rail links will experience traffic approaching or exceeding chartered capacity by the year 2006-07.'

18.7 Competition Concerns in Railways

18.7.1 *Monopoly of Concor*

Despite the various initiatives taken by the railways, there are certain issues that remain unresolved. Presently, the Container Corporation of India (Concor) enjoys a monopoly over container movement by rail to and from ports. Though, of late, Concor has failed to meet the growing demand for container movement in the country. A glaring example of this squeeze on availability of containers is provided by the recent congestion at JNPT, and the consequent decline in its performance, as mentioned above. Despite adding to its existing fleet, the supply of rakes by Concor has been inadequate to meet the growing demand.

It can be argued that freight forwarders have the option of moving cargo by road. Notwithstanding, this involves either a down payment of import duties when taking delivery of the goods, or furnishing of a bank guarantee in lieu, which is a costly process. On the contrary, the government follows a discriminatory policy if Concor is transporting the goods, as import duties can be paid at the final destination, i.e. the inland terminal. Thus, container movement via road becomes

---

BOX 18.1

Reasons Favouring Road Transport Versus Railways

- The rating policy of railways is commodity-based and, for certain commodities, like iron and steel, cement, freight rates by rail are more than that by road. Cross-subsidisation of passenger traffic distorts railway tariffs.

- Change in the nature of goods moved. It is not raw material alone, but semi-finished goods that are also placed on longer hauls.

- Centres for production of major bulk commodities like fertilisers, POL, steel are now spread throughout the country. This has resulted in reduction in lead for movement of these commodities.

- Trucks are more easily available than railway wagons.

- Railways lack flexibility in movement and do not provide door-to-door service.

Indeed, apart from reasons to do with the railways pricing themselves out of the market – freight rates have gone up faster than those for passengers, and the ratio of passenger to freight rates at 0.32 is the lowest in the world – the railways is too bankrupt to invest money in developing tracks. In the last ten years, the arrears in track renewal have increased from 3,500 km to more than 12,200 km, according to the Rakesh Mohan Committee on railways. Thanks partly to this, and partly to the supreme emphasis paid to passenger

that much more uncompetitive and serves to preserve the monopoly of Concor.

There are several reasons why the Concor monopoly has to go, the most obvious one being that it keeps freight rates too high. Equally important is the fact that Concor simply doesn't have the money required to be able to provide enough wagons for both exporters and importers.

Given this, a need has been felt for the participation of other players in the container movement over rail. It is also realised that competition with Concor can become effective only if other operators are allowed to run container trains.

In November 2004, the government took the first step towards breaking Concor's monopoly by allowing the Pipavav Rail Corporation Ltd. (PRCL) to transport containers by rail on some ten routes from Pipavav Port to all dry ports, including inland container depots. Interestingly, PRCL is a 50:50 joint venture between Pipavav Port in Gujarat and the Indian Railways!

This has been followed by an announcement in the Railway Budget of 2005-06 to allow private operators in movement of container trains, signalling an end to Concor's monopoly.

Railway tracks constitute a natural monopoly. With the entry of other operators who would be using these tracks, there is a need to establish an independent regulatory authority to fix the prices and control the quality of supply. Furthermore, with the entry of other operators in container movement by rail, they will have to be allowed equal access to engines to pull these wagons. This requires a neutral regulator to ensure that the railways do not squeeze out competition by not allowing them to move their wagons.

18.8 Way Ahead for Railways

With the road transport sector increasing its share in the total freight movement, there is a need for railway freight rates to become more flexible so that they can respond to competition through periodic adjustments. Once the Golden Quadrilateral is in place, railways will face an increased competition from the road sector.

A mechanism needs to be evolved (an independent regulator perhaps) to keep an eye on costs and revenues, to ensure freight is not as heavily overcharged as it is today. If the railways social burden is paid for through the budget or paid for by users, the freight

rates could be brought down by as much as 40 per cent. As a first step, certain operational streams, like transportation of oil or cement or iron ore could be licensed out to private operators, and then a view taken based on the experience.

The government has taken steps to break the monopoly of Concor by allowing private operators to operate container trains. In this context, it is worth noting that the Railways Act now allows only the Government of India to fix freight and also restricts the Railways liability for losses. Unless these provisions are changed, private sector cannot effectively compete with Concor.

18.9 Road Transport

The Indian road network of nearly 3 million kilometres is one of the largest in the world, although this should be normalised for geographical area, size of the economy or population. While the total length of the national roads network has increased 3.4 times between 1951 and 1995, the total vehicle fleet has grown from 0.3mn in 1951 to 12.5mn in 1998, and is currently estimated at 22mn.

The geographic coverage of India's highway network at 0.66 km of highway per square km of land area, is almost identical to the level of the United States (0.65) and much higher than that of China (0.16), Mexico (0.16), and Brazil (0.20). But India compares very poorly with these countries in terms of lane capacity and surface quality. While China has 15,000 km of 4 or 6 lane access controlled expressways, India has less than 5,000 km of four-lane highways.

According to a World Bank analysis, around half the national highway network is good, a quarter 'fair' and the rest 'poor'. Given the huge congestion, truck and bus speed average 30-40 km per hour on the highway against expected speeds of double that. It often takes five days for a truck to travel from Delhi to Kolkata', 1,500 km distance. While the formation of the National Highways Authority of India (NHAI) has been a big step forward in catalysing development of the national highways, it is estimated that there is a 43 per cent shortage in the funds required for maintaining the national highways.

In recent times, the government has laid great emphasis on the development of an adequate road network in the country. A vision of expressway connecting the far corners of the country has been projected. These projects may cost more than

Rs. 25,000 crore (nearly US$6bn). It is undeniable that this vital infrastructure requirement would have to be developed with private sector's participation.

18.9.1 Competition Concerns in Goods Transport

The majority of goods transporters in India are small operators owning one or two trucks. In a few cases, these operators own between 5 to 10 trucks. Most big transporters, in fact, have very few trucks of their own – the largest, Transport Corporation of India (TCI) has less than 400 trucks of its own. Indeed, over the last decade, the trucking industry has got even more fragmented. There is ease of entry and exit from the trucking industry. The Motor Vehicles Act only mandates registration of vehicles by owners and obtaining a permit for operation.

The prevailing situation may give an impression of the existence of a perfectly competitive market, since there are a large number of producers of trucking services and none of them is big enough to influence the price line. In reality, however, things are quite different.

An important aspect of the industry is the dependence of transporters on intermediaries. These include booking agents (also called transport suppliers or transport contractors) and brokers. These players basically perform the function of middlemen for truck owners. While the broker is a person (or a group of persons) who takes commission from truck owners and ensures the supply of trucks to the transport contractor, the booking agent engages in the business of collecting, forwarding or distributing goods carried. Small operators are involved only in the physical movement of goods and depend on booking agents and other fleet operators/transporters for obtaining business. According to industry sources, in only about 2-3 per cent of cases customers directly access the truck owners and book their goods.

As a matter of fact, the intermediaries control freight rates because they alone have the financial resources and market information necessary to influence the price line. The transport contractors quote and settle freight rates with consignors. These are negotiated rates and are valid for a given period of time. Truck owners depend on brokers, who have day-to-day arrangements with them, for obtaining goods for transportation. Brokers arrange the goods for truck owners from booking agents at the prevailing market rates, for which they charge their brokerage.

It has been observed that freight charges paid to truck owners have no relationship with the type and load of freight arranged through brokers. Booking agents/transport contractors and brokers are at present an unregulated lot, despite the fact that they act as powerful agents of the trucking industry. There exists no code of conduct for their modus operandi.

One way to break this practice is by encouraging large fleet owners. However, restrictive provisions in the laws relating to truck drivers, impair the formation of large fleets.

Alternatively, state governments can play an important role as they have the powers to fix freight rates under the Motor Vehicles Act. However, the state governments feel that the matter should be left to the market forces so far as goods freight rates are concerned. As of now, in most states, there is no price regulation and freight rates are presumably decided through forces of demand and supply.

There are also instances of cartelised operation of truckers' union around major production sites and factories (see chapter on State Government Policies and Competition).

18.9.2 Competition Concerns in the Construction of Highways

In the construction of highways, the National Highways Authority has not taken steps to introduce competition in the market, for example, by structuring the bid documents in an appropriate way. Generally, bids are structured in a way, which allows only a few large players to bid. For example, if certain flyovers and bridges are to be built, then all of them are put in the same tender. Though, two-three players bid, but more often, the one who is awarded the contract, sub-contracts the work to the other remaining players – the so-called competitors. This was brought to light in the case of Chennai flyover scam that had rocked the state assembly during late-1990's (see chapter on State Government Policies and Competition).

18.10 Transport Sector: The Way Forward

In the changing economic scenario, factors such as globalisation of markets, international economic integration, removal of barriers to business and trade and increased competition, have enhanced the need of transportation. It is one of the most important infrastructure requirements, which is essential for the expansion of opportunities and plays an important role in economic growth.

Transportation in India is a large and varied sector of the economy. This chapter has done a brief review of four sub-sectors viz., railways, roads, seaports and civil aviation to identify the competition and regulatory concerns. Despite the various initiatives undertaken by the government over the past few years, the transport sector remains very inefficient. The reason for this sorry state of affairs eventually boils down to policies that inhibit competition in and across the various sub-sectors.

The Central government has ministries to handle civil aviation, railways, marine transport and surface transportation. Counterpart agencies are found at the state and union territory level. In contrast, several countries have a single Ministry of Transport, covering all the modes of transport. Since this would be difficult in a large country like India, a permanent forum for ensuring inter-modal coordination could be set up where the policy-makers of all these modes of transport come together to learn from, and respond to, the latest developments in transportation in the country and abroad.

Although there is a large private-sector involvement in transportation in India, the government continues to play a large regulatory and developmental role, and is also the major service provider in case of certain sub-sectors. This leads to 'conflicts of interest', as brought in the cases of civil aviation, ports, and railways.

The increased role of private sector in the provision of transport infrastructure facilities and services does not eliminate the need for a regulatory oversight. Instead, such reforms have emphasised the need for effective regulation and regulatory institutions for a number of reasons, including:

- The existence of natural monopolies;

- The limitations of competition for the market;

- The existence of asymmetric information between transport operators and regulators;

- The need for private investment in infrastructure facilities; and

- The need to assign risks between operators and government.

However, there is no regulator in the transport sector in India, as in electricity or telecom or financial services. There is TAMP for the ports sector, but its role is limited and is not concerned about issues relating to efficiency or taking measures to create competition in the sector. For this reason, whatever needs to be done in the transport sector to make it more competitive has to be done by way of policy reforms.

Regulation in transport sector has been tried in several countries. In India, we need to consider if all the competition issues in the transport sector can be addressed as policy initiatives with the Competition Commission of India playing an active role with government or in addition, we need a transport regulator (may be a multi-sector transport regulator) to address all the regulatory issues.

Notes

1. Presentation by JNPT Chairman Ravi Budhiraja at World Bank-CII conference (web-address: http://lnweb18.worldbank.org/SAR/sa.nsf/Attachments/rbb/$File/rbb.ppt).

2. ICAO brochure, "Economic Contribution of Civil Aviation: Ripples of Prosperity", 2000.

3. Report of the Committee on a Roadmap for the Civil Aviation Sector, Ministry of Civil Aviation, Government of India, November 2003 (henceforth, Naresh Chandra report).

4. Naresh Chandra Report.

5. *ibid.*

6. Traffic levels at most of the destinations are very low, also reflected in the highly skewed distribution of air traffic, thus ruling out competition between airports. Furthermore, given the existing number of terminals even at major airports, there appears to be little scope for introducing intra-airport competition (Naresh Chandra Report).

7. Naresh Chandra Report.

8. Over 40 per cent of passenger traffic is concentrated in these two airports (Naresh Chandra Report).

9. Naresh Chandra Report.

10. *ibid.*

11. *ibid.*

12. *ibid.*

13. Economic Survey, 2004-05.

14. *ibid.*

15. http://lnweb18.worldbank.org/SAR/sa.nsf/Attachments/rbb/$File/rbb.ppt

References

"Flying Indian Airlines out of the red," *Business Standard*, December 23, 2002.

Economic Contribution of Civil Aviation: Ripples of Prosperity, International Civil Aviation Organisation (ICAO) brochure, 2000.

Container Rail Corridors: An Approach Paper, Department of Shipping, Ministry of Shipping, Road Transport and Highways, Government of India.

Debroy, Bibek and P.D. Kaushik, *Barriers to Inter-State Trade and Commerce – The Case of Road Transport*, Background Paper prepared for the National Commission to review the working of the Constitution.

Deshmukh, Atul, *Indian Ports: The Current Scenario*, University of Mumbai.

Firm Level Survey, CII-World Bank, 2002.

India Infrastructure Report 1996.

India Infrastructure Report 2001.

Report of the Committee on a Roadmap for the Civil Aviation Sector, Ministry of Civil Aviation, Government of India, November 2003 (Naresh Chandra Report).

Tenth Plan Document, Planning Commission.

The Indian Railways Report 2001: Policy Imperatives for Reinvention and Growth (Rakesh Mohan Committee).

Economic Survey 2004-05.

Indian Air Farce, Indian Express, January 16, 2005.

India's Transport Sector: The Challenges Ahead, World Bank, May 2002.

http://civilaviation.nic.in/moca/acvl.htm

http://lnweb18.worldbank.org/SAR/sa.nsf/Attachments/rbb/$File/rbb.ppt

http://www.indiacore.com

Personal interviews with Michael Pinto, former Shipping Secretary and Sunil Arora, CMD, Indian Airlines.

Part VII

Competition Policy in Services

19 Competition and Regulation in Financial Services

Shubhashis Gangopadhyay • Praveen Mohanty

19.1 Introduction

Competition in the financial sector is important for a number of reasons. As in the real sector, competition enables product innovation and the development and adoption of efficient practices. Financial product innovation manifests itself in the introduction of new financial instruments with different risk-return profiles to allow better risk management (or portfolio balancing) for individual and other investors. Efficiency gains mainly accrue in two ways. First, using modern information and communication technologies and by effecting organisational changes in financial institutions that reduce the transaction costs of operating in financial instruments. Second, new financial products at low costs improve the efficiency of the "real" sector. Benefits reaped by the non-financial sector include, among others, an improved access to capital, cheaper credit and housing loans for consumers, a better match between the financing needs of deficit and surplus units, etc.

While market forces mainly determine competition, it is important to have regulatory institutions that ensure that these forces operate effectively and are not circumvented, or blocked, by those participating in the market. This is true for both the financial and non-financial sectors, though the possibilities of such "capture", or market failure, are much higher in financial markets. This is largely due to the fact that information asymmetries (knowledge gaps between "buyers" and "sellers") are much higher in the markets for financial services than they are for real goods and services. Moreover, while a "commodity market failure" seldom leads to an economic meltdown, financial market failures have significant macro impacts.

The key measures used in most competition policies are:

(a) rules designed to deal with industry structure, or, what are more commonly known as merger or anti-trust laws.

(b) rules designed to prevent anti-competitive behaviour through oligopolistic price fixing, or more generally through collusion.

(c) rules that ensure that markets are contestable, i.e., free entry and exit.

It is important to note that contestability relies heavily on free exit as much as it depends on easy entry.

Since the initiation of reforms in 1991, the financial sector – covering banking, insurance, capital market, asset management and pensions – has seen a fundamental shift in its institutional structure. This shift has been brought about by a greater emphasis on competition, regulatory framework, supervisory oversight, and transparency. As a result, the financial sector has grown not only in size, but also through the introduction of innovative products aimed at meeting the financial intermediation needs of different segments of the economy. This chapter traces the reform path and evaluates its impact on the organisation of each segment, the nature and quality of the services it provides, and, on productivity and employment.

The reforms in the financial sector were initiated in an environment where many segments of economic activity were gradually freed from government control. It was realised early on that deregulated activities required liberalised financial systems to raise resources efficiently. As domestic reforms progressed, increasing integration with global markets became another catalyst for further reforms. Entries into banking, mutual funds, and later into insurance have been progressively allowed. The reforms have helped create a financial sector in India that is stable and growing. The financial markets and the institutional framework under which the markets operate have weathered a number of domestic and international crises. Such exigencies, triggered by disparate events in various countries, have alerted policymakers and regulators to the potential fragility of intermediaries in a deregulated environment and resulted in ongoing modifications and improvements in process and disclosure requirements. This has given the policymakers the confidence to continue with the reform process of reducing the government's presence in the sector, transferring power to independent regulators, and relying on market forces to chart new growth paths for the sector as well as the economy.

The entry of the private sector has instilled competition among public sector institutions, compelling them to improve product offerings and service standards, as well as adopt a more customer-friendly approach. Under competitive pressures, the financial sector has rapidly implemented technological advances in information and communication. The resulting productivity gains and reductions in transaction costs have been passed on to the customers in the form of better products and services. However, one thing is clear: we still have a long way to go. In spite of the reforms and the entry of the private sector, government-owned institutions continue to dominate banking, insurance, and pensions.

19.2 Measuring Reforms

Ideally, the success of reforms can be measured against the fulfilment of the objectives. The primary impact of reforms should be to perceptibly reduce inefficiencies in the delivery of financial services. Alternatively, any lowering of the cost to consumers and other users of financial services could be viewed as an efficiency gain. While there is no reliable quantitative estimate of such costs prior to the reforms, the structure of the industry in the early-90s suggests a very high-cost financial sector. The sector was dominated by the public sector – 90 per cent of banking assets were held by state-owned banks, while insurance, pensions and asset management companies were government monopolies. This lack of competition and the influence of political rather than business motives in management resulted in high transaction costs and poor services to the customers. Compared to other countries, the banking industry was relatively inefficient in its density and costs of branch banking, the mix of payment instruments, general insurance expense ratios and fund management costs.

The second impact of financial reforms can be judged by observing the capacity of the nation's financial system, and more importantly its regulatory authority, to adapt to the changing environment of the global financial system. Not only must the financial institutions be able to implement new technologies and practices, the regulatory authorities must also be in a position to understand the full implications of such changes. Without the latter, good innovative practices will either be disallowed by the regulators, or, what could be worse for an emerging market system, bad practices would go unchecked, leading often to major crises in the financial system. In either case, it becomes difficult to maintain the integrity and stability of a system that is essential for rapid investment and growth.

Against this general backdrop, one has to take into account the particular national environment within which the financial system has to operate. One can define three major drivers of development for the financial sector in India.

19.2.1 Changing Customer Needs

Changes in customer needs and profiles are gradual but have powerful influences in financial sector developments. In the decade of the 90s, Indian house-holds have been increasing their holding of financial assets as well as their financial borrowing – a process that is often described as "deepening" of the financial system. This is largely the effect of changing demographics, life cycle changes and increasing wealth. India has a very young population, with large numbers of new entrants to the working force. At the same time, the middle and high-income group has been ageing and has increased expectations of higher retirement incomes. Add to this the job mobility of the current work-force, more time spent in training and education by the young, shifts in work-leisure preferences, changes in family structure and you have a consuming class that is willing to spend now and pay later. It is not surprising that in such a society, con-sumer loans and other financial services for the house-holds will be in demand. This is fuelled by the younger generation's better access to information and familiarity with alternative and modern technologies. These also implied that the financial sector needed to gear itself to meet the increasing demands from consumers.

19.2.2 Technological Progress

The second major driver, and this is true for all economies, is technological innovation. Systems for processing, communicating and storing information – essential parts of the infrastructure supporting financial services – have undergone substantial changes. Technology has made it possible to access products and markets both domestically and internationally. It affords more effective means to analyse and monitor risk. Now financial service providers can disaggregate risk on a broad scale, price it more accurately and redistribute it more efficiently. Not only has the new technology led to falling costs, it has also enabled innovations that were not feasible without the possibility of secure electronic transactions. In particular, it has facilitated the conduct of financial activities from sites physically remote from the service providers – work, home, another country – resulting in a lowering of transaction costs and entry barriers for new entrants.

19.2.3 *Regulation*

Regulatory institutions profoundly influence the structure, scale and operation of financial sector activities. Not only do they decide what players can and cannot do, they also maintain the credibility of the system, so that more consumers of financial services are encouraged to participate in the market. It is the regulatory environment that controls the pace of opening up of the Indian financial sector to global markets and competition. The more developed the regulatory system, less would be the power and influence of the government – not only in the proportion of ownership of financial institutions, but also in the implicit and explicit government guarantees of various financial liabilities that inhibit healthy competition.

In this context, one can judge the success of the reforms by the degree to which regulatory oversight has enabled the realisation of consumer demands, through the adoption of a more dynamic and low-cost financial system. Quite independently, one can also evaluate whether the new regulatory system is transparent and flexible enough to deal with the changing conditions. Most importantly, the regulator should not hold up innovations because of its lack of understanding of how new instruments work. This can be very inefficient in the current environment where global companies under more dynamic regulators can out-compete domestic players, even if they are otherwise efficient.

19.3 Banking Reforms

Prior to 1991, the Indian banking sector was over-regulated and repressed. Predominantly government-owned, interest rates on deposits and lending were administratively determined and there was a high degree of Statutory pre-emption of bank deposits through high Statutory Liquidity Ratio (SLR) and Cash Reserve Ratio (CRR) requirements. SLR was at 38.5 per cent against a legal cap of 40 per cent; CRR was at 15 per cent and government bonds were issued at sub-market rates. Priority sector lending norms were used to channel cheap credit to the small-scale, agriculture and other identified sectors. At a more micro level, regulation extended to determining credit norms, mergers and acquisitions, restrictions on types of products and services, tenure of credit, consortium lending, etc.

Reforms led to the entry of private sector banks (nine in 1993 and two more in 2003). Interest rates (on both loans and deposits) were deregulated. Credit terms were no longer set by the government. Concomitantly, public sector banks were given greater autonomy. Instead, the regulatory authority, the Reserve Bank of India (RBI), moved towards a more arm's length monitoring through the application and tightening of prudential norms related to capital adequacy, income recognition and asset classification in accordance with international norms and improved disclosure practices. All this resulted in a significant increase in the use of information and communication technologies in the Indian banking industry. This revolution in technology use is evident in branch automation, ATM networks, multiple banking channels, etc. Also, changes in the core banking software have introduced many product and service innovations.

The branch distribution policy prior to 1991 had led to a number of inefficient branches in various regions of the country. E.g., the nationalised commercial banks had a large presence in rural and semi-urban areas. While only 34 per cent of their deposits were sourced from such branches and 23 per cent of their advances were disbursed in these areas, they accounted for 70 per cent of all their branches. This policy was relaxed and the bank boards now have greater autonomy in deciding on where branches will be opened and which branches need to be closed or transferred (unless a region becomes completely uncovered by any bank).

There are two product segments in banking, namely, retail and wholesale. Retail banking is directed towards the households and the small sector, while wholesale banking caters to larger firms and other financial institutions. Most banks provide both types of services, though there are some specialised institutions, like the housing finance corporations for retail, and development banks like the Industrial Development Bank of India (IDBI) for wholesale banking.

The benefits of reforms are the most pronounced in retail banking. Prior to reforms, retail services were restricted to taking deposits and supporting a small set of payments-related instruments. Deregulation, the freeing up of interest rates and types of lending activities led to a number of products becoming available, such as, vehicle, personal, housing or mortgage loans and credit cards. Though there are no definitive figures, some estimates put banks' total exposure to retail activities as high as Rs. 1000 bn. Indeed, such assets are said to account for 25 per cent of all banking assets of ICICI Bank.

A large part of this phenomenal growth was due to the fact that there was a widening demand gap in the availability of these services, given the changing demographics in the economy referred to earlier. The entry of private and foreign banks armed with new generation technologies and human capital, coupled with free competition among banks, led to an aggressive marketing of these products. The growth has been fuelled by increased consumer access and improved service quality brought about largely by the deregulation of credit terms that allowed lending rates to be determined by the cost of funds and the attendant risks of particular products. Anyhow, while such retail banking has spread from metropolitan centres to other urban areas, rural markets are yet to be adequately covered. This is largely due to the nature of rural markets and the distribution of wealth among rural customers.

Among the retail segments, the housing loan market has shown one of the highest growth rates. This has important implications for the entire economy. It fuels the construction sector, which generates extensive employment as well as boosting large segments of other sectors, like steel and cement.

Wholesale banking has also introduced a host of new products, like rupee interest rate swaps, forward rate agreements, interest rate futures and foreign currency options. The interest rate and currency derivatives have experienced greater liquidity and "finer" pricing due to the entry of a large number of banks into such activities. Corporate customers have gained from these changes, as they can now hedge their interest rate and currency risks, and hence, have greater flexibility in determining the conditions under which they borrow. In March 2003, the RBI issued draft guidelines for the introduction of credit derivatives in the domestic market. This will make credit a tradable item, leading to better risk management by banks and better pricing of risk.

However, wholesale banking is yet to notch up the spectacular growth achieved by retail banking. This is largely due to the debt recovery laws (or, bankruptcy laws) laying a misplaced emphasis on protecting current industries at the expense of the growth of new ones.

19.4 Insurance

Prior to the opening up of private participation in August 2000, the insurance sector was a government monopoly consisting of Life Insurance Corporation (LIC), and General Insurance Corporation (GIC) with its four subsidiaries for general insurance. Now, there are 13 new life insurance companies and 8 new general insurance companies. They are mostly joint ventures with major global insurance players. As a part of the reform package, the four subsidiaries of GIC were made independent and GIC became a re-insurance company. Private participants have been constantly gaining market share. The private company's share of the life insurance premium in 2001-02, the first year, was 2 per cent. This figure increased to 5.7 per cent in 2002-03 and to 11 per cent in the first half 2003-04. The premium share of private general insurance increased from 3.7 per cent in 2001-02 to as high as 13.7 per cent during the first half of 2003-04.

The reform process initiated in 2000 has enhanced competition, provided more choices to the customer, triggered innovations, allowed various insurance packages, improved the efficiency levels, increased coverage in terms of density and penetration, obligated the insurers to provide for the needs of the rural and socially disadvantaged sectors, and increased the awareness among customers, thus feeding the growth in demand for insurance.

Yet, by international standards, the Indian insurance sector is far behind in terms of its penetration. This is largely because of the lack of a knowledge base on risk factors. The history of government-owned insurance companies meant that no actuarial analysis, data collection and storage were undertaken. New insurance companies are, therefore, cautious. They deal first with less risky customers and products, while they collect information on the risks of other types of customers and products. Another hindrance to the faster growth of insurance is the necessity to have larger capital bases in the private companies. Here they are at a disadvantage *vis-à-vis* the government-owned companies, which often have a better portfolio of customers because of their national reach and depth. Relaxing the 25 per cent foreign direct investment cap on private companies may help in quickly increasing the capital base. The Finance Minister, in his July 2004 budget speech, announced a revision of this cap to 49 per cent. Unfortunately, some of the coalition partners of the present government strongly opposed such a move. This means that, except for those private companies that are sponsored by financial institutions (like ICICI Prudential, HDFC Standard Life and SBI Life), others will continue to be plagued by a shortage of funds that will constrain their growth.

Corporatisation of LIC, through an amendment of the LIC Act of 1934 is also necessary. As of now, the LIC operations are opaque to the public, and, more importantly, even to the Insurance Regulatory and Development Authority (IRDA). If LIC were to become a corporate entity under the Companies Act, it would eliminate the implicit government guarantee to all the LIC insurance policies, and, hence, usher in transparency in asset management. This would go a long way in "levelling" the insurance playing field and allow the private players to better compete with LIC.

19.5 Asset Management/Mutual Funds

The Unit Trust of India (UTI) was set up in 1963 under an Act of Parliament, and the first non-UTI mutual fund was launched a quarter century later in 1987, when State Bank of India (SBI) launched the SBI Mutual Fund. This led to some more mutual funds initiated by some of the other public sector banks and insurance companies. In 1993, there were less than 10 such funds. The nationalised Unit Trust of India dominated the market. The UTI and state-owned insurance firms and banks offered plain vanilla funds amounting to about Rs. 470 bn. India's first private sector mutual fund was launched in 1993 and was later acquired by Franklin Templeton. Many foreign players set up joint ventures with private Indian partners. The total assets under management have risen to more than Rs. 1.6 tn, with much of this growth occurring in the last two years. The funds are split evenly between stocks and bonds.

Even though private asset management companies were allowed before 1994, the UTI Act was finally repealed in 2001 when UTI became a corporate entity. This was followed by a number of Securities and Exchange Board of India (SEBI) regulations on the types of permitted schemes; e.g., after the recent UTI fiasco, assured return schemes are no longer allowed. SEBI also established entry and exit norms, enabled a number of mergers within the industry, started treating venture capital companies as similar to mutual funds,

implemented the dematerialisation of units and their listing on stock exchanges. From nothing in 1993, today in 10 years time, private sector funds and foreign fund joint ventures manage around 78 per cent of the industry's total assets. There are more than 30 mutual funds in India, offering slightly less than 400 different schemes, from plain debt or equity funds to more sophisticated ones that satisfy more idiosyncratic investors with different growth, safety and income requirements.

Still, on an international scale, our mutual funds industry is quite small. While the industry manages funds amounting to 6 per cent of India's gross domestic product, it continues to be a small fraction of what individual mutual funds manage overseas. One of the major problems faced by the Indian mutual fund industry is that the industry has not been able to excite the common investor. This has been largely due to the lack of awareness among investors and the plethora of tax-saving government savings schemes. Nevertheless, the industry is poised for more rapid growth, as investors become more market-savvy and deposit rates continue to fall. Add to that a rising middle class and a group of young Indians entering the labour market with relatively well-paying jobs.

19.6 Pension Funds

A new pension scheme has been introduced for government employees and is likely to be extended to the rest of the working population. Pension Fund Regulatory and Development Authority (PFRDA) has been appointed as a regulator for the sector, with a mandate to regulate the independent private asset managers and the central record keeping agencies.

Statutory contributions towards provident fund and gratuities have killed off the private pensions sector. The government and quasi-government pensions were not indexed against inflation and that prompted most retirees to opt for commuting their pensions to the maximum allowable amount. These pensions were mostly unfounded obligations. Not surprisingly, pension funds have never been important players in the Indian capital market.

The EPF, or the employees' provident fund, promised a lump sum payment at the time of the employee's retirement. This is more like a nest egg with both the employee and the employer putting in matching amounts. More recently, a part of this is being used for a limited pension plan. Here, too, the restriction on allowable investments has meant that the

EPF has had limited impact on capital markets. The PPF, or the public provident fund, is open to all Indians, employed and self-employed. It is an incentive for savings, offering a fixed tax-free rate of return with a maturity of 15 years.

As a first step, the government introduced a pension scheme for employees joining the Central government service from January 1, 2004. The scheme is based largely on the recommendations of the OASIS (Old Age Social and Income Security) Expert Committee, set up by the Ministry of Social Justice and Empowerment. The focus of the recommendations is to set up a more market oriented pension fund in the private sector and regulated by a Pensions Authority. The fund would be free to invest in the stock market and would enjoy favourable tax treatment.

A pension fund can be viewed either as something that offers old age security, or, a method of mopping up current resources to pay for various public expenditures that will pay dividends later. Some may find a government-run pension scheme more suited for the latter objective, especially in a country where infrastructure investment and social safety nets are woefully lacking. Though, with a well functioning capital market, and with pension funds being allowed to participate in it, a private pension fund can do just as well. The real issue is one of a regulatory structure that prevents a crisis of credibility so that investors are confident of putting in their money into pensions. One way of doing this is to ensure that pension funds offer a return corresponding to the long-term returns in the capital market. Obviously, well-regulated private pension funds are more suited for this. Different pension funds offering varied risk-return profiles can attract various types of players. More importantly, the same investor can distribute her/his savings across more than one pension fund.

Fortunately, the Indian Government is thinking precisely along these lines. First, the new pension proposal has moved away from that of defined-benefit to one where the returns are market determined. Second, it allows private fund managers to operate these funds. Third, it is not trying to "capture" these savings for government-run projects. If the government wants this money, it has to compete with all other demanders of finance in the market, and hence, pay the proper price of capital.

Be that as it may, the political economy of Indian policy making is rather strange. As is mostly the case, muddled thinking dilutes a good idea. So, now we hear that there will be a fixed number of fund managers who will be chosen – a maximum of six with at least one public sector institution. No one knows the significance of the magic number "six". No one knows why it is essential to have a public sector institution. Of course, an inefficient public concern can act as a low benchmark for the other five private sector concerns!

19.7 Non-Banking Financial Companies (NBFCs)

By the mid-90s, there were more than 40,000 NBFCs in India, including a mix of large and small companies in the unorganised sector. Instances of lack of sustainability, coupled with their mushrooming growth after 1991, prompted serious regulatory changes, and hence, a slight decline in their number. However, banks continue to dominate as financial intermediaries. The percentage of NBFC deposits to that of all scheduled commercial banks is less than 2 per cent.

NBFCs do not fall under the purview of banking regulations. Instead, these are licensed under a 1997 amendment of the RBI Act. Operationally, this involves compulsory registration with the RBI, which is more in the nature of an approval granted by it. For, existing NBFCs, with net owned funds (NOF) equivalent to Rs. 5 mn or more, can be registered with the RBI with a minimum capital of Rs. 2.5 mn. Subsequently, from 2000 onwards, new NBFCs will have to register with the RBI showing an NOF of at least Rs. 20 mn. The RBI (Amendment) Act, 1997, is also the most comprehensive attempt at regulating NBFCs. The focus of the regulatory structure is to safeguard depositors and at the same time allow greater flexibility to NBFCs so that they can help in the development of a diversified financial sector. Accordingly, entry-level norms for new and existing NBFCs have been laid down. In addition to compulsory registration with the RBI, the regulations impose conditions on minimum level of NOF, maintenance of certain percentage of liquid assets as per cent of public deposits in government bonds, creation of a reserve fund and subsequent transfers of a pre-determined percentage of profits to this fund, credit rating of deposits, capital adequacy, income recognition, asset classification, compulsory credit rating provision for bad and doubtful debts, exposure norms and other measures of financial reporting.

Operationally, regulators categorise NBFCs according to their size, the type of activity they perform, and, whether or not, they accept public deposits. Supervision is carried out through on-site inspection, off-site surveillance, reports from the NBFCs' statutory auditors and market data. For those NBFCs that accept public deposits, the regulatory structure treats them as if they are similar to banks. On the other hand, unlike banks, NBFCs are not allowed to sell demand deposits.

The question remains as to whether, for regulatory purposes, such NBFCs should be treated as banks. Given that banks sell demand deposits, they are open to an asset-liability mismatch. This may trigger a run on them by depositors. Further, all banks are an integral part of the payments system and a run on one bank could lead to contagion runs and a collapse of the entire financial system. Most economies have some sort of deposit insurance to prevent the start of such panic runs. Nevertheless, since deposits are insured, it often results in a moral hazard for bank managers, and hence, the need for third party regulation. NBFCs do not have the same possibilities of a "run" on their deposits, which are, in any case, not payable on demand. So, where is the reason to regulate them the same way as one would regulate a bank?

19.8 Conclusion

The Indian financial sector has experienced major changes since the reforms started in the 90s. For instance, prior to 1992, when the National Stock Exchange was set-up, the stock market consisted of a broker-controlled system of regional exchanges, with an open-cry system of trade execution, no transparency in the traded price, and high transaction costs. The "bear" and the "bull" operators could easily manipulate prices due to the low public float and the segregation of the markets by trading on the margin. This scenario has undergone a complete change with both National Stock Exchange (NSE) and Bombay Stock Exchange (BSE) being national markets where trades are electronically executed against an order book that is transparently available to all traders. The creation of depository institutions and trade guarantee by the exchanges have not only brought down the transaction costs, but also eliminated settlement risk and fraud risk from stock market transactions. All these developments have occurred within the regulatory oversight of the Securities and Exchange Board of India (SEBI), but without explicit directions by the regulator.

Of course, the financial market involves a lot more than the stock market. Consider the change in the behaviour of Indian banks. As described in the literature, banks can perform one of two opposing roles. One is the helping hand approach that corrects market failures; the other is the grabbing hands approach wherein the government regulates to satisfy political constituencies. At the expense of being graphic, one can say that post-reforms, India moved from the grabbing hand approach to that of a helping hand one. Earlier, through state ownership of banks, the government indulged in directed lending, financial repression and political influence. Now, even though there are state-owned banks, the introduction of private and foreign banks has resulted in more competition in the banking sector. Also, state-owned banks face less political influence and hard budget constraints, along with stricter income recognition and disclosure norms. A study of more than a hundred countries suggests that private control of banks, coupled with strict disclosure norms, performs best for stability in the banking sector.

In India, in the immediate future, banks and financial institutions (FIs) will have to play a big role in furthering investment and growth. There are two reasons for this. First, given the corporate governance and information disclosure structures in India, it is easier for an investor to use an asset manager who has greater resources to collect information and monitor those who use outside funds. Second, given our income levels and their distribution, there is little discretionary savings, and most individuals prefer fixed returns on savings, as given by banks, insurance companies and pension funds, to risky returns. Also, and this is true for most emerging markets, Indian stock markets are yet to be fully developed to meet the equity requirements of start-up businesses. The private equity market exists in a limited form for certain businesses, but not for others, especially those in the infrastructure sector. Companies, therefore, tend to rely more on FIs to fund their investments.

Anyhow, this leads to an increased concentration in the total amount of risk held by the FIs, and this they may not want to do. They may reduce the risk by lending less, or demanding collateral from prospective borrowers. The former is directly against the stated objective of greater investment. The latter is an inefficient mechanism as the presence of collateral transfers the risk back to the borrower, and, individual borrowers are expected to be more risk averse than FIs, and hence, should bear lower amounts of the total risk. In particular, the demand for collateral prevents start-up firms from accessing the formal credit markets more than it prevents the large and already established businesses. For a sustained growth rate of 8 per cent and more, we will need all profitable ideas to be funded, not simply those originating in the big industrial houses.

It is useful here to make a distinction between FIs that simply pass through the risk, like mutual funds, venture capital funds, hedge funds, etc., and those that intermediate risk through assured returns, like banks, pension funds, insurance companies, etc. The former group needs little regulation other than information disclosure norms. There is a feeling that the latter group, on the other hand, needs to be more closely regulated so that the investor feels protected, or assured. Of course, as universal banks become more common, this distinction between two different types of FIs will become more and more blurred.

In principle, as long as there are instruments like deposits, and FIs lend to risky projects, they will continue to want to unload their risks to those who are more willing to, and capable of, bearing them. If banks can lower their risks by passing them on to others, it will not only make the deposits more secure, but will also reduce the cost of adherence to regulations concerning capital adequacy. It is in this context that credit derivatives can play an important role. Recently, rules and regulations have been suggested for trade in credit derivatives.

It is common among many to view derivatives as highly risky instruments and that they create too much systemic risk exposure. Consequently, they feel that regulated institutions should not jump into these activities without proper safeguards, as listed by the regulatory authorities. This sort of reasoning can be counter-productive on two counts. First, the very basis of the view can be erroneous. To say that systemic risk exposure of derivatives is high, one must compare it with the risk of alternative financial structures that derivatives replace, rather than on any abstract, absolute measure. Consider the inter-bank foreign exchange market as against the over the counter (OTC) option market for foreign exchange. Given that the daily inter-bank market is close to a trillion dollars, the systemic risk potential from systemic failure is very high. The contract default on OTC options leads to a risk exposure equal to the difference between the strike price and the principal amount. In the inter-bank deals, on the other hand, the exposure is the total amount of the principal. Thus, while the options have a risk exposure, substituting them for standard forex transactions actually reduces the systemic exposure.

Second, the desire to get regulations in place before institutions can trade in derivatives may have the same results that we had in product markets during the license *raj*. That system hampered and delayed product and process innovations. Similarly, a "regulation, and hence, permission first" approach may result in Indian financial markets following the expertise and knowledge of the regulators, rather than being led by the creativity of the financial innovators.

In principle, when it comes to regulation, the approach must be comprehensive and not just an attempt to regulate specific activities. In financial markets, e.g., requiring a forced market-to-market collateralisation, but not requiring this on other traditional investments, like loans, is counter-productive for reasons similar to the one cited above on measuring risk exposures. Loans have principal and (gross) interest exposures, while swaps have only net interest exposures. Restricting derivatives only, and not other functionally equivalent alternatives, can actually increase the systemic risk exposure rather than reducing it.

If we continue further with this example, one sees the need to move from the current emphasis on regulating institutions to one of functional regulation. Merton gives the example of a standard investment objective of a levered position in the S&P 500 stocks. Starting with buying each of the individual stocks on margin in the cash stock market, to one where one borrows to buy a variable-rate annuity whose return is linked to the S&P 500, there are 11 different ways of taking up this position. All 11 of these transactions in his example are functionally equivalent, but involve different sets of agents and institutions, such as, brokers, mutual funds, investment banks, commercial banks, insurance companies and exchanges. If only some of the institutions are regulated, it will result in some of these alternatives becoming more expensive than others and give rise to unnecessary distortions.

Indeed, financial innovations, including many aspects of securitisation, can result from such regulations! Capital adequacy norms have opened up avenues of what is known in the literature as regulatory capital arbitrage. This is driven by the large gaps in the economic risks of assets held by the banks and that of the risk-weighted measure assigned to the loans by the capital adequacy regulations. For instance, in the US, the capital requirement on housing mortgages is four per cent. If, however, the mortgages were sold and the proceeds were invested in government bonds, the bank would have no capital requirement. Now suppose that the bank enters into an amortisation swap. It gets the total returns on mortgages, including amortisation and prepayments, while it pays the returns on US treasury bonds to the swap counter party. According to capital adequacy norms, the bank's capital requirements fall to 0.4 per cent. However, investing directly in the mortgages is functionally similar to the one that has the swap agreement, while in terms of the regulatory implications they are vastly different.

The Indian financial markets have matured significantly in the last decade. Today, the landscape of the markets contains a liquid national market for equity, public and private market for debt, derivative markets in equity, currency and interest rates, and insurance. A robust regulatory framework with independent market regulators oversees the growth of this market. Even then, given the interdependence of these markets, and the bundling or unbundling of risks in a manner that results in multiple regulators having jurisdiction over a particular investment offering, there is a need to ensure that there is an integrated policy framework underlying the regulatory institutions. The Financial Services Administration (FSA) of the United Kingdom was created to reduce the multiplicity of regulators and to ensure a common approach to regulation of the different segments of the financial sector.

No discussion of the financial sector is complete without some discussion on the recovery of financial claims. These become especially important when we consider the major objective of financial markets, i.e., reallocating risk so that capital can move to more efficient activities. An important element of this reallocation is contained in the bankruptcy laws, which, in principle, should enable the reallocation of capital from inefficient to efficient activities. In spite of the far-reaching achievements in the liberalisation of the financial markets in India, new projects find it difficult to access the public markets for investible funds. On the one hand, as discussed above, FIs' requirement of collateral discourages borrowing since many new businesses in the services sector do not have fixed assets that can be offered as collateral for borrowing. And on the other hand, in the absence of legal provisions for winding up bankrupt businesses, banks have to rely exclusively on the collateral to recover their dues from these firms.

20 Competition and Professional Services

T.C.A. Anant

This paper briefly analyses the role for competition policy in the market for professional services. In the first section, we briefly review the characteristics of professional services and the need for regulatory intervention. In these services, self-regulation has been developed, taking into account the unique characteristics of a given service. In the second section, we examine the nature of the self-regulatory codes for three major professional services, namely law, accountancy and (allopathic) medicine. We note how there are standards that create the potential for anti-competitive outcomes. We briefly summarise the experience of other countries in this regard. We finally conclude by outlining the importance of competition assessment, and regulation, in this critical sector.

20.1 The Market for Professional Services

Professional services refer to activities, occupations, or businesses of individuals that require specialised education, knowledge, and skills, and are predominantly intellectual. Thus, under the classification in use at the WTO, professional services include:

- Legal services
- Accounting, auditing and bookkeeping services
- Taxation services
- Architectural services
- Engineering services
- Integrated engineering services
- Urban planning and landscape architectural services
- Medical and dental services
- Veterinary services

- Services provided by midwives, nurses, physiotherapists and para-medical personnel
- Other services

The defining feature here is that the concerned service is supplied through individuals, and is highly *idiosyncratic in character*. Thus, the service purchased by one consumer is not the same as that by another. This feature of professional services then creates conditions for different types of market failure. The key aspects can be classified as either informational, both asymmetric and imperfect, or externalities.

Information: The consumer in these cases often does not know his own needs, as in medicine or law. The customer needs the specialist or expert to tell him both what is wrong, and what he needs to do about it. The service provider is important in both shaping the demand and for suggesting methods of meeting it. Thus, for instance, a doctor determines the patient's requirements as well as the specific medication needed. The scope for providers to supply misleading information to consumers arises due to the information asymmetry that exists between service providers and consumers; since the former tend to have better information on the prices, performance and availability of various products, than consumers. Thus, we hear of examples of a doctor asking a patient to get a test redone because he trusts a particular laboratory more; or prescribes the brand name, instead of a generic formulation, for some pharmacological drug. As a consequence, we find the market for professional services can have some very perverse outcomes. This could include the 'lemons problem', where differences in the consumers' and provider's perception, of the quality being provided, leads to market failure. There could also be Moral Hazard when the service provider seeks to *gold-plate* the services to the consumer, even when they do not need it, as with unnecessary tests, and so on.

Externalities: This concept, in economic terms, refers to those costs and benefits, which arise in a transaction but are borne by parties other than the buyer and seller. A good example of this would be in accounting services. Consider the case of accounts of a listed company. While the buyer of the service is the firm and the provider is an accountant/accounting firm, the beneficiaries are the people who rely on these audited reports to make their investment decisions. The consequences of collusion between the buyer and seller, or poor judgement on the service provider's part, can lead to serious consequences. There are several illustrations of this in corporate history, the recent example of Enron, or the case of the Global Trust Bank, exemplifies the problem. Furthermore, the benefit to the firm from having a credible, honest accountant may be less than the gain from a collusive one. We may see market failure in not just the market for accounting services, but also in related areas, like those of the markets for stocks and commercial paper.

Similar examples can probably be found for each and every professional service. These types of problems are then typically defined as the basis for market regulation or market intervention. However, the idiosyncratic nature of professional services now leads to the next level of difficulty. Conventional regulatory approaches, by focussing on prices, technologies and rates of return, are clearly inappropriate in dealing with these situations. The nature of service is so idiosyncratic that pricing of services, except in some limited aspects of service provision, is clearly not practical. Further specifications of technology and rates of return are similarly unproductive, as they are better suited for process activities. It is for this reason that, unlike other activities, a process of self-regulation has become a hallmark of this sector.

While there is no clear formal definition of self-regulation, it refers to things like codes of conduct and voluntary labelling initiatives, ethical and quality standards. Associations of professional service providers formulate the norms, standards or codes. Sometimes these associations have legal sanction, as in the case of the Bar council/medical council; in other cases, particularly in case of sub-specialities, they are voluntary. The advantages of self-regulation are primarily in the character of the service. Professional service requires specialised skills or training. Thus, only somebody, who is trained and skilled in this manner,

can evaluate the functioning of another professional. Where the association is sanctioned by law, membership of the association is necessary to practice the profession. Thus, the association can discipline its members by withdrawing their right to practice. In addition to formal discipline, the associations can bring moral and social pressure on their members to conform to these standards.

20.2 Competition Issues in Self Regulation

Before entering into a discussion of the issues in this section, a general caveat and disclaimer is in order. The ethical codes and conduct rules framed by the respective professional associations have, in general, the effect of reducing professional misconduct, improving disclosure of information, and improving client and social welfare. The examples, cited below, concern restrictions where the beneficial impact may be counter-balanced by competition concerns, which we will outline. It is not the case that such standards are unique to India, they have been, and are, being practised in other countries as well. But the critical issue is the need for a clear assessment of competitive impact. In some cases, the standards have been challenged and are in the process of being modified.[1]

20.2.1 Entry

The professional associations have an obligation to protect consumers from unqualified, unskilled persons, masquerading as professional service providers. For this purpose, the associations seek to certify qualification and competence of their members. This is done in two ways: some associations like those for Chartered Accountants, Company Secretaries and Cost Accountants conduct their own examinations whereas others, like the Bar Council and Medical Council, prescribe standards for training institutions and accept all qualified students as members. Both types of solutions raise questions. The first is a case where the council lays down standards for education, as in the case of the bar council for law. The problem here is that a number of universities and law colleges meet these standards only in a notional sense. The quality of instruction does not adhere to the standards expected. On the other hand, the ICAI style integrated course, offered by the institute takes a lot of time; and the training is not easily transferable,[2] in case the candidate opts out at an intermediate stage, unlike say, the possibility of switching to a science degree in medical training. A critical issue would be the opportunities given to those who have had their basic training in foreign universities. If the requirements imply a long period of coursework/apprenticeship, then this would be a significant barrier to a number of potential applicants in a globalised world. Indian professions do not have an explicit nationality requirement in their charters, but the absence of well-defined mechanisms, to recognise foreign training, is an implicit barrier.

Furthermore, Professionals have usually been required to practice as individuals or in partnerships with others in the same profession. The reason, usually given for these prohibitions, is to ensure the practitioner's personal responsibility to the client. The question of how this impacts the cost of doing business is not adequately addressed. The advantage of corporate forms is the advantage of raising funds, like equity. The question has been partly addressed by the idea of a limited liability partnership. But again, there appears to be no progress on this suggestion. In trying to understand the motivation and need for such reforms, it is instructive to examine the example in another professional service - "stock-broking". Stockbrokers, until recently, were functioning as partnerships regulated by a self-regulatory stock exchange. The consequence, of this and other public policies, was a relatively opaque, thinly traded system. Shifting to corporatised service providers has played an important role in deepening and strengthening the stock exchanges. While one cannot generalise, from such examples, it may be useful to examine alternatives to institutional assumptions.

There are explicit and implicit restrictions on the names that can be used in partnerships. There are also moves to explicitly restrict the use of foreign brand names[3]. This antipathy to brand names has some quality and efficiency implications. As has been seen in the case of other goods and services, brand identities help in quality control and facilitate consumer choice and decision-making. Furthermore, since brand identity is of a long-term nature, it promotes inter-temporal efficiency as well. The no-brand name strategy in India oddly creates a bias in favour of family or relational identities. The effect is to strengthen established family firms over new entrants to the profession.

The quality standards of the professions are an important tool in promoting market efficiency. It is important to see, that in their operation and implementation, they do not either unnecessarily limit entry or erode quality.

20.2.2 *Advertising*

There is a marked tendency for professional associations to restrict advertising by its members. A brief study of the guidelines issued by the associations for accountants, lawyers and doctors reveals all of them discourage or restrict advertising by its members.

Soliciting of patients, directly or indirectly, by a physician, by a group of physicians or by institutions or organisations is unethical. A physician shall not make use of him/her (or his/her name) as subject of any form, or manner, of advertising or publicity, through any mode, either alone or in conjunction with others, which is of such a character as to invite attention to him or to his professional position, skill, qualification, achievements, attainments, specialities, appointments, associations, affiliations or honours, and/or of such character as would ordinarily result in his self aggrandisement. [Indian Medical Council (Professional conduct, Etiquette and Ethics) Regulations, 2002].

Clause (7) - Practising member prohibited from advertising his professional attainments or services, or using any designation or expressions other than 'chartered accountant' on professional documents, visiting cards or sign boards, except permitted degree or title (ICAI Code of Ethics).

36. An advocate shall not solicit work or advertise, either directly or indirectly, whether by circulars, advertisements, touts, personal communications, interviews not warranted by personal relations, furnishing or inspiring newspaper comments or producing his photographs to be published in connection with cases in which he has been engaged or concerned. His sign-board or name-plate should be of a reasonable size. The sign-board, name-plate or stationery should not indicate that he is, or has been, President or Member of a Bar Council or of any Association, or that he has been associated with any person or organisation, or with any particular cause or matter, or that he specialises in any particular type of work, or that he has been a Judge or an Advocate General. (Bar Council of India Rules Chapter – II Standards of Professional Conduct and Etiquette).

These restrictions are justified on the ground of needing to protect the public from incompetents and from misleading information. The problem is, in a world with uninformed consumers, the restrictions on advertising have a number of anti-competitive effects. They restrict entry as the absence of information favours established firms. As a consequence there is also reduced price competition, and consumers are not adequately informed about specialists. Additionally, where referrals are necessary, the consumer is dependent on the advice of his primary consultant. This encourages the potential for collusive behaviour, and unethical practices like "kick-backs" and commissions.[4] For all of these reasons, especially given the asymmetric character of the information on professional services, the restriction on advertising seems counter-productive. In fact, given the intrusive character of other ethical standards, it is not clear why the professions do not opt for a method to lay down standards for informative advertising. This would mean that instead of outright bans, the associations could define clear parameters for truth in advertising; ruling out inducements, misleading claims, etc.

These types of restrictions are not unique to India. Till the 1970s, the American Medical Association's ethical standards prohibited physicians from engaging in various forms of advertising. In 1979, the Federal Trade Commission held that such restraints violated the antitrust laws.[5] Similarly, in the UK, during the 1970s, a number of references on advertising restrictions were referred to the monopolies commission, these covered cases relating to barristers/advocates; veterinary surgeons; surveyors; accountants; and stockbrokers. And in most of these cases, except those relating to the legal profession the restrictions were held to be anti-competitive.[6]

20.2.3 Price Competition/Collusion

In addition, the ethical standards often have clauses, which may facilitate collusion or reduce the possibility of explicit price competition. For example,

Clause (12) - Practising member prohibited from accepting a position as auditor, previously held by some other chartered accountant, in such conditions as to constitute under- cutting (ICAI Code of Ethics).

The impact of such clauses is to reduce the competitive pressure, and create a threat, on a firm seeking to promote lower costs. While price competition has its limitations and may impact quality, such embargoes can increase implicit collusion and raise customer costs. Given that the other standards explicitly address quality, it is not clear why there should be restrictions on pricing. In fact, we could ask for some mechanisms of transparent pricing, as in competitive bidding, say, for auditing contracts for large corporations.

20.2.4 Some Other Dimensions of Practice

In addition to conditions of entry, and information dissemination, some other standards have a bearing on market outcomes and innovation.

Both the accounting and legal professions restrict contingent fees.

Clause (10) - Practising member prohibited from charging or offering to charge, accepting or offering to accept, in respect of any professional employment, fees which are based on a percentage of profits or contingent upon the findings, or results of such employment, except permitted by the regulations (ICAI Code of Ethics).

20. An advocate shall not stipulate for a fee contingent on the results of litigation or agree to share the proceeds thereof. (Bar Council of India Rules Chapter – II Standards of Professional Conduct and Etiquette).

The bar is not significant in the case of accounting, as there is little risk associated with the service. However, in the case of the legal profession, this does have an effect on outcomes. By disallowing contingent fee contracts, the council raises the bar on liability cases. Where contingent fee cases are allowed, there is a significant rise in liability litigation. While this does have costs on Industry, it has played a major role in raising safety standards. It is true, that informal reports suggest a fair amount of unreported, or underhanded, contingent fee work takes place in insurance cases, especially those related to motor-vehicle claims. The problem with an official embargo is that it leaves clients at the mercy of unethical lawyers, who do not hesitate violating standards and are devoid of the protection associated with a legal, but regulated, system. An open contingent fee system would have the advantage that, like with advertising, it could be better regulated, and the consumers be offered protection from sub-standard professionals.

20.2.5 Nature of Practice

The ethical standards of Professional Conduct are formulated with certain assumptions about the nature of practice. Thus, in respect of legal services, the standards are centred largely around the litigative process, and with a view to regulating a profession focussed on legal and adversarial work. The effect of this approach is that the Advocates Act and the Rules of Professional Conduct do not appropriately or effectively regulate non-litigating lawyers, or set out a code of conduct appropriate and applicable to non-litigating transactional work and consultancies.[7]

Similarly, the medical standards have a view on the profession where an individual doctor deals with his patient. The standards are silent on the issue of group-care, or corporate or institutional practice. Thus, for instance, a critical requirement in obstetrics is the presence of a paediatrician to handle the post-delivery care of the new-born child. Most Gynaecologists operate in teams with identified paediatricians; it is a matter of assessment as to whether this would constitute a tied-sale. The rise of the medical practice in a corporate structure, and the role of doctors in promoting such corporate ventures, ends up in a regulatory black hole.

A related concern is the embargo on multi-disciplinary practices. This is most marked in the law and accounting services. For example,

Clause (2) - Practising member prohibited to pay or allow any share, commission or brokerage or profits of his professional business, to any person other than a member of the Institute or a partner or retired partner or the legal representative of deceased partner (ICAI Code of Ethics).

Clause (3) - Practising member prohibited to accept or agreeing to accept any part of the profits of the professional work of lawyer, auctioneer, broker or other agent who is not a member of the Institute (*ICAI Code of Ethics*).

Clause (4) - Practising member prohibited to enter into partnership with any person other than a practising member or members of recognised foreign professional bodies (ICAI Code of Ethics).

Likewise in legal services

2. *An advocate shall not enter into a partnership or any other arrangement for sharing remuneration with any person or legal practitioner who is not an advocate.* (Bar Council of India Rules Chapter – II Standards of Professional Conduct and Etiquette).[8]

However, as is obvious to any student of corporate consultancy, the nature of consultancy work requires collaborative advice from both professions. In value terms this maybe a major growth area for both professions. Once again, by embargoing the phenomenon, the associations have effectively restricted innovation. It is not clear why this standard benefits clients - since the formal right to audit or litigate is still regulated by the association, why should there be a need for a further restriction on the character of group practice?

The problem, in all these examples, is that standards have been evolved with old-fashioned perspectives on the nature and character of professional practice. These antiquated views restrict innovation and leave emerging areas of the market poorly or completely unregulated.

20.2.6 Regulatory Capture

The problem of capture of the regulator by the regulated is one of the sources of failure in all forms of regulation. In the case of self-regulation, since the regulated entity is, itself, in charge of the regulation process, the possibility of capture is enhanced. The possibility of this risk is borne out by examining one classic example that has ended up in the courts - strikes by lawyers. This matter was examined and conclusively dealt with by the Supreme Court of India in the case "Ex-Capt. Harish Uppal *Vs.* Union of India and Another [(2003) 2 SCC 45]". The judgement was pronounced by the Constitution Bench of the court, after a number of cases on the right of lawyers to strike. Some extracts, from this judgement, make powerful reading

> The above-mentioned Interim Order was passed in the hope that with self-restraint, and self-regulation, the lawyers would retrieve their profession from lost social respect. The hope has not fructified. Unfortunately, strikes and boycott calls are becoming a frequent spectacle. Strikes, boycott calls, and even unruly and unbecoming conduct are becoming a frequent spectacle. On the slightest pretence, strikes and/or boycott calls are resorted to. The judicial system is being held to ransom. Administration of law and justice is threatened. The rule of law is undermined.

The court observed that the bar had not restrained the lawyers; and in one case the state bar council had submitted that lawyers had a right to go on strike, or give a call for boycott, and that Courts had no power of supervision over the conduct of lawyers.

The court rejected these arguments and held that *"lawyers have no right to go on strike or give a call for boycott and even they cannot go on a token strike... It is held that no Bar Council, or Bar Association, can permit calling of a meeting for purposes, of considering, a call for strike or boycott, and requisition, if any, for such meetings must be ignored ...The functions of the Bar Council of India are to regulate proper functioning of the Bars and members thereof - It must frame appropriate Rules to deal with the situation arising due to frequent strikes of advocates"*

The ruling examined the various reasons, Bar councils had noted, for going on strike and held that most of them were baseless. The point of this example is to illustrate a wide spread unethical practice, and the unwillingness of the bar to restrict or discipline the profession. In cases like strikes, by virtue of limiting transfer of jurisdiction, the objective is not very different from cartels seeking to share the market. In fact, from the viewpoint of anti-trust, strikes by professional service providers have a flavour, similar to refusal to deal.

The larger question is the quality and nature of the disciplinary process of the respective associations, and their willingness to address customer concerns. In some cases, like accountancy, ethical standards have a public good character in that the benefits extend to a larger, dependent society. In this context, the failure to enforce standards has an impact on society at large. The most striking example of such a failure would be the recent collapse of Enron and the role played by its auditors in that event. Typically, such societal consequences may not be within the ambit of competition authorities, more imaginative use of clauses on collusion may be worth exploring. Moreover, by focussing on the associations as well as on consumer welfare and efficiency, the competition authority can bring to bear a class of disciplinary devices not available through ordinary civil or criminal challenges.

In nutshell, while ethical standards as a whole seek to promote consumer welfare and mitigate the effects of asymmetric and imperfect information, there are elements, which have the effect or the potential to promote anti-competitive behaviour. Thus, there is a clear role for a market regulator to assess the competitive impact of regulatory standards.

20.3 Experience of Other Countries in Self Regulation[9]

In the US, the anti-trust laws have been applied to the professions since the landmark Supreme Court decision in *Goldfarb Vs. Virginia*. Goldfarb established that the Sherman Act contained no exemption for the professions. Similarly, in the UK, the anti-monopoly provisions of the competition act apply to professional service providers. In France, the *Conseil de la concurrence* has made clear that professional organisation rules may not violate the rules as laid down in the competition law, notably those against price fixing agreements. These examples can be extended to many more. Furthermore, as we have seen in the discussion earlier, these powers have been used to restrict or embargo standards that have an anti-competitive impact.

In addition to formal actions and investigations of practices in the professions, many OECD competition authorities have been active in advocating more liberal regimes and intervening in official enquiries, to attempt to obtain changes in anti-competitive rules operated in certain professions. Thus, in addition to its explicit regulatory function, the US Federal Trade Commission

staff has submitted *amicus curiae* briefs to state, and self-regulatory, entities on competition issues relating to a variety of professions, including accountants, lawyers and architects.

These regulatory efforts have been complemented by the work in the WTO, where the working party on professional services have produced disciplines on domestic regulation, which seek to reduce barriers to entry through an application of the GATS rules on National Treatment.

20.4 Conclusion

In the absence of an effective debate on competition policy, the effectiveness of self-regulatory professional service associations has not been analysed in India. The purpose of this limited review is to illustrate the potential for anti-competitive consequences, from certain regulatory assumptions.

The professional service associations have played an invaluable role in developing and deepening critical professional services. However, as we have seen, their regulatory function has often involved assumptions and restrictions on behaviour that have not been consistent with principles of market functioning. Thus, restrictions on advertising and entry may not have given the desire outcomes to customers. The associations certainly have a transparent and open process for formulating ethical standards; they do not include market assessment, or have a way of assessing consumer impact of their norms.

Section 21 of the competition act provides for the possibility for Statutory authorities, which would include professional regulators as we have noted, to seek the advice of the commission. A more pro-active commission, by using its *suo-motu* powers to analyse anti-competitive behaviour, may make such advice-seeking more fruitful. Furthermore, in the case of regulatory capture, or failure, the competition authority, through its powers to fine, may provide an additional disciplinary device to improve regulatory functioning.

Notes

1. See the Report on Competition in Professional Services, Roundtables on Competition Policy OECD 2000 for some examples.

2. One must note that in recent years the institute has permitted the foundation courses to be done along side the undergraduate degree. The Institute could collaborate with universities/UGC to design curriculum that matches the requirements of the institute. In that case all the institute needs to arrange is the qualifying examinations.

3. See for instance the White Paper on Multinational Accounting Firms Operating in India published by The Chartered Accountants' Action Committee for Level Playing Field, http://www.ca-actioncommittee.org/content/index.html or the agitation against foreign law firms in Mumbai and Delhi.

4. Both of these are more widespread than the associations would like to acknowledge. In fact commissions promote collusion and unnecessary referrals.

5. Self Regulation and Antitrust Robert Pitofsky, Chairman, Federal Trade Commission, D. C. Bar Association Symposium, February 18, 1998.

6. OECD Report on Professional Services.

7. Report on "Trade in Legal Services" Dr. N.L. Mitra unpublished

8. In medicine the position is somewhat ambiguous since doctors are not discouraged from cooperating with other specialists and paramedical staff but they are discouraged from accepting rebates and commissions. Though in their case it is not clear what happens if they constitute a joint practice with other professions. In any case as we have noted the medical ethics are silent on the institutions of practice.

9. See the Report on Competition in Professional Services, Roundtables on Competition Policy OECD 2000 for a fuller description and details of the competition regimes in other OECD countries.

References

Report on *Competition in Professional Services*, Roundtables on Competition Policy OECD 2000.

Indian Medical Council (Professional Conduct, Etiquette and Ethics) Regulations, 2002.

Institute of Chartered Accountants of India (ICAI) Code of Ethics.

White Paper on *Multinational Accounting Firms Operating in India*, The Chartered Accountants' Action Committee for Level Playing Field, http://www.ca-actioncommittee.org/content/index.html

Bar Council of India Rules, "Chapter – II Standards of Professional Conduct and Etiquette."

Self Regulation and Antitrust, Robert Pitofsky, Chairman, Federal Trade Commission, D.C. Bar Association Symposium, February 18, 1998.

Report on Trade in Legal Services, Dr. N.L. Mitra unpublished.

Part VIII

Competition Policy in
New Economy Areas

21 Competition Issues in Information Technology Sector

K.J. Joseph

21.1 Introduction

It is widely recognised that Information Communication Technology (ICT), and associated innovations, could be instrumental in enhancing efficiency, productivity, competitiveness and growth, both in the developing and developed world. But as of now, the access to the new technology, and the capability to develop and harness it for development, is unequally distributed both between and within countries.

The current unequal access to Information Technlogy (IT) notwithstanding, it has been argued that in the current era of globalisation, the ability to harness this technology improves the capability of developing country firms to withstand competition from multinational corporations, or in developing partnerships with them. At the same time, IT poses a potential threat, that if unable to harness this new source of wealth, developing country firms will fall even more behind the developed countries (Pohjola 2001), resulting in an additional digital threat to development. In this context, it may appear paradoxical that a developing country, like India, has emerged as a global player in the ICT sector, showing remarkable vibrancy in terms of output and export growth.[1]

If the available statistics are any indication, the ICT software and service exports, from India, recorded an annual compound growth rate of over 60 per cent in rupee terms (at current prices), and around 45 per cent in dollar terms, during the last decade. A reduction in the observed growth rate in the recent past, notwithstanding, the IT and software sector has been able to maintain a growth rate of over 20 per cent even since 2000. This is unprecedented, not only in terms of the magnitude of the observed growth rate, but also in terms of its stability. As a result, about 0.6 million people working in India's information technology sector, today, create approximately $16 billion worth of wealth every year. Estimates show that IT exports during 2003-04 climbed up to $12.3 billion despite the recessionary conditions in the principal markets, like the US, and the less-than-friendly market environment faced by the ITES-BPO services. India exports IT and IT-enabled services to over 180 countries, and Indian firms are training people in IT in 55 countries. A single Indian firm - NIIT - today runs 100 training centres in, of all places, China! The Government of India, itself, is setting up training centres in other countries.[2] These achievements become all the more striking, considering that they were realised almost entirely by local firms.[3]

Nonetheless, India is yet to emerge as a major user of ICT in the domestic sectors of the economy. This, in turn, has to be seen *inter alia* in the context of competitive environment, both in the software and hardware segment. The new technology is considered as instrumental in enhancing international competitiveness, which is a *sine qua non* for survival in a globalised economy. The present paper explores, within the constraints set by data, competition issues in the ICT sector; and reflects its bearing on the diffusion of ICT into other sectors of the economy. In accomplishing this objective, the paper begins with an overview of the recent trends in the ICT sector.

21.2 Overview of the IT Sector

The value of output of India's software and service sector increased by more than 18 times, from less than $ 0.83 billion, in 1994-95, to $ 15.5 billion in 2003-04. During the same period, the software and service exports increased by more than 25 times, indicating the predominant role of exports in the growth process. Given the high growth of this sector, the share of the software and service sector (in total exports) increased almost seven-fold (from 3.2% to 21.3%) during 1996-2003. Also, as a percentage of GDP, the software and service sector, today, accounts for over 2.6 per cent, as compared to 0.5 per cent in 1996-97—an increase of over five times (Figure 21.1).

FIGURE 21.1

Share of Software and Services in GDP and Exports (in per cent)

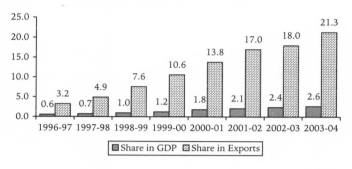

More importantly, India has established credibility in the international software and services market, which, in turn, makes India an attractive location for the off-shoring of services. The credibility has been established on account of the better quality services, and there is hardly an IT firm in India that does not hold necessary quality certification. As of December 2003, 65 IT firms are holding SEI CMM level-5 certification. In addition, it has been argued that the IT sector, has had a spill-over effect, in terms of promoting new entrepreneurial and management practices, in other sectors of the economy (Arora and Athreya 2002).

However, even today, the software and service sector is confined mainly to a few metropolitan cities, like Bangalore, Delhi, Mumbai, Hyderabad and Chennai, thus, remaining as enclaves with limited links with the rest of the economy (Kumar 2000 D'Costa 2002). At the same time, it may be noted that various state governments have initiated policy measures to attract investment, from metropolitan areas, to second and third level towns.

21.2.1 Changing Mode of Software and Service Exports

In the early years of its development, the software and service exports from the country, was carried out mostly in the form of onsite development (Heeks 1996). However, with the setting up of a number of Software Technology Parks, and liberalised policies towards the telecom sector, that led to the entry of a number of

private sector telecom companies, there has been a significant shift away from onsite development. Today nearly 60 per cent of the exports takes the form of offshore development (Figure 21.2). However, the figure also indicates that the share of software products and packages, wherein the profit margins and value-addition are known to be higher, has shown a decline in recent years. To illustrate, the share of software products and packages has declined from about 9.5 per cent in 1995, to 3.2 per cent in 2004.

FIGURE 21.2

Changing Mode of Software and Service Exports

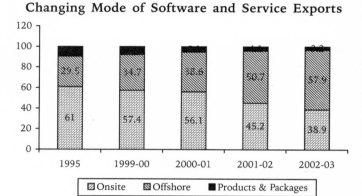

In terms of the destination of exports, in 2003-04, the US accounted for 67.8 per cent, followed by the UK, with 14 per cent (Electronics and Software Export Promotion Council 2004). The share of Asian countries is estimated at about 8 per cent, of which almost 3 per cent accounts for the Japanese market.

The higher export growth, during the last decade notwithstanding, it has been argued that Indian firms, by and large, operate at the low end of the value chain (Arora et al., 2001 D'Costa 2002). But a study (Joseph and Abraham 2002), that estimated firm level Index of Technological Competence, has shown that there has been upward mobility of firms in terms of their competence.[4] Similar conclusions were drawn by another study (Kumar 2001b) that explored the issue by analysing the value added per employee, profitability and net foreign exchange outflow.

21.2.2 Declining Growth of Software and the Rise of IT Enabled Services

The higher export growth of the 1990s, however, was followed by a decline since 2001 (Figure 21.3). Data obtained from the Department of Information Technology (2004) indicates that, while exports recorded an annual compound growth rate of over 54 per cent during 1996-2000, growth rate during the following three years was only of the order of 25 per cent. The period, since 2000, also witnessed the emergence of IT Enabled Services as a major component of Software and Service exports from the country. In 1999-00, the total ITES exports was only of the order of $565 million, and it is estimated to have increased to $3.6 billion in 2003-04. Thus viewed, the recorded growth rate of software exports, during 2000-03, was only of the order of 17.6 per cent. Hence, the upward trend in the annual growth rate since 2001 has been mostly on account of the increase in IT Enabled Services (ITES), and the share of ITES in total software and service exports more than doubled from about 14 per cent (2000) to more than 29 per cent in 2003-04.

FIGURE 21.3

Rate of Growth in Domestic and Export of Software and Services

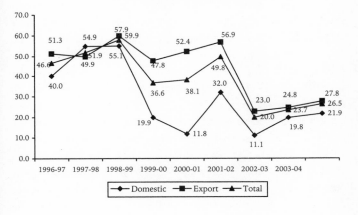

21.2.3 Use of ICT in the Domestic Economy

While the availability of reliable data makes any serious analysis, of the use of ICT by other sectors of the economy, difficult, the available evidence tends to suggest that the performance, in this respect, has been less impressive. This is especially when one compares it with the performance record in terms of export. In 1997-98, for example, the Nasscom estimate on the domestic market was of the order of $1152 million, and the export estimate was of the order of $1759 million. Thus, the domestic market accounted for about 65 per cent of the exports. As we move to 2003-04, the domestic market increased by $3374 million and the export was estimated at $12,200 million, leading to a situation wherein the domestic market accounts for only about 28 per cent of exports. At this juncture, it is worthwhile to note that countries like China and Brazil, though not known for their export performance, are

having a large software sector, almost comparable in size to that of India, catering mostly to the domestic market.

The limited use of software in the domestic sectors of the economy, in India, has been an outcome of a number of factors. To begin with, it may be seen from the national approach towards the use of computers, especially during the formative years of the computer and electronics industry in the country. In 1969, the Ministry of Labour, Employment and Rehabilitation, set up a high level committee to advise the Government on computerisation. The resolution, setting up the committee, noted the following:

"Government's policy in this regard has been that automation could be introduced as a selective basis... The criteria which determined such selectivity need to be more clearly defined, and for this purpose the Government have decided to set up a committee" (as quoted in Subramanian, 1992, p. 13).

The committee favoured a positive approach, and recognised the legitimate use of computers, in the fields of education, science, defence, and even in some commercial and industrial establishments. But the strict regulatory measures that they prescribed were contrary to their positive approach. It was laid down that all the computerisation proposals had to be scrutinised by two experts, case by case, and a justification report furnished.

As late as in 1984, while the Government adopted a liberalised policy towards the computer industry, the approach of Government, towards the use of computers, had not undergone any major change. To a question raised, in Parliament in 1984, on the use of computers, it was stated that the policy announced in 1978, which was highly restrictive, continued to be the basis for the induction of computer technology in India.[5]

The approach towards the use of new technology, however, has changed since then. Yet India, even today, is not known as a major user of IT in different sectors of the economy, despite the presence of a large number of e-governance projects initiated by the Government and IT initiatives undertaken by different stakeholders. The manufacturing sector, for example, wherein IT use could be instrumental in bringing down cost and enhancing international competitiveness, accounts for only about 15 per cent of the total IT market (Table 21.1).

Studies that analysed the product market (spending induced real appreciation) and factor market (resource movement effect) implications of IT export boom, have pointed towards a dampening effect on the cost and competitiveness of other sectors, through the resource movement effect. Thus, while IT has the potential of contributing towards productivity and growth, the export-oriented growth strategy of ICT, in India, seems to also have had adverse impacts on other sectors competing for skilled manpower, at least in the short run (Joseph and Harilal 2001).

TABLE 21.1

Distribution of Domestic IT Market Across Different Sectors, 2002-03

(Per cent)

IT/Telecom	22
Government	14
Energy	6
Small Office/Home	11
Education	11
Banking and Finance	21
Manufacturing	15

Source: Nasscom (2004).

The crucial issue is how to reconcile the low diffusion of IT across different sectors of the domestic economy, despite the country having an internationally competitive software industry. To address this issue, one needs to examine the present market structure and competitiveness of the IT market, both in hardware and software.

21.3 Market Structure and Competition in the IT Market

The IT industry is a multi-product industry, comprising of both hardware and software. IT hardware consists of a large number of products like computers, peripherals, network equipment, communication equipment, and so on. Similarly, in the case of software, there are software services and software products. Lack of detailed data prevents one to make a detailed analysis of the market structure and competition. Nonetheless, within the limits set by data availability, one could make a tentative exploration of software and computer hardware.

21.3.1 Computer Hardware

The computer industry in India has passed through different phases. In the 1960s, foreign firms dominated the industry, whereas the 1970's was a period of public sector domination. The 1980s witnessed the emergence of private, domestic firms dominating the industry.[6] The liberalised policies of the 1990s that

removed the entry barriers to the foreign firms, coupled with the emergence of software boom have had the following effects. First, many of the domestic hardware firms, like Wipro, HCL and others, who dominated the hardware sector during the 1980s, have diversified into software and service exports. Secondly, with the opening of the domestic economy, today, all the world leaders in hardware sector are having their presence in the domestic market. Thirdly, with easy availability of SKD/CKD kits with removal of tariff barriers, there has been a mushrooming of the non-branded market.

According to the Manufacturers Association of Information Technology (MAIT), the total sales of personal computers in the country, in 2003-04, reached 3 million - recording an annual growth rate of 32 per cent over the previous year. Indian brands account for 21 per cent, and the foreign firms' share is 26 per cent. The non-branded segment accounts for about 53 per cent of the market.[7] Thus, there appears to be strong competition between three major sets of actors. The foreign firms have been able to increase their share, and almost all the leading players in the world market like DELL, IBM, Acer, HP, etc., have their presence in the domestic market. Though there are a large number of domestic firms in the field, none of them appears to be enjoying any dominant position. In fact, it could be argued that the presence of a strong non-branded sector, accounting for more than 50 per cent of the total market, acts as a major factor in creating a highly competitive market structure. Hence, while the presence of a non-branded segment implies revenue loss for the Government, they appear to serve a very socially useful role as the catalysts in competition, in addition to generating employment.

The presence of a competitive market structure is evident from the fact that the high growth, recorded during the last year, has been an outcome of reduced custom duties, which in turn has been passed onto the consumers in the form of lower prices. To illustrate, the output growth during 2002-2003 has been about 32 per cent. This was in response to a reduction in prices (of the order of 8 to 12 per cent) on account of the cut in excise duty (from 16 per cent to 8 per cent), and the removal of the special additional duty (4 per cent). Had the industry not been competitive, the effect of reduced duty structure would not have reflected in prices. On the whole, going by the available evidence, the hardware segment of the IT industry appears to present characteristics of a highly competitive market structure.

21.3.2 *Software*

Computer hardware today, however, is a relatively less important segment of the IT industry. The more important segment, which facilitates the harnessing of new technology for development, is the software. The software, in turn, could be broadly divided into operating systems and applications software, either taking the form of software services or products. Each of these product segments has varying market structures and competitive environments.

In the case of operating systems, it is well known that a single firm in the world dominates the market for it. Microsoft operating systems – "Windows" - controls over 90 per cent of the desktop software market. Lack of competition in this crucial segment has its effect, not only on the price at which it is available, but also sets limits on the development of application software, based on this operating system, because of the lack of access to source codes. The interaction of both these factors leads to a situation wherein the new technology is made inaccessible to the domestic market of a country, like India, with low per capita income, leading to low domestic demand. High prices of software also induces software piracy, which dampens any efforts in the development of software products for the domestic market.

At the same time, the Indian ICT firms, given these constraints and having the option of either focusing on the local or foreign market, naturally opted for the booming foreign market. Also, the state policies and institutional interventions have provided a highly conducive environment for the exploitation of export opportunities. Thus, the increased export orientation (mostly catering to the high-income countries that could afford the high price of software) and the neglect of the domestic market, by the Indian ICT firms, has to be seen in the context of the existing market structure and competitive environment.

The software service is a highly labour intensive and skill intensive activity. No wonder software services fit well with India's endowments, and have emerged as a major player. India's software service sector consists of over 3000 firms and appears to present a long tailed distribution, wherein 7 firms in 2002-03 are found to be having an export of over 1000 crore, whereas 2644 firms were found to be too small with an export of less than 10 crore. (Table 21.2).

It is also found that the share of the top four firms in exports is only about 26 per cent, and even the top 19 firms listed in Table 21.3 accounted for about 40 per cent of the total exports. Given the fact that Indian firms are mostly export oriented, and they have to compete with large multinational firms, there appears to be the need for reaping scale economies to remain competitive. This calls for consolidation, such that Indian firms are able to enhance international competitiveness and are also able to venture into risky, and investment incentive, areas like software products. The recent trend, in terms of the incidence of a large number of mergers and take-overs, is to be seen in the context of the industry's attempt at consolidation. Our inquiry has shown that since 2003, 19 foreign firms were taken over by the Indian firms, other Indian firms acquired 13 Indian firms, and foreign firms acquired 8 Indian firms.

TABLE 21.2

Size Distribution of Indian Software Firms (2002-2003)

Size Class (crore)	No. of Firms	Share in Total
Less than 10	2644	87.23
10 to 50	244	8.05
50 to 100	73	5.71
100 to 250	43	1.40
250 to 500	15	0.49
500 to 1000	5	0.16
More than 1000	7	0.23
Total	3031	100.00

Source: Nasscom 2004.

TABLE 21.3

List of Top Software and Services Exporting Firms (2002-2003)

Name of the Company	Export (Rs. Mill)	Share
Tata Consultancy Services	4545.3	9.25
Infosys Technologies Ltd	3543.5	7.21
Wipro Technologies	2787.4	5.67
Satyam Computer Services Ltd	2003.3	4.07
HCL Technologies Ltd	1530.5	3.11
Patni Computer Systems Ltd	914.0	1.86
Mahindra British Telecom Ltd	634.7	1.29
IFlex Solutions	593.3	1.21
HCL Perot Systems Ltd	449.0	0.91
NIIT Ltd	426.3	0.86
Mascot Systems Ltd	421.0	0.85
Digital Globalsoft Ltd	415.3	0.84
Mastek Ltd	374.4	0.76
Polaris Software	367.2	0.74
Birlasoft Ltd	346.4	0.70
Mphasis BFL Ltd	335.6	
Pentasoft Technologies Ltd	296.5	
Hexaware Technologies Ltd	257.9	
Tata Infotech Ltd	256.0	

Source: Nassscom 2004.

On the demand side, the Indian market is less sophisticated and the domestic demand has been rather limited. The lower demand has to be seen in the context of higher prices for both software and hardware. While the policy reforms in the recent past have had the effect of bringing down hardware prices considerably, the same has not taken place in the case of software when compared to the income levels in India. It also appears that there is a lack of awareness among different segments in the Indian economy, in terms of the advantages of using ICT, which in turn calls for awareness creation, and the necessary training.

The "open source," or "free[8]," software movement is an attempt at making the software segment more competitive, and promotes the development of application software. India, being a country with abundant supply of skilled manpower, is well endowed to promote the development of open source software. As in the case of most products, demand constraint is bound to set limits to such initiatives. In such context, if past experience is any indication, government policy could play a significant role, which could make the software segment more competitive in structure. To begin with, government, being one of the major users, could promote open source software by opting for open source instead of the proprietary software. Secondly, government could subsidise the development and use of software applications, based on open source.

For promoting the use of ICT, it is imperative that the Indian IT companies acquire domain expertise, in various industry verticals. This calls for greater interaction among the ICT firms and the user segments. In inducing such interaction, and the development of domain expertise, the state policy could pay a constructive role. This could take the form of extending the incentives, today offered to software exports, to the domestic market as well, such that at least some of the firms that are, today, focussing on the foreign market turn to the domestic market.

First, from the software side, the state policy should explicitly promote the use of open source software and provide special incentives for such projects. Secondly, for promoting the domestic use of new technology - it is worthwhile to consider its development on par with any innovative activity, and receive all the incentives enjoyed by firms, undertaking in-house R&D, for the development of new products or processes. Thirdly from the hardware side, there are innovations like "simputer" that need to be further encouraged, such that the hardware prices could be brought down.

21.4 Concluding Observations

During the last decade, India has emerged as a major player in the field of information communication technology and, today, the IT sector makes significant contribution, not only to the GDP of the country but also to its export earning. The unprecedented growth performance of the IT sector, in terms of its export earning, not withstanding, the use of this technology in the domestic economy appears to be less remarkable. The efficiency and growth, of many sectors of the economy, could be enhanced, by harnessing the new technology. This, *inter alia* depends on the competitive environment and other strategies adopted by both IT firms, and the using sectors. Therefore, the present study looked at the nature and extent of competition in India's information technology. In accomplishing this objective, the study began with an overview of the recent growth performance of the IT sector, and the use of new technology in the domestic economy. This was followed by an analysis of the present structure of the IT software and hardware sectors, with a view to highlight the extent of competition that exists today.

Our preliminary inquiry suggests that, in the case of hardware, with the removal of entry barriers, almost all the leading players in the world market have a presence in India. The removal of tariff barriers and the presence of a large non-branded market, act as sources of increased competition. The situation appears to be different in the case of software. The high market concentration in some of the software segments, especially in operating systems, seems to have the effect of not only increasing software prices but also dampening the development of applications software, on account of the lack of access to source codes. The high price tends to make software beyond the reach of many, and adversely affects demand. In addition, it also promotes software piracy, which acts as a major disincentive for the development of software for the domestic market. The above factors, along with the lack of inducement mechanism to induce the IT firms to exploit the domestic market, has had the effect of limited use of IT in other sectors of the economy.

Given that the state played a proactive role, so far, in the development of the IT and software service sectors in the economy (Kumar and Joseph 2004), the paper makes the case for active state involvement in addressing these issues. To begin with, the study underscores the need for creating a more competitive environment in the software sector *inter alia* by promoting the open source software. Towards this end, the state could provide appropriate incentives for the promotion of open source software, and create demand by promoting its use in all the e-governance projects. In addition, the incentives and concessions offered to the export market may be extended to those firms developing software for the domestic market as well, such that the Indian ICT firms work together with other sectors of the economy and develop the needed domain expertise. From the hardware side, innovations, like "simputer," need to be encouraged such that hardware becomes more affordable and leads to greater demand.

Notes

1. This has attracted the attention of researchers and there are a large number of studies focusing on the different aspects of ICT growth. An illustrative list includes (Heeks 1996, Kumar 2001, Joseph and Harilal 2001, Arora et al., 2001, Nath and Hazra 2002).

2. See, the three-part article on Indian IT industry by India's former IT Minister Arun Shourie (2004a, 2004b, 2004c).

3. Out of the top twenty software and service firms in India in 1998-99 only six were subsidiaries of foreign companies (Arora and Athreya, 2002).

4. Since the conventional measures of innovation like R&D has its limits in capturing innovation in a service sector like ICT, the study developed an Index of Claimed Technological Competence (ICTC) using firm level information on their areas of specialization. The theoretical base of the index has been drawn from the literature on technological opportunity.

5. Ram Vilas Paswan, 'Computerisation Policy in the Country', IPAG Journal, Vol. 11, New Delhi, August 1984, p. 742, Lok Sabha Question, No, 4142, answered on 21 March, 1984.

6. See in this context Grieco (1984) BICP (1989) Joseph (1997).

7. See for details http://www.mait.com/industry.asp

8. Stallman clarifies that the word 'free' pertains to freedom, not price. "You may or may not pay for a program," he says. "Either way, once you have the software, you have three freedoms. First, the freedom to copy the program and give it away to friends and co-workers; second, the freedom to change the program, by having the full source code; third, the freedom to distribute an improved version, and thus help build this community." See for details, http://www.networkmagazineindia.com/200108/inperso2.htm

References

Arora, A., Arunachalam V.S., Asundi J. and Ronald F. (2001). "The Indian Software Services Industry" *Research Policy*, Vol. 30 (3), 1267-87.

Arora A. and Athreya S. (2002). "The Software Industry and India's Economic Development," *Information Economics and Policy*, Vol. 14, pp 25-273.

Bureau of Industrial Costs and Prices (1989). *Report on Computer and Peripherals*, Government of India, New Delhi.

D'Costa, A.P. (2003). "Uneven and Combined Development: Understanding India's Software Exports," *World Development* 31(1): 211-226.

Government of India (1985). "New Computer Policy" *The Gazette of India*, August 31, 1985.

———. (1986). *Policy on Computer Software Exports, Software Development and Training*, Department of Electronics, New Delhi.

Grieco, J. (1984). *Between Dependency and Autonomy: India's Experience with the International Computer Industry*, University of California Press, Berkeley, CA.

Heeks, R. (1996). *India's Software Industry: State Policy, Liberalisation and Industrial Development*, Sage Publications, New Delhi, Thousand Oaks, London.

India, Department of Electronics (1972). *Annual Report*, Department of Electronics, New Delhi.

India, NTIT&SD (1998). *IT Action Plan (in three volumes)*, New Delhi, National Taskforce on Information Technology and Software Development, http://it-taskforce.nic.in/

India, MIT (2000a). *Annual Report 1999-2000*, Ministry of Information Technology, Govt. of India.

———. (2000b). *Action Taken Report of the National Task Force on Information Technology and Software Development*, IT Action Plan: Part I.

Joseph K.J. (1997). *Industry Under Economic Liberalisation: The Case of Indian Electronics*, Sage Publications, New Delhi.

———. (2002). "Growth of ICT and ICT for Development: Realities of the Myths of Indian Experience," *Discussion Paper No. 2002/78*, WIDER-UNU August, http://www.wider.unu.edu/publications/publications.htm

Joseph, K.J. and Harilal, K.N. (2001). "Structure and Growth of India's IT Exports: Implications of an Export-Oriented Growth Strategy," *Economic and Political Weekly*, Vol. 36, No. 34, pp 3263-70.

Joseph K.J. and Vinoj Abraham (2002). "Moving up or lagging behind in Technology? An Analysis of India's ICT Sector," Paper Presented at the International Seminar on *ICTs and Indian Development - Processes, Prognoses and Policies*, Organised by the Institute for Human Development, New Delhi and Institute of Social Studies, The Hague, Nov 9-11, 2002, Bangalore. (Forthcoming in Aswini Saith (ed) *ICTs and Indian Development*).

Kramer, K.L. and Dedrick, J. (2001). "Information Technology and Economic Development: Results and Policy Implications of Cross-Country Studies," in Pohjola M. (ed) *Information Technology, Productivity and Economic Growth*, Oxford University Press.

Kumar, N. (2001). "Indian Software Industry Development: International and National Perspective", *Economic and Political Weekly*, Vol 36, (44).

Kumar, N. and K.J. Joseph (2004). National Innovation Systems and India's IT Capability: Are there any Lessons for ASEAN New Comers?, RIS Discussion Paper No. 72/2004, Research and Information System for Non-Aligned and other Developing Countries, New Delhi.

NASSCOM (2004). *The I.T. Software and Services Industry in India: Strategic Review 2000*, National Association of Software and Service Companies, New Delhi.

Oberoi, S.S. (1991). "Software Technology Park: Concepts, Procedures and Status," *Electronics Information and Planning*, Vol. 19, No. 3 pp 42-46.

Parthasarathi, A. and K.J. Joseph (2002). "Limits to Innovation with Strong Export Orientation: The Experience of India's Information Communication Technology Sector," *Science, Technology and Society*, Vol. 7, No. 1.

Pohjola, M. (2001a). "Information Technology and Economic Growth: Introduction and Conclusions" in Pohjola, M. (ed) *Information Technology, Productivity and Economic Growth*, Oxford University Press.

Shourie, A. (2004a). "In Infotech, We have a Headstart So Let's Not Put Up Our Feet" *Indian Express* January 3, 2004, New Delhi.

———. (2004b). "Indian Infotech Needs to Partner East Europe, Target China," *Indian Express* January 3, 2004, New Delhi.

———. (2004c). "IT's Written, Now Just Dot the Is, Cross the Ts, *Indian Express* January 5 New Delhi.

Subramanian C. (1992). *India and the Computer*, Oxford University Press, New Delhi.

22 Implications of Competition Policy on Biotechnology Industry in India

A. Damodaran

22.1 The Structure of Biotechnology Industry in India

India's biotechnology segment is emerging as one of the fastest growing industries, reckoned in terms of the volumes of investment attracted in recent years. During 2003-04, India's biotech sector is estimated to have attracted private investments to the tune of US$140mn. Infrastructure and R & D account for nearly 80 per cent of these investments. The two significant factors, which lie at the base of India's biotechnology potential, are the scientific and technical pool of human resources, and the rich biodiversity of the country. With an interesting demographic profile and a large agriculture sector, India also affords a large market base for new biotechnology products.

It is estimated that the total biotech industry in 2003-04 in India was US$720mn, according to the most authentic survey on the sector carried out by the biotech magazine BioSpectrum, along with the industry association, ABLE (Association of Biotechnology-Led Enterprises). The industry grew by 39 per cent. The industry is made up of approximately 235 companies, the majority of which commenced operations after 1999. In terms of their presence, the bio-pharma sector accounted for 76 per cent of the biotech industry, followed by bio-services (8.5 per cent), bio-industrial (7.5 per cent), bio-agri (5.5 per cent), and bio-informatics (2 per cent). The bio-services sector includes clinical research and related, contracted, research programmes (Kulkarni, 2003).

It is estimated that India's market size, for biotech products and services, would attain a level of US$1.5bn in 2007 and would leap to US$4.5bn by 2010. Exports of biotech products would add another US$4.5bn,

making India's biotech industry a US$9bn giant by 2010. India has acquired competence in the areas of bioprocess engineering, downstream processing and isolation methods, bio-material extracts, re-combinant DNA technology, and in the fabrication of bio-processing equipments including bio-reactors (ibid).

22.1.1 Bio-Pharma Sector

The vaccines segment is the most dynamic one in the bio-pharma area. It is estimated that vaccines account for US$100mn, and registered a growth of 27 per cent in 2004 as compared to the previous year (ibid). There is growing demand for new generation, and combination, vaccines such as Hepatitis 'A' and 'B', as well as rDNA and nucleic acid vaccines. With this growth, it is expected that bio-pharma companies such as Bharat Biotech, Bharat Serums, Biological E, Haffkine Bio-Pharmaceutical, Panacea, Pfizer, Serum Institute of India, Shanta Biotechnics, SmithKline Beecham and Wockhardt will achieve quantum jumps in turnover volumes in future. The second important segment in the bio-pharma sector is therapeutics, with a sales turnover of US$93mn in 2003. Biocon, Eli Lilly, and Wockhardt are the lead players here. The diagnostics sales market, at US$22mn in 2003, is the third important segment. The major firms are Bharat Biotech, Qualigens Diagnostics, Span Diagnostics, J. Mitra, and xCyton Diagnostics. There is a serious effort being made by these diagnostics industries, to bring in molecular medicines for cancer and cardiovascular disorders (ibid).

India has also attracted biotech majors such as Monsanto, Pfizer, Unilever, Dupont, and Bayer. Eli Lilly and Ranbaxy have set up a joint venture for marketing a range of biotech products for diabetes treatment.

22.1.2 Agri-Biotech Sector

During the year 2003-04, the agro-biotech market, was valued at US$40 mn in terms of sales. With the approval accorded to the first recombinant bio-agri product, Bollgard, a Bt cotton variety developed by Monsanto–Mahyco in 2002, there has been a spurt of new plant biotech products in the pipeline. Transgenics of rice, brassica, moonbean, pigeonpea, cotton, tomatoes, and some vegetables like cabbage, cauliflower etc., will complete field assessment, and some of them would be ready for large-scale production by 2005 (*ibid*).

22.1.3 Bio-Fuel

This sector has been mainly focused on ethanol-blended petrol, which is expected to be a major consumption fuel in India, with backward linkage effects, on sugar cane farmers. The major attraction of this product is its ability to save on our import bill for crude oil.

22.1.4 Industrial Bio-Tech Sector

India has always been a lead manufacturer of industrial enzymes, which is a significant export item as well. Biocon India has a tie up with Genencor International and Quest International (an ICI subsidiary) for the production of select food enzymes. Biocon has competence in the speciality enzyme markets of the world. The other leading companies in this sector are Novzyme, Advanced Biochemicals, Rossari Biotech, Maps India. There are emerging players such as Fermenta Biotech, Maple Biotech, Textan Chemicals, Pappayin Products, Lumis Biotech, Celgen Biologicals, Avon Organics, Resil Bitoech and Sangitah Biotechemicals. According to the BioSpectrum-ABLE survey, companies like Rossari Biotech, Biocon and Zytex (India) have received ISO certification for their manufacturing facilities and processes, and they meet other relevant international standards as well (*ibid*).

Unlike plant biotechnology, where bio-safety concerns have affected third generation products such as transgenics, the industrial biotech sector is relatively free from regulatory concerns.

22.1.5 Bio-Informatics

India's intrinsic advantage in the IT field has created a major possibility for advancement in bio-informatics. The Indian industry is small, currently accounting for just US$20mn. However, the sector is all set to capture a good chunk of the global bioinformatics market, which is expected to grow to US$6 bn by 2005. The focus of bio-informatics has mainly been on data handling, fingerprinting and DNA sequencing. Wipro Health Sciences, SysArris and Kshema are the companies that are active in this sector. One of the most interesting, innovative, business models in bio-informatics is 'Strand Genomics' - a spin-off company of the Indian Institute of Science, it has done pioneering work with high quality, patented products. Another significant player is SciNova Informatics from Pune, which is currently focused on the local market with bona fide products, including novel versions of Prometheus (*ibid*).

In mid-2004, one of the country's leading software companies, Tata Consultancy Services (TCS), launched the Tata Biosuite, a versatile software package for life sciences and drug discovery. This was developed jointly by the company, along with some of the country's leading academic institutions, as part of a public-private partnership initiative. The Suite is considered to be among the best in the world, and is likely to make waves in the global market place in a few years (*ibid*).

The bioinformatics industry is mushrooming around IT centres. There are many companies based in Bangalore, Hyderabad and Chennai. Some of these are Accelrys, Bigtec, Genotypic, Jalaja Technologies, Infosys, Kshema Technologies, and Systat Software in Bangalore. Hyderabad has promising players like Ocimum Biosolutions, Molecular Connections, Helix Genomics, Bijam Biosciences, GCV Biosciences, Caliber Technologies and Shakti Biosystems. In the North, companies like Mascon, LabVantage Solutions, and Fundastic Solutions have made great progress (*ibid*).

It is estimated that the Department of Biotechnology would be spending Rs. 90 crore on the bio-informatics sector during the period 2003-2007.

22.1.6 Research Services Sector

One of the potent areas of growth for this segment is out-sourced clinical trials. Overseas drug firms find India to be a proven base for clinical trials and associated data analysis, for drug discovery, on account of the country's strengths in bio-informatics and generic drug research.

The contract research and clinical business in India during 2003-04 was about US$55mn, which more than doubled over the previous year. India's contract and clinical research organisations are providing a broad range of clinical research services, including bio-equivalence, bioavailability, pharmacokinetic studies, and phase I to phase IV clinical studies.

Unfortunately, this area is bound to be problematic on account of ethical and regulatory concerns, that may arise, both from Government agencies and civil society. This is a highly competitive sector and companies sometimes tend to cut corners. Competitors are stated to use partial clinical trial data to undermine their rivals. PIL cases, involving Biocon India and Shanta Biotech, are popularly mentioned in the context (*ibid*).

The other area of concern is the tendency for fly-by-night operators who may undertake services without paying due importance to quality. Furthermore, the absence of data security is detrimental to the growth of the industry. Currently, Indian regulators approve home-made drugs that just cite the clinical trial studies done by their equivalent products here and elsewhere.

22.1.7 Bio-Suppliers

It is estimated that the world bio-supplier market is of the order of US$10-15bn per year (*ibid*). India's bio-supplier market was estimated to be of the order of US$190mn (Rs. 820 crore). Most of the key bio-suppliers are large multinational companies whose subsidiaries are located in India. According to the BioSpectrum-ABLE survey - of the top 10 bio-suppliers in India, 8 are multinationals. These include Millipore, Agilent, Becton Dickinson, BioRad, Alfa Laval, Sartorius, Thermo Electron and Amersham. These companies supply equipment to Indian biotech firms such as Biocon India Limited, Cipla, Novartis, Dr. Reddy's Lab., Wockhardt, etc., and have extensive manufacturing bases and marketing networks. The basic R&D work is done in their parent companies, whilst customised products are supplied to the Indian market. Indian firms, such as Chemito Instruments Private Limited, Scigenics, Thermo Electron, and LLS Indian Limited, are also in the fray to supply high quality products to clients, based on international standards (*ibid*, 2003).

These prominent suppliers are making significant investments in India to set up infrastructure and develop new marketing initiatives. They have invested over US$300mn in the past few years. These companies cater to the growing demand for high-quality products in separation, purification and membrane technology. Major supplies include bioreactors, bioprocess plants, autoclaves, analytical equipment, separation plants, analyzers, clean rooms, centrifuges, effluent treatment plants, purified water and heat exchangers.

22.2 Biotechnology Policies in India

Though biotechnology has been a major sector in India for over two decades, there is no National Policy on Biotechnology so far.

A few years ago, the Department of Biotechnology (DBT), the nodal agency of the Government, had formulated a 10-year vision document on biotechnology. Due to persistent demand from the industry for a cohesive national outlook on this important sector, the Government is currently evolving a national biotech policy. The policy is most likely to be made public in January 2005 (Anon, 2002b).

The vision document emphasises the significance of private-public partnerships in providing a significant fillip to the growth of the biotechnology industry in India. Infusion of foreign investments and the formation of joint ventures are amongst strategies outlined in the national policy paper. The DBT forms the nodal point for policy formulation and programme implementation in the biotechnology sector. This department was set up in 1985 and has, since then, undertaken major programmes for human resource and infrastructure development, for the biotech sector. The department has set up a technology development fund for the development of Small and Medium Enterprises (SMEs), which is expected to supplement private, venture capital funds in promoting promising micro-enterprises.

It is envisaged that during the Tenth Five Year Plan, a large number of SMEs would be promoted through the enabling financial infrastructure created by the Department of Biotechnology, focussing especially on agri-biotech products. The efforts of the Department of Biotechnology are supplemented by programmes undertaken by the Indian Council of Agriculture Research (ICAR); the Council of Scientific and Industrial Research (CSIR); the Indian Council of Medical Research (ICMR); and the Department of Science and Technology. Notable private and public R&D institutes such as the Indian Institute of Science, the Tata Institute of Fundamental Research, and State Governments sponsored R&D Institutes. Most notably, the Institute for Bioinformatics and Applied Biotechnology (IBAB) in Karnataka has also played a major role in the development of research programmes (Ruet *et al.*).

Apart from national policies and programmes, State Governments have also initiated major policy and industrial support programmes, to encourage biotechnology. Notable States, which have taken lead in this regard, are Andhra Pradesh, Karnataka and Maharashtra. The sub-national policies are focussed on providing physical infrastructure and financial support for developing biotech clusters, based on close twinning of R&D institutes with start-up firms, that would commercialise technologies churned out by the former. (Ruet *et al.*).

One of the most interesting features of India's biotech sector is the keen sub-national competition for attracting investments and industrial units. Andhra Pradesh, Karnataka and Maharashtra are locked in keen competition to advertise their industrial support mechanisms, in order to attract units both from within the country and without. However, the focus of the competition is on pre-production facilities, which enable new units to leverage external economies for attaining an edge in production and operational capacities. Whilst the States of Karnataka and Andhra Pradesh have tried to leverage their IT potential to attract IT-BT fusion projects, notably in the area of bio-informatics, there have also been interesting efforts to attract knowledge intensive enterprises through other enabling means. For example, the State Government of Maharashtra has gone a step further to set up biotech parks in Pune, to house pilot plant facilities, which could be availed of by biotech companies on lease basis, without having to make capital investments. This is in addition to the States efforts' to make forays in bio-informatics and bioprocessing. However, these efforts suffer from absence of leveraging effects and bias towards bio-informatics (Damodaran, 2002).

22.3 Backward Integration through Joint Ventures, Mergers and Acquisitions

In the developed world, joint ventures, mergers and acquisitions are commonplace phenomena, particularly in the biotech sector. Very often, mergers and acquisitions are propelled by the desire to monopolise market share and to avoid competition. When it comes to acquisitions, the situation could display unusual trends, and may be motivated by more than one consideration. Thus General Electric, which was a leading manufacturer of machines, such as Positron Emission Tomography and MRI scanners, acquired all outstanding shares of Amersham, which had expertise as a leading player in the market for scanners and contrast drugs used in X-rays, CT scans, Ultrasound, MRI and PET scans. Through the acquisition, GE's strategy was to create a health care company that could have a dominant position in common markets. More importantly, GE considered the deal to help it leverage

Amersham's knowledge base in the use of gene therapy for treating patients, and thus more effectively compete with Roche and Abbot Laboratories, the lead diagnostic and drug firms in the world (Anon 2003).

Mergers and acquisitions in the biotech sector, in India, will depend upon the functioning of the new Competition Act of 2002. There exists potential for mergers and acquisitions amongst subsidiaries of multinational companies (MNCs), which are functioning in India particularly in the bio-pharma, agri-biotech and bio-supplier segments. Moreover, Indian firms and R&D establishments definitely look forward to transferring their innovations to industries, through the joint venture route. Publicly funded Institutes, such as the Central Drug Research Institute, are also not averse to having collaborations with overseas entities, including MNCs, especially in the field of joint research. In the agri-biotech sector, the Indian Agricultural Research Institute (IARI) has already entered into successful pacts with The Energy & Resources Institute (TERI), New Delhi, and have been working with MNCs, such as Syngenta, to develop markets for third generation biotech products, including transgenics.

22.4 Regulatory Regime for Biotech Industry in India

Multiple regulatory authorities deal with bio-technology products and processes in India. This will be evident from the succeeding discussions.

22.4.1 Regulatory Framework

The regulatory environment in biotechnology involves the interplay of several administrative ministries, given the cross-sectoral implications of biotechnology. In the present state of affairs, there are seven regulatory bodies, of which one or more deal with any aspect of biotechnology in the country. These are:

- *Department of Biotechnology, Ministry of Science and Technology* - which is the administrative body of regulatory approvals for investment and technology activities in the sector.

- *Drug Controller General of India, Ministry of Health* - which is the official regulatory body governing manufacture, and commercial release, of pharmaceutical products, including recombinant products.

- *Genetic Engineering Approvals Committee, Ministry of Environment and Forests* - which deals with bio-safety aspects, and is the regulatory authority for trials and commercial release of all genetically modified organisms (GMOs).

• *National Biodiversity Authority, set up under the National Biodiversity Legislation 2002 by the Ministry of Environment and Forests*

• *Ministry of Chemicals and Pharmaceuticals* - which is the administrative ministry for the chemical and pharmaceuticals industry, and governs industrial regulation and foreign investment in these sectors (enzymes, Pharma, industrial biotech products, etc.).

• *Department of Animal Welfare* - Ministry of Health, which deals with the protection of animal rights, and use of animals for scientific research experiments.

• *Department of Agriculture Research and Education, Ministry of Agriculture* - which deals with all field research in agriculture crops.

Besides these apex authorities, several bodies are involved in administering the regulations, such as the National Pharmaceutical Pricing Authority of India; the Review Committee on Genetic Manipulation; Institutional Bio-Safety Committee; and Institutional Animals Ethics Committee. (Anon, 2002b, and Ruet *et al.*, 2003).

While the investment regulations are business friendly, the procedures are dilatory and overlapping. The involvement of more than one ministry in the Government of India, with overlapping jurisdiction, results in operators having to seek multiple clearances from different authorities at different stages. This leads to delays and uncertainties in decision-making.

As far as the agri-biotech industry is concerned, the following, according to Damodaran (2004), form the principal regulatory agencies and legislation:

a. Ministry of Agriculture/ICAR

• Plant Variety and Farmers Rights Act 2002.

• Seeds Act 1966.

• Plants Fruits and Seeds (Regulation of Import into India) Order 2003.

b. Ministry of Food and Civil Supplies

• Prevention of Food Adulteration Act.

c. Ministry of Environment and Forests

• National Biodiversity Legislation 2002 .

• Rules for Manufacture, Use, Import, Export and Storage of Hazardous Micro-organisms and Genetically Engineered Organisms or Cells 1989 which form the Bio-safety Regulations flowing from the Environment Protection Act 1986.

In 2003, a National Task Force was set up, under the Chairmanship Dr. M.S. Swaminathan, to formulate a new regulatory structure for bio-agri products. The Task Force has submitted its Report in May 2004, and the Government is in the process of implementing the suggestions after consulting all the stakeholders. The Swaminathan Task Force has essentially suggested the formation of a single agency – the National Biotechnology Regulatory Board – on the lines of the Space Commission, Telecom Commission, and Atomic Energy Regulatory Board, etc. to be run by professionals. The Board should have permanent members who specialise in various subjects of biotechnology and all the existing regulations will be harmonised, to provide a single window system, for biotech products.

Following this, the government had set up another Task Force, under the Chairmanship of Dr. R.A. Mashelkar (Director-General, CSIR), to simplify the regulatory procedures for recombinant pharma products. The Mashelkar Task Force Report is awaited.

22.5 India's Competition Act 2002

India's Competition Act of 2002, has been enacted to (a) prevent practices having adverse effect on competition (b) promote and sustain competition in markets (c) protect the interests of consumers (d) look into factors that suppress freedom of trade, carried out by other participants in Indian markets (Anon, 2002). To this extent, the act goes beyond a narrow consumer-focused vision that is typical, of competition policies, in certain other parts of the world. It is also noteworthy that, despite the legacy of the Monopolies and Restrictive Trade Practices (MRTP) Act of 1969, the Competition Act 2002, is not obsessed with preventing firms from protecting or expanding their market shares by non-efficiency factors. Finally, the Act is also careful to provide for advocacy, whereby branches of Government adjust their policies, so as to interfere least with market competition.

Thus the Act defines an enterprise as including a person, or a department, of the Government that is engaged in any activity that is related to production, storage, supply, distribution, acquisition, or control of articles or goods. Section 3 (1) of the Act, by prohibiting anti-competitive agreements that are non-efficient in nature, sends an important signal to the biotechnology community in India that would like to practice the 'terminator' or 'generic use restriction technologies'. Similarly, Section 4 of the Act, by restricting abuse of dominant position by an enterprise, has the capacity to prevent chances of predatory or unfair pricing of seeds, or drugs, as the case may be. Section 4 (2) (b), by excluding limitations or restrictions, of goods and services, that are favourable to consumers or public interest, provides greater legitimacy to the compulsory licensing provisions in the Patents Act 1970 (as amended in 2002), and the Plant Varieties and Farmers' Rights Act of 2001. Section 5 (b) of the Competition Act also prevents acquisitions that are restrictive in impacts on market access, and thus could play an important role in predatory acquisitions in the biotech sector.

22.6 Competition Issues

The competition issues in the biotech field would mainly arise from the application of Intellectual Property Rights over biotech products, by innovating companies. The phenomena of acquisitions and mergers would be the second important set of competition issues that may arise in India's biotech industry. Both aspects would encourage monopoly rights in production, distribution and marketing of biotech products. This would, in turn, impact on the consumers of biotech products, through higher pricing of products and restrictions on its multiplication. However, the presence of public plant biotech research institutions that seek to position their products, according to local conditions, could dampen the oligopolistic tendencies (See Nagarajan, 2003 for details regarding region specific products). Even in the bio-pharma sector, the trend towards seeking joint ventures in research needs to be welcomed, as they would serve to encourage joint commercial ventures in future (Gupta, 2003).

Similarly, in the bio-pharma sector, India's Patent Act, 1970, as modified through the first and second amendments, can adversely affect the ability of generic drug manufacturers to adopt alternative processes in developing new drugs. This is especially in view of the product patent regimes that would be fully operational by 1st January 2005. Even the interim exclusive marketing right regime, which is currently operational, acts to virtually confer monopolistic rights over distribution and marketing of new drugs, for which product patents have been obtained, in PCT (Patent Co-operation Treaty) countries.

The Plant Varieties and Farmers' Rights Act of 2001, accords plant breeders the rights for new, distinct, uniform and stable varieties of plants, whilst disallowing farmers to sell produce from protected varieties. To this extent, it would be possible for plant biotechnology companies, producing non-hybrid varieties of plants or seeds, to enforce full-cost and high-margin pricing systems for seeds that are considered essential for farming operations.

22.7 Flexibilities in India's IPR Regimes and its Impact on Competition

Intellectual Property Rights (IPRs), awarded through the India Patent Acts, and the Plant Varieties and Farmers Rights Act of 2002, prima-facie confer significant economic exclusiveness to producers of new biotech products and processes. Notwithstanding, it is a plain fact that these IPR regimes have the potential to restrict extreme cases of competition restriction. (Damodaran, 1999 and 2004). Thus the Patent (Amendment Act of 2002) provides the flexibilities of abridging rights of inventors whose primary or intended use, or commercial exploitation, of their invention would be contrary to public order or morality, or causes serious prejudice to human, animal or plant life or health, or to the environment. The Act is also notable for its opposition provisions, and for its requirement on the part of a potential inventor to disclose source, and geographic, origin of the biological material used in an invention. This clause, which is incorporated in Section 10 of the said Act, fortifies the 'previous approval' principles enshrined in India's National Biodiversity Act, 2002. Under the Plant Varieties and Farmers Rights Act of 2001, the Central Government reserves the right to enforce compulsory licensing, of protected varieties and seeds, in the larger interest of food security, livelihoods and consumer welfare.

To the extent that these flexibilities exist, it may be fair to surmise that the Indian IPR regimes do promote or facilitate a healthy competition law. It also follows that there is an implicit effort to coordinate the objectives of India's competition law with that of the country's IPR regimes, particularly in relation to biotechnology. It is quite possible therefore, to ensure that IPR rules do not act as a threat to competition concerns in the biotechnology sector.

To conclude, India's fast growing biotech sector has the potential of serious implications on the competition environment in the country. Even so, a constellation of pro-active legislations serves to ensure that competition is not impaired. India's IPR regimes, whilst affording protection to inventions that fulfil the criteria of novelty, non-obviousness and commercial application, do still carry with it the elements for regulating anti-competition behaviour, on the part of firms concerned. The flexibilities inherent in India's IPR regimes, coupled with the bio-safety, biodiversity and stringent food safety laws, could go a long way in promoting the biotech sector, in a manner that is sustainable and economically advantageous.

References

Anonymous (2003). "Bio Venture," *Biospectrum*, Vol. 1, 9 November pp 74-75.

—————. (2002a). "The Competition Act, 2002," *The Gazette of India*, Ministry of Law and Justice, New Delhi.

—————. (2002b). *Annual Report 2001-02*, Department of Biotechnology, Government of India, New Delhi.

Damodaran, A. (2004). "Economic Implications of Global Conventions and India's Regulatory Environment on Plant Biotechnology Industry," VRF *Monograph*, No. 393, Institute of Developing Economies, Japan, November.

—————. (2002). "Policy Dimensions of Plant Biotechnology, IPRs on Micro-organisms and the Issue of Strategizing" in *Round Table on IPR: Biotechnology and Agriculture* , *IIMB Management Review*, Vol. 14, No. 3, pp 95-97.

—————. (1999). "Regulating Transgenic Plants in India: Biosafety, Plant Variety Protection and Beyond", *Economic and Political Weekly*, XXXIV (13), March, A-34 – A-41.

Gupta, C.M. (2003). "Industry Participation is very Important for Research," *Interview*, *Biospectrum*, Vol. 1, 9 November.

Kulkarni, Narayan (2003). "Biotech Industry Changes the Fortune of Suppliers," *Biospectrum*, Vol. 1, 9, November.

Nagarajan, N. (2003). "Develop Region-based Transgenics," *Interview*, *Biospectrum*, Vol. 1, 9, November.

Ruet, Joel and Zerah, Marie-Helene (2003). *Biotechnology in India*, Report Commissioned by French Embassy in India, New Delhi.

Market Structure, Competition and Performance: The Analytical Background

K.V. Ramaswamy

Evaluation of the state of competition requires an understanding of how the relevant markets function in practice. Economic theory has developed many models for the analysis of markets. This section provides a non-technical exposition of these important concepts and models. A key question is what are the costs and benefits of deviation from competitive markets?

1.0 Meaning of Competition and Competitive Markets

The concept of competition can be defined in many ways. In common parlance, competition refers to rivalry between firms in a market for objects like market share and profits. Market power is the ability to raise market prices above competitive levels and exclude competition.

Policy intervention requires prior identification and assessment of the degree of competition in real life product markets? What are the standard guiding principles? For this we need to distinguish between competition in a market and competition for a market.[1]

Competition *in a market* refers to actions of incumbents in an established market and those potential entrants who would like to sell the same product. The instruments of competition would be price or capacity (quantity competition) and other non-price instruments like advertising etc. This involves erecting entry barriers, product differentiation, vertical integration etc.

Competition *for a* market is defined as a process of creating a new market based on innovative technologies and/or new standards (example new operating system for Windows). This involves challenging the sellers of existing products through the introduction of new products or creating potential competition by upfront investment in facilities to supply a new product. Here

the instrument of competition is not the price or capacity. Measurement of competition for a market is much more difficult than the measurement of competition in a market.

It is helpful to discuss certain standard models that economic analysis uses to understand competition and competitive behaviour.

2.0 Perfect Competition

A market is said to be perfectly competitive when firms perceive that they individually have no noticeable influence on market price. The outcome in such an industry is efficient in the sense that the cost of the last unit of output (marginal cost) would just equal what consumers would be willing to pay for that unit.[2] Perfect competition is regarded as a benchmark market structure for evaluating other market structures.

3.0 Monopoly and Imperfect Competition

The polar extreme of perfect competition is monopoly, that is a market with only one producer of the product with no close substitutes. Here the producer enjoys the power to influence market outcomes by his or her actions. This is called market power or monopoly power. He or she restricts output so as to raise the price above the efficient level (perfect competition level). The market price is above the marginal cost of production leading to efficiency loss or inefficiency of monopoly.

Intermediate degrees of competition between perfect competition and monopoly that exist are shown to be more complex. Oligopoly is an example of such a market structure defined as a market with a *few* or a limited number of firms. The fewness character results in strategic interaction of participant firms. In this type of market each firm takes into account the likely response of its competitors to its output or pricing decisions. Most models of imperfect competition predict that firms charge prices above marginal costs. Each firm has some market power to influence the market outcomes. Resource allocation will be less than social optimal as price is greater than marginal cost of production.

Oligopolistic market structures are predicted to give rise to collusive behaviour in price setting. National laws prohibit explicit collusion among participant firms to raise prices or restrict outputs. However, oligopolistic firms may take recourse to implicit collusion using a variety of business strategies like threat of price cuts, parallel pricing and implicit geographic distribution of markets etc. In many cases a market consists of a few big firms and a number of small firms. In such markets a single large firm or a few big firms are often found to dominate.[3]

4.0 Structure Conduct and Performance Approach

A useful organising framework to think about competition and market power is provided by the structure conduct performance paradigm.[4] In this framework, structure determines performance. The market structure (measured by market share or concentration ratio) is exogenously determined and conditions the conduct (prices, advertising expense etc.) of the firms and that in turn determines the market performance (profitability, productivity etc.). A simple diagram can be used to illustrate the inter-connections between the key variables as shown in Figure 1.

FIGURE 1

Modified S-C-P Paradigm

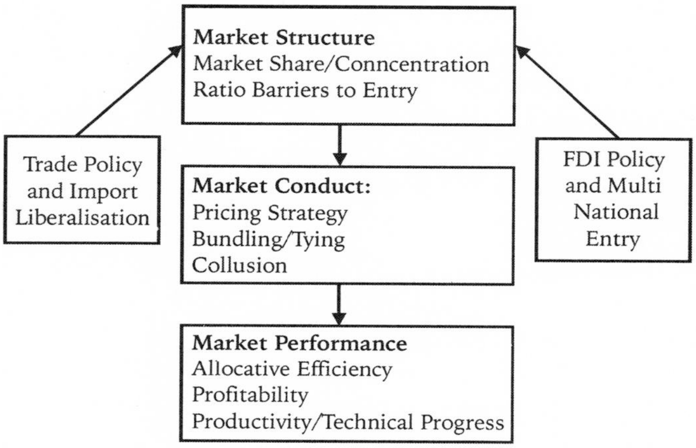

A limitation of this paradigm is that it assumes the causation to be unidirectional as indicated by the arrows. Later analysts have pointed out that it is not necessarily be so. For example, market performance can have feedback effects into market structure. Market size obviously influences the market structure and the equilibrium market structure is argued to be endogenous.[5] The traditional framework of S-C-P paradigm has been modified by accommodating the impact of foreign competition on market structure. A further elaboration on the conceptual basis of these three components will be useful.

5.0 Market Structure and Competition

The market structure tells us about the environment within which an enterprise functions and the nature of external pressure on the enterprise. The elements of market structure that we look at are concentration ratio, stability of market shares, conditions of entry and exit of firms. Knowledge about the prevailing market structure tells us how closely it resembles either a competitive or monopolistic structure. An industry wherein few firms have a large share of the total market is supposed to be concentrated industry. This concentrated structure is supposed to encourage collusive practices (coordinated price and output decisions).

5.1 Concentration Ratio

This is defined as the market share of the top 'n' firms in the industry. A widely used measure is the per cent of industry sales accounted for by the top four firms, that is the 4-firm concentration ratio. A drawback of this measure is that it does not use information contained in the remaining part of the market share distribution. An alternative index is the Hirfindahl-Hirschman index (HH index). The HH index is defined as sum of the squares of market shares (percentage share) of all the firms in the industry. The HH index declines with increases in the number of firms and increases with rising inequality in market share among a given number of firms. The US justice department considers an HH value of 1000 as critical in its evaluation of merger proposals.

5.2 Stability of Markets Shares

A limitation of the above summary measures of concentration is that they ignore the dynamic changes in the market shares of individual firms. Market shares of dominant firms may increase or decline over time. Greater churning of market shares in given market suggests greater intensity of competition. Whether the dominant firms' leadership persists over time is another indicator of persistence of market power.

5.3 Entry and Exit Conditions

There may be legal barriers (example, industrial licensing) or natural barriers that restrict entry of firms that could provide alternative supply. The condition of entry into an industry is important in the assessment of competition for two reasons. First, the number of firms in an industry is influenced by cost of entry and consequently influences the level of concentration. Secondly, the conditions of entry determine the extent of potential competition. Exit conditions are important because it influences the original entry decision of a firm. If firms anticipate that the cost of future exit, perhaps due to unfavorable business conditions, is likely to be high then they may not enter the industry at all. This is likely to diminish the threat of potential competition.

Two important barriers to entry are scale economies and excess capacity[6]. The existence of economies of scale implies that production facilities must be of certain minimum size. This minimum efficient scale varies from industry to industry. Market size or size of the national market for a particular product may not be large enough to support more than few firms. That is the minimum efficient scale (MES) of a production unit may be large relative to the total market. A new entrant with an MES plant will cause post-entry prices to fall and this makes an entry decision unattractive. The extent of this barrier to entry may be measured by the ratio of output corresponding to MES plant to total plant capacity in the industry. Imperfect competition is unavoidable in many developing country product markets simply due to small size of market for those products.

Firms may build excess capacity for both strategic and non-strategic reasons. Holding excess capacity to meet contingencies of cyclical demand is an example of non-strategic reason. If firms build excess capacity either to deter new entry or to pre-empt existing competitors then it is regarded as strategic reason. Strategic excess capacity enables incumbents to threaten potential entrants with output expansion and price-cutting to prevent their entry. In this situation incumbents prior to announcement of entry hold excess capacity.

6.0 Market Conduct and Competition

Market conduct refers to the ways in which the firms in a market interact with each other and the business practices that they adopt to achieve their competitive objectives. Market conduct of firms is a reflection of competitive activity in terms of pricing strategies, policies toward product design and services, how they advertise and promote their products like bundling, tie-ins etc. An examination of market conduct is supposed to reveal the sources of observed conduct. The origin of an observed conduct may be the attainment of monopoly position or superior competitive capabilities attained. What can be regarded as anticompetitive and what is pro-competitive conduct is arrived only after a detailed examination of the given industry.

7.0 Market Performance and Competition

Market performance is the outcome of the market conduct of the participating firms. Is the observed outcome closer to the one that is expected to occur under perfectly competitive conditions? The two standard measures of market performance are: (1) rate of return on capital: Value of output minus total costs divided by total assets and (2) Price cost margins: value of output minus total costs divided by value of output. This is a measure of margin of price over average cost. These two measures are estimated for firms in an industry and compared with the industry-wide average return or margin on sales. This would shed light on the existence of excess profits or above normal returns. The persistence of profits over time is another issue that may be addressed in this context.

It is suggested that instead of studying profitability it is preferable to study the relationship between price and concentration (Weiss, 1986). Do higher prices persist in concentrated industries, is a relevant question in any assessment of the state of competition.

Another significant performance indicator is total factor productivity growth or technical progress. Competition is supposed to improve efficiency and productivity of firms in order to sustain competitive positions. The relationship between market structure and productivity growth is a relevant issue in this context.

Notes

1. Geroski (2003).

2. Such a market is shown to achieve efficient allocation of resources in the Pareto sense. It is impossible to make anyone better-off without making anybody else worse-off.

3. Such a market structure is called the dominant firm and competitive fringe model.

4. Scherer and Ross (1999) provide an excellent exposition.

5. The relationship between market size, market concentration and sunk costs is enriched by the recent contributions of John Sutton (1996).

6. The third factor is product differentiation. Product differentiation makes competition less perfect by reducing the degree of substitutability between products that are essentially same. This gives some power to the individual supplier of the product to influence the market price. However, benefit aspect is that it satisfies consumer preference for variety.

References

Geroski, P.A. (2003). "Competition in Markets and Competition for Markets," *Journal of Trade, Competition and Trade*, Vol. 3, No. 3, pp151-166.

Scherer F.M. (1970) *Industrial Market Structure and Economic Performance*, Rand McNally, Chicago.

Scherer, F.M, and D. Ross (1990). *Industrial Market Structure and Economic Performance*, Houghton Mifflin, Boston.

Sutton, John (1996). *Sunk Costs and Market Structure*, The MIT Press, Cambridge.

Annexure:
National Competition Policy

(Draft 2005.03.29)

GOVERNMENT TO TAKE COMPETITION SERIOUSLY

The Government of India has made 'competition' a serious policy issue. Extracted below are relevant excerpts from the President's Address to the Parliament on 7th June, 2004:

"Revival of industrial growth is of paramount importance. Incentives for boosting private investment will be introduced. Foreign Direct Investment will continue to be encouraged. Indian industry will be given every support to become productive and competitive".

"Competition, both domestic and external, will be deepened across industry with professionally run regulatory institutions in place to ensure that competition is free and fair".

"The Government will establish a National Manufacturing Competitiveness Council to provide a continuing forum for policy interactions to energise and sustain the growth of the manufacturing industry".

"The Government is committed to a strong and effective public sector, whose social objectives are met by its commercial functioning. But for this, there is need for selectivity and a strategic focus. My government will devolve full managerial and commercial autonomy to successful, profit-making companies operating in a competitive environment".

"My government believes that privatisation should increase competition, not decrease it".

The National Common Minimum Programme adds: "It will not support the emergence of any monopoly that only restricts competition. All regulatory institutions will be strengthened to ensure that competition is free and fair. These institutions will be run professionally".

1. Preamble

1.1 The Government of India recognises that efficient, well functioning competitive markets are key to rapid economic and social development of the country. Competitive markets are essential to ensure that the ownership and control of the material resources of the community are so distributed so as best to subserve the common good; and that the operation of the economic system does not result in the undue concentration of wealth and means of production. Efficient and competitive markets are essential to ensure that the fruits of development are received by all citizens regardless of caste, creed and gender.

1.2 The National Competition Policy is being formulated to ensure that markets in the country function under the principles of free, fair and unrestricted competition. The National Competition Policy shall provide guidelines to different branches of the Government and agencies at all levels in maintaining the appropriate competition dimension, while taking any step or decision which will have an impact on the economy and consumers. The National Competition Policy seeks to maximise social welfare. The National Competition Policy Statement will be a medium-term document, subject to a parliamentary review every three years.

2. Need for a National Competition Policy

2.1 The rationale behind the National Competition Policy stems from Article 39 of the Constitution of India, which has enshrined the Directive Principles to be followed by the State, to ensure all-round welfare of the citizens of the country. In Article 39 (b) and (c) the Constitution adds: "(b) that the ownership and control of the material resources of the community are so distributed as best to subserve the common good; (c) that the operation of the economic system does not result in the concentration of wealth and means of production to the common detriment.

2.2 Since early-1990's the Government has initiated the process of greater market orientation through a series of reform measures. The key objective being to promote competition and ensure efficient use of available resources.

2.3 In spite of this, there exist distortions in the economic management of the country, as often policies are framed without acknowledging the market process. Moreover, there is no consistent approach followed in the various policies that affect competition.

2.4 There are also several competition concerns in the market place, which adversely affect consumer welfare as well as business welfare.

2.5 India has had a competition legislation, the Monopolies & Restrictive Trade Practices Act since 1969, which is to be replaced with the Competition Act, 2002. India has also enacted a consumer protection legislation: Consumer Protection Act in 1986 (COPRA) which recognises the rights of consumers and provides for an easy and simple redressal system. It is one of the most unique legislations in the world.

2.6 Efforts are ongoing to bring in competitive outcomes in various infrastructure sectors through regulatory reforms and establishment of new independent regulatory regimes.

2.7 The government has also established a National Manufacturing Competitiveness Council to examine and promote competitiveness of the Indian industry. However, the Council's remit is not to examine the competition scenario in the country, which covers a much wider range of issues.

2.8 Competition promotes competitiveness, but the reverse is not true. It is affected by various policies of the government such as: trade policy, investment policy, labour policy, consumer policy, environment policy, policy on intellectual property rights, sectoral regulatory policies etc.

2.9 Though the country has a Competition Law and various Sectoral Regulatory Laws, there is a need to frame a Competition Policy, to harmonise the various policies of the Government (both Central as well as States). This would ensure a consistent approach and ensure that Governments and other economic regulatory agencies are aware of and take into account the competition dimension while formulating or implementing any policy.

2.10 The National Competition Policy does not prevent government from increasing expenditure on welfare or levels of government-funded or subsidised social services, or maintaining government ownership of businesses. It explicitly recognises the need for government intervention in markets, where it is justified.

3. Principles

3.1 The Constitution of India seeks to ensure for its citizens—social, economic and political justice. However, as consumers face imbalances in economic terms, education levels and bargaining power, the

National Competition Policy aims to promote and protect economic democracy for just, equitable and sustainable economic and social development. Taking this into account, the National Competition Policy, while promoting a healthy competition culture, will endeavour to uphold the following principles:

- **Free and fair market process:** The policy will be to protect free, fair and contestable markets rather than welfare of any individual participant in the market place.

- **Removal of distortions and barriers:** The policy will emphasise on making market conditions congenial for entry of new players by removing both policy induced and private barriers.

- **Justification and Notification:** When, for reasons of economic or social welfare, there is a need to deviate from the accepted principles of competition this will be done only through notification and public justification of the measures.

- **Balancing competition and intellectual property rights:** Intellectual property right holders will be put under reasonable restrictions if their behaviour amounts to abuse of monopoly rights.

- **Competitive neutrality:** adopting policies which establish a 'level playing field' where the public sector competes with the private sector.

- **Access to 'essential facilities':** When, for reasons of technology or other public purpose it is desirable to continue a monopoly, it will be incumbent on the owners of such monopoly to grant to third parties access and use of their infrastructure at an agreed and fair price and on agreed terms and conditions

- **Competition Audit:** The Policy will encourage all Ministries, Departments and other bodies, Government and Non-government at the Centre and the States to promote accountability, transparency and good governance, and to periodically conduct a "Competition Audit" of all policies, existing and proposed.

- **Respect for international obligations:** Adherence to this policy will be subject to non-conflict with international obligations accepted by the country.

- **Involvement of stakeholders:** attempts will be made to consult all relevant stakeholders and take on board their concerns while making policy changes that affect competition.

4. Objectives

4.1 Taking into account the needs of and priorities for promoting a healthy competition culture the objectives of the National Competition Policy are to:

a. **Reform regulations and policies which unjustifiably restrict competition,** i.e. tightening the examination of regulations which reduce efficiency by shielding businesses, both in private sector and public sector, from competition through a 'competition audit'; public interest tests would be used to assess the desirability and proportionality of policies and regulations, and these would be subject to regular independent review;

b. **Encourage policies and programmes to enable better and healthy competition in the market place, and to bring about competitive outcomes;**

c. **Protect the market players** from anti-competitive practices and abuse of dominance;

d. **Provide adequate resources to competition authority and other economic regulators,** so that they are well-equipped to perform effectively;

e. **Develop an effective working relationship between various agencies and institutions that seek to promote and protect competition;**

f. **Structural reform of public utilities to facilitate competition** i.e. opening up of public utilities to competition, where possible using independent review processes;

g. **Promote assessment of competition impact in every area of governance** where consumer and business interests are affected;

h. **Promote local, national, regional and international co-operation** in the field of competition policy enforcement and advocacy; and

i. **Promote a healthy competition culture** in the country through formal as well as non-formal education systems, which will include capacity building programmes for various stakeholders.

5. Measures

5.1 Bearing in mind the costs and benefits of proposed measures; the economic, social, cultural and technological diversity of the country; and the needs of its population, to evolve time bound programmes for the promotion of competition and realisation of competitive outcomes. These measures will apply to the market of indigenously produced goods, services and technology as well as to imports.

5.2 *Policy Statement:* The Government will formulate, adopt and disseminate this Statement widely so as to inform every citizen of India about the seriousness of the government to promote a healthy competition culture in the country.

5.3 *Competition Agencies:* The Government will establish and resource agencies, such as the National Competition Policy Council; State Competition Policy Councils, Competition Authority, Independent Regulatory Agencies to promote and protect competition in the market place.

5.4 *Representation:* Enable representation of consumers and business' views in the decision-making process:

a. Provide and strengthen representation to consumer and business organisations in the decision-making process of the Government at all levels; and

b. Promote and encourage an independent consumer movement in the country by providing assistance to consumer groups to form their organisations and giving them the opportunity to present their views in the decision-making process.

5.5 *Public Education:* To help various stakeholders in their decision-making:

a. Promote information dissemination programmes on competition as an integral part of the formal education system at school and college levels;

b. Encourage business to undertake publication of educational material for mass distribution; and

c. Enable consumer organisations to undertake capacity building programme for consumers, activists and others.

5.6 *Research and Advocacy:*

a. Develop and strengthen competition analyses of markets and sectors and dissemination of information through research and academic institutions, media and consumer organisations; and

b. Encourage consumer organisations to review the implementation of competition regulations by competition agencies, and of providers of goods, services and technology and verification of claims.

5.7 *International Exchange of Information on Competition Policy*

a. Initiate and implement systematic exchange of information on measures of competition enforcement and advocacy, regionally and internationally; and

b. Encourage participation of competition agencies in information exchange programmes with international organisations and other competition agencies.

6. Monitoring and Evaluation

6.1 In view of economic, social, cultural and technological diversity of the country, it is essential to adopt and strengthen monitoring and evaluation mechanisms by involving consumer and other interest groups, and business in the process of implementation of the aforesaid measures to achieve the objectives.

6.2 Government will establish an apex National Competition Policy Council with the Prime Minister (or his/her nominee) as its chairperson, Chief Ministers of the States or their nominees, and members drawn from Business, Consumer Organisations, Media and Academia so that competition issues receive the highest consideration in every area of governance.

The Steering Committee

Towards a Functional Competition Policy for
India (FunComp Project)

S. Sundar   **Chairman**

Distinguished Fellow,
The Energy and Resources Institute (TERI)
New Delhi.

Shankar Acharya   **Member**

Honorary Professor,
Indian Council for Research on
International Economic Relations (ICRIER),
New Delhi.

T.C.A. Anant   **Member**

Professor, Deptt. of Economics,
Delhi School of Economics, University of Delhi,
Delhi.

Suman Bery   **Member**

Director General,
National Council of Applied Economic Research (NCAER),
New Delhi.

B.B. Bhattacharya   **Member**

Vice-chancellor,
Jawahar Lal Nehru University
Delhi.

S. Chakravarthy   **Member**

Adviser/Consultant on Competition Policy and Law,
and Fellow, CUTS Centre for Competition,
Investment & Economic Regulation (C-CIER).

V.K. Dhall   Special Invitee

Member
Competition Commission of India
New Delhi.

Shubhashis Gangopadhyay   Member

Director, India Development Foundation (IDF),
Gurgaon.

Subir Gokarn   Member

Chief Economist, CRISIL Ltd.,
New Delhi.

Pradeep S. Mehta   Member

Secretary General,
CUTS International, Jaipur.

Shrawan Nigam   Member

Adviser, Planning Commission,
Government of India, New Delhi.

Manoj Pant   Member

Professor, School of International Studies,
Jawaharlal Nehru University, New Delhi.

T.C.A. Srinivas Raghavan   Member

Consulting Editor, Business Standard,
New Delhi.

S.L. Rao   Member

Chairman,
Institute for Social and Economic Change (ISEC),
Bangalore.

Pronab Sen   Member

Adviser, Planning Commission,
Government of India, New Delhi.